Visualizing Jewish Narrative

Also Available from Bloomsbury

The Power of Comics: History, Form, and Culture
Randy Duncan, Matthew J. Smith, and Paul Levitz

Black Comics: Politics of Race and Representation
Sheena C. Howard and Ronald L. Jackson II

Visualizing Jewish Narrative

Jewish Comics and Graphic Novels

Edited by
Derek Parker Royal

Bloomsbury Academic
An imprint of Bloomsbury Publishing Plc

B L O O M S B U R Y
LONDON · OXFORD · NEW YORK · NEW DELHI · SYDNEY

Bloomsbury Academic
An imprint of Bloomsbury Publishing Plc

50 Bedford Square   1385 Broadway
London   New York
WC1B 3DP   NY 10018
UK   USA

www.bloomsbury.com

BLOOMSBURY and the Diana logo are trademarks of Bloomsbury Publishing Plc

First published 2016
Paperback edition first published 2017

British Library Cataloguing-in-Publication Data
A catalogue record for this book is available from the British Library.

ISBN: HB: 978-1-4742-4879-2
PB: 978-1-3500-5630-5
ePDF: 978-1-4742-4881-5
ePub: 978-1-4742-4880-8

Library of Congress Cataloging-in-Publication Data
A catalog record for this book is available from the Library of Congress.

Cover design: Eleanor Rose
Cover image © Ben Katchor

Typeset by Integra Software Services Pvt. Ltd.

In loving memory of my mother, Nancy Lipe Royal.

Unlike the case in most families, it was you, Mom, who strongly encouraged me to read comics.

Contents

Contributors   x

Foreword *Danny Fingeroth*   xv

Acknowledgments   xvii

Introduction: Visualizing Jewish Narrative
Derek Parker Royal   1

Part 1 Picturing Jewish Identity

1   Thinly Disguised (Autobio)Graphical Stories: Will Eisner's
      Life, in Pictures
      Lan Dong   15

2   "Not a Word for Little Girls!": Knowledge, Word, and Image
      in Leela Corman's *Unterzakhn*
      Tahneer Oksman   29

3   Jewish Sexualities in J. T. Waldman's *Megillat Esther*
      Matt Reingold   41

4   "You Wouldn't Shoot Your Fellow Jews": Jewish Identity and
      Nostalgia in Joann Sfar's *Klezmer*
      Nicole Wilkes Goldberg and James Goldberg   55

5   Feiffer's Jewish Voice
      Ira Nadel   67

6   There Goes the Neighborhood: Cycling Ethnoracial Tensions in
      Will Eisner's *Dropsie Avenue*
      Derek Parker Royal   81

"Jews and Superheroes"
Eli Valley   95

Part 2 Jewish Engagements with Comic Genres

7   The Servant: Marvel Comics and the Golem Legend
      Robert G. Weiner   101

8   "America Makes Strange Jews": Superheroes, Jewish Masculinity,
     and Howard Chaykin's *Dominic Fortune*
     Brannon Costello   115

9   Converting Schmaltz into Chicken Fat: Will Elder and the
     Judaization of American Comedy
     Daniel M. Bronstein   129

10 The Third Temple: Alternative Realities' Depiction of Israel in
     Israeli Comics and What it Tells Us about Political Consensus
     in Israeli Society
     Ofer Berenstein   141

Part 3 Jewish Comics, the Holocaust, and Trauma

11 *The Search*: A Graphic Narrative for Beginning to Teach
     about the Holocaust
     Wendy Stallard Flory   157

12 Picturing "The Holiest Thing": Joe Kubert's Children of the
     Warsaw Ghetto
     Samantha Baskind   171

13 Trauma in Gaza: The Israeli-Palestinian Conflict through
     the Eyes of the Graphic Novelist
     Ellen Rosner Feig   185

14 "To Night the Ensilenced Word": Intervocality and Postmemorial
     Representation in the Graphic Novel about the Holocaust
     Jean-Philippe Marcoux   199

"How Shaloman Was Born"
Al Wiesner   213

Part 4 Representation of Israel, Biblical Text, and Legend

15 The Art of Persuasion and Propaganda: The Israeli-Palestinian
     Conflict in Comic Books and Graphic Novels
     Chantal Catherine Michel   221

16 Strange Encounters in Rutu Modan's *Exit Wounds* and "Jamilti"
     Stephen E. Tabachnick   231

17   The "Outsider": Neil Gaiman and the Old Testament
     Cyril Camus   241

18   Jewish Giants: Nephilim, Rephaim, and the IDF
     Tof Eklund   257

Bibliography   269
Index   290

Contributors

Samantha Baskind, professor of art history at Cleveland State University, is the author of several books, including *Raphael Soyer and the Search for Modern Jewish Art* (2004) and a solely authored encyclopedia, *Encyclopedia of Jewish American Artists* (2007). She also coauthored *Jewish Art: A Modern History* (2011) with Larry Silver and coedited, with Ranen Omer-Sherman, *The Jewish Graphic Novel: Critical Approaches* (2008). Her newest book, *Jewish Artists and the Bible in Twentieth-Century America* (2014), was funded by a year-long National Endowment for the Humanities Fellowship. She served as editor for US art for the twenty-two-volume revised edition of the *Encyclopaedia Judaica* (2006) and is currently series editor of "Dimyonot: Jews and the Cultural Imagination," published by the Pennsylvania State University Press.

Ofer Berenstein is a PhD candidate in the Department of Communication, Media, and Film at the University of Calgary, where he studies visual political culture. He is a comics writer, editor, and critic, and he is a founding member of the Israeli Comic Books Readers and Collectors' Society. He has written and presented on Israeli comics internationally, including at such venues as the Royal War Museum in London and the US Library of Congress.

Daniel M. Bronstein is an ordained rabbi and holds a PhD in Jewish history. His dissertation "Torah in the Trenches: The Rabbi Chaplains of World War II, 1940–1946" (2009) examines intra-Jewish relations in the context of world war and the Holocaust. Having served as a congregational rabbi, he is an independent scholar and educator and currently teaches for the Departments of History and Sociology at Hunter College, among other venues. Dr. Bronstein has also published on a variety of topics and is a contributor to *Jews and American Popular Culture* (2006), *The Cambridge Dictionary of Judaism and Jewish Culture* (2011), and *Jewish Theology in Our Time* (2012).

Cyril Camus teaches English in the Pyrenees, in a prep course for future students of business and engineering schools. He is a former teaching assistant and doctoral student at the Université de Toulouse-Le Mirail, where he wrote a thesis on Neil Gaiman's works in comics, literature, and cinema, earning him a PhD in Studies of English and English-Speaking Cultures. His writings on Neil Gaiman, Alan Moore, and postmodern fantasy have been published in the French journals *Otrante* and *Caliban*, the US journal *Shofar*, the British journal *Studies in Comics*, and the edited collection *Mountains Figured and Disfigured in the English-Speaking World* (2010). Other articles are scheduled to be featured in the journal *Studies in the Novel* and in an e-book about intersemioticity published by Presses Universitaires du Midi.

Brannon Costello is an associate professor of English at Louisiana State University, where he also directs the Master of Arts in the Liberal Arts program. His research and teaching interests include US Southern studies and comics studies, and he is the author of *Plantation Airs: Racial Paternalism and the Transformation of Class in Southern Fiction, 1945–1971* (2007), the editor of *Howard Chaykin: Conversations* (2011) and *Conversations with Michael Chabon* (2015), and the coeditor of *Comics and the U.S. South* (2012). He is currently at work on a book-length study of cartoonist Howard Chaykin.

Lan Dong is an associate professor of English at the University of Illinois Springfield. She is the author of *Mulan's Legend and Legacy in China and the United States* (2011), *Reading Amy Tan* (2009), and a number of journal articles, book chapters, and essays on Asian American literature, children's literature, and popular culture. She is the editor of *Transnationalism and the Asian American Heroine* (2011), *Teaching Comics and Graphic Narratives* (2012), and *Asian American Culture: From Anime to Tiger Moms* (2016). Currently she is working on a project on comics and Asian American experiences.

Tof Eklund is a non-binary transgender scholar and author. They teach creative writing and game design at Full Sail University, focusing on the combination of creative technique, technical proficiency, and critical awareness in new media. Their publications include *Autumn Harvest: Maiden* (2015), a postcolonial feminist fantasy romance; *The Unconventional Dwarf* (2013), a tabletop role-playing book; and edited special issues of comics studies journal, *ImageTexT*. Their first commercial computer game, *Autumn Harvest: Rites of Spring*, is due out in 2016.

Ellen Rosner Feig is an associate professor of composition and literature at Bergen Community College in New Jersey. As the codirector of the Center for Peace, Justice, and Reconciliation, Dr. Feig develops workshops, programming, and courses focused on peace studies, genocide studies, restorative justice, and historical context. In addition, as the founder and director of the college's TEDx event, Feig has created four large-scale events that have brought together well-known figures such as Gabriel Bol Deng, Gary Lucas, and Peter Nelson, NY Director of Facing History and Ourselves.

Danny Fingeroth was the editorial director of Marvel's Spider-Man comics line and writer of many comics featuring Spider-Man, Iron Man, Superman and other iconic characters. He is the author of *Superman on the Couch: What Superheroes Really Tell Us About Ourselves and Our Society* (2004), *Disguised as Clark Kent: Jews Comics and the Creation of the Superhero* (2007), *The Rough Guide to Graphic Novels* (2008), and co-editor (with Roy Thomas) of *The Stan Lee Universe* (2011). Fingeroth is a consultant to Will Eisner Studios and Wizard World Comic Conventions, and has spoken on comics-related topics at Columbia University, the Smithsonian Institution, The New York Historical Society, and many other venues. For more info go to www. DannyFingeroth.com.

Wendy Stallard Flory is Professor of English at Purdue University. Her article, "The Psychology of Antisemitism: Conscience-Free Rationalization and the Deferring of Moral Choice," appeared in *Antisemitism in the Contemporary World*, edited by Michael Curtis (1986). She has published *Ezra Pound and the Cantos: A Record of Struggle* (1980) and *The American Ezra Pound* (1989), both with Yale University Press. Her completed book manuscript, "Inside Stories: The American Romance and Its Characters in Depth," presents an original critical approach that it demonstrates with eleven chapter-length readings of individual romances.

James Goldberg's family is Jewish on one side, Sikh on the other, and Mormon in the middle. His plays, essays, and short stories have appeared in *Shofar*, *Drash*, *The Best of Mormonism: 2009*, *Sikh Chic*, and other publications. Goldberg has taught persuasive and creative writing at Brigham Young University and now writes web content for the LDS Church History Department.

Nicole Wilkes Goldberg earned an MA in English literature in 2009 at Brigham Young University. She has presented at the Jewish American and Holocaust Literature Symposium and the North American Levinas Society. She currently divides her time between teaching English at Brigham Young University and raising her children.

Jean-Philippe Marcoux is a professor of American literature at Université Laval in Québec, Canada. He is the author of the monograph, *Jazz Griots: Music and Historiography in the 1960s African American Poem* (2012), and he has published in the journals *MELUS*, *Re-Marking*, *The Langston Hughes Review*, *College Language Association*, and *Canadian Poetry*, among others. He is currently working on book-length study of the Umbra poets and workshops that will focus on the literary production of the group. The working title is *"Prophets of the Planets: The Umbra Poets and the Shaping of a Black Aesthetic."*

Chantal Catherine Michel studied media and cinema studies at Université Paul Valéry (Montpellier, France), Montclair State University (NJ) and in 2010 received her PhD from Freie Universität (Berlin, Germany). She attended many national and international conferences with lectures on Yiddish cinema and published several articles about this topic as well as her book, *Das Jiddische Kino* (2012). Having always been interested in comic books and graphic novels, she taught several classes on the comics medium, film versions of comic books and on political comics.

Ira Nadel, Professor of English at the University of British Columbia, is the author of biographies of Leonard Cohen, Tom Stoppard, David Mamet, and Leon Uris. He has also published *Joyce and the Jews: Culture and Texts* (1989) and *Modernism's Second Act: A Cultural Narrative* (2013), as well as edited *The Cambridge Companion to Ezra Pound* (2007) and *Ezra Pound in Context* (2010). Forthcoming from him are both a critical biography of Virginia Woolf and a short study of Pound's *Cathay*.

Tahneer Oksman is an assistant professor and director of the Writing Program at Marymount Manhattan College. Her book, *"How Come Boys Get to Keep Their Noses?": Women and Jewish American Identity in Contemporary Graphic Memoirs*, will be published in 2016 by Columbia University Press. She has published articles in *a/b: Auto/Biography Studies, Studies in Comics*, and *Studies in American Jewish Literature*, as well as in *The Forward, Lilith*, and the *Los Angeles Review of Books*. She is currently the graphic narratives reviews editor at *Cleaver Magazine*.

Matt Reingold teaches in the Judaic Studies program at TanenbaumCHAT in Toronto, Canada. He is a recent doctoral graduate from York University's Faculty of Education, where he was a Wexner Fellow and Davidson Scholar. His areas of research are arts-based learning in secondary Jewish education and Jewish graphic novels.

Derek Parker Royal is a professor in the School of Arts, Technology, and Emerging Communication at the University of Texas at Dallas, and also the general editor of Bloomsbury Academic's new "Bloomsbury Comics Studies Series." He is the coauthor of *Philip Roth's American Pastoral* (2011) and the editor of *Philip Roth: New Perspectives on an American Author* (2005) and *Unfinalized Moments: Essays in the Development of Contemporary Jewish American Narrative* (2011). His essays on comics, American literature, and film have appeared in a variety of edited book collections as well as scholarly journals, including *College Literature, Modern Fiction Studies, Contemporary Literature, MELUS, Critique, Post Script, Literature/Film Quarterly, Poe Studies/Dark Romanticism, The Mark Twain Annual, Nathaniel Hawthorne Review, Texas Studies in Literature and Language, Midwest Quarterly, ImageTexT, International Journal of Comic Art, Modern Drama, Modern Jewish Studies/Yiddish, Shofar*, and *Studies in American Jewish Literature*. He is the founder and former executive editor of *Philip Roth Studies*, and he has guest edited eight different special issues of scholarly journals, covering topics such as contemporary Jewish narrative, multiethnic comics, the Hernandez brothers, superheroes and gender, comics and world politics, and Woody Allen's post-1990 films. His books *Coloring America: Multi-Ethnic Engagements in Recent Comics* and *The Hernandez Brothers: Conversations* are forthcoming from the University Press of Mississippi. He is also the cohost and cocreator of the popular podcast, *The Comics Alternative*, which can be found at ComicsAlternative.com.

Stephen E. Tabachnick is a professor of English at the University of Memphis and has been teaching courses in the graphic novel for more than twenty years. He is the editor of *Teaching the Graphic Novel* (2009), the coeditor of *Drawn from the Classics: Essays on Graphic Adaptations of Literary Works* (2015), and the author of *The Quest for Jewish Belief and Identity in the Graphic Novel* (2014). He is also the author of *Fiercer Than Tigers: The Life and Works of Rex Warner* (2002), and the author or editor of several books about Lawrence of Arabia and Charles M. Doughty (author of *Travels in Arabia Deserta*).

Eli Valley is a writer and artist whose work has been featured in *The New York Times, New York Magazine, The Nation, The New Republic, The Guardian, The Daily Beast,*

The Intercept, *Gawker*, *Saveur*, and elsewhere. His art has been labeled "ferociously repugnant" by *Commentary* and "hilarious" by *The Comics Journal*. The 2011–2013 Artist in Residence at the *Forward* newspaper, he has given multimedia performances fusing comics with personal narrative in the United States, Europe, Africa, and Israel. His website is www.EliValley.com.

Robert G. Weiner is associate humanities librarian at Texas Tech University, where he is the liaison for the College of Visual and Performing Arts as well as film studies. He is on the editorial board for the *Journal of Graphic Novel and Comics* and has published in the *International Journal of Comic Art*, *Journal of Popular Culture*, *Texas Library Journal*, and the *Journal of Pan African Studies*, among others. He is the author of *Marvel Graphic Novels: An Annotated Guide* (2007) and editor of *Graphic Novels and Comics in Libraries and Archives* (2010) and *Captain America the Struggle of the Superhero* (2009). He is also the coeditor of such collections as *The Joker: A Serious Study of the Clown Prince of Crime* (2015), *Graphic Novels and Comics in the Classroom: Essays on the Educational Power of Sequential Art* (2013), *Web Spinning Heroics* (2012), and *James Bond in Popular and World Culture* (2010).

Al Wiesner is a writer, illustrator, and publisher. He created *Shaloman* in 1983, a series now spanning forty issues across five volumes. In 2010, Wiesner was honored with an Inkpot Award, and he has been recognized in numerous journals and scholarly literature as an advocate for Judaic awareness within the comics industry.

Foreword
What Hath Will Wrought?

If you've ever wondered, "Is Superman more like Moses or Jesus?" or "Is the Spirit really Jewish?" or "Is it really appropriate to discuss the Holocaust in comics form?" then this is the book for you. Through a variety of approaches, *Visualizing Jewish Narrative* examines the many and varied aspects of Jewish comics and graphic novels, all of them offering thought-provoking insights into what could broadly be called "Jewish comics" (the sequential art type; not Shecky Greene and Buddy Hackett).

Of course, just like defining, "What is a Jew?" can lead to all sorts of strange permutations of thought and emotion, ditto for, "What makes a comic Jewish?" I have no more idea than anyone else, but I am somewhat obsessed with the question, as are the smart people writing in this book like Daniel Bronstein, Robert G. Weiner, Brannon Costello, Samantha Baskind, Catherine Michel, Stephen E. Tabachnick, and the rest of the remarkable roster of writers brought together by Derek Royal (which seems to be his real name, not one chosen to disguise his Jewishness—he claims he's not—or his superhero secret identity—he likewise claims he's not one of those, either—but I have my doubts about the latter).

But whether or not he's from the planet Krypton, Derek has devised a working definition of visual Jewish narrative that encompasses stories with some kind of Jewish theme or connection—be it the wise-guy humor of Will Elder's "chicken-fat"-infused *Mad* comics, or the quest for identity that is embarked upon in Marvel and DC's superhero comics, as well as in memoir-style graphic novels like *How to Understand Israel in 60 Days or Less*.

An especially strong aspect of *Visualizing Jewish Narrative* is that while it certainly helps to have read the comics and graphic novels cited, the authors manage to bring them to life as they comment on them. Ideally, this will create a feedback loop where people interested in the comics will read the book, and people intrigued by the book will seek out the comics.

Worth noting as well as a subtext of the book is how the narrative works cited, "Jewish" in whatever way, have become of interest to large segments of society that are by no means Jewish. Perhaps, as with Jewish American novels and films, "Jewish" is a metaphor for "human." Philip Roth's *Portnoy's Complaint* may be about a specifically Jewish narrator and his relation to his ethnic and religious background, but really, it's about everyone's weird family and how growing up in it affects one as an adult.

So what this book's essays and the works they comment on perhaps have in common is the need we all have to be different and yet to fit in, to be individuals while simultaneously part of a community.

In this light, since there are two essays about Will Eisner in this book, Eisner may be a reasonable figure to take a moment to examine and to keep in mind while reading the essays within.

Broadly speaking, Eisner (1917–2005) had two phases to his career that were relevant to this book. In his first phase, he created the weekly *Spirit* comic that appeared as a newspaper insert from 1940 to 1952, and is generally considered a high point in the development of comics. Set in a version of New York he called Central City, Eisner populated *The Spirit* with various ethnic types, including Yiddish-accented, urban Jews. While many, notably Jules Feiffer, have described the Spirit himself—a masked crime-fighter who has some attributes of a superhero—as being Jewish, this is something that has to be read between the lines to discern.

However, starting with 1978's *A Contract with God*—Eisner's collection of comics stories that helped jumpstart the modern graphic novel movement—the cartoonist focused on Jewish life in America in the twentieth century, a topic that he would explore until he passed away in 2005. Like prose novelists Roth, Saul Bellow, and Bernard Malamud, Eisner found fertile storytelling ground looking back with insight at the world from which he had emerged. Eisner also became passionately concerned about anti-Semitism, which he especially addressed in his final graphic novel, *The Plot: The Secret Story of the Protocols of the Elders of Zion*, the history of the notorious fraudulent document that continues to plague the world to this very day.

In these two phases of his career, Eisner goes from telling "coded" Jewish stories in *The Spirit*—including the Feiffer-scripted "Ten Minutes" about an ill-fated hustler from a seemingly (although not explicitly) Jewish neighborhood in the 1940s Bronx—to graphic novels, such as *To the Heart of the Storm*, that specifically deal with issues relating to Jewish life in America and Europe in the 1930s and 1940s as recalled decades later. One could say that Eisner, as much as any individual creator can, embodies the development of visual Jewish narrative. I would even go so far as to suggest that many of the comics and graphic novels discussed in this book are highly involved with Eisner, somehow engaging with his work, either continuing from it, expanding on it, or arguing with it—sometimes all three simultaneously. Food for thought, I hope, even if you don't necessarily agree.

In any case, I'll close by saying *mazel tov* to Derek and the rest of the writers of the book. May it sell 120,000 copies and open 120 million minds. Now, dear reader, go forth and explore this fascinating volume.

Danny Fingeroth

Acknowledgments

It is with deep gratitude that I acknowledge Daniel Morris and Zev Garber, who were the coeditors of *Shofar: An Interdisciplinary Journal of Jewish Studies* when this project first appeared as a special issue of the journal in 2011. Nancy Lein, *Shofar*'s managing editor at the time, was indispensable in helping me to pull everything together, and in a coherent and visually attractive manner. It was their support and encouragement that drove me to transform that seven-essay study into this much more expansive collection.

Thanks also to those friends and colleagues who have served as sounding boards for this project as well as exciting discussants on the topic of Jewish comics. These include Danny Fingeroth, Ben Katchor, Steven E. Tabachnick, M. Thomas Inge, Steven M. Bergson, Harry Brod, Ranen Omer-Sherman, and my fearless cohost of *The Comics Alternative* podcast, Andrew J. Kunka.

Of course, I could not have brought this collection to fruition without the help of everyone at Bloomsbury Publishing, specifically David Avital and Mark Richardson. I thank you guys, as well, for being the home of the new Bloomsbury Comics Studies Series, an idea that I first hammered out with David back in 2012. I am proud to be the series' general editor. Here's wishing us years of productive collaboration on comics-related scholarship!

The following essays in this collection were originally published in the 2011 special issue of *Shofar* devoted to Jewish comic and graphic novels (volume 29, number 2), most in shorter form:

Lan Dong, "Thinly Disguised (Autobio)Graphical Stories: Will Eisner's *Life, in Pictures*."

Wendy Stallard Flory, "*The Search*: A Graphic Narrative for Beginning to Teach about the Holocaust."

Robert G. Weiner, "The Servant: Marvel Comics and the Golem Legend."

Cyril Camus, "The 'Outsider': Neil Gaiman and the Old Testament."

Nicole Wilkes Goldberg and James Goldberg, "'You Wouldn't Shoot Your Fellow Jews': Jewish Identity and Nostalgia in Joann Sfar's *Klezmer*."

Derek Parker Royal, "There Goes the Neighborhood: Cycling Ethnoracial Tensions in Will Eisner's *Dropsie Avenue*."

Introduction
Visualizing Jewish Narrative

Derek Parker Royal

Over the past several years, there has been rapidly growing interest in Jews and comics—not comics of the Groucho Marx, Woody Allen, and Larry David variety but those as presented on the paneled pages of the newspaper funnies, comic books, and graphic novels.[1] In the past ten years alone, there have been no less than ten titles devoted exclusively to the history and analysis of Jews and comic art, and these books do not even include the many recent comics-related texts with substantive portions devoted to specific Jewish authors.[2] Part of this interest can be read as an outgrowth, or the natural consequence, of scholarly studies in Jews and popular culture. The past couple of decades have seen a number of significant studies that highlight the presence, and even the essential contributions, of Jews in a variety of popular media.[3] Comics, the argument goes, is one of those mass outlets—along with television and Hollywood films—in which Jews could not only thrive but also largely define according to particular ethnic themes and sensibilities. This nascent interest in Jewish comics and graphic novels can also be linked to another recent phenomenon, a broader scholarly focus on comics and the ways in which they represent ethnoracial identity.[4] Many of these analyses have not only chronicled the history of racial and ethnic caricatures in American comic strips, comic books, and film animation, but they have also explored the relatively recent rise in ethnic ownership of the comic image, that is, how traditionally marginalized writers and illustrators have become more a part of the comics industry and have thereby exerted more control over representations of their own ethnic communities.

In terms of Jewish Americans, this involvement in the industry has been in place since the comic book's inception. As comics historian Arie Kaplan points out, Maxwell "Charlie" Gaines (née Max Ginsberg) put together what many consider the first American comic book. In 1934, he, along with his friend Harry L. Wildenberg, persuaded Eastern Color Printing to collect the comic strips that had previously been published in Sunday newspapers, print them in half tabloid size and distribute them first through chain department stores, then when that proved successful, sell them on newsstands. There had been earlier attempts to collect and distribute comic strips in magazine form, but this was the first time anyone had done so on the retail level and not as a promotional giveaway (*From Krakow to Krypton* 2–3). The result was *Famous Funnies*, and as critics such as Kaplan, Danny Fingeroth, and Paul Buhle have pointed out, thus began the Jewish association with comics and their shaping of the medium. Indeed, many of the early pioneers of American comics were Jews, including Jerome Siegel, Joe Shuster, Bob Kane, Bill Finger, Jerry Robinson, Joe Simon, Jack Kirby, Stan Lee, Larry Leiber, Gil Kane, Will Eisner, Jules Feiffer, Will Elder, Harvey Kurtzman, Al Jaffee, and Joe Kubert. This brief list of artists and writers created, or famously illustrated, most of the memorable characters of the 1930s and 1940s, including Superman, Batman, Captain America, the Guardian, the Boy Commandos, the Fantastic Four, the Hulk, the X-Men, Iron Man, the Green Lantern, the Spirit, and Sgt. Rock. And editors such as Stan Lee, Mort Weisinger, Julius Schwartz, William Gaines, Al Feldstein, and Harvey Kurtzman put their indelible stamp on most of the significant comic books coming out of the industry's leading publishers: DC Comics, Marvel, and EC Comics.

One of the reasons for this Jewish dominance in the comics industry is due in large part to the occupational opportunities, or lack thereof, in the first half of the twentieth century. As both Kaplan and Fingeroth have pointed out, most of the prominent and "respectable" fields where artists and writers could express their creativity—such as magazines, newspaper strips, and advertising—were closed to Jews at the time, or at least difficult to enter, due to anti-Semitism, both overt and subtle. So those with backgrounds and training in the illustrative arts were limited to the less desirable, and more lowly regarded, jobs where there was no discrimination, such as in pulp magazines and comic books. According to Al Jaffee, one of *Mad* magazine's legendary artists, only the rare "super-Jew" could break through into newspaper strips and magazine art, and for everyone else, they were confronted with the gentleman's agreement:

> In a lot of firms, there was an unwritten policy that no Jews need apply .... You went in and you sat down with your portfolio and the message came through clearly, especially when you ran into very nice people who would say, "Look, your work looks pretty good and I wouldn't mind taking you in, but there's a policy here. We don't hire too many Jewish people." ... But the comic-book business did not discriminate. In fact, a lot of the comic-book publishers were Jewish, so the opportunities for getting work [were there], because you got rid of that one big bugaboo! (qtd. in Kaplan, *From Krakow to Krypton* 28–29)

Will Eisner put it more bluntly when he pointed out that comics was "a medium that was regarded as trash, that nobody really wanted to go into." And explaining the overriding presence of Jews in the industry, he states: "There were Jews in this medium because it was a crap medium. And in a marketplace that still had racial overtones, it was an easy medium to get into" (Brownstein and Schutz 211).[5] According to this understanding of history, the Jewish presence in comics was not only a fortuitous accident but a culturally defining one as well.

However, such readings are not without their detractors. Ben Katchor, a frequent contributor to *The Forward* and *Metropolis Magazine*, as well as the author of the comic strip *Julius Knipl, Real Estate Photographer*, is not entirely comfortable with the assertion that Jews have been among the most prominent innovators in comics. He states that this understanding of comics is a simplification of history made by people who think that comics were invented in 1938 by Siegel and Shuster [the creators of Superman]. The best American newspaper comic strips artists at the early twentieth century—Chester Gould, Windsor McCay, Harold Gray, and George Herriman—were not Jewish .... If there was some vital connection between Jews and comics, why were there so few comic-strips in the Yiddish press?

Katchor admits that many Jews were involved in the creation of American comic books in the late 1930s and 1940s, but he believes that the subject matter at the time—for example, superhero, detective, and funny animal comics—was more of a liability to the medium than an asset. He agrees with Eisner, stating that comics was "the lowest level of commercial art open to the children of immigrant Jews," but his assessment of their contribution stands in stark contrast with that of recent critics who highlight the Jewish presence in early comics: "These people set picture-stories [Katchor's preferred term for comics] back a hundred years and turned comics into a low-level commercial art-form directed at children and adolescents. It's taken sixty years to shake off the stigma they imposed upon comics."

Katchor's critique raises a series of intriguing questions. First, if, contrary to what critics such as Kaplan, Fingeroth, and Buhle have argued, Jews were not the primary driving force behind early comics, then what makes an emphasis on Jewish comics so special? Here, we should make a distinction between comics as a medium—an emphasis that Katchor is apparently making—and comic books as a specific form, or package, of delivery and marketing. There is no question that many Jews were involved in the development of the comic book as a consumable cultural product, but what Katchor seems to be suggesting is that the distinction between the comic book and the comic strip is more fluid than many would care to admit. After all, the first comic books were nothing more than previously published strips collected together in magazine form. This being the case, arguing that one community of individuals is largely responsible for the existence of a cultural phenomenon—American comics— is dubious at best. This kind of critical analysis runs the risk of essentializing a narrative form according to nation or ethnicity, such as arguing that the novel is English or that trickster tales are African American. It is the kind of assertion, according to Laurence Roth, that "has become the hallmark of the 'sociopolitical' approach to interpreting the Jewish presence in American popular culture" (465).[6] In observing that Jews have contributed greatly to the history of comic art, one must resist the temptation to define the medium solely or even primarily through this involvement. Such an interpretive stance can lead to a nostalgia that privileges a false, or at least a biased, understanding of history. For example, almost every recent book on Jews and comics has taken as its critical springboard Michael Chabon's *The Amazing Adventures of Kavalier & Clay* (2000), a novel inspired and largely informed by the Golden Age of comics and its wealth of Jewish creators. What is more, Chabon has lately become the "high literary" darling of comics fans and writers, contributing commentary, forewords, introductions, and endorsements to a variety of comics-related media. This is not to take away from the significance of Chabon's Pulitzer Prize-winning novel, an engaging narrative that adeptly incorporates the early history of American comics into its fictional world. But it is curious how so many pop culture-based studies, especially those devoted to comics, have referenced the novel as a way of almost legitimizing their projects.

A second question stemming from Katchor's assertion runs thus: what *exactly* is Jewish about comics? In addition to the "career argument"—that the contributions of so many Jews to the inception of the comic book *in effect* makes it a special case— some have pointed out that specific Jewish sensibilities and experiences have defined American comics. Some, such as Kaplan and Mel Gordon, have argued that Jewish humor—its Yiddishisms, its sarcasm, its self-mockery—was a defining feature of such artists as Harvey Kurtzman and *Mad* magazine's other "usual gang of idiots" (as its regular contributors have been called), and that their legacy led directly to the underground comix movement of the 1960s and to contemporary Jewish artists such as Art Spiegelman, Daniel Clowes, and Kim Deitch.[7] Others have read the superhero genre as having direct roots to the Jewish experience.[8] For these critics, figures such as Superman, the Thing, the X-Men, and even the goyish Captain America can be best understood through a Jewish lens. The origins of Moses, passing and assimilation, the legend of the golem, the Diaspora, Kabbalism, the history of Israel, the Holocaust, the Hebrew Bible, and former Israeli Prime Minister David Ben-Gurion are just some of the facets of Jewish experience that have gone into the construction of superheroes. The problem with such an approach is that it runs the danger of being applied too freely and in ways that stretch credibility. It is one thing to see in Superman's origins, a child sent in a vessel from a doomed people and adopted into a world where he must hide his true identity, a retelling of the Exodus story. It is something else entirely to read Thor, a superhero straight from Norse mythology, and his ill-fated romance with human Jane Foster as an analogy to marrying outside of the tribe. One may also fall into the trap of reading with ethnic blinders, of only seeing the "Jewish" parts of a comic and ignoring any other possible similarities and influences. Such a prejudiced approach to comics could then lead to legitimizing only those interpretations that best fit your schema.[9]

In his recent *Jewish Comix Anthology: Volume 1* (2014), Steven M. Bergson collects over forty graphic tales with some sort of Jewish subject matter, and it would be difficult to argue that the stories' contents are ethnically questionable in any way. But with other texts, the issue is not as clear-cut. Yet another question—or series of questions— generated by Ben Katchor's objection relates not only to Jews and comics but also to Jewish cultural production as a whole. How specifically do we define Jewish literature, Jewish art, Jewish film, and Jewish music? Must it have a Jewish "sensibility"? And what exactly is that sensibility? Is it primarily Ashkenazi or would it also accommodate Sephardic and Mizrahi temperaments? What do we do with comics created by Jews but that have little or no Jewish cultural or religious content? For example, Jewish-born Trina Robbins inserts practically no overt ethnic subject matter in her *GoGirl!* comics (2000–2006), yet she's also the writer of the graphic biography, *Lily Renee, Escape Artist: From Holocaust Survivor to Comic Book Pioneer* (2011). Is the former "less Jewish" because it does not engage directly with Jewish themes? Conversely, how do we read comics with clear and overt Jewish content but which were created by non-Jews? The latter is a question that could easily apply to Robert Crumb. He is married to the self-consciously Jewish cartoonist, Aline Kominsky-Crumb, has collaborated with her on

Weirdo magazine (1981–1993) and *Dirty Laundry Comics* (1993), and is often seen as possessing a Jewish sensibility (his fascination with strong Jewish women is almost legendary). What is more, his *The Book of Genesis Illustrated* (2009) is a complete graphic adaptation of the first book of the Torah and garnered much attention in the Jewish press. Or what about Seth Kushner's *Schmuck* (2015), a collection of short narratives whose ethnic marker is more or less confined to its title? There is nothing "Jewish" at all about the individual stories, and without the titular Yiddishism, one would be hard pressed to discern anything ethnic within the text. And then there is the case of Steve Niles (a non-Jew) and his *Breath of Bones: A Tale of the Golem* (2014). The narrative premise has everything to do with Jewish legend, but Niles intentionally left his story free of any direct cultural references and ethnic signifiers because, according to the creator, "I wanted to make [the story] universal .... I wanted to come up with a way so that everyone felt comfortable with it." Does this extrication of ethnic context, what some might call a "whitewashing" of the narrative, automatically disqualify the graphic novel from any Jewish comics reading list?[10]

Indeed, the golem figure is a useful springboard into problematizing any attempts at essentializing Jewish comics. American comic-book history is rich with golem references, direct and indirect, overtly Jewish and tangentially suggestive. Classic superheroes such as Superman and Captain America have been critically framed by the legend, yet with neither is the comparison crucial. More overt, or at least less masked, links to the golem have also defined mainstream American comics, such as Benjamin "the Thing" Grimm of the Fantastic Four (beginning in 1961), the vigilante Ragman (first appearing in 1976), the Golem (created by Len Wein and John Buscema in 1974), and even arguably Swamp Thing (also created by Wein, along with artist Berni Wrightson, in 1971). (In fact, Robert G. Weiner's contribution in this collection focuses on Marvel Comics' use of the golem legend.) One might even be tempted to read Paul Chadwick's character, Concrete (first appearing in 1986), through the lens of the Jewish legend, albeit, several times removed. And in addition to the aforementioned *Breath of Bones*, there are more recent uses of the golem figure, to greater and lesser degrees of ethno-mythic verisimilitude, that complicate any precise definition of a comic's "Jewishness" including Scott Barkman, Alex Leung, and Mark Louie Vuycankiat's *Golem* (2012), Hilary Goldstein and Giovanni Timpano's *The Golem* (2013), Olga Volozova's *The Golem of Gabirol* (2013), William Exley's *Golemchik* (2015), and David G. Klein's *The Golem's Voice* (2015). What all of these examples underscore are the complex cultural negotiations that go into illustrating, and sequentializing, Jewishness. Origin points can be unstable, and narrative trajectories can result in surprising points of impact.

Instead of attempting to pinpoint the "Jewish" in comics and graphic novels, we would do well to heed the advice of Danny Fingeroth, who, in his study of Jews, comics, and superheroes, concludes that the connection is one that "when looked at directly, almost disappears. One has to look at it from the corner of one's eye to catch a glimpse of something that, by its nature, evades detection" (155). Such an approach would certainly provide a more complete understanding of Jewish comics in all of its manifestations. It would allow for the work of early comics artists, with the "masked" ethnic identities of their superheroes, to be set alongside more overt Jewish creations such as Marvel Comics' Magneto and Kitty Pryde of the X-Men titles, the Fantastic

Four's the Thing, the Israeli superheroine Sabra, the fortune-seeking adventurer Dominic Fortune, and the gunslinger Two-Gun Kid; DC Comics' Colossal Boy of the Legion of Super-Heroes, the Justice League's Atom Smasher, and the golem-inspired vigilante Ragman; Howard Chaykin's Reuben Flagg in the *American Flagg!* series; Alan Oirich's Jewish Hero Corps, a team of Orthodox super-powered crime-fighters; and Al Wiesner's "man of stone" superhero, Shaloman (an inanimate rock who comes to life whenever someone cries out for help, "Oy vey!"). Given a more expansive definition of Jewish comics, readers could better appreciate the comedic roots of *Watchmensch* (2009), Rich Johnston and Simon Rohrmüller's parody of Alan Moore's classic take on the superhero genre, *Watchmen*. Furthermore, it would provide the tools to explore the critical crossroads of identity, adaptation, and metafiction found in Michael Chabon's hero, the Escapist: a comic-book character created (by two fictional Jewish artists) in a traditional novel, that spawned the comic-book series *Michael Chabon Presents the Amazing Adventures of the Escapist* (2004–2005, and whose hero had the gentile-sounding name, Tom Mayflower), that subsequently lead to a comic-book mini-series called *The Escapists* (2006), about a Jewish writer who buys the rights to recreate the hero … similar to the way Chabon's fictional Kavalier and Clay constructed their protagonist in the Pulitzer Prize-winning novel.

Indeed, the diverse nature of Jewish comics becomes even more apparent in its graphic novel form. Along with the groundbreaking and prolific work of Will Eisner—for example, *A Contract with God* (1978), *The Dreamer* (1986), *A Life Force* (1988), *To the Heart of the Storm* (1991), *Dropsie Avenue* (1995), *Fagin the Jew* (2003), and *The Name of the Game* (2003)—there is Milt Gross's wordless Yiddish humor-inspired masterpiece from 1930, *He Done Her Wrong: The Great American Novel (with No Words)*, Jules Feiffer's "novel in cartoons" *Tantrum* (1979), as well as more recent works such as Peter Kuper's *Stop Forgetting to Remember: The Autobiography of Walter Kurtz* (2007), Neil Kleid and Nicolas Cinquegrani's *The Big Kahn* (2009), and James Sturm's ethnic-inspired *The Golem's Mighty Swing* (2003) and *Market Day* (2010). Episodic narratives make up a sizable proportion of Jewish comics, as we find in Harvey Pekar's *American Splendor* stories (1976–2008), Steve Sheinkin's *Rabbi Harvey* books (2006, 2008), Ben Katchor's Julius Knipl strips (collected 1996), and Evan Dorkin's *Dork* series (1993–2001) and *Milk and Cheese: Dairy Products Gone Bad* (2012). And there are also instructional comics that provide histories of the Jewish people—for example, Stan Mack's *The Story of the Jews: A 4,000-Year Adventure* (1998), David Gantz's *Jews in America: A Cartoon History* (2002, rev. ed., 2006), and Harvey Pekar and Paul Buhles's *Yiddishkeit* (2011)—J.T. Waldman's graphic adaptation *Megillat Esther* (2006), as well as child-friendly comics such as Leibel Estrin and Dovid Sears's original *Mendy and the Golem* series (1981–1984)—yet another golem-related title—which uses adventure stories to teach ethical lessons. A more recent series for younger readers, a mash-up of Jewish legend and fantasy, is Barry Deutsch's *Hereville* series, featuring as its protagonist a time-traveling, monster-fighting Orthodox Jewish girl: *Hereville: How Mirka Got Her Sword* (2010), *Hereville: How Mirka Met a Meteorite* (2012), and *Hereville: How Mirka Caught a Fish* (2015).

Stories of the Holocaust are plentiful, many of them memoirs. Following Art Spiegelman's Pulitzer Prize-winning *Maus: A Survivor's Tale* (vol. 1, 1986; vol. 2, 1991) was Joe Kubert's *Yossel: April 19, 1943* (2003), Pascal Croci's *Auschwitz* (2004), Martin Lemelman's *Mendel's Daughter: A Memoir* (2006), Miriam Katin's *We Are on Our Own* (2006) and its follow up *Letting It Go* (2013), Bernice Eisenstein's *I Was a Child of Holocaust Survivors* (2006), David Sim's *Judenhauss* (2008), Eric Heuvel's *The Search* (2009) and *A Family Secret* (2009), Reinhard Kleist's *The Boxer: The True Story of Holocaust Survivor Harry Haft* (2014), Jeremie Dres's *We Won't See Auschwitz* (2013), and Rutu Modan's *The Property* (2013).[11] There are also many examples of Jewish gangster and crime comics, including Brian Michael Bendis's *Goldfish* (2001), Howard Chaykin's erotic thrillers *Black Kiss* (2002) and *Black Kiss II* (2013), Judd Winick's twelve-part maxi-series *Caper* (2003–2004), Joe Kubert's *Jew Gangster: A Father's Admonition* (2005), and Neil Kleid and Jake Allen's *Brownsville* (2006).

And while these Holocaust and crime narratives tend to define the ethnic self through specific events or even occupations, there are other artists whose works occasionally foreground Jewish identity but rarely make it an essential component of their narratives. These include such creators as Harvey Pekar (*American Splendor, Our Cancer Year* [1994], *The Quitter* [2005], and *Harvey Pekar's Cleveland* [2012]) and Bob Fingerman (*Minimum Wage* [1994–1999, 2013–present], *White Like She* [1994], and *From the Ashes* [2009]). Then there are other figures who, to varying degrees, appear to be ambivalent, if not silent, when it comes to their Jewish roots. These include the comic books, graphic novels, and caricature art of Daniel Clowes (author of *Wilson* [2010] and *Mister Wonderful* [2011], as well as the *Eightball* comic book series which generated *Ghost World* [1997], *Like an Velvet Glove Cast in Iron* [1997], *David Boring* [2000], and *Ice Haven* [2005]), Kim Deitch (*The Boulevard of Broken Dreams* [2002], *Shadowland* [2006], *Alias the Cat* [2007], and *The Search for Smilin' Ed* [2010]), and Drew Friedman (*Any Similarity to Persons Living or Dead Is Purely Coincidental* [1989], *Warts and All* [1990], *The Fun Never Stops!* [2007], and *Heroes of the Comics: Portraits of the Pioneering Legends of Comic Books* [2014]).[12]

While male authors largely populate the superhero realm, many Jewish women have defined their work far outside of the mainstream. These personal, at times autobiographical, comics include Ariel Schrag's high school chronicles, *Definition* (1997), *Potential* (2000), and *Likewise* (2009); Leela Corman's *Subway Series* (2002), *Queen's Day* (2003), and *Unterzakhn* (2012); Vanessa Davis's risqué *Spanish Rage* (2005) and *Make Me a Woman* (2010); Miss Lasko-Gross's *Escape from "Special"* (2007) and *A Mess of Everything* (2009); Aline Kominsky-Crumb's graphic memoir, *Need More Love* (2007); Liana Finck's *A Bintel Brief: Love and Longing in Old New York* (2014); Miriam Libicki's *Jobnik!* (2008); and Sarah Glidden's *How to Understand Israel in 60 Days or Less* (2010), the latter two being perspectives of Israel through American eyes.[13] A similar lens can be found in Boaz Yakin and Nick Bertozzi's *Jerusalem: A Family Portrait* (2013); Jack Baxter, Joshua Faudem, and Koren Shadmi's *Mike's Place: A True Story of Love, Blues, and Terror in Tel Aviv* (2015, although Faudem is Israeli), as well as Harvey Pekar's more critical *Not the Israel My Parents Promised Me* (2014, illustrated by J.T. Waldman).

Finally, there are those who represent Jewish identity from different international perspectives, such as the French comics artist Joann Sfar—*The Rabbi's Cat* (2005) and *Klezmer: Tales of the Wild East* (2006)—Italy's Vittorio Giardino (his three *A Jew in Communist Prague* volumes, 1997–1998), as well as Israel's Rutu Modan (*Exit Wounds*

[2007], *Jamilti and Other Stories* [2008], and *The Property* [2013]) and Tomer and Asaf Hanuka (the *Bipolar* series [2001–2004] and *The Divine* [2015, along with Boaz Lavie]). There is also the Actus Tragicus Comics Collective (of which Modan was a founding member), a group of Israeli artists that published such works as *Flipper 1 & 2* (2000), *Happy End* (2002), *Dead Herring Comics* (2004), *How to Love* (2007), and graphic adaptations of five stories from Israeli writer Etgar Keret, *Jetlag* (1999).

Given all of this, attempts to definitively define Jewish comics are quixotic at best, ever running the risk of being counterproductive and even critically stifling. As such, the focus of *Visualizing Jewish Narrative* is broad and inclusive, reflecting the diversity found in the medium. The essays that follow approach comics not only in terms of their ethnic content or the degree to which they display a Jewish sensibility (however that might be defined) but also regarding their engagements with the Old World, religious tradition, the Holocaust and trauma, cultural legends, representations of Israel, historical events, ethnic identity, urban spaces, assimilation, and the teaching of these various topics. Some of the authors discussed are self-consciously aware of themselves as cultural and/or religious Jews and create their narratives accordingly, others are less sure about representing their ethnic roots. The first section, "Picturing Jewish Identity," is made up of six essays that explore what it means to be Jewish in a variety of comics-related contexts. The first contribution, appropriately enough, is a study of the legendary Will Eisner, one of the most influential comics artists in history and considered to be, if not the true father of the graphic novel, then the one who popularized the form. In her essay, Lan Dong focuses on Eisner's autobiographical comics and how he combines both fiction and life writing as a way of examining social prejudice. Next, Tahneer Oksman discusses Leela Corman's *Unterzakhn* and its links to Mary Antin, her sister Frieda, and early immigrant narrative. Matt Reingold's study of J.T. Waldman's *Megillat Esther* explores issues of sexuality and Jewish identity, set against the story of Mordechai and Esther in the Book of Esther. Nicole Wilkes Goldberg and James Goldberg are also interested in Jewish identity, specifically in the ways it manifests itself through the ways comics artists rewrite or reimagine the past. In their essay, they read Joann Sfar's *Klezmer: Tales of the Wild East*, as a subversion of the kind of nostalgia found in a lot of Jewish cultural production, especially those works that emphasize a more conservative continuity with the past and its perceived traditions. Ira B. Nadel's essay explores one of America's legendary cartoonists, Jules Feiffer. His study investigates the particular Jewish voice Feiffer's comics, a topic that has received almost no critical attention. My own contribution in this section brings us back to Will Eisner, this time focusing on the author's views of American ethnic relations in a broad sense, not only as it relates to Jewishness. Specifically, I look at the ways in which the recurring visual themes in *Dropsie Avenue* underscore the process of assimilation—and the dynamics of becoming "white"—and how they contribute to Eisner's neo-naturalistic, if not outright cynical, retelling of the melting pot myth.

The second section of this collection, "Jewish Engagements with Comic Genres," is devoted to the ways in which artists have used popular genres—for example, the superhero comic, adventure, comedy, and science fiction—to investigate Jewish culture and identity. Robert G. Weiner leads off this section with a survey of perhaps the most influential Jewish legend in mainstream comics: the golem. In his essay, he examines the many uses of the golem in the Marvel Universe, especially as given form through the Hulk, the Thing, and the aptly named character, the Golem. Following this is Brannon Costello's study of Dominic Fortune, Howard Chaykin's adventurer/ hero, and what this character tells us about Jewish masculinity and the limitations of manhood. Next, Daniel Bronstein discusses one of *Mad* magazine's legendary creators, Will Elder, and the uses of "visual schmaltz." Specifically, Bronstein looks at Elder's philosophy of "chicken fat," the abundant, over-the-top satirical art that largely defined Elder's style and had its roots in traditional Jewish humor. Finally, Ofer Berenstein explores Israeli science fiction, distinguishes it from its western counterparts, and demonstrates its links to Zionist ideology.

The third section of the book, "Jewish Comics, the Holocaust, and Trauma," begins with Wendy Stallard Flory's close reading of Erich Heuvel, Ruud van der Rol, and Lies Schippers's Holocaust narrative, *The Search*. Specifically, she is interested in the text as an effective educational resource introducing students to the *Shoah*. Samantha Baskin is also interested in the Holocaust in graphic narrative form, and her essay focuses specifically on the Warsaw Ghetto uprising as represented in a series of mainstream and alternative comics. Next, Ellen Rosner Feig looks at the Israeli-Palestinian conflict through the graphic novels of Joe Sacco, Rutu Modan, Sarah Glidden, and Ari Folman. Rounding out this section is Jean-Philippe Marcoux's study of second-generation witnessing. Specifically, he looks at the comics of Art Spiegleman, Bernice Eisenstein, and Martin Lemelman and the ways in which they employ a second-generation voice to bear witness to the unrepresentable trauma experienced by their parents.

The final section of the collection, "Representation of Israel, Biblical Text, and Legend," includes four essays that look outside of the United States and its western counterparts. For example, Catherine Michel takes on the Israeli-Palestinian conflict, but she does so by going beyond American artists such as Joe Sacco and Miriam Libicki. Instead, she is interested in the comics of Maximilien Le Roy and Philippe Squarzoni, lesser known artists who use their work as propaganda and establish a political position in this historical conflict. Stephen E. Tabachnick is also interested in the Israeli-Palestinian conflict, but he limits his scope to the work of the Israeli artist, Rutu Modan, and how her comics voice a message of hope, even in the darkest days of the Intifada. One of the leading figures of the "British Invasion" of American comics in the 1980s, Neil Gaiman, is the subject of Cyril Camus's critical examination. He argues that although Gaiman is known primarily for this acclaimed DC Comics series, *Sandman* (1989–1996, 2009, 2013–2015), there is yet another side of his work that gets relatively little attention. Beginning with Gaiman's outsider status—being an Englishman currently living in America, being a Jew raised with an Anglican educational background—Camus looks at the ways in which the author's comics become intertextual links to, and at times even rewritings of, Hebrew Bible narratives. Finally, Tof Eklund looks at the work of three comics and gaming artists—Joann Sfar, Rutu Modan, and Kristoffer Osterman—and their representations of Jewish giants, the legendary Nephilim and Rephaim. Specifically, Eklund links this emphasis on gianthood to Israeli statehood, political power, and security and attempts to overcome the past. In addition to these essays, readers will find original works of comic art by such illustrators as Eli Valley, a regular contributor to *The Forward*, and Al Wiesner, the creator of the superhero, Shaloman. Their efforts illustrate—quite literally—the full potential of Jewish narrative art.

Taken together, all of these essays, along with the original illustrations, offer a useful introduction to Jewish comics and the criticism surrounding them. What is more, the authors' diversity of topics and of critical approaches all suggest the rich potential of this ever-growing field. As such, *Visualizing Jewish Narrative* stands alongside other recent contributions to the scholarship on ethnicity and comic art, not only as it relates to Jewish culture but as it intersects with that of other communities as well. Perhaps most important, it draws our attention to the fact that the history and the significance of Jewish narrative is more than mere words on a page. Will Eisner once observed with regret that his own graphic novels were relegated to the comics or the young adult sections of bookstores. He believed that his work, and that of others producing a more visually based literature, could stand alongside the books of such writers as Saul Bellow, Philip Roth, and Cynthia Ozick. If the scholarship over the past several years—including the current study—is any indication, then it would appear that Eisner's is a wish whose time has come.

Notes

1   "Graphic novel" is a problematic term, but I am using it here not only because of its widespread and common acceptance, but also in order to distinguish it from comic books as a publication format or delivery system. In this sense, "comics" applies to the medium as a whole, regardless of the form it takes (e.g., the editorial cartoon, the single-panel gag, the newspaper comic strip, the comic book, and the graphic novel). Furthermore, I use "graphic novel" to refer to long-form comics—as opposed to the typical American comic book which runs roughly 22–32 pages—regardless of genre. This could include long works of fictional comics that are "novelistic" in scope, collected issues of previously published comic books or strips, comic memoirs, comics-based journalism, and even expository comics.

2   For studies devoted solely to Jews and comics, see Simcha Weinstein, Danny Fingeroth, Samantha Baskind and Ranen Omer-Sherman, Paul Buhle (*Jews and American Comics*), Arie Kaplan (*From Krakow to Krypton*), Joël Kotek, Thomas Andrae and Mel Gordon, Frederik Stömberg (*Jewish Images in the Comics*), Harry Brod, and Stephen E. Tabachnick. Other works with significant portions on individual Jewish comics artists include Joe Simon, Gerard Jones and Will Jacobs, Arie Kaplan (*Masters of the Comic Book Universe Revealed!*), and of course the University Press of Mississippi's "Conversations with Comic Artists" series, which includes volumes devoted to Stan Lee (2007), Art Spiegelman (2007), Harvey Pekar (2008), Daniel Clowes (2010), Will Eisner (2011), and Howard Chaykin (2011).

3   For a sampling of recent titles on Jews and popular media, see Michael Rogen, Lawrence J. Epstein, Vincent Brooks, J. Hoberman and Jeffrey Sandler, David Zurawick, Andrea Most, and Paul Buhle's three volume *Jews and American Popular Culture*.

4   Paralleling the increased attention in Jews and comics, there has been flowering of titles related to other particular ethnic communities and comics, or multi ethnic

comics in a broader sense. Some of the most notable studies and anthologies include Jeffrey A. Brown; Frederik Stömberg (*Black Images in the Comics*); Michael A. Sheyahshe; Frederick Luis Aldama; Jeff Yang, Parry Shen, Keith Chow, and Jerry Ma; Damian Duffy and John Jennings; Sheena C. Howard and Ronald L. Jackson II; and my own special issue of *MELUS*.

5   For a fuller discussion on the socioeconomic and discriminatory issues surrounding Jews in the comics industry, see Kaplan, *From Krakow to Krypton*, 27–31, and Fingeroth, *Disguised as Clark Kent*, 25–29.

6   Roth cites as examples of this problematic approach Paul Buhle's work on Jews and Hollywood and Andrea Most's study of the Broadway musical. He asserts that "one needs to avoid the old trap of simply arguing for the special case of Jewish writers or the special status of Jewishness within cultural products" (465).

7   See Kaplan (*From Krakow to Krypton* 73–74) and Andrae and Gordon (14–23), for discussions on Jewish humor and its links to comics.

8   The best examples of this are Weinstein and Fingeroth.

9   I am reminded here of Ozzie Freedman's dilemma in Philip Roth's short story, "The Conversion of the Jews." In trying to understand why Jews, according to Rabbi Binder, are so special, he recalls his family's obsession with picking out Jewish names as a way of finding meaning.

> Then there was the plane crash. Fifty-eight people had been killed in a plane crash at La Guardia. In studying a casualty list in the newspaper his mother had discovered among the list of those dead eight Jewish names (his grandmother had nine but she counted Miller as a Jewish name); because of the eight she said the plane crash was "a tragedy." (141–142)

10   The examples of Crumb and Niles are not dissimilar to the case of John Updike and his Bech stories. In *Bech: A Book* (1970), *Bech Is Back* (1982), and *Bech at Bay* (1998), Updike writes the adventures of a fictional Jewish American novelist reminiscent of Bernard Malamud, Saul Bellow, Norman Mailer, and Philip Roth. The content—character, subject, theme, and even setting—are overtly Jewish in nature, but could one call these Updike narratives instances of Jewish American fiction?

11   The latter two are reassessments of the Holocaust from a more contemporary perspective, the grandchildren of survivors. One may be tempted to include Carla Jablonksi and Leland Purvis's "Resistance Trilogy" in this list—*Resistance* (2010), *Defiance* (2011), and *Victory* (2012)—although those books have more to do with the French Resistance than they do with the Holocaust directly.

12   Friedman's caricature series on Jewish comedians—*Old Jewish Comedians* (2006), *More Old Jewish Comedians* (2008), and *Even More Old Jewish Comedians* (2011)—are obviously more ethnically aware in their intent.

13   For a broader overview of female Jewish comics artists, see Sarah Lightman.

Part One

Picturing Jewish Identity

Thinly Disguised (Autobio)Graphical Stories:
Will Eisner's *Life, in Pictures*

Lan Dong

Is it autobiography if parts of it are not true? Is it fiction if parts of it are?
—Lynda Barry (*One Hundred Demons*)

Life is not what one lived, but what one remembers and how one remembers it in order to recount it.

—Gabriel Garcia Marquez (*Living to Tell the Tale*)

As Helena Frenkil Schlam has argued, at every point in the history of American cartoon arts some Jewish cartoonists have contributed their talents and ability to innovation and development, bringing "the sharpened perspective and moral anxiety to this artistic expression" (94). Will Eisner (1917–2005, born William Erwin Eisner) undoubtedly stands among such landmark figures. Jules Feiffer might have understated Eisner's influence when he called him "a cartoonist other cartoonists swiped from" (35) and in 1965 considered *The Spirit*, a weekly comic series published as supplemental inserts for Sunday newspapers from 1939 to 1942, as the "high point" of Eisner's career (37). 1965 was, after all, more than a decade before Eisner became known as a graphic novelist. With a career stretching from the 1930s to the new millennium, Eisner has been respected as a pioneer and godfather in the field of comics. Not only has he broken new ground in developing the visual language and text narrative of comics but also advocated for this medium to be a form of art and of literature that is capable of addressing serious subject matters and expressing a wealth of content. He also has explored the possibility and has paved the way for the use of comics for educational and vocational purposes.[1] Furthermore, Eisner has theorized comics as a "sequential art" and has examined its principles, concepts, and creative process in book-length works.[2] In addition, he has helped popularize the graphic novel as a unique generic category.[3] Robert C. Harvey's remark is one way to summarize Eisner's legacy—he is "a colossus in the history of 20th-century American cartooning" who stands athwart the century "one foot firmly planted in the conceptual genesis of the comic-book medium, the other resolutely striding into the future of the art form" ("An Affectionate Appreciation" 80). The numerous prestigious awards bestowed on him are only small tokens of recognition of Eisner's lifetime contribution to and achievement in the field of comics.[4] The Eisner Awards, created in his honor, are among the most esteemed tributes to cartoonists today. They are acknowledged as the "Oscars" of American comic books, covering more than twenty categories and have been presented each year since 1989 at the largest comics convention in the United States, the Comic-Con International.

During his long career of over seven decades, Eisner explored the potential of comics in various ways: from syndicated newspaper serials to magazines, from instructional manuals to book-length graphic novels, and from fiction to life writing. Indeed, life writing, particularly in the form of autobiography and memoirs, has become an integral part of contemporary graphic novels. In academia, scholarly discussions on graphic novels in general, and autobiographical comics in particular, have generated a variety of perspectives and approaches.[5] Eisner is considered the first cartoonist to demonstrate how "sequential art" can give voice to complex, socially aware characters and stories while marshaling powerful arguments about collective self-representation (Roth 465). This chapter explores the interactions between autobiographical writing and the graphic novel through a critical analysis of Eisner's collection *Life, in Pictures: Autobiographical Stories*. This study hopes to demonstrate how Eisner's work challenges the conventional conceptualization of autobiography as well as breaks new ground in creating, reading, and theorizing the graphic novel, thus expanding the ways the reader reads and understands both genres. At the same time, it reveals the techniques through which Eisner examines the complexity of social prejudice in visual and textual narratives.

Eisner's *Life, in Pictures: Autobiographical Stories*, published posthumously in 2007, gathers a collection of tales that by and large draw inspiration from his life experience. The story "A Sunset in Sunshine City" opens the volumes with a vignette related to the artist's life in Florida in his final years, although the tale is not completely autobiographical. Next, *The Dreamer*, originally published as "a graphic novella set during the dawn of comic books" in 1986, reflects Eisner's formative years as a young cartoonist who was trying to launch a career in New York City in the 1930s.[6] The lead character's dreams, optimism, insight, and innovation bear a lot of threads from Eisner's life. The next narrative in the collection, *To the Heart of the Storm*, first published in 1990, draws on the artist's experience as a soldier during the Second World War as well as casts light on anti-Semitism in New York City and Europe. The story as a whole leads the reader to contemplate social prejudice in its various forms. Originally published in 2001, *The Name of the Game*, inspired by the family history of Eisner's wife, Ann Louise Weingarten, is a multigenerational saga of the Arnheims, a fictional and prominent clan in the East Coast German Jewish community. Another short piece, "The Day I Became a Professional," which originally appeared in Dark Horse's *Autobiographix* (2003), concludes the collection by recounting a moment in Eisner's early career. In merely four pages Eisner portrays an episode unique enough to be a personal story while at the same time universal for cartoonists of different generations. These five stories, all printed in Eisner's signature sepia tone of which *A Contract with God* set a precedent, are presented not in the chronological order of the events they narrate but in the order in which Eisner created them. Bearing a strong sense of "witnessing history" ("Will Eisner's *Life, in Pictures*" 43), some of the narratives make direct reference to Eisner's life and career; others, though relating to the artist's personal experience, incorporate more fictional elements.

Overall, this collection of autobiographical fiction provides an intriguing example of the intersection of life writing and the graphic novel. Instead of telling the tales as fiction or autobiography, Eisner presents selected episodes that are related to "aspects" of his life, career, and people surrounding him (McCloud, "Introduction" 11). Part fictional and part autobiographical, his depictions of the characters—based on himself, family members, and friends—are, according to Eisner's friend and former publisher, Denis Kitchen, "usually not sparing in warts, but he stopped short at truly intimate detail" (59). Two narratives in this collection, *The Dreamer* and *To the Heart of the Storm*, are particularly significant for the purposes of this chapter: they demonstrate how Eisner explores the potential of the graphic novel form by incorporating fiction and life writing, thus expanding the domains of both genres; they reveal how he depicts and contemplates not only anti-Semitism but also broader social issues regarding prejudice.

During the past three decades, there has been a surge of life writing in North America. This trend has extended beyond the realm of words-only texts into works that combine visual and verbal elements such as graphic novels (Jacob 59). Indeed, autobiography has been an important part of comics since the underground comix in the 1960s when Robert Crumb and other cartoonists began to use the medium as "a means of personal and political expression" (Jacob 61). By blending facts with fiction, Eisner's work in "autographics" offers a departure from the confessional comics—prime examples including Harvey Pekar's *American Splendor* and Joe Matt's *Peepshow*—as well as from the narratives of trauma and crisis—for example, Art Spiegelman's two-volume *Maus: A Survivor's Tale* and David B.'s *Epileptic*—by effectively combining his personal experience with the life of a cartoonist in general.[7] As Kitchen has remarked: "Being a product of the Great Depression, a New York Jew, a workaholic loner and a self-made man were all characteristics reflected strongly in his work, both autobiographical and fictional, and are critical to understanding Eisner the man, but they could be ascribed to most of the numerous other cartoonists of his era" (17).

As a child born and raised in the Jewish ghetto in New York City, Eisner inherited a "dreaming" quality from his Austria-born father who valued creativity but was unable to make a living in the arts and struggled to provide for his family. Eisner also embraced a down-to-earth attitude from his mother who was born on a ship when her parents were en route from Romania to the United States and then was orphaned at a young age. Eisner's early years of pursuing a career in comics that started at the age of nineteen are reflected in the main themes of *The Dreamer*: in particular, his search for a publisher, rejection and frustration, the establishment of his first studio, and the breakthrough moment of launching a serial publication of weekly newspaper comic inserts.[8] To some degree, *The Dreamer* is a compact version of what Kitchen has called "Will Eisner's Personal History of Comics" (15). In his introduction to *The Dreamer*, Eisner wrote:

This is a story about a dreamer. It is a walk alongside a young cartoonist on the threshold of his career. It is an examination of hope and ambition. The events take place during a time when cartoonists found themselves on fallow ground, the dawn of the modern comic book industry during the mid-1930s .... *The Dreamer*, intended as a work of fiction, ultimately took on the shape of a historical account.

> In the telling, it was inescapable that the actors would resemble real people ....
> It all comes out of the cluttered closet where I store ghosts of the past, and from
> the yellowing memories of my experience. (*Life, in Pictures* 51–52. Hereafter cited
> parenthetically.)

Here Eisner uses the designations of "a dreamer" and "a young cartoonist" to
foreshadow the personal as well as universal aspects of the tale. It is his story; yet
it is also the story of many artists who share similar hopes and ambitions. Eisner
points to the hybrid nature of *The Dreamer*, first through his intention (fiction) and
second through his creation (a historical and autobiographical account). Instead of
using a visual self-representative avatar (like Art Spiegelman and Marjane Satrapi's
autobiographical avatars Artie and Marji), Eisner features fictional characters, some
of whom have obvious roots in history and reality. Kitchen's annotations, added to the
2007 Norton edition, guide the reader in bridging the characters and episodes in the
story to real people and events. The protagonist, Billy Eyron, a dreamer and young
artist, is as much autobiographical as fictional. His experience in launching a career
as a cartoonist bears much resemblance to Eisner's own. Not to mention, his name is
an altered form of "Will." The fictional Eyron & Samson Studio, established by Billy
and Jimmy Samson with Eyron's personal investment of $30, doubtless will remind
the reader of the Eisner & Iger Studio that Eisner co-founded with Samuel "Jerry" Iger
in the 1930s—a significant landmark for Eisner's career in comics. Moreover, Billy's
persistence for ownership of his comics creation echoes Eisner's insistence on owning
the copyright to *The Spirit* and to his later works, an ownership that was not only
"almost without parallel in comics at that time" but also "almost without parallel on
any popular basis for several decades to come" ("Will Eisner Official Web Site" n.p.).
Just like young Eisner, Billy is optimistic and ambitious in his career while challenging
common practices in the comics business by his retaining copyright control. When
recollecting the copyright issues in the early years of comics, Eisner once commented
that a "healthier arrangement does not come like the gentle rain from heaven. You
have to get it .... The early syndicate contracts were *really* enslavement .... They
owned the copyright. The contract gave the syndicate a right to give the work to
someone else if they felt that you were incapable of continuing" (Eisner *Eisner/Miller*,
245; original italic). Despite all this overlapping between the tale's graphic fictional
episodes and Eisner's life, between the cartoon persona and the creator, Billy's journey
as a young artist trying to find his way in his career, as well as in his pursuit of comics
as a professional in the 1930s, tells more than a personal story. Billy's dreams, hopes,
struggles, long hours, and lonely nights spent in the studio during these workaholic
years speak for and to many artists of that time.

The opening page of *The Dreamer* features at the top a torn piece from *The New
York Times* that indicates the story's date as Thursday, January 21, 1937, and its site
as New York City. The newspaper headline illustrates the historical backdrop of the
Great Depression: "Roosevelt pledges warfare against poverty, broader aid for 'those
who have too little ... '" (53). Under the newspaper image comes Billy, standing
outside a cafeteria holding a portfolio in one hand and a couple coins in the other;
he is positioned right below the title "The Dreamer." As Eisner has pointed out in

Comics and Sequential Art, words can convey intensity and tone. Lettering, usually hand-drawn or created in carefully chosen types of fonts in comics, functions as an extension of the imagery, emphasizing or implying mood (3–4). The excerpt from the newspaper, as an image hanging over the story title as well as the protagonist, evokes the connection between the character's experience and the social environment. Also on this page, Eisner's use of text as image reflects what Scott McCloud has discussed as motion produced between panels in the gutter (*Understanding Comics* 107, 66). The reversed word order of the window label, "Horn's Cafeteria," in the bottom frameless panel suggests the character's movement from outside to inside of the café.

Eisner's arrangement of panels displays constant change in size, shape, and position, posing a challenge to his audience. As a result, readers have to negotiate the ever-changing layouts while examining the individual panels and pages. More specifically, in negotiating Eisner's visual rhythm, the reader becomes an active participant in the text's meaning. In reflecting on this process as related to his works (as well as to other comics), Eisner emphasizes the connection between the comic artist and the reader and stresses that comics be a "participatory form" (*Eisner/Miller* 88). According to him, "[i]n comics, reader control is attained in two stages—attention and retention. Attention is accomplished by provocative and attractive imagery. Retention is achieved by the logical and intelligible arrangement of the images" (Eisner, *Graphic Storytelling* 51). In *The Dreamer*, Eisner portrays a young artist's life as well as presents the character's mental activity in a series of small panels within the limited space of one page. After Billy enters the cafeteria, a fortune-teller approaches him and sells him "a dream" for a dime: "I see you are going to be famous …. Yes, a successful artist … with all that it will bring" (54). The young artist's response is subtly depicted through a number of gestural indicators: laughing, shoulder shrugging, and waving hands. It is quite clear that he is not taking the "dream" he just bought seriously. Nevertheless, the four panels on the bottom of this page present a twist. The message Billy receives from a "Penny Fortunes and Your Weight" machine—"you will be a success in your chosen career"—prompts the overarching theme of the story. In the last panel Billy is reading the Penny Fortunes message carefully as he enters a subway station. His facial expression is visibly different from the panel above when he leaves the cafeteria and dismisses the fortune-teller's words. Thus, this page provides a point of entry into the story of how an artist might pursue the unfolding of his dreams.

After mapping the ups and downs in Billy's career, the story concludes with an episode of his again receiving the same message from a "Penny Fortunes and Your Weight" machine. The last panel, framed without borderlines, shows Billy still holding his portfolio, but now he is walking in long strides with a smile on his face. Now he is a young artist who already has realized some of his dreams. Furthermore, he now is a believer in his own abilities and success who will continue his journey. Besides closing the story on the cusp of Billy's rising career as a cartoonist, the last page of the story also alludes to an upcoming, and unexpected, change in the character's life path (Figure 1.1). The headline of the *New York Times* on Sunday September 3, 1939, shown on top of this page, reads: "Britain and France in war at 6 a.m.; Hitler won't halt attack on Poles; Chamberlain calls empire to fight"; meanwhile the boy at the newsstand shouts, "Heeyar … Git yer late paper … Jomans invade Poland!" (98). All these media indicate the subsequent storm of the Second World War and its effect

Figure 1.1 Reprinted from *Life, in Pictures* by Will Eisner, 98. Copyright © 2007 by Will Eisner Studios, Inc. With permission of the publisher, W. W. Norton & Company, Inc.

on many—cartoonists and others—that the next story, *To the Heart of the Storm*, will explore. The layout of the page, with the newspaper piece on the top, reminds the reader of the opening page of the story and once again frames the character's personal story within the historical context.

When Eisner was born in Brooklyn, New York, in 1917, many immigrants had come from Europe to the United States and settled in New York City largely in ethnic neighborhoods. Eisner came of age during a time of "social awakenings and pervading concern with economic survival," when "one could hear the rumblings and feel the shock waves from the distant Holocaust" (107). Beginning with his groundbreaking

A Contract with God and Other Tenement Stories, first published by Baronet Books in 1978 and followed by a number of graphic novels, Eisner's works have presented the reader with the multifaceted lives of Jewish immigrants and their offspring in the United States, challenged racial and ethnic stereotypes, and inspired further thoughts on social prejudice at differing levels. The fictional Dropsie Avenue in the Bronx that is the setting of *A Contract with God Trilogy* (including *A Contract with God and Other Tenement Stories*, *A Life Force*, and *Dropsie Avenue: The Neighborhood*) has become a literary and visual micro-cosmos of the Jewish community in New York City—a representation of the Great Depression as well as a mirror of American immigration history. Laurence Roth has observed that "the fulcrum for [Eisner's] analogy is Jewish life in America [which] puts him in company with contemporaries such as Saul Bellow, Herman Wouk, Bernard Malamud, Grace Paley, and Philip Roth" (473). Indeed, Eisner received the Lifetime Achievement Award from the National Foundation for Jewish Culture in 2002, recognizing his contribution to the cultural representation of Jewish communities in the United States.

As part of Eisner's artistic exploration of Jewish Americans, *To the Heart of the Storm* draws inspiration from the events that he and his family experienced. Eisner has stated that when writing this book, he intended "to deliver a narrowly focused fictional experience of that [pre-World War II] climate, but in the end, it metamorphosed into a thinly disguised autobiography. In such a work, fact and fiction became blended with selective recall and resulted in a special reality. I came to rely on the truthfulness of visceral memory" (107). *To the Heart of the Storm* represents a combination of the universal and the personal in Eisner's work. It opens with new recruits sitting on a troop train heading to an unspecified army training camp in 1942, resembling a film setup. The opening page presents the top panel of a train from a long shot against the backdrop of the silhouette of city skyscrapers and a looming storm, and then it zooms in to portray the characters in a medium shot in the bottom panel. Willie, a young comics artist whose name reminds the reader the connection between the author and main character he creates in this story, is staring out of the window while Mamid, an editor of a Turkish newspaper in Brooklyn, is reading a newspaper whose headline reads, "British fight for Singapore," an indicator of the historical setting of the story. Then the narrative quickly shifts to flashbacks and reveals how Willie's family encountered anti-Semitism in Europe as well as in America. In this story-within-a-story framework, Willie recalls the tales of Fannie and Shmuel, mostly based on the life experiences of Eisner's parents, giving the graphic novel a broad sweep, from 1880 to 1942 and covering events that take place in Romania, Vienna, New York, and New Jersey. In this sense, Eisner's work reminds the reader the important role memory, both personal and collective, plays in ethnic American memoirs. For example, the parental and communal memory of China and Chinese immigrants' life in the United States filters into Maxine Hong Kingston's *The Woman Warrior: Memoirs of a Girlhood among Ghosts* (1976) and *China Men* (1980). History of both Ireland and the United States informs Frank McCourt's *Angela's Ashes* (1996). The embellished memory of Iran and the recollection of her childhood in California contribute to the narrator's struggles to come to terms with her bicultural heritage in both countries in Azadeh Moaveni's *Lipstick Jihad: A Memoir of Growing Up Iranian in America and American in Iran* (2005). The interaction between memory and reality in *To the Heart of the Storm* pointedly speaks to the history of Jewish immigrants and prompts further contemplation of the storm of fascism in the 1930s and 1940s.

Son of Jewish immigrant parents himself, Eisner's childhood and experiences living in the tenements in New York City offer a wellspring of inspiration for his work. To him, "the city is a collection of neighborhoods …. And each of those neighborhoods is a world into itself" (Eisner, *Eisner/Miller* 261, 263). As Toni Morrison tells us, to lift the veil and reveal the past a writer depends on his/her own recollections as well as those of others. In the writing process, imagination plays as much an important role as memories (191–192). Eisner structures his narrative and visualization through a blending of the autobiographical and the fictional. The image on the third page in *To the Heart of the Storm* shows Willie staring at the train window, which leads the narrative back to 1928 when his family was moving from Brooklyn to the Bronx. The first adventure of Willie and his younger brother, Julian, in the new neighborhood involves, because of their "difference," an encounter with a bully, demeaning name-calling, and a street fight with Irish American youth. As a means of both survival and assimilation, Willie gives Julian the nickname of "Pete." As Ronald Takaki has observed, in the wave of immigration after the turn of the century, many Jews changed their names as a means to assimilate, thereby defining themselves as "Americans" (299–300). Eisner argues that "the comic maker working in modern times must deal with a reader whose life experience includes a substantial amount of exposure to film" (*Graphic Storytelling* 72). In *To the Heart of the Storm*, Willie's flashbacks—framed in the train window against a dark background—have a cinematic quality, and they guide the reader to view selected episodes from his past. Throughout the story, the sights that Willie sees out of his window trigger recollections from the past, which then serve as connecting points between the past and present as well as between historical anti-Semitism and the looming American participation in the Second World War.

As in his previous works, *To the Heart of the Storm* showcases Eisner's literary agility and graphic mastery. The *New Yorker* book review, for example, applauds the work: "Whatever the subject, Eisner manages a light touch: every page is sure-handed, carried out with subtlety, grace, and wit" ("Life, in Pictures" 167). For a book mostly made up of episodes from the past scattered across time and locations, the narrative structure holds particular importance in presenting a compelling and coherent story. As Eisner has emphasized repeatedly, despite the high visibility and attention that his artwork compels, "the story is the most critical component in a comic. Not only is it the intellectual frame on which all artwork rests, but it, more than anything else, helps the work endure" (*Graphic Storytelling* 2). The stories that Eisner has created are usually "built on truths" that he feels necessary to point out (Eisner, *Eisner/Miller*, 96). *To the Heart of the Storm* is no exception. In setting Willie's recollection against the backdrop of the increasing problems at the local, national, and international levels, Eisner steers clear of a linear narrative. Instead, he resorts to reconstructing an array of events and anecdotes as the characters grapple with prejudice of various kinds and uses such visual elements as uneven lines, white space, shading, perspectives, and distance to portray characters and narrate stories. The power underlying the visual language is more evident when placed in the context of race and ethnicity since comics, as a heavily coded medium, rely on stereotyping to achieve narrative effectiveness (Royal 7). In reflecting on growing up in the Bronx, Eisner considers his most indelible memories to be those of "the insidious prejudice that permeated my world. Resisting it brought me to the realization that primal prejudice has different meanings. To other than whites, it is racism; to the ethnically different, it is nationalism; to Jews, it is anti-Semitism" (107). Thus, Eisner structures his narrative with a focus on anti-Semitism both in history and in reality and in the process takes a closer look at the social prejudice at various levels. His usage of visual and textual language helps the flow and development of the story.

Moreover, through his characters of different generations and backgrounds, Eisner addresses the perception of Jewish identity from a number of angles. Ironically Jewish immigrants' success in the United States seemed to fuel anti-Semitism since the beginning of the twentieth century and long before the Second World War. Their accomplishments in education, business, and other social arenas incurred resentment and complaint (Takaki 305–308). For example, in *To the Heart of the Storm*, Willie's uncle Irving is fully aware that his Jewish heritage is an obstacle to his medical studies and his chances of becoming a doctor. As he says to Fannie, his half-sister: "I'm only Jewish if they think I'm Jewish! That's how prejudice works …. I've changed my religion! I'm a Christian now! So I can no longer be involved with you or even identified with the family" (165). The bold lettering in Irving's speech balloons indicates an increased volume of the speaker's voice and highlights how he perceives and deals with prejudice, which is important for their dialogue and the overarching theme of the book. Such emphasis is significant, for as David Carrier points out, "[t]he speech balloon is a defining element of the comic because it establishes a word/image unity that distinguishes comics from pictures illustrating a text" and therefore is essential for the story (4). The gestural indicators accompanying the siblings' dialogue, such as the characters' motion, posture, and facial expressions, clearly and effectively portray what is happening physically and emotionally in the scenes. Irving's hand gestures reinforce his words and help reveal his determination to shun his Jewish heritage, whereas Fannie's wide-opened eyes, hands held up to her chin, and blank stare suggest surprise and helplessness. Using such juxtaposition, Eisner points to the complexity within Irving's coping mechanism and portrays his character paradoxically as both a victim and a perpetrator of racism. If his reality— "where I work they don't hire Jews! … The school I want to go to has quotas to keep out Jews!"—clearly refers to the anti-Semistic climate at the time, his denial of heritage in order to earn a "pass" accepts and reinforces the discrimination. Yet, as Eisner shows in another episode later in the story, being Jewish is far more complicated than just a religious matter, and conversion will not change who a person really is. As Aunt Goldie's husband puts it, after converting to Catholicism, Goldie is "not entirely" Jewish but "underneath … she's still a Jew … Y' can't change the stripes on a zebra!" (245–246).

Like his relatives, Willie has his fair share of struggles with his Jewish background. As a teenager he befriends Heidi, only to find out that her family are nationalist German immigrants from Coblenz and forbid her to go out with Italians and Jews. His first meeting with Heidi's family is embedded with many between-the-line messages, largely coded within the scene's visuals, and foreshadows the failure of their friendship. As Robin Varnum and Christina T. Gibbons point out: "The elements of the representational code which comics employs—including both images and texts, and also such specialized features as word balloons, zip ribbons, and even the panel frames which enclose scenes or segments of a narrative—can be manipulated with great sophistication" (ix–x). While the visuals on this page show the hospitality of Heidi's family, the larger narrative context of this scene indicates multiple layers of meaning. Willie "passes" because his father is from Vienna, "not quite German ... but close" (259). Conversational topics such as the fatherland, the rise of Germany, and *untermensch* not only trouble Willie but also call for the reader's attention. In order to hold on to his social "pass," Willie decides to attend Heidi's graduation party alone, although his parents also are invited; as such, he denies his Jewish heritage. Besides bullies and verbal abuses, as portrayed at the beginning of *To the Heart of the Storm*, racism can surface in other forms. Eisner depicts the revelation of Willie's secret at the party "off stage" and without direct confrontation and reveals the character's emotional turmoil in a subtle way. This indirectness suggests the subtlety and ubiquity of social discrimination in everyday life. As Gillian Whitlock has proposed, new meanings can be generated in "an active process of imaginative production whereby the reader shuttles between words and images, and navigates across gutters and frames, being moved to see, feel, or think differently in the effort of producing narrative closure" (978). Through unintentional eavesdropping, Willie finds out that Heidi is crying to his friend Buck because she feels "so humiliated" for inviting him, a Jew, to the party (266) (Figure 1.2). The visual layout of the panels on this page—comprising repeated images of Willie standing outside a darkened doorway—underscores the emotional turmoil he experiences while overhearing Heidi. Shadows, space, and light are deliberate efforts to signal the character's feelings. Willie's gestures successfully reveal the emotional violence that he experiences.[9] The reappearance of the older woman in one of the bottom panels reminds the reader of how a moment ago Willie responds to her question: "Your parents didn't come, young man," with a lie: "No, my mother had a headache" (264). The last panel, and the only one framed in borderlines on this page wordlessly produces the "loudest" effect: as others enjoy the gathering, Willie slams the door, leaving not only the party but also the social circle to which he has tried so hard, yet failed, to belong.

The failed friendship between Willie and Heidi is but one example of how social bias can permeate people's everyday lives. As teenagers, Willie and Buck were best friends. They built a boat together from scratch, enjoyed summer sailing at the harbor, and then bought a used car by selling their boat. At the time they never discussed ethnicity, religion, and social belonging. Yet, years later, when they run into each other as adults on the street, Willie listens incredulously to Buck's speech against Jews. Although it is clear that Buck holds no ill-will toward Willie, his words reflect the social prejudices of the time: "Why do you think Hitler is trying to rid the world of Jews? They don't join up like we do .... They eat away at every society they infest .... Let me tell you. The Jews in this country don't have long to wait! Soon they'll be found out and ..." (296–297). In these panels Willie's facial expression and body gesture change from those of excitement to shock, anger, and disappointment. The overlapping panels of this scene—Buck is drinking coffee and talking to an vacant seat, while Willie walks alone

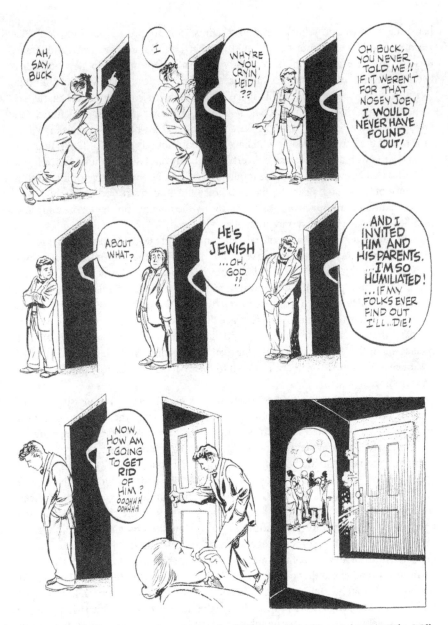

Figure 1.2 Reprinted from *Life, in Pictures* by Will Eisner, 266. Copyright © 2007 by Will Eisner Studios, Inc. With permission of the publisher, W. W. Norton & Company, Inc.

in the rainstorm—suggest the characters' movements occur concurrently. Since Buck is so intoxicated by the political topics, he does not notice that Willie has already left.

If young Willie's social dreams are smashed by German immigrants' bias against Jews, his encounters with other characters go further to reveal prejudices of different kinds. On one level, Willie's mother, an immigrant Jew from Romania, does not hide her disdain for Cousin Julius's family and claims: "I'm not prejudiced. I just don't like German Jews! They're snobs" (284). On another level, Julius's wife feels humiliated to settle among Russian, Polish, and other Eastern European Jews in New York City because they are "such peasants" while her family has a better educated, better cultured, German Jewish origin (285). In his social collage, Eisner also incorporates characters who are caught "in-between" and belong to none of these national, social, ethnic, and religious divisions. As one of the workers in his father's fur business reveals to Willie, he is one of the confused people who have "a trouble nobody can help" (288). In order to marry the woman he loves, he converts from being an Italian Catholic to become a Jew. Now that his wife has died, his family and friends no longer accept him. To find his sense of belonging again, he has no choice but to convert back to Catholicism. All these different perspectives prompt young Willie to contemplate the meaning and complexity of social identity and prejudice.

When the troop train reaches its destination, Mamid's words help the reader revisit the overarching theme of the narrative and remind Willie that prejudice is not a Jew's "private ghetto," but a much broader issue that "takes years to cultivate until it becomes part of the anatomy" (309). Like many others, Mamid tried to assimilate and evade the pains of prejudice when he emigrated from Turkey. Although he experienced shame, anger, and denial, he eventually made peace through optimism and bits of recall from his past: that is, "a selective memory and the tyranny of eternal hope" (309). The final scene of the graphic novel calls for further reflection on the incessant nature of prejudice as the new Army recruits march to their barracks as thunder and lightening brew in the distance (312).

A long-term believer in and advocate for the literary as well as artist merits of comics, Eisner wrote as early as in 1941 that comics were the "embryo of a new art form ... an illustrated novel. It is new and raw in form just now, but material for limitless intelligent development. And eventually and inevitably it will be a legitimate medium for the best of writers and artists" (Kitchen 17). In his keynote address at the "Will Eisner Symposium: The 2002 University of Florida Conference on Comics and Graphic Novels," Eisner stated that comics as a medium is indeed coming of age and comic artists have been recognized in the rooms of academia, but not yet accepted ("Keynote Address" n.p.). Now the graphic novel and related themes are examined at conferences and academic journals and books, an indication for the institutionalization of this medium in scholarly work.[10] Marianne Hirsch, for example, has suggested that in the new millennium this form offers a vital model for the "visual-verbal literacy" needed to "respond to the needs of the present moment" (1212). This chapter has strived to address the intersection of life writing and the graphic novel while exploring the inherent complexities in using comics to recount personal experiences as well as to address historical, cultural, and social issues. Several autobiographical works have garnered critical acclaim and discussion during the past years. Among them are Joe Matt's *Peepshow*, Art Spiegelman's two-volume *Maus: A Survivor's Tale* and *Breakdowns: Portrait of the Artist as a Young %@&*!*, Marjane Satrapi's two volumes of *Persepolis*, David B.'s *Epileptic*, and Alison Bechdel's *Fun Home: A Family Tragicomic*. Similar to these authors, Eisner also explores "the tangled relation of self to family stories and settings" with extraordinary complexity (Miller 543). His American Jewish historical writings and his autobiography are essential "in shaping not merely a canonical oeuvre but also the contours of a new and rapidly expanding medium" (Dauber 279). By presenting "thinly disguised autobiography" or "thinly fictionalized portraits of actual figures,"[11] Eisner's approach to the graphic novel—enriched by life stories—is one of the progressive steps that may open the doors for others to further explore the potentials of this particular generic category.

Notes

1   The instructional pamphlets, books, and magazines that Eisner and his American Visuals Corporation developed for the U.S. Army and other companies are examples of such.

2   Will Eisner's *Comics and Sequential Art* (1985) and *Graphic Storytelling and Visual Narrative* (1996) are among the earliest book-length works that examine comics through a critical and theoretical lens.

3   The term graphic novel has been used to "designate publications that differed from comic books only in number of pages and thickness of cover stock" (Harvey, *Art of the Comic Book* 116). Although Eisner did not invent the term "graphic novel," which was coined by Richard Kyle in 1964 to refer to comic books in general, he has played a significant role in advocating for this genre and introducing it to a broad range of readers. His *A Contract with God and Other Tenement Stories* (1978) is commonly considered one of the first American graphic novels.

4   Some of these awards include Comic Book Artist of the Year from National Cartoonists Society, 1967; Best Artist from National Cartoonists Society, 1968–1969; International Cartoonist Award, 1974; inductee into Hall of Fame of the Comic Book Academy, 2001; and the Eisner Award in the category of Best Graphic Album–new in 2002 for *The Name of the Game*.

5   For example, *Modern Fiction Studies* published a special issue in 2006, "Graphic Narrative," edited by Hillary Chute and Marianne DeKoven, discussing the literary and critical aspects of the graphic novel. In 2007, a special issue of *MELUS*, edited by Derek Parker Royal, facilitated discussions on the multiethnic engagements with the graphic novel. *Biography: An Interdisciplinary Quarterly* devoted a special issue in 2008 to addressing autobiographical comics, edited by Gillian Whitlock and Anna Poletti. Lynda Barry invented the hybrid term "autobifictionalography" to describe her work *One Hundred Demons* (2002). When discussing alternative comics as emerging literature, Charles Hatfield addresses the issues of authenticity and self-reflexivity in autobiographical comics with particular emphasis (108–151).

6   The cover page of the 1986 edition calls the book "a graphic novella set during the dawn of comic books" (Eisner, *The Dreamer* n.p.).

7   Using Art Spiegelman's *In the Shadow of No Towers* (2004) and Marjane Satrapi's *Persepolis* 1 (2003) and *Persepolis* 2 (2004) as textual examples, Gillian Whitlock coined the word "autographics" to refer to graphic memoirs that call attention to the visual and verbal rhetoric in this generic category and the negotiated position of the narrator in comics (966).

8   In 1983, Cat Yronwode (born Catherine Manfredi), Eisner's assistant at the time, encouraged him to do a story about how he became a comic book artist. In this

sense, *The Dreamer* came out of Yronwode's "perpetual requests that he buckle down and put his memories on paper" (Andelman 226).

9   Eisner uses the term "emotionally violent" (as opposed to physically violent) to describe his portrayal of the characters and events in *The Name of the Game* (*Eisner/Miller* 101). This concept is certainly applicable to some of his other works as well.

10   For example, Gillian Whitlock and Anna Poletti's introduction to the winter 2008 *Biography* special issue dedicated to graphic memoirs notes this trend (xii–xiii).

11   Eisner calls *To the Heart of the Storm* "a thinly disguised autobiography" despite his intention to create a fictional tale in his introduction (Eisner, *Life, in Pictures* 107). In his review for the *Booklist*, Gordon Flagg remarks that with "its thinly fictionalized portraits of actual figures from the industry's freewheeling early years" *The Dreamer* should appeal most to Eisner's fans (56).

"Not a Word for Little Girls!": Knowledge, Word, and Image in Leela Corman's *Unterzakhn*

Tahneer Oksman

In his introduction to Mary Antin's famous autobiography, *The Promised Land* (1912), Werner Sollors points out that although Antin claimed to have written a book representing the experiences of thousands of immigrants, in reality "her story does not even resemble that of her own sister" (Sollors xv). The key difference between Antin and her sister Frieda, both born in a *shtetl* in the Russian Pale, was that Antin received an education in America, inevitably leading her to become a successful writer, while Frieda labored in a sweatshop in large part to support Antin's career. Sollors points out that the frontispiece to the book, featuring an image of a young Antin beside Frieda, emphasizes that significant omission: the disparate yet interconnected path that Frieda trod, a path that had to be silenced in order for Antin to frame her narrative as a "success story."[1]

In his more recent essay on *The Promised Land*, Babak Elahi focuses on what he views as this crucial subtext of the book, that is, the interrelationship of Antin's and her sister's life paths. Elahi reads several passages in *A Promised Land* as exposés revealing Antin's reliance on Frieda, and Antin's "uncomfortable realization that it is her ... sister (literally and figuratively) who makes her own assimilation possible" (45). For example, in one scene, Frieda sacrifices the fabric of what was supposed to be her wedding dress to make a graduation dress for Mary. Elahi sees the inclusion of this and other scenes as Antin's way of subtly but unmistakably fusing together what might otherwise be identified as a "division of agency along lines of labor and consumption" (46).[2] In effect, Antin's text, if read in this manner, is a story of the communal education and work of the Jewish and female immigrant rather than one of an individual's striving and achievement. Mary's story, the story of an immigrant who joins the literate and educated middle class, *is* Frieda's story, the story of a garment industry worker who spends her life as part of the laboring class, even if Frieda's voice is never directly heard.

Leela Corman's graphic novel *Unterzakhn* (2012), set mostly in the 1910s and 1920s, traces the lives of sisters Esther and Fanya as they grow up on the Lower East Side of Manhattan. *Unterzakhn* can be read as a retelling of Antin's narrative, this time as a fictional tale told through the comics medium, with Frieda's point of view incorporated directly into the visual narrative.[3] Read in this way, Corman's work reveals how the graphic medium can visualize, in a literal sense, the interconnectivity of this Jewish immigrant community and especially the interdependent, though often invisible, community of women.

Unterzakhn threads together the life story of Fanya, who receives something akin to a formal education, with that of her sister Esther, who survives, and in some ways thrives, without one. While neither sister goes to public school due to their mother's insistence that they do not need "goyish schooling" (33), Fanya, the "smarter" sister, is taught how to read by the local "lady doctor," Bronia, and eventually becomes her apprentice. Fanya transmits some of her learning to her sister, including the ability to read, but Esther additionally experiences a very different form of knowledge while working in a brothel and later in a burlesque theater, where she eventually becomes a star. Instead of a narrative of schooling as "success"—a plotline that emphasizes individual strivings and achievements—this graphic novel examines the various non-traditional avenues of education open to the young immigrant woman, whether or not these avenues were sought out by her or arrived at through her consent. The text emphasizes the informal transmission of knowledge as the mode by which the characters' most powerful and influential education occurs. Although in the end, this informal education cannot save the sisters from their somewhat inevitable fates, it contrasts with the isolation of the domestic sphere, as well as with the solitude of the rare turn-of-the-century immigrant woman's acquisition of a formal education.[4] The urban setting binds the sisters to each other and to other women, for better or worse. Through its emphasis on unconventional modes of knowing and telling, of interactions that take place between and among women, the book openly confronts the limited options available to most immigrant women at the time and stresses the relational nature of each and every seemingly individual trajectory.

Corman's graphic novel contains various formal strategies to reflect this communal theme. The structure of the book plots the sisters' stories alongside one another, sometimes without formal transitions. This format reflects how each life path is embedded in the other, a dynamic that often plays out through illustrations as well as words. The story of the uneducated Esther, a character somewhat analogous to silenced Frieda in Antin's memoir, plays a key role in Fanya's story, and in the end neither sister's narrative stands alone. The cover of the book immediately signifies this relational narrative configuration.[5] The title, *Unterzakhn*, is portrayed in large red letters contained within a black rectangle, which divides the page. At the top of the cover, there is an image of the young twins, drawn at the age depicted in the opening of the book, and a large close-up of their matured faces fills the bottom half of the page. The two sets of drawings of the nearly identical sisters—made that much more similar by the simple black and white coloring—stress the way their faces and, by extension, their stories lay claims on one another. The top depiction shows their faces huddled close together, with similarly prominent noses and short hair styles, as well as nearly identical neutral expressions. The main feature that differentiates them is Esther's birthmark. This mark is significant for the reader early on in the story, when the sisters are young and there are no other visual distinctions to differentiate one from the other. In the larger image of the sisters at the bottom of the cover, they are more readily distinguishable. Esther's face is prominently featured, with her sister, Fanya, portrayed in profile, this time with the left side of her face fully visible, clearly lacking any birthmark, and with one eye aimed at her sister. The mole on Esther's face is more obvious in this second depiction of the pair and serves, along with her heavy eye make-up, lipstick, and bold haircut, to distinguish the two of them, reflecting their divergent life paths. Yet, even in this second image, in which their faces now point in different directions, their heads still merge to form one encompassing mass. The unreciprocated look from Fanya to Esther reinforces this visual affiliation between the two women, even as it reveals that there cannot ever be an easy connection between two people whose lives, at least for a time, splinter off so dramatically one from the other.

In addition, on this cover, both sets of the characters' faces are juxtaposed against a background of buildings, a visual synecdoche for the city of New York. The incorporation of these drawings of the two sisters against the same tenement backdrop unites their stories with those of the various immigrant communities existing and moving through the Lower East Side over time. In an interview, Corman herself stressed the importance of the setting of the book: "I'm interested in any part of New York that's gone through so many changes, with so many people living there. The imprint of those people is still there, and not just the Jews, but everyone who lived here."[6] The city represents a unifying force in the lives of these two individuals, as well as in the many other varied communal and individual histories, both real and fictional, that take place within its streets. There is not always a clear division between the so-called educated and laboring classes in *Unterzakhn* because the lines between the two are often revealed to be hazy and indistinct for immigrant women, who remain on the margins of both communities. Instead, through the framework of animated city streets, the voices of a vast network of women, who contribute to and influence the sisters' life paths, are woven visually and verbally into the storylines of the two main characters, thereby allowing the narrative to trace the journeys of countless related subjectivities. The graphic format of the book, and especially its visual emphasis on the multidimensionality of street life, locates the pivotal experiences of immigrant women in often unexpected encounters with others. Incorporating New York City into the comic as a constant, thriving, and interactive presence, *Unterzakhn* is a book that graphically foregrounds the communal nature of the story that Antin's *The Promised Land* only indirectly addresses.

With the tops of tall buildings hinting at the worlds of activities resonating within them, the images on the cover also reflect the novel's attention to what happens below the surface, as the title of the book, "unterzakhn," which can be translated to mean "underthings," similarly suggests.[7] The fates of the sisters are dependent not primarily on whether or not they have access to a formal education in America, a causal relationship that Antin and other immigrant writers of the early twentieth century, such as Anzia Yezierska, tended to focus on.[8] Instead, a more informal and often overlooked, though equally significant, form of knowledge holds the key to determining their futures. This knowledge of the everyday, which is both withheld from them and offered up to them at various points in their stories, emerges from their experiences on the streets of New York City and, more specifically, from the visual and verbal worlds that they encounter there. The telling of the immigrant story through the medium of comics in this way reinforces the significance of how much power there was in what could be seen and heard in everyday life, and how seemingly insignificant characters could withhold, concede, or generally abuse access to such knowledge.[9] To be aware (or unaware) of the "inner life" of the streets—the complex economic and sexual forces compelling the behaviors of friends, family, and neighbors—was a determinant of the trajectories that these women's lives would follow. Through its focus on the vernacular, on everyday encounters with oral and visual forms of knowledge, Corman's graphic novel therefore reflects how comics can emphasize aspects of those experiences that have yet to be fully explored or reflected: the unmentionable—and unofficial—schooling that took place in the day-to-day, and which in many ways is most effectively and powerfully conveyed through images as well as words, and especially through the intersection of the two on the page.[10]

From its opening scene, the book is focused on such often illegitimate transmissions of knowledge that occur as the sisters engage with the city around them. The novel begins by tracking a monumental incident that Fanya witnesses on the street. She is accompanying her mother, a corset-maker (creator of literal "underthings"), on a trip to pick out new fabrics when they chance upon a woman who is fallen, in both senses of the word: her body lies across the pavement of the sidewalk with her hair splayed and a large pool of blood staining the back of her dress and the ground beneath her. When Fanya's mother, Minna, directs her—"Fanya, go get Bronia the Lady-Doctor!"—it is the first time we are told either of the sisters' names. Fanya stands, wide eyed, behind her mother, grasping at the roll of fabric she has been assigned to carry. This image associates the material labor of the immigrant woman, the fabric that Fanya's mother will make into a corset, with the knowledge of the street that will eventually pull Fanya away from the laboring class and unsteadily and precariously into the educated middle class: she herself will become a "lady doctor."[11] The incorporation of the bottom half of other bodies into the scene, some standing and observing, others merely going on with their lives, situates Fanya as one of a larger crowd, even as she is singled out as the only child witnessing the scene, a symbolic representation emphasizing how this particular occurrence will play a paramount role in the direction of her future. The exaggerated size of her eyes—an impressionistic visual tactic that differentiates comics from other ways of telling—also reflects the importance that the encounter assumes within the rest of the narrative. As witness to this street scene, a chance occurrence, Fanya's life story is, in a single moment, dramatically differentiated from that of her sister. She starts out on a path that will unravel and distance her from Esther, just as, for the reader, she has been named while her sister's presence has, as yet, only been hinted at with her silent and immobile inclusion on the cover. The sister who is not marked literally—on her face—becomes the sister who is figuratively marked by what she sees as a young girl.

Fanya's moment of witnessing introduces her to a whole new cast of characters. One of these characters is the "pickle lady," a peddler who forces her way into Fanya's story by way of her interruptions. "For what you're looking?" she asks a frightened and anxious Fanya, who wanders the streets in search of Bronia. In this panel, which is the first time we are introduced to the pickle lady, only her words, and not her body, are presented to the reader, in the form of a speech bubble. The accidental collisions and intrusions of street life are thereby conveyed on the page, as per this example, through a visual architecture particular to comics. The pickle lady's speech bubble reflects the lurking presence of strangers, prepared to intrude on the girls' lives at any point in time, even as it emphasizes the general invisibility of such potential presences. In this way, the comic makes evident what is hidden or "under the surface" of city life. The pickle lady appears several pages later, once the incident with the fallen woman is over. This

Figure 2.1 Leela Corman, *Unterzakhn*, p. 22. Courtesy Leela Corman.

time, she takes on the role of a knowing mentor or of a teacher imparting knowledge to one of her students. In the first of two panels set side-by-side in the middle of the page, Fanya sits beside the pickle lady, looking up at her as she explains: "That Bronia, she's a pritze. You stay away from her and you'll be better off" (Figure 2.1, 22). The peddler's words here evoke the close association of disparate members of the community and the open channels of gossip—of judgment and common knowledge—that join that community together. "We all know from Bronia," she asserts in an earlier panel, summoning an imagined community of women in order, in part, to initiate Fanya into that world. The creation of a "we" also brings to the surface, and makes audible, the presence of a community without borders—a group of Yiddish speakers without a clearly defined separate or distinct space to call their own, whose interactions and street talk are rooted in a scattered and unpredictable urban life.

As the pickle lady's "student," Fanya, arms folded and at attention, is not satisfied with the warning that she stay away from Bronia. Instead, she pushes the matter, asking: "What's a pritze?" This desire to know more is rejected by the pickle lady, who chases Fanya from the scene, cutting the lesson short and leaving the girl with more questions than answers. She directs her finger off to the side: "Not a word for little girls! Now gey a veg!" prompting Fanya to seek answers elsewhere, perhaps on other street corners. Beside her pointed finger, various tiny shapes and figures can be seen in the panel, indicating new potential pockets of knowledge hidden in the shadows and waiting to emerge.

The Yiddish word "pritze"—a derogatory term for women roughly translated as "whore"—remains uninterpreted, hanging in the air, as Fanya mutters to herself: "Oy! That pickle lady is crazy!"[12] The word crops up at various points throughout the text, often, though not always, when women are speaking of Bronia. For example, when a woman who works at a brothel comes to try on dresses in Minna's store, and Minna sees her talking to Esther, she tells her daughter (in private): "You stay *away* from her and pritzes *like* her unless I *ask* for your help!" (25). Later on in the novel, discussing Bronia, Minna tells her friend that "[s]he's just a pritze who likes to mix in!" (36). Fanya's early interaction with the pickle lady and, more generally, both of the girls' encounters with the derogatory Yiddish word "pritze" at various points in the text highlight a theme that persists throughout the book: namely, the lack of practical knowledge about sex and birth control available to women at the time, and the general disdain applied to people, like Bronia, who were interested in providing such information. By using one Yiddish term to label women who (relatively speaking) overtly engaged in a wide range of sexual "practices"—from sex workers to a "lady doctor"—the word comes to stand for an entire underworld of knowledge about sex and the economy of sex as it was rooted in everyday tenement life. Fanya's particular introduction to the word, as something uttered but not defined, exemplifies the sisters' initiations into this underworld as somehow both inevitable and uncertain. While such street knowledge—specifically, information about the realities of sex and women's lives—unavoidably transforms the sisters, it does not free them from the confines of the shadows that are cast around women who openly challenge the rules of propriety that have been put into place. For these sisters, then, while sex and sexual knowledge are a means of escape from the conventional domestic futures outlined for them by their community—of growing up to become Jewish wives and mothers whose lives are rooted in the home—they also determine their limitations, the economic, social, and cultural realities that make it impossible for them to completely make their own choices, to leave such predictable and confining domestic fates behind.

Throughout the course of the novel, the word "pritze" and the sexual transgressions that it implies comes, ironically, to be associated with the secret lives of both sisters, however divergent those worlds seem on the surface. Fanya becomes Bronia's apprentice, and even surpasses her mentor in her desire to free women from what she comes to view as the binds of marriage and the consequences of sexual naiveté/ignorance. Esther goes to work at a brothel for a woman named Miss Lucille, and, with her help, eventually transforms into a burlesque theater star who flatters men in order (at least in part) to help her career. She becomes Miss Lucille's protégé, just as Fanya becomes Bronia's. The informal education of the two sisters—each obtained from an older woman in an informal setting—therefore reveals how their lives are similar and interdependent, despite the fact that they seem to be following autonomous and contrasting paths.

This connection between the sisters is exemplified in two panels that picture the girls talking to one another, as young girls, in the privacy of their bed. These illuminating panels are featured just before they each pursue their divergent careers. In the intimacy of a single bed, looking at one another as their hands touch, Fanya tells her sister, "Esther, I'm never gonna have babies." Fanya's declaration is likely based on what she gleans from the scene she witnessed early on in the novel, introducing her, though surreptitiously, to the horrors of an unwanted pregnancy and a deadly abortion. Esther agrees with her sister but then adds that "Babies make you ugly. I wanna be pretty forever!" (50). This vital declaration that each of the sisters makes—the decision not to have children—is what inevitably unites them, even as they come to it for very different reasons. It is a significant and improbable option for girls whose life circumstances make it much more plausible that they will follow in the footsteps of their mother, who is clearly unhappy with her role as both a mother and a wife. The sisters here re-envision their individual though ultimately interconnected fates in the private space of their bed, even as their domestic rebellions are rooted in the city streets.

By the end of the novel, it becomes apparent that the desire not to have children is never a real choice for women under these circumstances. Rather, it is a privilege tied not only to whether or not a woman has basic access to certain information and materials (as the fallen woman that Fanya encountered on the street most likely did not) but also to whether a woman is capable of and willing to navigate the contradictory expectations thrust on her by those invisible presences around her, especially in the face of her own needs and desires. At the novel's conclusion, Fanya, the sister with the means and knowledge necessary to prevent an unexpected pregnancy, ironically ends up with an unplanned child. Hers is a fate narrowly avoided by Esther, whose sex work often leaves her unprotected and highly vulnerable, and who deals with an unwanted pregnancy early on in the novel with her sister's help. "Maybe I'll just throw myself down your staircase," Fanya unhappily tells Esther, once they have been reunited and the reality of her pregnancy finally hits her (191). Fanya's sexual knowledge ultimately cannot save her from this destiny; indeed, as the ending of the story reveals, nothing could have prevented a fate that is as tied to her as the history that she shares with her sister.

Mary Antin's *The Promised Land* famously begins with the narrator intoning: "I was born, I have lived, and I have been made over" (1). For Antin, the person that she was before her immigration to the United States, and her subsequent assimilation, is someone else completely. "I am just as much out of the way as if I were dead, for I am absolutely other than the person whose story I have to tell," she continues. How, one wonders, does Frieda fit into this narrative? Is she also other than the person that she once was? Has she too experienced a "second birth," even though she never gets the opportunity to tell her own story? In *Unterzakhn*, Fanya and Esther both experience transformations, but, as the cover of the book illustrates, their stories remain forever entwined both in the same present and over time. Despite its somber conclusion, the end of the book is redemptive in the sense that the sisters inevitably find themselves in each other's company. Fanya moves into Esther's home, and before she dies the sisters share a bed once again. There are no suppressed narratives in *Unterzakhn*, and Fanya's death is neither the end nor the beginning of Esther's story.

This communal ending contrasts with the conclusion of Antin's autobiography, in which she describes visits to her sister's home in East Boston. As she explains, after her sister's husband and baby go to bed for the evening:

> Frieda took out her sewing, and I took a book; and the lamp was between us, shining on the table, on the large brown roses on the wall, on the green and brown diamonds of the oil cloth on the floor, on the baby's rattle on a shelf, and on the shining stove in the corner. It was such a pleasant kitchen—such a cosey, friendly room—that when Frieda and I were left alone I was perfectly happy to just sit there …
>
> I read aloud from Longfellow, or Whittier, or Tennyson; and it was as great a treat to me as it was to Frieda. Her attention alone was inspiring. Her delight, her eager questions doubled the meaning of the lines I read. (263)

In this passage, Antin's close attention to the details of Frieda's domestic life—the baby's rattle, the stove—reveals her desire to portray a life that she is estranged from, to convey herself as a tourist in relation to such an environment. In reading aloud to Frieda, Antin attempts to bridge this gap between their worlds, and perhaps even unite their stories. Instead, the act serves to enhance the distance that has emerged, over time, between the two women, Frieda attentive, docile, and fully domesticated, and Mary Antin the lone storyteller, the "I" of the story. Soon after this passage, she writes of feeling "ashamed to remember all of the beautiful things I had and did not share with her" (263). This reflection at the end of the book reinforces the one-sidedness of Antin's *The Promised Land* and the remorse that must inevitably accompany what had to be silenced in order for her to tell that story. Blind to the reality of the lives of so many immigrant women like her sister, Antin relegates Frieda's roles, as mother, wife, and domestic worker, to the margins in order to focus on the ins and outs of her own life, her assimilation into a new world, free from the ties that bind her to other women including Frieda.

The end of *Unterzakhn* finds these sisters, too, paired together, as one reads to the other (Figure 2.2, 192). Esther reads aloud from *The Odyssey*, a book that is part of

Figure 2.2 Leela Corman, *Unterzakhn*, p. 192. Courtesy Leela Corman.

their family legacy, passed on to the women by their father. Unlike Frieda, Esther has been taught to read by her sister early on in the novel, and she now uses this knowledge to reinforce their connection to one another. The distance forged between the two women melts away as they sit together, soaking, in the intimate space of the bath. The sisters have each managed to escape isolation; here they are, together, asking questions and relying on one another mutually and completely. With her pregnancy, Fanya has not escaped her mother's life, and, with her domestic partnership with her agent, Meyer, Esther has not either. However, in sharing a home, even under less than ideal circumstances, these sisters collectively take on the role of storyteller—an undertaking that turns their narratives into a shared tale belonging to a community of women whose stories have remained, for too long, untold.

Notes

1   Betty Bergland discusses the photographs in Antin's memoir, including, very briefly, this frontispiece, in her essay, "Rereading Photographs and Narratives in Ethnic Autobiography: Memory and Subjectivity in Mary Antin's *The Promised Land*." Additionally, over the past decade or so, many critics have written about Antin's work not simply as a story of the "success" of assimilation, but rather as a more complex text that criticizes even as it praises the immigrant experience in the United States. Some of these essays and book chapters (besides Sollors's introduction) include Lori Jirousek's "Mary Antin's Progressive Science: Eugenics, Evolution, and the Environment," Jules Chametzky's "Rethinking Mary Antin and *The Promised Land*," and Hana Wirth-Nesher's "Linguistic Passing: Mary Antin." The publication by Evelyn Salz of the *Selected Letters of Mary Antin* also shed light on Antin's personal history, in many ways in contrast to her published autobiographical works.

2   Antin writes most directly about this topic when describing her first day at school after her family has immigrated to Boston. She recognizes that her older sister must have been as disappointed as Mary was excited on that first day of school. "Whose hand was in mine, as I stood, overcome with awe, by the teacher's desk, and whispered my name as my father prompted? Was it Frieda's steady, capable hand? Was it her loyal heart that throbbed, beat for beat with mine, as it had done through all our childish adventures? Frieda's heart did throb that day, but not with my emotions. My heart pulsed with joy and pride and ambition; in her heart longing fought with abnegation" (157).

3   This is not the first time a contemporary work of literature about immigration has been read in some way as a revision of Antin's seminal autobiography. For example, in Steven G. Kellman's essay, "Lost in the Promised Land: Eva Hoffman Revises Mary Antin," he reads Hoffman's memoir, *Lost in Translation*, as a revision of *The Promised Land*. For Kellman, Hoffman's book is a more overtly critical version of the immigrant story than Antin's, one that focuses on the process of assimilation as always "tenuous and incomplete" (152).

4   Most immigrant women at the time did not have the opportunity to obtain the advanced formal education that Mary Antin received and then wrote about. In Sydney Stahl Weinberg's *The World of Our Mothers*, she devotes an entire chapter to education and the Jewish immigrant woman at the turn of the century and beyond. See Chapter 9: "Education: Dream and Reality," pp. 167–183. As Weinberg attests,

"most young immigrant women could not attain the goal of an advanced education because of the economic hardships of immigrant life. If they were able to attend school at all, only a few lucky ones could afford to remain until they reached fifteen or sixteen, when they usually graduated and went to work" (170). Susan A. Glenn's *Daughters of the Shtetl* includes a chapter that focuses on the alternative forms of education that women received in their work environments, a crucial factor given that many of them wanted to but could not receive formal schooling. See, for example, Chapter 4: "'All of Us Young People': The Social and Cultural Dimensions of Work," pp. 132–166, and especially the sub-chapter, "The Factory as School," pp. 154–159.

5   Reading the cover images of graphic novels created by a single author/illustrator can tell us a lot about the works contained within, as the cartoonist generally has more command in determining the design of the cover than authors of works of prose. At the very least, the central image on the cover of a graphic narrative is almost always drawn or designed by the cartoonist herself.

6   The association between comics and the city of New York was recently emphasized at a two day conference presented by Columbia University Libraries, entitled "Comic New York: Cartoonists & Scholars Talk NYC Comics." Organized by Jeremy Dauber, Danny Fingeroth, and Karen Green, the symposium took place on March 24–25, 2012, at Columbia University.

7   This definition comes from Yiddish scholar Eddy Portnoy, who pointed out to me that there is no such single word ("unterzakhn") in Yiddish. The definition here comes, instead, from the juxtaposition of two separate words. As he explained over email, the actual word for undergarments is "untervesh," although "unterzakhn" could easily "imply that it represents the underside of things."

8   In her stories and novels, Yezierska's characters often emphasize the potential for education to transform their fates, or, in the words of the character Shenah Pessah from the short story "Hunger," education is what would allow someone like her "to make from myself a person" (29). As another example of the importance of education in Yezierska's works, when registering for night school and asked what she wants to learn, the main character in *Bread Givers*, Sara Smolinsky, replies, "I want to learn everything in the school from the beginning to the end" (162). This "hunger" for learning is matched by the desire of these main characters to become entangled (romantically or otherwise) with men who are educators or at least highly educated in formal institutions of learning. Mary Antin similarly idealizes educators in *The Promised Land*.

9   *Yiddishkeit*, edited by Harvey Pekar and Paul Buhle, calls attention to the link between comics and the vernacular (in this case, the link between comics and Yiddish language and culture). As Neal Gabler argues in its introduction, "Yiddishkeit seems to luxuriate in its own lack of elegance and its own marginalization, which is why a book of comics art, another outsider form, seems especially appropriate to describe it ..." (9).

10 The works of the famous Jewish American cartoonist Will Eisner also focused on the often graphic (in both senses of the word) lives of those living in immigrant neighborhoods. See, for example, his well-known set of books, *The Contract with God Trilogy: Life on Dropsie Avenue (A Contract with God, A Life Force, and Dropsie Avenue)*. These graphic novels all deal with tenement life in the Bronx.

11 While acting as a "lady doctor" was by no means a respected or officially recognized position (and, in fact, would have resulted in the disparagement of this title holder),

it allowed these women access to a way of life that would have affiliated them more closely with a middle, rather than a laboring, class.

12   The word "pritse" literally translates to a landowner's wife, or a lordess. In a vernacular context, the word has come to be used as a derogatory name for a woman who thinks she can act like a wealthy woman and be served. For example, the expression "zany a prits/pritse" translates into "to be vaInglourious." Additionally, the word often also implies immorality and can refer to what are deemed to be immodest behaviors. I thank Agi Legutko, Eddy Portnoy, and Zipporah Oksman for their help in translating the word. The simplified translation that I use in this article comes from the "*Unterzakhn* Guide to Yiddish," which can be found on the Pantheon Books website.

Jewish Sexualities in J. T. Waldman's
Megillat Esther

Matt Reingold

Ori Z. Soltes writes that the Book of Esther received a radically different treatment than all of the other canonized books of the Bible in relation to the ways in which the text was visualized. Unlike the other books in which tradition was "reticent with regard to embellishing the text of the Torah," where "the Scroll of Esther is concerned, the situation has been completely different" (Soltes, "Images" 142). Dating to the ancient synagogue at Dura Europos (141), the Book of Esther has been illustrated on the walls of synagogues and used as an opportunity for crafting beautiful scrolls for personal use as illuminated and illustrated manuscripts (143). To explain the difference between the treatment of the Book of Esther and other sacred scriptures, and what made it particularly apt for visualization, Soltes suggests that the "fact that the name of God is never mentioned in the text makes its extensive visual decoration feasible" (142) given Judaism's resistance to visual representations of God and that the text was always part of the "fun-making" holiday of Purim (143).

Following the historical trend of illustrating the Book of Esther, J. T. Waldman's graphic novel *Megillat Esther* is a visual rendering of the Biblical text that includes Hebrew, English, and visual presentations of every verse of the book. In his rendition of the text, Waldman weaves Rabbinic and Middle-Ages Jewish exegetes' commentaries on the Book of Esther into the narrative, in addition to offering his own original commentary on the text. By including and adding to classical texts, Waldman situates his own *Megillat Esther* as an informed contemporary commentary on the text, best demonstrated in his presentation of the sexual relationship between Mordechai and his wife/niece Esther. The following essay will explore the ways in which Waldman makes use of classic texts while presenting his own commentary on the text through the statements that he makes about contemporary Jewish sexuality. First Rabbinic and Medieval commentaries about the relationship between Mordechai and Esther will be analyzed and the ways that Waldman makes use of them will be identified. Next, the original additions to the text that Waldman makes will be analyzed in order to demonstrate how Waldman's

The author wishes to gratefully thank the suggestions and feedback of Professor Josh Lambert.

reading is framed by contemporary Jewish sexual politics and the way in which Jews, particularly men, navigate sexuality and relationships in the twenty-first century. By analyzing Waldman's visual and textual choices, it becomes evident that he presents two contemporary readings through his presentation of Mordechai. First, he suggests that Mordechai can serve as a model for masculinity in which male strength can be demonstrated not only through physical heroics but through acknowledging and giving voice to the females around them. Second, by emphasizing an aspect of Esther's rise to the palace that has otherwise been unexamined, Waldman forces the reader to consider the sacrifices that Mordechai and Esther made in order to ensure the Jews' safety.

The starting point for a discussion on the commentary found in Waldman's *Megillat Esther* begins with first recognizing the way in which he acknowledges and makes use of earlier commentaries and sources. Throughout the text he indicates where and what is borrowed, and as a result, it becomes possible to make inferences into where Waldman makes additions to the text. In no fewer than four places does Waldman indicate the importance of citing sources and that sourcing is a rabbinic imperative for redeeming the world. Significantly, this idea is learned by the Talmudic rabbis from the Book of Esther's Queen Esther, whose willingness to credit Mordechai with saving the king's life in Chapter 2 (instead of taking the credit for herself) ultimately helped lead to the Jews' triumph in the story.

To demonstrate his commitment to sourcing, Waldman includes a bibliography, a paragraph explaining that his *Megillat Esther* "locates [itself] within the framework of rabbinic literature" (157) and endnotes embedded within images that correspond to the specific rabbinic teachings that he cites. Furthermore, given his choice of crafting a visual document, Waldman also creates a visual representation of his sources. On the page in which the king's would-be assassins are hanged on a tree (58), the tree's foundation in the ground is a matrix of all of Waldman's bibliographic entries. Combined, the image and the other written sourcing tools show that the foundation for Waldman's text is not his own understanding of the Book of Esther but rather the understandings of earlier exegetes who have already explicated the text (Figure 3.1).

Waldman's inclusion of sources does more than just give credit and indicate what inspired his interpretation. Soltes writes that "the involvement of the reader is intensified by Waldman's swaying interweave of passages *from* the story with passages *commenting* on the story that reinforce the notion that it is part of a larger narrative" ("The Graphic Novel"). The additions of commentary place the reader within a framework of Jewish textual history and force him to recognize that this story does not end with the conclusion of the narrative in Chapter 10 but continues through thousands of years of commentary, including the book in his very hands.

Understanding Waldman's textual approach allows for an understanding of the way in which he works with the sexual dynamic between Mordechai and Esther. The seeming innocuousness of the relationship between Mordechai and his niece Esther, as presented in Chapter 2, pales in comparison to the high drama that occurs in the rest of the narrative. In the text, the reader is informed that following the death of her parents, Esther was taken in as Mordechai's adopted daughter. However, the Jewish sages that composed the midrash between the years 400–1200 CE (Holtz 178) crafted a radical revisioning of the dynamic in their midrashic compilation on the Book of

Figure 3.1 Tree depicting Waldman's sources.

Esther found in the Babylonian Talmud's *Tractate Megillah*. There the sages suggest that Esther was not only Mordechai's niece but also his wife (Megillah 13a). This is suggested through a rereading of the Hebrew word *bat*, the word that Chapter 2 uses to describe Esther's relationship as Mordechai's daughter. By playing with the word *bat*, the midrash suggests that it should instead be read as *bayit*, home or wife.[1]

Waldman makes extensive use of the marriage motif by showing the couple in a sensual embrace in which Esther's face rests on Mordechai's bare chest (38). At the same time, by positioning Esther's face against Mordechai's chest, Waldman hints at an additional midrash in *Tractate Megillah* in which the midrash's authors provide a vivid description of Esther moving from bosom to bosom, and sexual partner to sexual partner, between Mordechai and King Ahasuerus (13b).[2]

A final way that Waldman engages with the midrashic treatment on Esther's sexuality occurs where he addresses Esther's sexual passivity with regard to her sexual relationship with King Ahasuerus (48, 53). A midrash in the Babylonian Talmud's *Tractate Sanhedrin* (74a–b) notes that Esther was passive "like the ground" when having sex with Ahasuerus. With this, the writers were suggesting that Esther was not guilty of adultery since she did not initiate a sexual relationship with him and was instead passive when she engaged in sex with the king. The implication of this was that she was therefore still permitted to engage in sexual relations with her Jewish husband Mordechai. Waldman's text (48) makes use of this midrash when he presents three panels involving three different scantily-clad women sexually pleasuring the king. These three images act in stark contrast to his depiction of Esther with the king in which she sits passively on a chair with her eyes focused on the ground and away from the king with her arms crossed across her chest while wearing a shawl to further cover herself (53). By depicting Esther in this way, Waldman reinforces and makes use of the midrash that argued in defense of Esther's chastity and moral virtues and suggests that she was disinterested in being with King Ahasuerus.

Esther's passivity at this point in the narrative in both midrash and Waldman stands in marked contradistinction to the Esther who enters the king's throne room to save the Jews in Chapter 5 verse 1. The midrash in *Tractate Sanhedrin* suggests that Esther's decision to approach the king to save the Jews would have involved initiating a sexual encounter, and in that moment of action, Esther was no longer passive in her sexuality with Ahasuerus, and with that action, Esther forsook her relationship with Mordechai forever because she would then become an adulteress. The reading of Esther offered by both the midrash and Waldman presents a woman who is no longer passive but instead is a female that knows what she is doing as she tries to shape policy in her efforts to save the Jews. While Waldman's text does not show any explicit sexuality in relation to Esther and Ahasuerus, the image of Esther preparing herself for the king is the only panel in the entire text to be drawn from behind the character (84). Through this act of visualization, the reader sees through Esther's eyes and sees the world as she does as an active heroine who will shape her people's destiny through her choice to come before the king and initiate a sexual encounter to curry his favor.

The midrashic statements about Esther and Mordechai, and their presentations in Waldman, are overtly sexual, religiously compromising, and are a far departure from the original storyline. The creative license taken by the midrash's authors is all the more striking since the text does not overtly allude to sexual indiscretions. In trying to understand the nature of these religiously challenging midrashim and why they were written, Barry Dov Walfish suggests that perhaps the rabbis wanted to make the story as implausible as possible in order to show God's miraculous providence in interceding, that the story legitimates niece-marriage as modeled through the marriage of Mordechai and Esther, or that the story becomes more emotional or complex through the dramatic inclusions (Walfish, "Kosher Adultery"). It is important to add that the focus and tone of many of the midrashim is often of a legal nature. The sages accept that Mordechai and Esther were married but then emphasize the legal nuances of the relationship as opposed to the psychosocial dimension of their partnership. They focus on when she can have sex and when she cannot, how the act was performed, and what its implications are for her other sexual relationships. The focus is never how Mordechai or Esther felt about the situation or how their relationship was negatively affected beyond the legal technicalities of their sexual expression. The closest the sages come to this is Esther's acknowledgment that Mordechai will be lost to him because of her sexual advances on the king as relayed by R' Abba. The reading of the story offered in the Talmud does not delve into the impact of the dissolution of their relationship or the impact that it would have on Esther and Mordechai. This is a point that will be returned to later in the paper as Waldman does address this topic in his treatment of Mordechai and Esther.

Whereas Waldman's work with the early midrashim indicates acceptance of the premise that Mordechai and Esther were married, as well as a willingness to engage with traditional texts, he makes minimal use of the Central European Middle Ages commentary on the topic despite their prevalence and importance in the cannon of Jewish exegetical scholarship. This is most likely because, as Walfish notes, many medieval commentators ignored the midrashim about Mordechai and Esther's relationship entirely.[3] However, Waldman does make use of Spanish and Portuguese Kabbalistic commentaries, which reflect an exegetical line of inquiry that differs from the midrashic emphasis on legal matters. In the Iberian approach, questions about the way in which Mordechai behaved when Esther was taken from him and how Esther behaved while in the palace as a Jew became topics for conversation and debate.

Ibn Shoshan and Abraham Saba each wrote particularly striking commentaries on the relationship between Mordechai and Esther. When considering why the midrash would allow Mordechai to continue his sexual relationship with Esther despite her marriage to the king, Ibn Shoshan writes that through her sexual relationship with Mordechai, Esther is able to maintain her Jewish identity (Walfish, "Esther" 131), which would otherwise be lost while living in the palace with a non-Jewish king. Additionally, Abraham Saba wonders why Mordechai didn't risk his life to save Esther from being taken to the king and how the midrash could justify her marriage to a non-Jew when she was already married. Why, Saba asks, did she not kill herself in the same way that Jews in Portugal did when they were given a similar choice, as marrying a non-Jew should be prohibited, especially if it involved adultery (Walfish, "Esther" 131)? Saba's source for his line of inquiry is most likely the *Targum Sheni* which scholars date anywhere between 300–1100 CE (Komlosh 515). This Aramaic text holds that Mordechai did hide Esther until a royal edict threatens his life whereupon he willingly gives Esther to the palace.[4] Saba, most likely, wonders why Mordechai capitulated to the edict and did not fight for Esther or encourage her to kill herself. Despite the harsh line of questioning, Saba, like the Kabbalists of his time, would not move beyond skepticism toward the midrash, and he ultimately accepted the rabbis' version of Esther and Mordechai as righteous and justified in their actions (Walfish, "Esther" 122–123).

Walfish suggests that the socio-political dynamics of Iberian Jewry and the threats of expulsions and conversions affected the exegetes' writings. For commentators like Ibn Shoshan and Saba, Esther is no longer just a Jew married to a non-Jew; instead, she is a crypto-Jew who, by secretly observing Judaism, could maintain her Jewish identity (Walfish, "Esther" 125). Along with this, Mordechai is no longer a man who just married his niece and let her leave; instead, he becomes someone who should have fought for his wife or been killed instead of letting her be defiled by a foreign power in the same way that other Iberian Jews fought for their families or accepted martyrdom.

Unlike the Kabbalists whose worldview was such that midrash is "the words of the sages [which] contained kernels of mystical truth about the essence of the divine … and that all the traditions of the sages were authentic and reliable interpretations" (Walfish, "Kosher Adultery" 134–135), Waldman does not need to accept verbatim and with absolute certainty the infallibility of the midrash. Furthermore, Waldman's surrounding socio-political climate is different than his exegetical predecessors. Not only is religious freedom an accepted value in Waldman's America, but so too are notions of fidelity and women's rights. These new realities actively shape the way in which Waldman crafts his own visual commentary on the Mordechai–Esther relationship as his commentary pushes the Megillah in ways that were never indicated before since "Waldman follows the tradition of rabbinic enhancement, but on his own terms" (Soltes, "The Graphic Novel"). Waldman's reading directly addresses the way in which Mordechai behaved toward Esther, and through his presentation, it becomes clear that he intentionally adds new material that shows a greater awareness of Esther's precarious situation, Mordechai's feelings toward losing Esther, and the nature of masculinity.

Waldman's presentation of the Mordechai and Esther relationship spans two pages, and there he picks up on the thread of Targum Sheni's reading of the text by showing Esther hidden below ground looking up at Mordechai. However, unlike Targum Sheni's version, Mordechai does not willingly give Esther to the king. Following an embrace in which Esther is shown to be leaning on Mordechai's chest, Esther says that even though she has "been hiding here for just three years, it feels like … seventy-five years!" (39). The scene then moves to outside of Mordechai's home and two guards barge in to his house and discover Mordechai and Esther hiding together below ground whereupon Esther is taken away (Figure 3.2).

This short scene provides multiple departure points for considering Waldman's visual commentary on the text. First, the speech that Esther delivers about waiting for seventy-five years is not in the Hebrew text. As Waldman cites, there is a midrash that says that Esther was seventy-five years old when she was brought before the king (160), but that too is a commentary and not in the original text. Thus, Waldman's use does not reflect the tenor of the original commentary. The artist's insertion here of dialogue that is not actually in the original text is an example of what Soltes refers to as "places where Waldman deliberately wanders from literally translating to allow the words of his characters to articulate the *sense* of the Hebrew narration" (Soltes, "The Graphic

Figure 3.2 Scene showing Mordechai and Esther hiding Underground.

Novel"). Waldman's way of using Hebrew and English is what Roland Barthes and others refer to in their analyses of images and texts as signifiers and signifieds. Barthes writes that when looking at images and text, there are signifiers, which are the literal image or text, and signifieds, which are the symbolic messages behind the picture or text. In Waldman's case, the Hebrew acts as the signifier and the English as the signified since the English presents the subtext or real intentions of the Hebrew. With Mordechai and Esther, Waldman is arguing more than just the idea that Esther was seventy-five years old before she was brought to the king; instead, and through working with the Hebrew, he plays with the idea that not only are Mordechai and Esther married but that because of the king's edict, Esther feels that she has been kept away from Mordechai for so long and that their relationship has suffered as a result through her loneliness. This act of hyperbole shows the love and feelings that Waldman believes Esther has toward Mordechai and that being taken away to the palace will not be an exciting opportunity; rather, it will be a moment of extreme loss for her.

A second way that Waldman comments on the story is the way in which masculinity is addressed through Mordechai's role as protector of Esther. Waldman's presentation of the Mordechai and Esther dynamic is limited because of the textually difficult position he is in as exegete. The artist is unable to create a radical Esther who refuses to go to the palace or a hyper-sexualized Esther who emphatically wants to go to the palace, as these readings would undermine the pulse of the story since they are not in consonance with the original text, given Esther's ultimate presence in the palace and role as savior to her people. As a result, Waldman cannot rewrite Esther as a fully decisive female voice in the text. Furthermore, he creates in the shadow of feminist critics who are challenged by Esther because of her lack of action and the types of messages that she communicates to female readers. For example, Timothy K. Beal writes that the very way in which Esther is described in the text as a Jewish female orphan who was exiled from Judah "emphasizes her potential status of an object of exchange among men" (35). Additionally, Beal cites scholars who argue that Esther "undergirds patriarchal assumptions that women should be deferential, obedient, and beautiful objects for men"(35) or that Esther is a model for how to "operate within a system in order to bring about social and political transformation" (45) despite her stereotypical femininity. Moreover, Ayelet Brenner combines the above two readings and suggests: "danger can be averted by mixing attractiveness, sense, and faith. A pretty and resourceful woman, although she is enclosed by predominantly androcentric norms, can survive and even prosper" (13). Beal challenges all of these readings and encourages a more holistic understanding of Esther's character. To do this, he examines the entire narrative and as a result of looking at all of the pieces of the story together, Esther can be seen as a three-dimensional character who experiences a "role-reversal in which she does the commanding" (Beal 48). Through this reversal, Beal argues that Esther moves beyond gendered stereotypes and establishes herself as a character with fully formed motives and one who develops throughout the narrative. Integrating a feminist approach into his narrative would be challenging for Waldman, given how much Esther is acted on and controlled throughout and that the true intention of the text is difficult to ascertain as evidenced by the myriad voices that speak about her.

Given his limitations in rewriting how Esther appears in the scene where she is taken away, Waldman instead shifts his focus toward Mordechai and how he behaves in the text. Waldman's reading of the text, and his bibliographic entry of Walfish's book about Medieval Esther commentary, suggests a familiarity with Saba's critiques of Mordechai. However, his reading moves Mordechai from passive to active in his role as Esther's spouse and protector. No longer are the commentaries theoretical "what if" and "what should be" statements about how Mordechai should have protected Esther and not given her away to the king; instead through visualization, Waldman actualizes the earlier commentaries and writes them into his narrative in relation to how Mordechai behaves.[5]

Lilian Rae Klein notes of the original text that "Mordechai does not direct Esther to enter the beauty contest and remains uninvolved in this un-Jewish behavior. Nevertheless, he does nothing to interfere with Esther's entering into a situation foreign to Jews or her potential loss of shame" (157). Despite this critique, Waldman decides for his Mordechai not only to hide Esther but also to not hand her over to the guards when they bang on his door. Instead, she is taken from him against his will. Waldman's Mordechai is an active figure who, while ultimately capitulating to the guards' force, does not willingly hand her over and attempts to protect her. Given the original text's sparse information on how Mordechai behaved in relation to Esther, by presenting a new visual narrative that challenges Mordechai's passivity and by focusing on the way in which his character is developed, Waldman presents an argument on the notion that masculinity can be demonstrated through affection and constructs a new reading on Jewish gendered relations. Through this shift in focus from Esther to Mordechai, Waldman moves the Esther narrative to a point that is more progressive than his predecessors. He does this by having Mordechai refuse to give Esther away. Waldman's visualization of the scene actualizes the questions on the text raised by earlier exegetes like Saba.

In support of Waldman's presentation of a masculinity that shows affection and protection toward women, it is valuable to consider Jackson Katz's recent article on the nature of Jewish masculinity. He writes:

> For thousands of years, the rabbinic tradition praised humility before adversity, and interpreted Jewish victimization as a punishment from God for insufficient adherence to his commandments. But instead of embracing a nonviolent masculine ideal rooted in Talmudic texts and a long Jewish cultural tradition, more and more Jewish men were finding themselves attracted to the idea of becoming real men, as defined in physical terms by Gentile culture. (60)

Instead of praising this construct, Katz notes that male Jewish violence against women and children increased through involvement in American wars and as a result of their own persecution as minorities in the United States. He writes, "Jewish men have a choice about how to respond to rage. On the one hand, they can respond with the armor of conservative masculinity and an unrestrained embrace of violence. On the other hand, they can champion nonviolence, even as they continue to wrestle with the question of when and where violence might be necessary or even appropriate" (73).

Waldman's presentation of Mordechai both challenges and reinforces the idealized version of masculinity that Katz outlines. His depiction of Mordechai shows a physically strong and robust man as evidenced by his sculpted physique and toned muscles. Despite Mordechai's appearance, Waldman's character does not in any way enter the fray against Esther's kidnappers. To further emphasize to the reader that Mordechai was capable of fighting with the men yet chose not to, Waldman drew one of the guards as overweight and doughy with a weapon to aid him in combat (39). The contrast between Mordechai and the kidnappers is stark and begs the question of why Waldman did not have Mordechai engage in any type of physical confrontation and instead appear weak. Beyond the obvious need to adhere to the story in which violence might compromise Mordechai's later role, Waldman apparently wants his Mordechai to be read not as weak but instead as one who has *chosen* not to fight because he has calculated the risks and determined that in this situation, violence would be an inappropriate choice that could cause danger not only to himself but, more importantly, to Esther. Through the juxtaposition of aggressive non-Jews who act savagely along with Mordechai who chooses to not fight but instead clings to his beloved underground, Waldman presents a strong case for a masculinity that can be powerful through its non-violence. By thinking of Esther's needs and safety, Mordechai actualizes Katz's articulation of positive masculinity as one who has calculated when violence is necessary and when it is not in the hope of later finding a way to ensure Esther's safety.

Additional support for this reading of Waldman's Mordechai as a trope for the potential of contemporary Jewish masculinity is found in the way that dialogue is presented in this scene. It is Esther, and not Mordechai, who dictates the situation as she is the only character with dialogue throughout. Susan Zaeske writes that "a central feature of the exilic rhetoric of Esther is the risky nature of the act of speaking … the contrast between the weak position of the rhetor and the all-powerful position of the audience represents the rhetorical environment of the Persian court as pervaded by risk" (199). Waldman challenges this reading in his scene despite Esther's position as the one secluded. It is Esther who initiates dialogue and it is Mordechai who eagerly and happily embraces her. Waldman's Mordechai is not the later Mordechai of Zaeske's reading that is "powerless" and "feminized" (198). Through the use of dialogue, body language, and physique, Waldman presents the key plotline of the classic text but locates within it an opportunity to construct a modern commentary on idealized Jewish sexual politics and, specifically, a masculinity that chooses to not perform violence or weak passivity yet still be strong. Like Katz's formulation of masculinity, Waldman's presentation of Mordechai also presents a strong masculinity that is at once both confident and strong without resorting to violence.

The second set of scenes where Waldman presents the relationship between Mordechai and Esther is through the denouement in Chapter 8 when Esther reveals her religion and relationship with Mordechai to Ahasuerus, and Mordechai is placed in a position of power within the kingdom. The midrash suggested that Esther's decision to appear before the king ended her sexual relationship with Mordechai (*Tractate Sanhedrin* 74a-b). Walfish notes the irony of the situation in which Mordechai and

Esther are now placed in as colleagues who must hide their past relationship and ignore their mutual feelings while working side by side for the king. Yet none of the classical commentators suggest that Esther revealed to the king that Mordechai was anything more than her uncle despite the ambiguity of the Hebrew phrasing in the text[6] (Walfish, "Kosher Adultery"). The socio-political climate of midrashic and medieval commentary was such that the idea of Esther revealing her marriage to Ahasuerus would be absurd and, as Walfish indicates, potentially perilous for other Jewish women ("Esther" 124). Yet, in spite of that history, Waldman's text twice suggests that their relationship is revealed or at least strongly hinted at to individuals of the palace.

The first time Waldman alludes to Mordechai and Esther's relationship is when the reader is informed that every day Mordechai would visit the palace to learn about Esther's welfare and what would happen to her in the king's harem (46–51). Whereas the Hebrew text informs the reader of this through narrative, Waldman structures it as a dialogue between Mordechai and a woman who works at the palace. The woman's narrative ends when she asks Mordechai whether "the turn of [his] beloved arrived" and after answering no, she asks "is she [his] daughter?" to which Mordechai emphatically responds: "No! She is the daughter of Avichayil, my uncle. I have taken her as my ... well it's hard to explain" (50). The second scene in which Esther and Mordechai's relationship is strongly hinted at occurs at the end of the story following Esther's revelation that she is Jewish. Waldman takes the ambiguous Hebrew text of Mordechai and Esther's relationship and has Esther strongly hint to the king that she and Mordechai were married. In Waldman's text, Esther explains that Mordechai is her "cousin once removed ... and [her] adopted parent and ... well ...," to which King Ahasuerus interjects by saying, "so that makes him your ...... oh ... who cares!" (117–118). Waldman's use of ellipses, a common convention in the comic medium, allows him to avoid directly saying that Esther was married to Mordechai and to completely break with the original text. But because there is no other relationship that any of the earlier commentators suggest, the ellipses make it clear that he is indicating that they were in fact married.

It is important to consider what messages Waldman is conveying as a result of directly addressing Mordechai and Esther's marriage in the text through parapraxes or Freudian slips which hint at what Waldman believes are their true desires and frustrations. He is suggesting here that a new reading of the traditional story needs to be created for the modern reader, making him, in essence, a twenty-first century commentator in the same way that the midrashic and Iberian authors reflected their societies. Unlike the midrash which was concerned with legal matters and therefore crafted commentaries which reflected legal themes or the Iberian communities which struggled with conversion crises, Waldman's characters reflect some of the issues that affect Jewish life today: masculinity and relationships.

Returning again to the theme of masculinity and how the text presents it, by addressing their marriage openly, Waldman's text humanizes Mordechai through the loss that he has endured and shows that despite Esther's role as savior to the Jews, she is no longer able to be his wife. This break with the original ensures that the reader not misread Mordechai as a character unaffected by Esther's move to the palace; instead, he is shaken by the loss of his wife given his willingness to share confidential and damaging information with a stranger. His Freudian slip suggests a disappointment with the situation and a longing for the return of his wife.

Moreover, Esther's willingness to share this information with her new husband suggests her discomfort with her new marriage and how she, too, has been affected by the loss of her husband despite her role as queen and savior to her people. Given that both Mordechai and Esther allude to their relationship and its termination, it is evident that Waldman raises important and challenging questions about the nature of service to the community and the responsibility that individuals should have toward their people. In the case of Mordechai and Esther, Waldman's characters have triumphed given Esther's role as queen, Mordechai's role as vizier to the king, and their saving of the Jews; however, neither character seems truly happy. Hemmed in by commitments to the original text, Waldman's Mordechai models Katz's comments about eliminating violence toward women and increasing consideration toward them. Yet, through the subtle allusions to their relationship, the reader is ultimately left wondering whether all of Waldman's textual and artistic choices hint at a deeper desire for Mordechai to have acted differently in the situation in order to protect Esther and their relationship, even at the cost of saving the Jewish community. Ultimately, both Mordechai and Esther do choose their community and their responsibility to their people, but through the textual emendations, Waldman argues that genuine sacrifice involves loss and that the loss of their relationship was a catastrophe for the star-crossed lovers. Waldman's additions, which are built on the earlier readings of his predecessors, focus on the themes of psychology and relationships in ways that earlier exegetes' never considered. This reading is uniquely a twenty-first-century one and reflects the time of its composition. Through his comics text, Waldman forces the reader to conceptualize the relationship in a new way and consider the fact that while the reader might be a direct benefactor of Esther's heroics, the heroes of the tale are ultimately losers of what they held most dear.[7]

Reading Waldman through the prism of masculinity is a reflection of the rabbinic imperative to craft commentaries that are relevant to the communities for which they are written. His artistic work is, in the words of Nissim Gal, similar to Israeli photographer Adi Nes who is not "only a storyteller or producer of images, but also a commentator on the text" (90). Despite its radical revisioning, Waldman's approach to the text is in consonance with the thematic imperative of the earlier commentators' works about how to maintain Judaism in a world of tension. The specific issues might have changed, but the need to find appropriate solutions that speak to each generation continues. Waldman's commentary directly responds to a world of hyper-masculinity and the negative impact of it for women. His work actively engages with these challenges while modeling an alternate approach, through Mordechai, to understanding what strength is and can be. Waldman's reading is, ultimately, an affirmation of Danna Nolan Fewell's comment on feminist Bible criticism when she argues that the "task is not to produce a woman's reading to oppose or to parallel a man's reading; [the] task is to produce a closer reading, an inclusive reading, a compelling reading that allows for a sexually holistic view of human experience" (85).

Notes

1   Despite the difference when rendered into English, the difference in Hebrew is
     minimal and the two words look very similar and can even be spelled the same but
     pronounced differently in some contexts.

2   Ever wise to defending Esther's honor and preserving the sanctity of marriage, this
     passage from *Tractate Megillah* also suggests that following each sexual encounter,
     Esther would ritually purify herself in the *mikvah*.

3   Notable exeptions include Ibn Ezra who refutes the midrash and suggests that
     Mordechai *wanted* to marry Esther but Ahasuerus took her first since virgins were
     preferable to the king (s.v. *l'bat* 2:7). Rashi accepts the midrash's explanation in
     his commentary when he writes that Esther and Mordechai were married (s.v. *lo
     l'bat* 2:7) and that Esther's decision to appear before the king effectively ended her
     marriage with Mordechai (s.v. *v'qaasher avadeti avadeti*) but he does not include any
     of the other passages from the midrash.

4   s.v. *va-yehi bhsma davar hamelech*.

5   It is important to note that for the reader who does not possess Hebrew or exegetical
     background or even familiarity with the *Megillat Esther* narrative, Waldman's
     presentation becomes the authoritative version of the story. While Waldman's
     footnotes help inform the reader, they don't offer explanations on every point
     he makes and one might think that the absence of footnote will, all the more so,
     demonstrate that it is not rabbinic text but the original text as opposed to the
     alternative in which the absence of footnote can indicate original commentary. This
     problem is, ultimately, unresolvable, and not only creates tension in understanding
     the narrative, but also allows for a sense of freedom so that each reader can
     understand the text in their own way based on their own experiences. The act of
     not knowing becomes, in a sense, the lens through which different audiences can
     appreciate and approach Waldman and discover, at their own pace and interest, the
     layers that are presented in his commentary on *Megillat Esther*.

6   In Chapter 8 verse 1, Esther tells the King what "[Mordechai] was to her" (מה הוא לה).
     The ambiguity leaves open the possibility that Esther told the king that they were
     married but this is highly unlikely.

7   It is interesting to note that this reversal of fortunes reflects a theme of the text in
     which winners end up losers and losers winners as in the case of the wicked Haman
     who thinks he has defeated the Jews and ends up dying and the Jews who think they
     will die end up celebrating. Here, however, the traditional victors, Mordechai and
     Esther, are, in fact, losers.

"You Wouldn't Shoot Your Fellow Jews": Jewish Identity and Nostalgia in Joann Sfar's *Klezmer*

Nicole Wilkes Goldberg and James Goldberg

What do most people associate with the prewar eastern European Jewish community? For many Americans, the song "Tradition" from *Fiddler on the Roof* would likely come in at the top of the list. Many may not remember the musical's larger themes of tension and transition, but the sense of continuity, community, and coherence in "Tradition" has captured the popular imagination and continues to inform contemporary perceptions of *shtetl* life. Perhaps that song has become prominent in our cultural memory because it provides us with a clear sense of how to relate from a decentered, uncertain present to a past we've pastoralized. Perhaps it stays with us because we feel a need to imagine some kind of calm on the other side of the storm of the Holocaust. While we remember that pogroms raged well before the Second World War, and that European Jewish life was not without its challenges, romantic images of Jewish unity and simplicity persist.

In French Jewish graphic novelist Joann Sfar's *Klezmer: Tales of the Wild East*, such images are largely absent. The book opens with a scene of Jews slaughtering Jews. No longstanding feud is involved: members of an established local klezmer band simply murder a wandering band of potential competitors. The two groups have barely encountered each other when the violence erupts (Sfar 4). Through his visual depiction of this violent encounter, Sfar jars us into the sense of tenuousness that permeates the work. When the two bands meet, the illustrations are standard for comics: watercolor cartoons with less-defined lines. The moment the violence erupts, however, the colors and lines explode into disarray. The abrupt loosening of Sfar's illustration style heightens the sense of chaos and unpredictability inherent in the violence. The lack of definition, distance from the human action, and sudden shift to stronger colors allow the violence itself, rather than any character, to dominate these images. The harsh angles of the horse's head in the third and fourth panels accentuate the shock of the violence; the rendering of the head without the body in the third panel and of eyes and teeth falling out with leg bent in an impossible arc hint at a fundamental collapse in order and logic. In the fifth frame, the loose rendering of the fire and the image of an isolated survivor evoke other images of violence and trauma from Jewish memory.

This is a far cry from "Tradition."

Klezmer follows the sole survivor of the violent encounter, Noah Davidovich, who calls himself "the Baron of My Backside" (17). The baron reluctantly allows a beautiful young woman from the village to join him in his wandering; Chava is confident in her sexuality and bored with *shtetl* life and sees singing with the baron as a means of escape from marrying "stupid," "ugly … idiot" boys from the village (15). The story jumps from the baron and Chava to a yeshiva where the rabbi's coat has been stolen. Yaacov, "a boy wonder" and the "rabbi's favorite student," is expelled from the yeshiva with only the stolen coat—a mournful gift from the rabbi—and a sack of belongings to accompany him in the snow (22). Yaacov unwittingly follows the baron's path, meeting the murdered musicians, three men in a cave longing for their deceased rabbi, a nervous, sleepwalking former yeshiva student named Vincenzo, and a gypsy whom the two students save from being hanged by the Cossacks. Tschkola, the gypsy, convinces Yaacov and Vincenzo that the three of them can play Jewish music together because "Jews are constantly getting married, circumcised, engaged. There's some money to be made" (78). The five characters' lives intersect at a bar in Odessa when they play together for the first time. In the "Notes" that follow the narrative, Sfar describes the characters in *Klezmer* as outsiders, both from the dominant culture and from Jewish establishments: "Yaacov tries his best to be a bad Jew, Vincenzo lives with the terror of his yeshiva experience, Chava hates the backward traditions of her shtetl, and the Baron of My Backside tries hard to forget his dead." Sfar adds: "They make a fine gang of freethinkers!" (VII). The romanticized, mythologized unity of the shtetl is shattered within the text, and the world the characters inhabit is, indeed, a "wild east," full of danger and doubt. As Sfar points out: "In the end what makes those characters Jewish in spite of everything is this awareness of their frailty: nobody's there for them" (IX).

Klezmer is not Joann Sfar's first work grappling with Jewish identity and the irrecoverable fragmentation of the past. Born in Nice, France, in 1971, he began publishing graphic novels during the 1990s through l'Association, a progressive publishing house founded by French and Belgian comic artists. While l'Association opened opportunities for many talented European graphic writers such as Marjane Satrapi (creator of *Persopolis*), David B., and Guy Delisle, most of the founders and many writers, including Sfar, have since left the publishing house (Bérubé). Sfar is most noted for his graphic novel *The Rabbi's Cat* (2002, English translation 2005), a mystical tale about a cat who eats a talking bird and gains the power of speech. The cat deeply desires to be bar mitzvahed and become Jewish. Set in French-occupied Algiers before the Second World War and focalized through the eyes of a cunning, sinful, and devoted cat, Sfar explores his father's Sephardi roots in Setif, Algeria. According to Sfar: "*Klezmer* is the flip side of the story. The Cat was for my dad's family" (VII). *Klezmer* reimagines the Ashkenazi world of his maternal family, who came to France from Ukraine in the 1930s.

Writing *Klezmer* presented both unique challenges and opportunities because of the lack of direct access Sfar felt he had to his Ashkenazi family's past. "My mother's family is a snow covered desert," he explains. "My grandpa and grandma told me lots of stories, but never about their ancestors. I don't know anything about Poland or Ukraine" (VII). Because of the vast gap in the transmission from memory to written narrative, Sfar seeks connection to the lost world of Ashkenaz in other ways. He explains that practicing klezmer music[1] gives him "the feeling of nestling in my hands a few nearly cold embers and carefully blowing on them to try to make them burn once again" and attempts to infuse that feeling into the work (I).

Despite its jarring dissimilarities with more obviously nostalgic depictions of Ashkenazi past, *Klezmer* shares a fundamental investment in recovering that past. A song like "Tradition" and the loosely illustrated outsiders who inhabit Sfar's graphic novel greatly differ because the works are driven by divergent nostalgic modes. In contemporary colloquial American usage, the term "nostalgia" typically refers to a wistful, often shallow or sentimentalized, longing for the past. Nostalgia's etymological roots, however, suggest something deeper: the term first appears in a 1688 medical dissertation by Andreas Hofer[2] to describe "the particular kind of melancholy experienced by Swiss mercenaries when removed from their homeland," an affliction which led to deep depressions and even suicide (Grainge 19). Hofer formed this diagnostic label out of the Greek words *nostos*, which means "return home" and *algos*, which means "pain" (19). Historically, then, nostalgia was less mood than malady—a painful dilemma for those separated from a sense of home. Although the everyday usage of the term has shifted, there is still a critical utility to exploring crises of memory as such separations and by acknowledging the pain and uncertainty inherent in the original definition. Paul Grainge believes that "as a commodified style, the nostalgia mode has developed, principally within postmodern theory, a theoretical association with *amnesia*" and that "forms of stylized nostalgia have been framed in relation to an incumbent memory crisis" (21). It should not be surprising, then, that many Jewish writers facing accentuated memory crises associated with the Holocaust write with particular urgency about the past.

The modes in which such writers approach the past vary greatly, however, as do modes of response to the fundamental dilemma of nostalgia. Svetlana Boym suggests that most nostalgic expressions fall into one of two basic categories: restorative nostalgia and reflective nostalgia (41). Boym explains: "Restorative nostalgia puts emphasis on *nostos* and proposes to build the lost home and patch up the memory gaps. Reflective nostalgia dwells in *algia*, in longing and loss, the imperfect process of remembrance" (41). Restorative nostalgia is concerned primarily with *continuity* within a community and/or physical space and tries to hide decay and the passage of time. This is, perhaps, the impetus behind the nostalgic draw toward "Tradition": the concept of shared rituals and values articulated in that song is one in which culture presents itself as largely immune to the stresses of history. Boym suggests that, in fact, it is the stresses of history themselves which contribute in some cases to the transition from adaptable organic "customs" to more strict and overtly constructed "traditions" which then present themselves as continuous with past practices (42). Especially when undeniable ruptures occur, Boym argues, restorative nostalgia tries to fill in the gaps and create certainties, often through literal reconstructions or prescribed social practices within historically significant physical spaces, in order to re-establish a sense of continuity (45).

Reflective nostalgia shares restorative nostalgia's concern for the relationships between present and past, but it is primarily concerned with *connection* rather than continuity. "*Re-flection*," according to Boym, "suggests new flexibility, not the reestablishment of stasis" and thus "is more about individual and cultural memory" (49). Because of its focus on connection and its acceptance of the ambiguous space between the present and memory, reflective nostalgia leaves room for fragments, uncertainties, irony, humor, and narrative play, longing less for the literal homeland than for a lost "potential space of cultural experience" (53).

In *Klezmer*, Sfar accepts the constant ruptures of history in order to look for such spaces. In a key scene, Yaacov, who is trying to forget God after he is expelled from the yeshiva, seeks shelter from the cold in what turns out to be the dead musicians' wagon. He feels he should bury the musicians, but is too frightened to do so, and reasons "The snow is doing the job for me." He says a prayer for the dead in spite of his new attempt at atheism, telling God: "If you don't exist, someone has to think of them." He even says the Kaddish for the musicians, though he is alone, because "Tomorrow, they'll be lost under the snow" (27). Only after Yaacov has wrestled with his conflicting beliefs, does his focus shift to their instruments. In this scene, Sfar captures some of the essential elements of reflective nostalgia: continuity in memory associated with restorative nostalgia becomes illusive and is replaced by attention to the ways in which time obscures the past, in the text quite literally through the snow. A focus on *nostos*, the return home, is precluded by an acute awareness of the depth of loss (*algia*), accentuated in the text by the constant presence of the skeletons, especially through the starkly juxtaposed text and images, such as the illustration of the burned skeleton of the violin player captioned: "It's not as if I were robbing a dead man. I'm robbing the snow" (28). An insistence on absolute adherence to traditional practices is replaced by an ability to deal in fragments and an open playing space for the ways in which those fragments will be integrated into the future, as seen in Yaacov's unconventional prayers and in his willingness to take the instruments without a specific plan for how he will use them.

Yaacov's reflective approach to the dead musicians echoes not only Sfar's approach to the prewar Ashkenazi world ("Notes" VI) but also the approaches that shaped the 1970s klezmer revival. Christina Baade argues that between the end of the Second World War and the years leading up to this revival, klezmer was "aimed at a nostalgia market" made up primarily of aging immigrants and lost some of its immediacy as "a general transition from experiencing the music interactively through dance at a social function to a more individualized, nostalgic listening experience at home" took place (211). In the 1970s, according to Christina L. Baade, just as klezmer was dying out, Jewish musicians who had been trained in other forms began to turn toward klezmer in search of their own Jewish musical heritage (212–213). The heritage they found themselves turning toward, however, had been irrevocably disrupted by the Holocaust "in which most of the *klezmorim* [klezmer musicians] were murdered" and because of which the Ashkenazi immigrant population American klezmer served had gone unreplenished for three decades (211). Instead of an anchoring body of musical mentors and a clear audience base, revivalist musicians were confronted by fragments of a compelling musical form accompanied by implicit reminders of the violent past. They could have attempted to preserve the form by carefully defining it but did not do so. Definitions of klezmer since the late 1970s have varied widely and have often been broad, even impressionistic. According to Baade: "The common thread between these definitions ties klezmer music to Jewish identity. Other characteristics of the genre as it is known today–instrumentation,[3] form, and history, for example–are open to debate among klezmer scholars and to different performances by klezmer bands" (209). More than codifying any formal or physical element of the form to create *continuity* with past *klezmorim*, contemporary practitioners have focused on the ways in which the music lends them a dynamic *connection* to Ashkenazi history. This combination of significant flexibility with a deep sense of connection and commitment to an obscured past has made klezmer a music people once again gather to dance to in great numbers. As Baade notes, "there is a sense that klezmer has a special quality which is tied to Jewish identity but accessible to and consumable by others" (217). Sfar interprets this as an indication "that plenty of people are willing to carry a bit of Jewish memory on behalf of the Jews" ("Notes" XII).

Sfar's emphasis on memory and revivalist klezmer's grounding in reflective nostalgia provide a counterpoint to the prominence of Zionism in discourses on Jewish identity. Some have speculated that the complicated discourse on the role of Zionism in Jewish identity helped fuel the klezmer revival. Baade points out that "as Slobin and Svigals have observed, this mode of Jewish musical identity could exist without the Zionism associated with Israeli folk music in a period when the relation of American Jews to Israel became more problematic" (214). This search for an alternative to Israeli folk music is not simply a matter of surface political differences; rather, it reveals tensions between restorative and reflective nostalgias that shape debates over Jewish identity.

Judaism itself has arguably been defined since the destruction of the Temple of Jerusalem in terms of the dilemma of nostalgia: a pain to return home has been so profoundly imbedded in Jewish religious and cultural practice as to be one of its central ideological features. Because asking Jews to abandon nostalgia effectively requires Jews to abandon their Jewishness, questions over differing manifestations of deeply ingrained nostalgic tendencies constitute the core of debates over Jewish identity. Some respond to these questions in more restorative modes, defining Jewish continuity either through careful performance of certain traditions that claim strong historical grounding or else, during the past century, through a literal return to a geographically defined homeland. Others value reflective nostalgia more, focusing on elements of Jewish practice that encourage connection, even when they do so through undisguised adaptation, and valorizing diaspora over the allure of a pre-Messianic physical return.

The question of which mode of nostalgia best suits Jewish identity has significant political implications and, as such, has been the subject of significant critical discussion. Daniel and Jonathan Boyarin argue that "the solution of Zionism ... seems to [be] a subversion of Jewish culture and not its culmination" and call for greater valorization of diaspora within discourses over Jewish identity (101). In his "Notes," Sfar explains:

> The secularizing of Judaism is the idea that people are more Jewish in Israel than in the Diaspora. I love Israel, because it's a beautiful country and I have family there, but give me a break! Israel is the opportunity to transform my fellow Jews into ordinary people: Jewish farmers with a fence around their field, with an army–regular people, in fact. From a quality of life standpoint that's a good thing, but I

don't see what I have in common with them. *They are far less Jewish than I am.* (II, emphasis added)

For Sfar, as for the Boyarins, to conflate Israeli national identity with Jewish identity is unsatisfactory because it "represents the substitution of a European, Western cultural-political formation for a traditional Jewish one … that takes on entirely different meanings when combined with political hegemony" (Boyarin and Boyarin 101). Sfar expresses greater sympathy for such a project from a standpoint of livability than the Boyarins do but is equally insistent that Zionism not be identified as a culmination of Judaism. He writes:

> A Jew who has nothing else to do but protect his land, that's a bit too much like a Pole. Not that I mean to detract in any way from the merits of Poland. Everyone should be entitled to be in an old country, to own one's land, to place one's trust in priests, to want to live in peace within secure and recognized borders. Humanly and politically, that's a beautiful project. It so happens that it's the opposite of what my ancestors have been doing since the destruction of the Temple of Jerusalem.[4]
>
> *People who don't like Jews* never asked them to do anything else: go home! And live like everyone else. And forget your dreams and your ecstasies and your wanderings. ("Notes" II–III, underline in original)

Perhaps the differences between Jewish and European ways of approaching identity contributed to the process through which "the Jew [became] the very sign of discourse and disorder in the Christian polity" (Boyarin and Boyarin 88). Perhaps Sfar's "people who don't like Jews" were motivated in part by the very real sense in which, according to the Boyarins: "Jewishness disrupts the very categories of identity because it is not national, not genealogical, not religious, but all of these in dialectical tension with one another" (109). Historically, it may have been precisely Jews' reflectively nostalgic ability to intermix with others without surrendering their intensely felt connections to a lost past that created so much tension whenever restoratively nostalgic hostland regimes and/or populations attempted to return to a "purer" past in which invented versions of a supposedly closed ethnic tradition could be preserved. This historical ability to maintain difference dynamically appears to be one thing that draws Sfar toward Jewish tradition in his writing.

This is not to say that Jews never engaged in their own restorative nostalgic projects before the advent of Zionism. The desire for cultural continuity is not limited to any particular group. In minority Jewish communities with little political power, however, restorative impulses often manifested themselves in re-entrenchments of orthodoxy whose tools were limited to excommunications instead of expulsions and to theoretical discussions over the Jewish soul rather than temporal discussions over how to dispose of Jewish lives. Although, as *Klezmer* suggests, sometimes even the marginalized patrol their boundaries through violence.

Many passages in *Klezmer*, in fact, can be read as discussions of the tensions between reflective and restorative approaches to nostalgia—which, ultimately, valorize reflective approaches. Take, for example, the baron's "revenge" for the murder of his friends. Careful to keep hidden, he follows the murderers and observes that they are preparing for a wedding. "That's why they were worried," says the baron to himself. "I'm not going right away. I'll let them act like stars for a bit. I'll wait till it's in full swing. We're gonna give them some joy" (6). This "we" suggests that in some sense, the baron sees himself as still connected to his dead band members and expects to draw some sort of power through that connection. In the book's first extended "musical" sequence,[5] the local band plays as people dance—until the baron slips in and begins to play his harmonica in a way that elevates the dance experience to a new level, far outshining the local musicians. "Even the musicians had to clap," and for the first time, the rabbi invites a musician—the baron—to his table (10). After embracing and thanking the baron, the rabbi rejoices in the baron's ability to bring unpredictability and energy to klezmer music. As the rabbi tells him: "[O]ur dear musicians are just predictable. They make the right motions on their instruments. But I don't' call that music. To me that's just good craftsmanship" (11).

In these expressions of the nature of music, Sfar allows the rabbi to problematize the concept of continuity through cultural ossification. Just as making the right motions on instruments doesn't qualify as music, cultural vibrancy is lost when identity is placed solely in a codified set of performances. Music exists from a point of possibility, even uncertainty—closer to Boym's "potential space of cultural experience" (53) than to any fully prescribed notion in which manufactured tradition solely constitutes culture. The rabbi, perhaps feeling a temporary relief for his nostalgia in the baron's music, proceeds to climb up on the table to make a public proclamation stating that the baron will "become the leader of the musicians, that way he can teach them to seek the tragic rhythm of life in their art" (Sfar, *Klezmer* 12). The baron refuses, however, and the rabbi immediately reverts to a prescriptive, restorative attempt to force continuity with the experience he has just lost. Still standing on the table, the rabbi declares, "from now on all our musicians must learn to play the harmonica. For celebrations, for prayer, for joy and for tears, all I want to hear is harmonica" (13). As the baron departs, the rabbi attempts to maintain, or *restore*, the baron's unpredictability and energy in the *shtetl*.

Sfar's portrayal of the rabbi's attempt to locate "klezmer soul" in the harmonica parallels his dismissal of those who "think the Jewish soul is to be found in compliance with dietary rules" (Sfar, "Notes" II) and those who believe that Jewish identity is to be found in immigration to Israel. Sfar believes searching for Jewish identity in tensions and paradoxes instead:

> If I'm my grandfather's student, I can't join the camp of those who try to make Judaism sensible. Finding a place for Jews, explaining how to be a good Jew, that's not Jewish at all. Believing that the Bible will solve men's problems, that's good for the Vatican. Saying that you've been in mourning since the destruction of the Temple and that life doesn't last long and it's sad but that perhaps one day the Messiah will come, and all the while implying that he won't but that you should still await him expectantly, that's more to my liking. ("Notes" IV–V)

While Sfar locates the tensions and paradoxes as internal to the religious components of Jewish identity in this passage, he also sees power in the tension between religion and disbelief.

Various scenes with the baron and Yaacov illuminate the power of this paradoxical space to preserve a place for memory. For example, in a dream the baron sees himself as "a black goat lost in the snow ... smoking an earthenware pipe from which flames are escaping" (Sfar, *Klezmer* 18), and he is visited by his dead friends. The baron is haunted by the guilt of abandoning his fellow musicians to be buried in the snow, but his irreligious nature justifies leaving them. The musicians complain that the baron failed to bury them, which is "shutting them out of heaven" (19). Infuriated, the baron, as a goat, protests: "Oh, shut up! You're not any more religious than I am. There's no such thing as heaven" (19) (Figure 4.1). Here, the space between religion and disbelief becomes the site of the baron's connection to the past. The baron's professed irreligiousness and personal disbelief in heaven do not undo the religious imagery that figures him as a goat or the inherited idea of heaven and spirits that has allowed this dream to take place—the tension between religiosity and disbelief, in fact, becomes an important space for memory. Such spaces, defined by their tensions, become important sites for a sort of improvisational mode of relating to reality. Improvisation, which exists in the space between the rigidity of order and disconnection of total freedom, seems to be one of Sfar's central metaphors for healthy cultural practice.

One clear example of this is in his depiction of Vincenzo, who, like Yaacov, is wandering after being thrown out of his yeshiva. Unlike Yaacov, however, Vincenzo is devastated and wants to go back. Vincenzo feels "lost outside of [his] yeshiva" and begs Yaacov to bring him to another yeshiva to regain a sense of continuity (62–63). The restorative nostalgic impulses Vincenzo feels are associated with neurosis, and Vincenzo is depicted as a stock character shlemiel for as long as he clings to them. Things change drastically, however, after Vincenzo finds out about Yaacov's violin. The young man who wished himself into a "kosher" mental hospital is suddenly confident and at ease. His timidity evaporates. The way Sfar draws him changes. In the ensuing musical sequence, Vincenzo begins to play with increasing abandon and complexity. In one frame, he is rendered impressionistically, his body arcing around the violin. In another, he holds the violin up at an improbable angle such that it appears to be lifting him—in this frame, he is colored pure green. The climax of the sequence is in three frames that alternate close-ups from Vincenzo to Tshokola (who accompanies him on the banjo) and then back to Vincenzo. The blur of their movements obscures any background. Tshokola throws all his energy into the accompaniment. Vincenzo begins to sweat. His need for strict order against the chaos of the world has given way to a deep sense of connection and orientation in the playing space of klezmer music.

Significantly, this playing space is also open to the non-Jewish Tshokola. This insertion is not ahistorical: Baade confirms that "non-Jews played in early [klezmer] bands" (210). That Eastern Europe's ethnic communities were not hermetically sealed off from one another is evidenced by the musical influences still present in klezmer. In the difficult economic circumstances Europe's *klezmorim* faced, "the musicians' flexibility helped them survive, and early klezmer was influenced extensively by Gypsy, Turkish, Polish, Ukrainian, Magyar, and Russian musics"[6] (Baade 210). That such mixing occurred is an important aspect of what reflective nostalgia and diaspora offer at their best. As Boyarin and Boyarin observe, "the same figure, a Nagid, an Ibn Gabirol, or a Maimonides, can be simultaneously the vehicle of the preservation of traditions

Figure 4.1 Reprinted from *Klezmer: Book One: Tales of the Wild East* by Joann Sfar, trans. Alexis Siegel. 19. Copyright © 2006 by Joann Sfar. With permission of the publisher, First Second.

and of the mixing of cultures …. Diasporic cultural identity teaches us that cultures are not preserved by being protected from 'mixing' but probably can only continue to exist as a product of such mixing" (108). Sfar pays tribute to the potential vibrancy of such intercultural spaces in *Klezmer*. In one scene, Yaacov coaches Tshokola on how to convert Gypsy and Russian stories into "Jewish" ones: he should tell the stories he knows but replace non-Jewish cultural references with Jewish ones. Yaacov says, "instead of Gypsy caravans you say that it's Moses and the caravan of the Israelites in the desert … instead of princes you say 'the rabbi's son,' instead of princess you say 'a rabbi's daughter who lived holed up indoors because her father was very strict.' … And if the story has a really happy ending, the rabbi's son becomes the second most important figure of the realm, he buys back his *shtetl* and does away with taxes and forbids pogroms" (95–96). Although Tshokola's initial response to Yaacov is "we'll be better off if you tell the Jewish stories" (96), it isn't long before he is left to tell one on his own (Figure 4.2). The use of vibrant colors underscores the engaging text to suggest the playfulness that can occur in this mixing space is cause for celebration. The story is not an example of some idealized hybridity; it is an awkward creation but one with the power to surprise and to call positive attention to difference as well as to common ground. While it does nothing to recreate or accurately perform Gypsy-ness, Russian-ness, or Jewish-ness, it nurtures a sense of connection with each of them. The story points toward an ideal state which R. Radhakrishnan envisions for his son: "For my part" he says, "I hope that his future and that of his generation will have many roots and many pasts. I hope, especially, that it will be a future where his identity will be a matter of rich and complex negotiation and not the result of some blind and official decree" (129).

Such negotiations are made possible by reflective nostalgias that find meaning in the fragmentary rather than striving for a more internally coherent whole. From the standpoint of restorative nostalgia, Tshokola's story is a corruption, a subversion of its authentic antecedents. From a reflective nostalgic viewpoint, such incomplete and ironic narratives have greater authenticity than complete narratives because, as Boym points out, "only false memories can be totally recalled" (54).

By inverting standard tropes of Jewish nostalgic approaches to the Ashkenazi past, Sfar presents a reflective nostalgic project that creates spaces for narratives to survive within the "snow-covered desert" ("Notes" VII). He redirects our cultural memory of *shtetl* life from "Tradition" to the unpredictability and improvisation of klezmer music. Because violence, death, and doubt continually interrupt the restorative nostalgic impulse, Sfar's characters challenge and redefine concepts of faith, loyalty, and home. Each one of Sfar's outsiders brings unique instrumentation to the irrecoverable past: voice, harmonica, guitar, violin, piano, and banjo. Accompanied by Sfar's loose illustrations, they perform in a space between unity and cacophony, unsure of whom or what to trust and yet confident enough to embrace the fragmentary nature of living in the diaspora. Through their movement and music, *Klezmer* raises important and practical questions about the nature of Jewish identity. Is Jewish identity primarily to be found through communal unity and strong shared objectives? Or is Jewish identity more closely related to the tensions and uncertainties of a diasporic condition?

Perhaps, above all else, the Jewish soul is to be found in sites of displacement and paradox.

Figure 4.2 Reprinted from *Klezmer: Book One: Tales of the Wild East* by Joann Sfar, trans. Alexis Siegel. 106. Copyright © 2006 by Joann Sfar. With permission of the publisher, First Second.

Notes

1   The designation "klezmer music" is, of course, technically redundant because "klezmer" is the Yiddish word for music. We have chosen to retain it in this instance to distinguish klezmer from *Klezmer*.

2   Grainge and other English-language critics list the source as Johannes Hofer, but a recent translation of work by Jean Starobinski explains that in fact the dissertation in question was "defended by Andreas Hofer of Mulhouse and presided over by Johannes Jacob Harder of Basel."

3   In her discussion of instrumentation, Baade suggests that "conscription and the service of Jews in military bands" in the nineteenth century may have been the reason for a shift from string-dominated ensembles to the clarinet-led, more woodwind-heavy ensembles most commonly associated with klezmer (210). That the baron's klezmer group is described as having met in a Polish army marching band suggests significant integration of details from actual klezmer history on Sfar's part (*Klezmer* 3).

4   Boyarin and Boyarin take this point even further back in Jewish history, pointing out that "the biblical story is not one of autochthony but one of always already coming from somewhere else" (104), reminding us that "the father of Jewry was deterritorialized" and that thus "there is a sense in which Israel was born in exile" (Davies qtd. in Boyarin and Boyarin 106). They also spend significant time on Davies's discussion of tensions between the more land-oriented "Davidic" biblical texts and the "Mosaic" texts of wandering (106).

5   "*The idea of doing a musical graphic novel* appeals to me hugely," says Sfar, "because the graphic novel is a world of silence" (XIII, underline in original). Sfar uses a variety of visual techniques to give the feeling of music, but also often includes song titles and snatches of lyrics in the text proper and a list of suggested listening in the "Notes."

6   In *Klezmer*, Yaacov's group looks for Jewish audiences, but they are flexible in the way that Baade states that early *klezmorim* had to be. As Tshokola says at one village, "you can't pick and choose your audience" so "he knows tons of Russian songs" (86).

Feiffer's Jewish Voice

Ira Nadel

The title of this essay not only puns on Jules Feiffer's fifty-one-year contribution to the *Village Voice* but is also a statement of the sustained and continuous Jewish outlook, if not imagination, in his work. Whether directly or indirectly, Feiffer's themes and characters reflect a persistent sensibility alert to the conditions and struggles of Jewish urban survival while being satirical and topical. Kafka he is not, but he is certainly a mix of Shelley Berman, Mort Sahl, and Woody Allen.

As neurosis reached a new level with Berman's routines, Sahl's complaints and Allen's anti-heroes, Feiffer became the visual poet of interior angst and the choreographer of urban tensions. Complex aspirations take on reductive form but never lose their mordant humor and cogency. While the children in his comics have adult angst and his adults display childish tantrums, their longings remain genuine. The wan despair of his characters expresses a flirtation, if not fixation, on Jewish worry translated to the secular world. Embodying the burdens of the family and adulthood are Feiffer's Bernard and Dancer, two of his most representative characters: a youthful but shy yuppie wannabe looking for romance and an artistic type devoted to her art. They confirm the travails of Joseph from Saul Bellow's *Dangling Man* (1944) while anticipating that of Philip Roth's Neil Klugman ("Goodbye, Columbus," 1959). Indeed, Bellow's character sharply summarizes Feiffer's impact when he says "trouble, like physical pain, makes us actively aware that we are living" (Bellow 55) (Figure 5.1).

Guide to non-confident living

What Feiffer explains is the inability to explain. His characters collapse into self-defeat. The explanatory agencies of family, institutions, and psychology fail to help. The self is left flailing: neither politics nor the single life brings direction or relief. A sequence from 1997, for example, begins with "an answer to the world's problems" but ends with a decision to erase this resolution with the question: "Why make trouble?" "What's left but gossip?" ("Op-Art"). A 1998 strip concludes expressing the deflation of values shared by many ("Opinion"). Such an impasse punctures the expectations of a society making the title of Feiffer's 2007 omnibus collection of *Village Voice* strips from 1956 to 1966, *Explainers*, wonderfully ironic.

Figure 5.1 "Then I Guess That's It," *The Village Voice*, February 21, 1963. Rpt. from Feiffer, *Explainers: The Complete Village Voice Strips (1956–1966)*. Seattle, WA: Fantagraphics Books, 2008. 338.

Angst and anxiety characterized post-war Jewish humor inherited from the Yiddish theater and late nineteenth-century Eastern Europe experiences. Self-mockery blended with insecurity, leading to self-deprecation. Relationships always fail as men never quite connect with women in Feiffer's world. In a strip from February 24, 1960, a comely date tells Bernard that occasionally, when she has hurt him and he gets that lost little boy look, she wants to run over and squeeze him. "But that doesn't mean I want **your** hands on **me**" she cries two panels later (*Explainers* 174). By the 1960s, such satire became ingrained in popular culture as this exchange from Woody Allen's movie, *Play It Again Sam* (1969), reveals. Attempting to pick up a woman at an art museum as they stand before a Jackson Pollock, the Allen character asks "What does it say to you?" "It restates the negativeness of the universe," the hippie-styled woman begins, and she goes on to explain in a flat voice its embodiment of nothingness emphasizing its existential power. "What are you doing Saturday night?" Allen responds. "Committing suicide," she answers. "What about Friday?" is his rejoinder (qtd. in Epstein xvi). Feiffer illustrates such colliding perspectives of urban life, individual angst, political confusion, and social manners.

"Sick, Sick, Sick," his early *Village Voice* series subtitled "A Guide to Non-Confident Living," set the tone, described by Feiffer as a satiric comment on "the young urban middle class, their work habits, sex urges and family antagonisms" (*Jules Feiffer's America* 10). The six to eight borderless panels focus on Greenwich Village people obsessed with explaining themselves "in an endless babble of self-interest, self-loathing, self-searching, evasion" (*Jules Feiffer's America* 11). Without background illustration, just white space, the text dominates the thin figures; talk is everywhere. One panel from 3-2-60 shows a thirtyish woman assessing movies vs. theater. Now that she is dating Ernie, she has been attending theater opening nights but finds the audiences befuddled and her own taste overturned: what she thought was terrible, the papers find superb. And then she realizes that movies are not better than plays. It only "seems that way because if it's a really GOOD play it CLOSES in two days." In the final panel she concludes that "if they'd only make the GOOD plays a little bit rotten for the critics, we might have some REAL theatre in this country" (*Explainers* 175). Bernard, as Feiffer explained, was an urban liberal given "to anxiety attacks, stomach aches and obsessive confessionals." And he always felt guilty about sex (*Jules Feiffer's America* 11). The Dancer was his counterpart, a demoralized and misused woman seeking self-expression through movement.

And then there was guilt. How could Feiffer overlook it? His own upbringing engendered it, especially as experienced through his mother, who repeatedly criticized his unreliable and unsuccessful father and constantly berated her son for preferring to draw rather than throw a ball. She would always find excuses for her own failings and blame others for her mistakes. One of her most devastating moves was giving away the young Feiffer's dog because he supposedly couldn't (or wouldn't) take care of it properly. His protests at her willful and pre-emptory act met no sympathy. And if he did offer any criticism, she steamrollered him with the sacrifices *she* had to make as breadwinner, householder, and educator because his father only went from one failed business to another (*Backing into Forward* 20–22).

On December 17, 1958, Feiffer published his first Jewish Mother cartoon in the *Village Voice* emphasizing a supposedly sacrificial mother who gives her son money for his psychiatrist, first apartment, and "extras." But one day, he courageously calls her to say that she had given him all this money just so he could feel guilty and she stops. Within a month he is dispossessed, can't find a job, and is being sued by his psychiatrist. With devastating sarcasm, the mother mutters in the final panel: "But listen—so long as he's happy" (*Explainers* 109). Despite Feiffer's care in drawing the woman so that she would *not* look like his own mother, she called to complain. He denied it was she, lying to her which was his tactic: "The choice was either lying to her or never seeing her again .... confronting a woman who never in her life admitted she was wrong would [not] make for a satisfactory relationship." He compromised, withholding his opinions, feelings, and judgments (*Backing into Forward* 34). His father was no better: he preferred to leave the room whenever a confrontation occurred. It is no surprise to learn that Feiffer underwent therapy on and off for some eighteen years.

At this moment, Feiffer was, as he repeats in his memoir *Backing into Forward*, caught in a Jewish mother joke—anticipating Alexander Portnoy who tells Dr. Spielvogel exactly the same thing.[1] What did he have against her she asked him when she called and he immediately knew that even at thirty, he was trapped. He thought he would escape by saying whatever happened happened long ago and he had forgiven her. After five seconds of silence, she bitterly replied: "Is that the thanks I get?" Knocked down "for the eight-count" by her remark, all he could think of with admiration and pride was "'My God, she can still do it!' She was seventy five" (*Backing into Forward* 33).[2]

Feiffer did not want to be Jewish. He found his family's Judaism hypocritical, attending synagogue only on the High Holidays and paying no more than lip service to the religion. The height of duplicity was his Bar Mitzvah: he had not been to Hebrew School and realized that the event was only for his relatives. But he dutifully went through with it, even though he was not allowed to invite any of his friends. His mother, repeatedly schooling him in her heartbreak from the hardships of her working life from the broken promises of her husband to her own long hours, soon became the caricature of a Jewish mother. And strangely, her heroes all seem to have been named Bernard: Bernard Shaw, playwright; Bernarr Macfadden, body-building publisher; and Bernard Baruch, successful investor and advisor to presidents. Bernard was also the name of the neighbor's boy in *Death of a Salesman* (1949) which Feiffer saw with his mother at the Windsor Theatre in the Bronx. Her incessant lecturing about these men drove Feiffer to think of running off to sea, and was it any wonder, he writes, that when he wanted to create a character who represented him at his weakest, he chose the name "Bernard" (*Backing into Forward* 86)?

Ashamed by their near impoverishment, Feiffer's mother, who sketched and irregularly sold fashion designs in the garment district, never let up telling him how poverty held her back. Refinement was her goal but it was impossible to achieve. Broadway was too expensive but not the Windsor Theatre on Fordham Road. Such a life of complaint and discontent intensified Feiffer's wish to leave it and even to leave his Judaism which he associated with such behavior: "I wasn't meant for these parents. I wasn't meant to be Jewish. I was Episcopalian, or whatever that church was where movie stars dressed up to go in MGM movies" (*Backing into Forward* 87). But he knew it was not to be, at least not until he left home or turned twenty-one—a magical number for him. "Don't" was her watchword, enforcing a kind of protective Maginot line around him, assuring his safety in the city. As a consequence: "I treated myself as breakable" (*Backing into Forward* 88). He was cautious, vigilant: cars, trolleys, and even subways were threats and dangerous, a fear Bernard exhibits in "Sick, Sick, Sick."

Feiffer grew up knowing that the only strategy for a child that worked with grownups was surrender. Adults never listened, they only lectured. Adults, as his cartoons reveal, were judgmental and righteous when it came to discussions with children—"and guilt provoking," something that the adults of his parent's generation could instill with perfection, never admitting blame (*Backing into Forward* 24). A Feiffer cartoon in the mid-1960s expresses this clearly: a baby, hardly old enough to walk, catalogues the grievances inflicted upon it by its parents, each indignity accompanied by a soothing "Mommy loves baby. Daddy loves baby." "Whatever that word 'love' means—" says the baby, essaying its first steps, "I can hardly wait till I'm big enough to do it to THEM" (July 15, 1965; *Explainers* 463).

The complacency and conformity of the Eisenhower years quickly became the backdrop for Feiffer's figures. This mix of self-satisfaction and Cold War anxiety—generating what he calls in his memoir "America's near nervous breakdown" (*Backing into Forward* 29)—created nervous stomachs for all, producing arrogance but little self-worth. It was the period of *The Lonely Crowd* by David Riesman (1950), a sociological study which identified three cultural types: the tradition-directed, inner-directed, and other-directed. The other-directed person, Riesman noted, sought love rather than self-esteem, not necessarily to control others but to relate to them. The other-directed needed assurance that they were emotionally in tune with society. This need became a feature of Bernard's character.

The Organization Man (1956), *The Man in the Grey Flannel Suit* (1955), and *The Art of Loving* (1956) similarly emphasized self-examination and conformity. But people were beginning to question their social identity, looking for instruction and example.

Feiffer reacted by exploiting that need and exposing the falsity of responsibility, conformity, and regularity imposed from without rather than coming from within. Preferring the radical, oppositional position of those who had if not dropped out at least became skeptical of middle-class values and security, Feiffer exhibited themes that echoed the worries of the time.

A comic panel published on March 9, 1961, is symptomatic. Alone at a café table, a Bernard-like character recites his failed relationships with woman after woman trying to justify each and find a lesson. One relationship matures him, another gives him insight; collectively, he rationalizes that such experience makes him wiser. As he slinks down further in his chair in the final panel, he crowns himself with this ironic justification: "I've come to look on myself as the Renaissance man of the Rejectees" (*Explainers* 230). Disappointment turns on its head forming a dismal victory.

Constant discontent and a feeling of being conflicted, coupled with misunderstanding language, provides the substance of Feiffer's texts and imagery as expressed in this Yiddish joke: "Are you comfortable?" the hostess asked when the writer sat down on the sofa in her New York apartment. "I make a living" he answered, shrugging his shoulders. Yiddish inflections and cadences are embedded in Feiffer's texts, their syntax of inversion echoing the themes of Feiffer's style which expands the self-accusatory and contradictory dimension of Jewish humor. Or as the father in Feiffer's *Tantrum* (1979) says: "I think like a young man, still everything hurts" (39). Or as the child Leo advises another child at an airport in the same work:

1. Get the grades but don't trust what they teach you.
2. Don't tell them what you're thinking. They'll use it against you.
3. Never be rational if you want to have your way. Ignore logic: it'll cripple your spirit. (106)

The final directive is "Don't mature! Mature people do the shit work!" (107). A hatred of responsibility runs through his strips—as well as a sustained sense of humor which unites Feiffer's work. His comic ideal incorporates missteps and confusions as this exchange illustrates when two year old Leo in *Tantrum* visits his successful brother Charlie at his office: "What's new?" Charlie asks. "I'm two years old." "I've always said so. What else is New?" (50).

Kafka in shirtsleeves

Judaism, despite its supplying the roots of Feiffer's humor, is ironically more noticeable by its absence than presence. In his comic strips, innuendo rather than direct statement conveys a Jewish tone or outlook: direct references or content are infrequent. It is an attitude or perspective associated with a Jewish sensibility akin to an intellectual Jackie Mason, a mediated Lenny Bruce, a hipper Woody Allen—all expressed in language and drawing that is spare, with only one or two characters, in an elongated style in six or eight panel monologues of the self-absorbed. What Feiffer conveys indirectly and directly are the ironic inflections and nuances of a Jewish joke, in syntax and

Figure 5.2 "I'm Too Demanding," *The Village Voice*, June 30, 1974.

expression closer to Yiddish than English with characters akin to the Schlemiel but as contemporary misguided liberal humanist.

For Feiffer, the Schlemiel has donned a tie or dancer's tights, moved to the Village and confronts a universe filled with social hesitation, doubt, and misunderstanding. The dancer in a panel of June 15, 1961, moves from communicating with the world to a state of withdrawal because no one understands her movement. Bernard remains incomplete, ineffectual, neutered. In a strip of July 2, 1964, a middle-aged Bernard, hoping at last to confirm his maturity, gives himself the acid test: visiting his parents. But almost immediately, his mother complains that he isn't eating enough and his father tells him he shouldn't be such a wise guy. Why don't they see him more often they ask but he knows that if he can get through the evening without feeling ten years old—"I'm a man!" (*Explainers* 408).

Vulnerability and fear (cited by Feiffer as his youthful nemeses) characterize his figures from the *Voice* transferred to the loser as a reluctant winner. One becomes mature by virtue of failure.[3] A strip of December 13, 1962, illustrates this when a single young woman complains of self-hate because of her apparent superficiality. But she then discovers that even her self-hate is superficial and that "at bottom I really like myself" (*Explainers* 326). This is Schlemiel humor which turns hardship into laughter through recourse to the irrational (Wisse 74). The anti-hero becomes the essence of Feiffer's America in the 1950s and 1960s because his characters address individual limitations and reflect the shrinking opportunities for renewal or improvement in relations or status. The failure of artists, or those with artistic temperaments, to be seen or heard compounded the dilemma. Self-pity surfaces in Feiffer as a distinctive urban trait, the result of emotional self-indulgence. Through irony bordered by an anti-romantic, defeatist view, Feiffer intensifies the condition of the schlemiel-manqué as exhaustion replaces ambition.

The Jewish roots of Feiffer's urban angst are, and are not, expressly present in the strips. They are there but repressed. They do not dominate but infiltrate the culture, as Henry Adams sensed as early as 1914 when he wrote that although "we are anti-everything and we are wild up-lifters; yet we somehow seem to be more Jewish every day" (Adams 540). Feiffer's characters exhibit similar traits without being outwardly or nakedly Jewish. This is Feiffer's Jewish voice, masked in the urbanity and self-pity of the "urbanista" of the 1950s and 1960s echoed in a popular advertisement of the time which had a close-up of non-Jews eating a corned beef sandwich with the caption: "You don't have to be Jewish to love Levy's," a popular New York rye bread.

A new neutrality replaces the negative implications of being Jewish: characters act and sound Jewish but are not openly Jewish. Their attitude may be Jewish but they don't look Jewish. Their Judaism exists only by innuendo, as in the television sitcom, *Seinfeld*, where the characters appear to be but are not actually identified as Jewish. Mort Sahl did not speak of his Jewishness and neither did Jerry Seinfeld. The achievement of this strategy was to make Jews of the gentiles.

Israel—surprisingly, little addressed in Feiffer's work—appears only in a political context. In a strip toward the end of *Jules Feiffer's America*, a young man outlines the positions of his relatives who are angry over reaction to Israel's self-defense: "more is made in the media over Israel in Lebanon than the Russians in Poland or Afghanistan," one says. Others commiserate over the misrepresentation of Israel's position and how many countries avoid condemnation when they defend *their* borders. But then, Uncle Max, Uncle Jake, Aunt Gossie, Uncle Irving, and his mother all develop illnesses from colitis to high blood pressure. "Hypocrisy is not good for the Jews," is the disillusioning ironic conclusion (*Jules Feiffer's America* 250). On the same page is a panel presenting a figure dancing to "begin the Begin" (a reference to Cole Porter's "Begin the Beguine") celebrating Israel's revenge through bombing, wiping out the PLO, ending with an ironic verse critiquing Israel's militarism, and the wish for "a middle east serene with F-16—when I begin the Begin" (*Jules Feiffer's America* 250).

As metropolitanism dominated popular culture, the tension of maintaining faith in democratic processes while living in a political quagmire—something Feiffer increasingly exposed—was "not at all unlike the ironic traditional tension of the Jews" subject to the threats in previous generations of pogroms or governmental exploitation (Wisse 79). In the era of what Bellow called "hardboilded-dom" (9), witnessing the self-pity and social criticism of Feiffer's characters is both a relief and a threat. But the outward exposure of an awkward inner life increasingly became Feiffer's subject. No longer would or could one be tightlipped. The emotive came forward in all its inadequacies. The erratic and irrational became the city norm.

Feiffer's drawing style reflected his self-effacing manner, especially as a child. His strategy of withdrawing from battle with his mother and fear of expressing his dreams or desires resulted in a natural preference for the hesitant, withdrawn, and anxious. The style itself became "soft," undemonstrative, unobtrusive. A strip from December 5, 1963, thematically and visually expresses this as a businessman, pummeled by screams of "MOVE OVER, OUT OF THE WAY, WATCH YOUR STEP," enters a bar and asks for a double. He then tells the bartender that he will invent a new birth control pill to insure survival: "You swallow one and for a whole day it's as if you were never born" (*Explainers* 378). Obliteration or disappearance become the new goal. An early psychosomatic condition of stomach aches when Feiffer began to work at Will Eisner's studio caused by guilt over misrepresenting his situation to his mother—he lied to her about earning $10 a week when in fact he worked for free—became his first *Voice* strip. The confessional openness in his art, which soon distinguished it and his characters, came after his years at Eisner's studio and then the army which, he says, turned him into a satirist.

Incompleteness defined Feiffer's simple drawings of figures, the result of a soft line with amoebic rather than hard characters. He connected this to an odd combination of talent and fraud, his ambivalence "more of a comfort than a cause" (*Backing into Forward* 60). If he messed up, he would blame himself but also forgive himself: he had talent, but he was a fake. But again, his style marked inadequacy rather than a finished technique. Recounting his early art classes at the Arts Students League, he acknowledged that he could passably draw the human figure (only in pencil), but a fluid brush line was beyond his manageable skills: "it wasn't thick and thin, it was splotchy and hamhanded" (63). He also could not master layout. His characters did not move dramatically across the page but seem to hang out "leadenly" from their panels "as if standing on a street corner" (63). Eisner knew this so tried Feiffer on backgrounds but that also did not work: he was inept at streets, docks, bridges, and automobiles. He was then assigned simple things: borderlines, scalloped balloons, inking in shadows, eventually coloring photocopies of the entire *Spirit* section. He was seventeen and one year out of high school, absorbing everything he could from Eisner and his staff.

Feiffer began to grow in confidence but with words rather than images. And he soon sensed that Eisner was losing interest in the story aspect of *The Spirit*. Character, incident, conflict, and resolution, combined with humor and suspense, were declining. In his second year with Eisner, Feiffer intimated that the old punch of *Spirit* was gone. Eisner told him that if he could do better, he should. Feiffer then researched, drafted, and wrote his first *Spirit* story, earlier strips plus the radio acting as influences as he combined mood with terse dialogue. Drawing on his own Bronx background—life on Stratford Avenue with scenes at Pensky's candy store—Feiffer fashioned his story. The cartooning side remained weak, but the story side grew strong. Eisner liked the eight-page layout and story and gave the green light to do more, and soon Feiffer took over the *Spirit* stories becoming over time the sole writer. He had no intention in becoming the writer of these stories but, as Feiffer suggests in his memoir, it was another example of how he backed into a situation that allowed him to move ahead. By imitating, or at least echoing, Eisner and his sensibility, Feiffer found his own (*Backing into Forward* 68).

The army completed Feiffer's education as a cartoonist. Recognizing that most of his life until he was drafted he delayed choices, the army made that easier by telling him what to do. But this often infuriated him. He did not like taking orders and often found himself bored. One day during formation at Fort Monmouth, New Jersey, he thought of *Munro*, his cartoon narrative about a four-year-old boy drafted by mistake into the army, although no one in the service would admit it. He drew the story in 1952, but it was not published until 1959 (no publisher knew how to market it), becoming then a bestseller and an animated cartoon which won an Academy Award. It highlights the bureaucracy, inhumanity, and confusion of authority, a persistent theme in Feiffer's work.

Feiffer characterized the freedom to create this and subsequent cartoons as being able to "treat my career as a series of mood swings …. wandering into seductive and scary neighborhoods and getting lost …. circling around with no sense of where I was headed, just as in real life, until I discovered a way out and the way home" (*Backing into Forward* 161). This explained his dipping into relationship cartoons, political cartoons, plays, novels, screenplays watercolors, and children's books.

Dissent also became a focus. Marginalized in the 1950s, it seemed to exist only in small magazines like *Partisan Review*, the *New Republic*, and *I.F. Stone's Weekly*. But in late October, 1955, the *Village Voice* began, founded by Ed Fancher, publisher, Dan Wolf, editor and Norman Mailer, silent financial backer who supposedly came up with the name of the paper. Judy Feiffer, Jules's wife at the time of its founding, explained that the *Voice* would be "an uncensored forum … a kind of great underground, the equivalent of a European newspaper of intellectual expression" (qtd. in Manso 222). Mailer wanted the paper to be a "hip shock sheet" (qtd. in Manso 225).

Feiffer first appeared in the *Voice* in October 1956, following his failure to sell cartoons to conventional markets for almost four years. He started by giving them free to the paper in exchange for an independence of style and subject matter. However, his actual motive was to get noticed and then to interest a publisher, because he could show he had an audience. For the first several months he tried a different style for almost every strip, although he knew he wanted to introduce an "I" character who gives way more than he means to. He thought of this as "comic strip psychotherapy, laugh while you wince, wince as you laugh," akin to core Jewish humor rooted in Yiddish jokes and idioms: "the more painful the subject the funnier it should look" (*Backing into Forward* 212). This was the period of Sick Humor, or Black Humor, the work of Bruce Jay Friedman, Mike Nichols and Elaine May, and early Woody Allen getting noticed. The zeitgeist was angst ridden, filled with guilt, and surrounded by psychotherapists who were, at least in the mind of popular culture, decidedly Jewish in manner if not mood.

But Feiffer still lacked a distinctive drawing style. William Steig was soon an influence, however, especially with his book, *The Agony in the Kindergarten* (1950). But instead of imitating his one-line captions, Feiffer would do a series of panels presented as monologues focusing on everything he disliked about himself: self-doubt, self-questioning, self-pity. He also imitated the styles of Robert Osborn and the United Productions of America animated cartoon studio where Feiffer worked briefly (think Mr. Magoo). But it took him nearly six months for his head and line to agree. His graphic style changed to looser inking and more rounded forms with more spontaneous lines. Feiffer attributed this in part to a new inking tool: sharpened wooden dowel sticks. It gave him a line that was dry and brush-like, unconventional and artful. He used the dowels for years but eventually, fed up with eccentricities of the line, went back to pen and ink (Groth xiii).

He was also in psychotherapy, scaring himself, he remarks, by his anger and politics (*Jules Feiffer's America* 12). But he was lucky because he timed himself with a generation of young educated urbanists also confronting introspection while looking for their place in society and discovering that "their parents' place [was] uninhabitable" (*Backing into Forward* 215).

Alienation, suppression, conformity dominated but the new assault was internal, an onslaught of doubt, insecurity, and neurosis. This was coupled with a character—Bernard or others—so conformist that he could transform himself physically and psychically into the several subcultures he encountered almost simultaneously. Not surprisingly, then, Feiffer's first published cartoon for the *Voice*, appearing October 24, 1956, dealt with a character's chronic stomach ache which always occurred when he faced a deadline or worry. Two newspaper readers at the bus stop who listen with surprise to the wailing suddenly shout "SHUT UP!" and hasten away. Urban disinterest trumps emotional empathy. The city will not tolerate psychosomatic problems.

Offsetting the timid Bernard was the over-sexed, Brando-influenced Huey, the two the twin poles of masculine immaturity. Contrasting with Bernard's sexual neuroses was Huey's sexual magnetism. Marriage in the strips was no panacea partly because each party has unrequited needs that neither partner satisfies. Fractured, distrustful, and resentful relationships become the norm.

"Sick, Sick, Sick" took off. Feiffer's aim was satirically precise: the silent generation of college students, the conformist young professionals, and the status-seeking elders. Focused initially on the world of Greenwich Village with its wine-and-cheese parties, modern dancers, and would-be writers, Feiffer soon broadened his aim to politicians, bureaucrats, and the military. Self-interest, self-loathing, and self-searching matched by evasion dominated the babble which formed the texts of his panels. He feasted on victim-heroes, Bernard the most prominent, a young urban liberal given to constant anxiety attacks and stomach aches. Whether he had sex or not, he felt guilty. He sought, but virtually never found, meaningful relationships. The Dancer was his counterpart. Abused and exploited by men, she, nevertheless, kept her faith in art and self-realization. She danced, fell, got up, tripped, but continued. And on occasion, she sailed aloft.

The *Voice*, itself a new counterculture venture, was the appropriate outlet for Feiffer's illustrated narratives of the unfulfilled and neurotic summarized in this sentence from Feiffer's memoir: "Jill and I had very little to say to each other, but it took three months to find out," duplicated in panels from a February 21, 1963, cartoon from the *Voice* in which a couple admit they're finished. "It's not right anymore. I'd give almost anything if it were different" laments the woman but the last panel shows them heading in opposite directions with tremendous smiles of relief on their faces (*Backing into Forward* 191; *Explainers* 338). Feiffer, social critic, found the differences between how people behaved and their self-serving rationales a mix of the amusing, irrational, and, at times, enraging (*Backing into Forward* 186).

The *Voice* would settle his style and career using his own inadequacies as its subject matter. Finding himself inept with girls and inept at a career, Feiffer saw his early years as the apprenticeship of his future character Bernard Mergendeiler, the luckless-with-women nebbish. Feiffer's own natural shyness worked into the character he created. He lacked an opening line with women, but without one he paradoxically knew he had to become famous because once you are famous you didn't need one (*Backing into Forward* 184). One of his few dates, however, who to his surprise became his "steady girl" for a while, was a modern dancer, a student at NYU. She became the source of Feiffer's successful dance cartoons, although it was "the pretension and not the dance" that drove him to his dancers (*Backing into Forward* 186).

Dance-speak became his new fascination, the convention of the solo or lead dancer often trudging out at the start of the recital and offering a barely audible talk that was generally incomprehensible. Only her hands expressively spoke. What Feiffer began to do in his dance cartoons was offer his version of what he thought the dancer said, the subsequent leaps, falls, crawls, contortions, and anguish echoing her statements or not. This established "the first tentative, flat-footed beachhead toward a counterculture" he wrote (*Backing into Forward* 187). Disenchantment but persistence characterized the dancer's actions.

By the 1970s, however, frustration dominated his dancer. In her dance to 1971, she repeats her dances for the past three years until she stands erect and realizes in the final panel that "Nothing else gets better—why should I?" The positioning of the statement is telling. The first part "nothing else gets better" is on the left side of her body as we look at her, the second on her right, the body acting as a kind of semaphore separating the two (*Jules Feiffer's America* 142). In a later strip, "A Dance to Autumn," the dancer expresses a new freedom to break old molds and escape the past but after displaying new twists and contortions; and thinking about her statements, she anticlimactically and disenchantingly concludes in the final panel, sitting huddled over and comforting herself, that "it's not worth it." Deflation replaces idealism, a characteristic Feiffer response duplicating Jewish humor's comedy of self-defeat (*Jules Feiffer's America* 150).

Initially planning to focus on the personal and psychological disorders of the urban middle class, Feiffer found himself pulled to politics, and once he started, he couldn't stop. Moral outrage at governmental stupidity forced him to continue. Eisenhower's obtuse comments on the *Brown v. Brown* decision incensed him, as did the growing reliance on political double-speak. Politics, combined with male–female relations, became his subjects which he often intertwined.

Defining the texture of a Feiffer cartoon is language. Indeed, he always felt more confident with the writing than the drawing, the language confrontational and honest. What he achieved was a balance between the gestural drawing and text, one not overpowering the other, although he has said that he didn't want the drawings to be noticed at all. The art had to be minimalist to concentrate on the story (Groth xiv). The drawings are simple, as he himself so often acknowledged, but they gain resonance through the dialogue which possesses a dramatic rhythm and actually structures the panels. And as the tempo picks up, the language becomes more complex, and the voices vary from disillusioned urban professionals to mothers, bigots, reactionaries, and housewives, as well as military personnel and presidents.

His portrait of a single woman who finds searing self-analysis through an evening of theater (the satirical review "stripped bare all my illusions, pretensions, hypocrisies"), as well as a nightclub comic and a cartoon, finds balance through an early morning appointment with her analyst. But satisfaction comes not through addressing her crisis but the weather. "One needs some escape," she concludes in this strip from February 28, 1963. This satire of reversal underscores the power of Feiffer's work achieved through his texts as much as his illustrations (*Explainers* 339).

The political Feiffer supplanted the anxiety-ridden Feiffer. From his youth onward, he was aware of injustice and political abuse, aware partly from his older sister who became a Communist. As he adjusted his Jewish radicalism, he soon turned against bureaucracy, complacency, interference. First Eisenhower, then Kennedy, Johnson, Nixon, Reagan, and Carter became his targets, always with satiric precision. *Jules Feiffer's America* (1982) valuably collects this work in which no leader escapes critique. Again, text balances image. One bullheaded law and order type, for example, pledges a million dollars to "the Indicted States of America and to the corruption for which it stands," completing his pledge with "one Nixon under guard—invisible, with liberty inoperative—for all" (*Jules Feiffer's America* 163). Another featuring Nixon reveals his steely determination to uphold justice fully and impartially: "impeachment with honor" he concludes (*Jules Feiffer's America* 163). In another, a ruminative Nixon explains that Watergate was not criminal but self-defensive (*Jules Feiffer's America* 162). Nixon, as Feiffer wrote, was "a genius of the second-rate, the Mozart of mediocrity" who managed to redefine Feiffer's radical political agenda through what he labeled "the great soap opera of American public life" (*Jules Feiffer's America* 125).

Near the end of *Jules Feiffer's America*, the cartoonist writes that Reagan and his kind teach us "what not to, where not to, and how not to. They give negative lessons" excellent for satirists. But surviving our leaders "is not just a struggle, it is a joy; that is the irony of the work I do. The more outraged I am as a citizen, the more fun I find as a cartoonist" (*Jules Feiffer's America* 230). The cartoon "continues the illusion of hope," and that is what keeps him going. Drawing humanizes him: "the more outraged I am as a citizen, the more fun I find as a cartoonist." But it also "galvanizes" him "into combat" (*Jules Feiffer's America* 230). The roots of this moral outrage and eagerness for justice are in Jewish ethical thinking transferred in Feiffer's hands to the politics and social life of mid-twentieth-century United States. Jewish exile, covenant, and existence (often expressed through Israel) are central parts of his psyche and imagination. Although he declared his separation from Jewish practice, his ideas and art never left it.

Feiffer's heroes, like those of Jewish comedians, are victims of misfortune and heroes of endurance. The Dancer still dances and Bernard continues to labor. His use of macaronic language, at times streetwise or intellectualized, reflects the duality of Feiffer's characters, educated but bewildered. Elevated diction jostles with colloquial expression, the professional with the dropout or, as Irving Howe summarized, "gutter vividness with university refinement, street energy with high-culture rhetoric" (Howe 15). Everyday speech in Feiffer's work vibrates with cultural ambition dominated by self-irony. Feiffer transferred the humiliations and fears of Jewish life to his urban sophisticates, while ironic deflation established the satirical humor of his style.

In one of his late dance strips, Feiffer's dancer renounces movement and energy for torpor in her dance to summer. Contradicting her movements, she celebrates sitting, lying, getting a tan, and turning over. But four simple words in the final panel comically justify her inaction and Feiffer's success: "Thank God for Art" (*Jules Feiffer's America* 153). Feiffer, as Maurice Sendak commented, is "that rare artist who can draw an idea" (Sendak 7).

Notes

1   "This is my life, my only life, and I'm living it in the middle of a Jewish joke! I am the son in the Jewish joke—*only it ain't no joke!*" Philip Roth, *Portnoy's Complaint* (New York: Random House, 1969) 36–37.

2   Mike Nicholas and Elaine May were at the same time exposing the Jewish mother on stage. When Nichols defends not calling his mother, May replies "Someday, someday, Arthur, you'll get married, and you'll have children of your own, and honey, when you do, I only pray that they make you suffer. That's a mother's prayer." When he says he feels awful, she responds with "Oh, honey, if I could believe that, I'd be the happiest mother in the world" (in Epstein 182).

3   Malamud's "heroes" come to mind, their suffering, loss, humiliation and fears dominating their behavior. See "The Lady of the Lake" or *A New Life*.

There Goes the Neighborhood: Cycling Ethnoracial Tensions in Will Eisner's *Dropsie Avenue*

Derek Parker Royal

In his *Contract with God* trilogy, Will Eisner, one of the earliest and most vocal advocates of the graphic novel, sets out to narrate the life of Dropsie Avenue, a neighborhood in the Bronx housing residents of diverse ethnic backgrounds. His first two books in the trilogy—*A Contract with God* (1978) and *A Life Force* (1988)—focus primarily on the lives of Jewish families caught in the struggles of Depression-era United States, reminiscent of both Isaac Bashevis Singer's shtetl portraits and the kind of Jewish social realism found in the work of Anzia Yezierska and Michael Gold. However, the third book in the trilogy, *Dropsie Avenue: The Neighborhood* (1995),[1] is strikingly different from its predecessors in that it is not restricted to an individual family or a cast of three or four characters. What is more, and also unlike the previous works in the trilogy, *Dropsie Avenue* does not primarily concern itself with Jewish issues, culture, or families. Instead, Eisner's story is projected onto a much broader canvas, American ethnoracial relations as a whole and the process of urban assimilation.[2] The narrative sweep of the graphic novel[3] encompasses Dropsie Avenue residents from the 1870s to the late twentieth century, revealing its multi ethnic evolution and the turmoil generated by such diverse encounters. What is significant about the last in Eisner's trilogy is the ways in which the author uses comics to represent the ongoing dynamics of the modern ethnic neighborhood. Through both word and picture, Eisner offers a critical—if not downright cynical—reading of the traditional "melting pot" myth, resistant to any romantic notions of multicultural nationhood that any "cartoony" representations might initially suggest. On the contrary, the very form of his efforts—the fluid sweep of his graphics, his non-traditional uses of framing, and his employment of contrastive tones—reveals a rather stark, even neo-naturalistic, analysis of relations between American ethnic communities. As Laurence Roth says of the Dropsie Avenue narratives, which also include *A Contract with God* and *A Life Force*, "the special contracts promised between America and its citizens ... are redrawn by Eisner as distinctly unglamorous and unfulfilled agreements" (466). What is more, Eisner's bittersweet rendition of the Dropsie Avenue neighborhood (much like the one in which the author grew up) is further complicated by what he apparently sees as the cyclical nature of ethnoracial tensions—a fitting metaphor, given the fact that the book itself is part of a larger graphic narrative cycle.[4]

In drawing together the various actions that occur and recur, cycle-like, throughout the text, Eisner employs several highly revealing, and visually sophisticated, graphic signifiers that dramatically underscore the violence and alienation that can result within multiethnic communities. They include a metaphoric emphasis on windows, references to fire, and the presence of "For Sale" or "For Rent" signs, and it is the use of these visual themes that will be the focus of the current essay. These cyclically recurring images function as a form of illustrated shorthand, coded disclosures of the seemingly neverending, and apparently futile, attempts of diverse populations to work out their differences and live in mutual respect. They serve as visual leitmotifs that not only underscore the pessimistic tone of the graphic novel but also interlink the sprawling action of the narrative—assorted sequences that, taken together, can certainly be read as a metaphor for the breakdown in American ethnoracial relations. In other words, the many references to windows, fire, and signs serve the paradoxical function of binding together into a cohesive whole a series of varied and disjointed episodes that are intended to emphasize social fragmentation.

The plot of *Dropsie Avenue* is fairly simple. It begins in 1870, in the living room of the Van Dropsies, a Dutch family from New York's earliest wave of immigrant settlers, where they are discussing the relatively recent arrival of the English into their neighborhood, a region that we now know of as the Bronx. Dirk Van Dropsie complains that the English are gaining the economic upper hand on the Dutch residents, and on one drunken night sets fire to a neighbor's crops as an act of protest. In the process Dirk accidentally kills his niece by immolation, is then shot by his brother-in-law, the Dropsie family goes into seclusion until their house is eventually destroyed by fire, and then soon after a "For Sale" sign is placed on the property. Several years later, the newly rich O'Brien family purchases the lot, wanting desperately to move up in social circles and enhance their lifestyle in the now predominantly English neighborhood, and then just as the Van Dropsies had earlier scrutinized the English, the O'Briens are scrutinized by the English neighbors across the street. These early scenes in this graphic novel set the stage for many of the images and themes that will recur throughout. "Established" residents will become unsettled by the arrival of newer immigrants, complain about the "colorful" changes—color as signifier of difference resonates throughout this work—eventually sell their homes and move away from Dropsie Avenue. The newer immigrants will then become the "established" neighbors, eventually bemoaning the fact that an even newer and more "colorful" group of arrivals have started to move in. This continues throughout the graphic novel, with the English being replaced by the Irish, being replaced by the Italians, and then followed by German, Jewish, Hispanic (primarily Puerto Rican), and then finally African American arrivals.[5]

The central figure in this drama is the Dropsie neighborhood itself, a setting that becomes a character, metaphorically living and breathing with a life force all its own. In fact, several times throughout the graphic novel individuals comment on how neighborhoods have a life cycle much like people. As one of the book's dominant figures, Abie Gold, speculates: "Maybe a neighborhood has a life cycle … like people!" (141). And if the neighborhood is the central character in this novel, it's one that is as chaotic and fragmented as the relationships among its inhabitants. What binds these various episodes together are a series of interlocking themes and images—such as those of fire, signage, and windows—that connect, or cycle, its long string of individual stories. In this way, *Drospie Avenue* is much like Eisner's 1978 graphic novel, *A Contract with God*, a text that relies on the short-story cycle form as a way of bringing together its seemingly disparate narratives.[6] However, *Dropsie Avenue* is more, and in the fullest sense, novelistic than the earlier work, with its more tightly woven scenes and its structuring imagery. In fact, it is a graphic novel whose visuals dramatically outweigh its verbiage in narrative significance.[7]

Inside looking out, outside looking in

Perhaps the most common theme in *Dropsie Avenue* can be summed up by the fatalistic adage: "There goes the neighborhood." Individuals from one ethnic community are constantly throwing up their hands at the arrival of individuals from another ethnic group, and this throwing up of the hands can be read at different times as resignation, resistance, and relocation. The resignation comes in the form of moderate voices within an established community, accepting the presence of a new group of residents and aware of the potential for growth and progress among different people. In Eisner's text, this pragmatic approach to ethnic diversity is often clothed in religious garb—for instance, there are occasions when Father O'Leary (67), Father Gianelli (142), Rabbi Goodstein (78), and the African American reverend Dr. Washington (143) acknowledge the reality of the changing neighborhood and adjust their outlooks accordingly—but it also comes in more secular forms. Abie Gold and Polo Palmero, a lawyer and a political boss, are two of the most developed characters in the novel and understand the social necessity, as well as the personal profits, that come of good community relations.

While examples of resignation and even understanding can be found throughout *Dropsie Avenue*, scenes of resistance and relocation are far more plentiful. One way in which Eisner represents ethnoracial discord is through the use of windows as a visual theme.[8] The artist uses windows and glass imagery not only to illustrate (literally) the various barriers separating one ethnic group from another but also as a commentary on the process of obtaining "insider" status. In this way, we can read *Dropsie Avenue* as a visual discourse on whiteness, or the means through which certain individuals and groups identify themselves as "white," thereby positioning themselves within a perceived middle class—or at least distinctly separate from what they see as common laborers or recent immigrants—and assuming the various entitlements and privileges such a status provides.[9] Window imagery functions as a way of representing both insider and outsider status, and the graphic novel is filled with examples of "privileged" characters inside their domains looking out at others or perspectives of individuals outside looking in on those in positions of authority. As such, Eisner provides us not only with examples of ethnoracial identity formation, how individuals contextualize themselves within certain ethnic and racial groupings, but also with the process of what Karen Brodkin calls "ethnoracial assignment," which is "about popularly held classifications and their deployment by those with national power to make them matter economically, politically, and socially to the individuals classified" (3).

The opening episodes of *Dropsie Avenue* are an effective demonstration of this. In the first scene, Hendrik Van Dropsie, the Dutch landowner whose father bought the property from the Van Bronks, is looking out of his window and talking with his family about the growing presence of the English. Hendrik's brother-in-law, Dirk, complains that the English are buying up everything and, standing by the window, claims that soon the new residents will "make things bad" for the Van Dropsies (4) and damns them for not belonging (6). A similar context is drawn after the Van Dropsie house is burned to the ground. When Sean O'Brien, a nouveau riche Irish owner of a construction company, builds a mansion in the neighborhood, the Skidmore family (part of the now dominant English presence on Dropsie Avenue) stands by their window and bemoans the O'Briens' presence. Looking out at their unwanted neighbors, they complain that Mrs. O'Brien walks down the street "as if she owns the neighborhood," and laugh at them because "they don't even know they don't belong" (14). This use of window imagery occurs repeatedly throughout the graphic novel, linking together the separate episodes and demonstrating patterns of exclusiveness among the various ethnic residents of Dropsie Avenue.[10]

Windows are also used to establish authority and privilege from an inverse perspective. There are a number of scenes where Eisner forces the reader, through visual framing and perspective, to look in on those with economic power, individuals who have "made it" in the neighborhood and who now have some political voice. One of the most frequently recurring characters in the graphic novel is the Ashkenazi ragman, Izzy Cash, so called because of his singsong cries as he pushes his cart down the street: "I cash clothes" (65). He becomes the central economic power on Dropsie Avenue, and even his name suggests as much. He is one of the only figures in the novel who is observed through windows from an outside perspective. When he buys his first building from the borough bank, we are introduced to this transaction as if we were standing outside the bank window looking in (73). When he is present at a hearing because he is accused of being a slumlord, we observe the action from the outside and through the door's windows (90). And before Izzy begins selling off his property, having a "bad feeling about Dropsie Avenue" and realizing that it is going downhill, we see him discussing this matter with his assistant as if we were looking through the window of his office door (Figure 6.1). The latter example is particularly telling, in that as we observe Izzy Cash through the door window—as if we were outside of the room— he is looking outside of his office window at the crumbling neighborhood below. In other words, the distance between the haves and the have nots is compounded. In these scenes with Izzy, the outsider is the focalizer. It is as if the reader is serving as a narrative proxy for the disempowered other as he or she looks in on, and is separated from, those with economic clout.

Eisner also uses windows to represent the pent-up rage that can result from prejudice, fear, and imposed ethnic divisions. These come in the form of broken glass. Soon after the United States enters the First World War, Irish children overhear their parents talking about the "krauts" and the "damn huns" who have moved into the neighborhood. They act out by throwing rocks through the German immigrants'

Figure 6.1 Reprinted from *Dropsie Avenue* by Will Eisner. 131. Copyright © 1995 by Will Eisner, Copyright © 2006 by the Estate of Will Eisner. Used with permission of the publisher, W. W. Norton & Company, Inc.

window (32). When Italian youth retaliate after the Puerto Ricans beat up one of their own, the ensuing fight shatters the plate glass of Herman Gold's tailor shop (96). Later, the glass storefront of Joe Leone's shoe repair business, next door to Gold's shop, is smashed by Puerto Ricans enraged by what they perceive as disrespect from an Italian priest (124). And finally, Gold's shop window is once again destroyed when his landlord tries to burn him out so that he can get the lease back and legally increase rents (146).

Indeed, windows are also thresholds of transgression, the crossing of which can be linked to urban poverty. Rowena Shepard's future husband, Prince, is first seen climbing through a window after he is caught stealing from a tenement apartment (46–47). Six pages later, Prince catches three young thugs, intent on robbery, as they climb through the window of Rowena's new flower business (53). In Sven Svensen's former building, now owned by a major drug dealer aptly named Bones, homeless men can be seen through a broken windowpane. Their drunken carelessness causes a fire that destroys the building, and flames are shown shooting out the apartment window (130). This image of a flaming window is repeated seventeen pages later when an African-American father sets fire to his own apartment so that he can qualify for public housing assistance, which includes clothing and moving costs, as a burned out family (147).

As these many examples clearly demonstrate, Eisner's use of windows emphasizes the economic and social divisions resulting from ethnoracial turmoil, and it reveals the almost cyclical process through which immigrant communities establish themselves in order to be considered "white" ... or the violence that can result from being excluded from such social privilege. The window imagery also helps to give form to his sprawling narrative, with the repeated use of windows binding together the book's many episodes. In fact, one can even read the recurring image as a metafictional device. It is as if Eisner is drawing our attention to his project by showing us that windows are visually similar to the various panels that make up the comic page. This becomes apparent toward the end of the graphic novel, when we see the last remaining tenement building minutes before it is demolished. And at the Dropsie Avenue Reunion, the arrangement of the pictures on "The Old Neighborhood as We Remember It" display board (161)—the sequential layout resembling the visual of broken-out windows—recall the multi-paned building just three pages earlier (158). The reunion photographs can even be seen as "windows" into the past. Yet, as these final visual references suggest—the boarded up windows and the pictures of a dead past—Dropsie Avenue no longer embodies the dreams of its earliest residents. Even the final attempts to revive the neighborhood, bankrolled by the Rowena Plant Corporation, fall prey to the suspicions of and prejudices against the ethnic other.

Firestorms of ethnoracial animosity

Another way in which Eisner reveals fear and bigotry in *Dropsie Avenue*, as well as gives form to his narrative, is through fire imagery. Throughout the text, fire is directly linked to the anger and discontent among the neighborhood residents, and they come in a variety of forms, from budding embers of personal resentment to full-scale emotional explosions from the community at large. In fact, the graphic novel more or less begins with such imagery. In the opening scene, Dirk's anger at the growing English presence is expressed through conflagration. He attempts to destroy the English crops, thereby removing any economic threat that the new arrivals may pose. Screaming "Burn them out!" (7), Dirk literalizes the inner fires of his hatred, and in doing so he ignites a flame that consumes not only the English crops but also his niece, Helda Van Dropsie. In these opening pages of his graphic novel, Eisner is pointing out, rather overtly, the underlying nature of the Dropsie neighborhood, illustrating through its very namesake the fire-laden forces of destruction that will propel the rest of the narrative.

While the opening scenes with the Van Dropsie family may be a rather heavy-handed way to symbolize hatred, other scenes in the book reveal a more nuanced use of fire imagery. One such episode occurs in a brief exchange between Coleen O'Brien and her brother Neil (20). It is around 1900, approximately thirty years after the opening crop fire, and the O'Brien family currently owns the old Van Dropsie property, now centrally located within a largely English population. In this scene Coleen tells her brother about her affair with Charles Livermore, from well-to-do Anglo ancestry, which ended because the Livermore family wouldn't let their son marry, in Coleen's words, "a low class Irish girl" (19). What is significant about this series of panels is the way in which Eisner uses Coleen's cigarette smoke as a means to revealing ethnic resentment. As she pours out her story to Neil, her words are literally framed by the smoke that she exhales. Unlike the opening scenes with Van Dropsie, the hate portrayed in this episode visually begins as a small flame at the top of the page and then is slowly revealed through the burning down of Coleen's cigarette, the smoke of which encompasses the insult and rumor leveled against the young Irish woman.

Eisner uses a similar technique several pages later, when a group of neighborhood residents, now primarily Irish, congregate to discuss the recent immigrant arrivals (30). It is the early days of the First World War, and the "Dropsie Avenue Property Owner's Association" has gathered to discuss a possible solution to the growing German population. "Them Krauts is movin' in," one resident exclaims, and the men decide to hold a patriotic block party as a way of "cleaning up the neighborhood" (31). Their frustrations, as well as their unfounded fears, are initially revealed through their tobacco smoke, and this framing device immediately follows the image of a "For Sale" sign, a panel that serves as a segue between Neil O'Brien's story and the owner's association's clash with their German neighbors (more on the use of signage later in the essay). Tobacco smoke is also closely associated with Big Ed Casey, the owner of a construction company that builds the neighborhood's first tenement houses. In every instance of his brief appearance in the graphic novel (36–42), he is shown with a cigar. Not only is Eisner visually stereotyping the powerful and crooked fat cat—the cigar as a sign of authority and consumption—but he is also directly linking Big Ed's cigar smoke to much of the abuse and violence underlying the narrative. It is Big Ed, after all, who corrupts the idealistic city-planning director, Danny Smith, and who indirectly causes the death (or murder) of the city investigator. Perhaps even more significant, Big Ed's cigar smoke is visually linked to the construction of the Dropsie Avenue tenements, an event that will accelerate ethnoracial discord. It is as if the chances of harmony and stability within the neighborhood have gone up in smoke, disappearing into thin air like Danny Smith's integrity.[11] It is no accident that the final panel of this event—as with the previous O'Brien episode—foregrounds a "For Sale" sign, with Danny and his wife deciding to move out of the Dropsie neighborhood now that they can afford to do so.

Such visual links to animosity and strife seem tame compared to many of the images that follow. Elsewhere, Eisner uses much more dramatic means to express ethnic discontent. In illustrating the United States entering the Second World War (83), he juxtaposes images of Dropsie Avenue (the street shot at the top part of the page) with scenes of destruction from the war, a conflict that was largely waged over issues of ethnoracial differences. With both the newspaper headlines screaming war and the mushroom cloud on the left hand of the panel, Eisner links the ethnic resentments on Dropsie Avenue with images of war-ravaged Europe. What is more, the bright streetlight at the bottom right of the page not only pulls the eye downward from the pre-war scenes of Dropsie Avenue, thereby facilitating a condensed temporal segue, but it also centers the subsequent action in the midst of ruins.[12] This is the only time in the graphic novel that Eisner takes his story, albeit briefly, outside of the Dropsie Avenue setting. And it is significant that it is Berlin, of all places—now a burned out shell of a city—that becomes the symbolic embodiment of destruction and is directly linked to the Dropsie neighborhood. These images of fiery destruction gain even more import when compared to scenes near the end of the novel, when the last standing building along Dropsie Avenue is destroyed (159). In an effort to stem crime and further economic decay, the city planners decide to demolish what is left of the "bombed out" (157) neighborhood so as to start anew—a situation that parallels the decimation of the Nazi capital. The parallel is thematic as well as visual. The explosive cloud from the demolition is a graphic echo of the atomic cloud seen earlier in the book (83)—down to its mushroom shape—and the aerial shot of the leveled buildings on Dropsie Avenue are likewise a direct link to the bombed out buildings of Berlin.

Other images of conflagration are even more straightforward. In one episode, for instance, the inner frustrations of the neighborhood's residents are given outward expression in the form of an explosion (Figure 6.2). At one point, Sven Svensen, the owner and super of one of Dropsie Avenue's tenement buildings, is bombarded by complaints from his occupants. His is perhaps the most ethnically diverse residence on the block—Svensen was one of the first owners to integrate his building—and here Eisner is showing how the slow growth of ethnically generated animosity (revealed through grumblings over rent, utilities, and undesirable tenants) can build into a much more destructive force, something on a metaphorical scale of a boiler explosion. This graphic allegory is given more direct expression twenty-four pages later, when Abie Gold and Polo Palmero ruminate on the changes in the neighborhood. Abie, now a city councilman for the Dropsie Avenue district, is talking with Polo about the growing problem of drugs. In this scene, Abie waxes philosophical about the cyclical nature of neighborhoods, and Polo equates the chaotic "jungle" of the streets with the growing presence of even more ethnic and racial minorities. They have just had the police jail the drug dealer Bones, and in retaliation the dealer has someone rig Polo's car. Not only does Eisner use these fiery explosions to represent the extremes of ethnic tensions—the underlying animosity and hatred that can at any time express itself in violent and unpredictable ways—but he does so by linking them visually, thereby underscoring their effects in the narrative. Visually, the fiery death of Polo (141) directly parallels explosion in Figure 6.2, down to the very detail of both sharing the same lower right-hand space on the page. Furthermore, these explosions come at two key moments in the text. The explosion at the Svensen building leads directly to neighborhood's downward spiral at the hands of Bones, and the assassination of Polo immediately follows Abie's musings on the neighborhood's "life cycle" and its death as a "force of nature" (141).

References to fire and ethnoracial discord appear more frequently in the last half of the text, as if the graphic novel is building to a crescendo ending with Dropsie Avenue's final destruction. Abie breaks up a brawl between Italian and Puerto Rican

Figure 6.2 Reprinted from *Dropsie Avenue* by Will Eisner. 117. Copyright © 1995 by Will Eisner, Copyright © 2006 by the Estate of Will Eisner. Used with permission of the publisher, W. W. Norton & Company, Inc.

gangs by asking women to boil water and pour it down on the heads of fighters below their windows (97). The old Svensen building is burned to the ground due to the drunken carelessness of vagrants (130–331). Another tenement building is destroyed when its owner hires finishers to strip all of its plumbing and heating fixtures, in an attempt to force out its undesirable—ethnic—residents. A fire occurs as a result of a tenant igniting a trash barrel in order to keep warm and then having that barrel knocked over during a fight with one of the "dopers from upstairs" (136). As referenced earlier, Abie Gold's father, a tailor and a refugee from the Nazis, has his business burned out (he suspects) by his own landlord. As the firemen extinguish the flames, Abie's father screams "It's Berlin again! Berlin again! Again!" (146).[13] And finally, the aforementioned African American sets fire to his apartment building so that he can receive public assistance (147). In each of these cases, Eisner uses fire imagery to reveal the underlying animosity in our modern and ethnically diverse urban space.

Sign, sign, everywhere a sign

Given the violence and the desperation that seems to permeate the text, it should come as no surprise that an outside force, some deus ex machina, may be needed to bring any promising change to Eisner's neighborhood. This "saving" force comes in the form of Rowena Shepard—and her suggestive surname—a once youthful and innocent gardener who lived in the shadows of the tenements, occupying the neighborhood's last remaining private home. In the 1970s, after demolition teams have completely leveled the area, she returns to work with Abie Gold and Rubie Brown, an idealistic African-American City Planning Director who had grown up on Dropsie Avenue, in rebuilding the neighborhood. Rowena is now an aged millionaire, having successfully transformed her love of gardening into a thriving floral company, and she wants to use her money to recreate the neighborhood. Abie reads Rowena's letter about her memories of Dropsie Avenue (169), and these remembrances are framed in dream-like text bubbles (although one could also read these "airy" remembrances as visually akin to smoke, thus linking these images to the fire and destruction seen earlier in the narrative). Throughout the text, Rowena is associated with magical transformation—in earlier scenes in the novel she sits in her wheelchair among her many roses, calling herself the princess of a "magic garden," a place where she meets a young mute boy whom she calls her "prince from an enchanted kingdom"—and "magic" is what she attempts to bring back to Dropsie Avenue. It is here where Eisner's text flirts most closely with sentimentality, potentially providing unrealistically easy answers to the complex problems underlying his fictional landscape. Indeed, Eisner has been known at times to stray into the world of schmaltz, turning otherwise serious and provocative premises into maudlin storylines. This can be seen in such texts as *Fagin the Jew* (2003), his graphic narrative revision of Dickens's *Oliver Twist*, or even *The Dreamer* (1986) and *Minor Miracles* (2000), stories that rely heavily on the melodramatic.

However, although *Dropsie Avenue* may at times threaten to become sentimental, the text ultimately resists such trite responses to ethnic turmoil. Eisner does this with another visual motif that runs throughout the text: the "For Sale" or "For Rent" sign. Whenever there is a dramatic change in the neighborhood, the threat of racial hatred, or a new ethnic minority moving into a building or onto a block, "For Sale" or "For Rent" signs are never far behind. This signage functions as an almost fatalistic counterweight to the optimism that springs from the neighborhood's more hopeful residents. As mentioned previously, these signs appear immediately after the episodes with Neil O'Brien (30) and Danny Smith (43). They also occur after a German family is shunned by their Irish neighbors (34), in the wake of the stock market crash of 1929 (71), when Izzy Cash decides to integrate his buildings (112), after Svensen rents to gypsies and other "undesirables" (113), and when Rafa Gorgol—an abusive and unkempt man who is drawn to represent an East European "other"—is shot by his wife (116). And as with the window and fire imagery, the repetitive use of "For Sale" or "For Rent" signs brings together the diverse episodes that make up the narrative.

Eisner uses this image most effectively in the final pages of the graphic novel. One day, after the Rowena Corporation has used its millions to "magically" create Dropsie Gardens, a residential community of affordable single-family homes, two neighbors, one black and one white, are out doing yard work and comment on their recently arrived neighbors. We never see these new residents, but according to the homeowners they are families who have arrived "on leaky boats" and who decorate their houses in "weird colors" and "dinky ornaments" (171–172). Again, "color" has infiltrated Dropsie Avenue, the neighbors are resentful, and the "For Sale" signs begin to go up. It is a "there goes the neighborhood" attitude all over again, and residents are once more suspicious and unsettled by ethnic diversity. As if to drive this point home, in the most recent edition of *Dropsie Avenue*—published in 2005 as a single-volume trilogy and including *A Contract with God* and *A Life Force*—Eisner added two new illustrations. These are the final graphic commentaries of the graphic novel, and they show the Dropsie Gardens community slipping into disorder. In the first of these illustrations, the new houses on Dropsie Avenue are shown in disarray. Accompanying this image are the words of an extradiegetic narrator explaining:

> As it often happens to neighborhoods[,] Dropsie Avenue's ethnic mix began to change. The simple inexpensive home attracted a new group of people. Poorer and immigrant, they came with different cultural tastes and a less responsible attutude [*sic*] toward ownership and community. Soon they added brightly colored improvised structures to accommodate their large families. As earlier residents moved out, its character changed … visible evidence of implacable growth. (173)

This detached, almost clinical, voice-over is then immediately followed by the book's final image (174). In it, we see the rain-drenched neighborhood sprinkled with "For Sale" signs, moving vans standing ready to assist in the relocation.[14] It appears that the "fairytale" quality of the planned community is undermined once again by the cycles of violence and distrust, and not even Rowena's magic can change this fact.[15]

Will Eisner's message in *Dropsie Avenue* isn't uplifting. Unlike the endings of some of his other graphic novels, this one is dark, blunt, and uncompromising. One could even call it neo-naturalistic, a fatalistic reading of ethnoracial relations in the United States. It is significant to note that this is the final text of *The* Contract with God *Trilogy*, a series of narratives that explore interactions among disparate individuals and systems of faith. But whereas the earlier stories in the trilogy may have held out for the possibility of personal redemption, either through faith or even through art, there seems to be little chance of that happening within the larger community. *Dropsie Avenue* shows us a localized neighborhood trapped in the grips of ethnic intolerance, and even if its message is bleak, it is one that we should nonetheless heed, especially given our country's continued acts of racial intolerance, our ongoing rhetorical posturings concerning patriotism, and the current heated debates on immigration.

Notes

1   Throughout this essay, I will reference the most recent Norton edition of *Dropsie Avenue*, since not long before his death Eisner provided four brand new illustrations for the new version, and, as I will argue, some of those additional drawings are important when determining the book's tone.

2   In this way, my reading of *Dropsie Avenue* differs from that of comics critic and artist, Danny Fingeroth. He reads the book as part of a series of graphic novels in which "Eisner was preoccupied with Jewish subjects" (140). While I would agree that many of Eisner's later works such *A Contract with God* and *To the Heart of the Storm* (1991) directly engage with and are primarily focused on issues of Jewishness, *Dropsie Avenue* provides a much broader context, with Jewish concerns being only one of many ethnoracial voices heard in the text.

3   The term "graphic novel"—a label commonly applied to a variety of comics, regardless of genre, length, and subject matter—is highly problematic and raises a number of challenging questions within comics studies. However, despite the baggage of this label, I will nonetheless use it when referring to *Dropsie Avenue*, if for no other reason, then because Eisner himself employed the term and is (mistakenly) seen by many as its originator. As Bob Andelman points out in his biography, although Eisner was not the first to use apply "graphic novel" to his work, he is largely responsible for popularizing the term, thereby lending more "legitimacy" to comics as a literary form (295–296).

4   In 2005 all three of Eisner's interconnected Dropsie Avenue narratives were for the first time collected in one volume, *The* Contract with God *Trilogy: Life on Dropsie Avenue*.

5   Asian immigrants are curiously absent from *Dropsie Avenue*, but at the very end of the novel there is an ambiguous reference to new and even more "colorful" boat arrivals, which could include Vietnamese, Chinese, or any number of other ethnic figures. See, for example, final dialogue in the book (171–172).

6   For a further discussion of *A Contract with God* as a graphic cycle, a comics equivalent of the short-story cycle, see my essay, "Sequential Sketches of Ethnic Identity: Will Eisner's *A Contract with God* as Graphic Cycle."

7   Not all graphic novels do this. Marjane Satrapi's *Persepolis: The Story of a Childhood* (2003) and Alison Bechdel's *Fun Home: A Family Tragicomic* (2006), for instance, are works that rely more heavily on dialogue and "voice-overs"—what Thierry Groensteen calls "the voice of the reciter" (88)—as a thematically propelling force, and Eisner's final work, *The Plot: The Secret Story of the Protocols of the Elders of Zion* (2005), is by and large a text built more upon words than graphics. These are what Scott McCloud would call examples of "word-specific" comics—where pictures illustrate, but do not significantly add to the text—or "duo-specific" combinations—where words and pictures generate essentially the same message (153).

8   I wish to thank a former student of mine, C. J. Stephens, for initially drawing my attention to Eisner's abundant use of window imagery and its thematic import.

9   "White," in this sense, is not necessarily defined through (Western) European ancestry or skin pigmentation—although skin color does figure into a larger understanding of "whiteness"—but much more importantly, is a privileged social position that is understood in contrast to an "other," usually those who have been associated with "blackness" and/or have been traditionally excluded from various social, economic, and intellectual arenas. As such, race is regarded as a social constructed, and that which is defined as "non-white" is used as a justification for discrimination. For further discussions on whiteness and the process under which individuals are considered white, see Michael Omi and Howard Winant, Noel Ignatiev, Karen Brodkin, and Matthew Frye Jacobson.

10   Other notable examples include Sean O'Brien looking out his window at the up-and-coming O'Leary family (17); his son Neil looking out at the factories across town (29); Rowena Shepard's grandmother looking out of her window—one of the few remaining private houses on Dropsie Avenue—at the tenements that crowd her (45); neighbors, bootleggers, and prostitutes looking at the protest, and subsequent death, of Lilly O'Reily (57, 59); Rowena's neighbors watching her and Prince as they leave Dropsie Avenue (62); the Irish residents looking at the newly arrived Italians as they move into a tenement building (67); Father Gianelli, Rabbi Goldstein, and their neighbors looking out onto the streets that have "abandoned" their children (81); politician Polo Palermo looking out his window as he plans on getting the support of the Jewish population (92); white residents looking out their windows as African Americans move into their building (112); tenants looking down on Puerto Rican and Italian gangs fighting (125); kids looking out their windows as they drop a water balloon on the new Hasidic arrivals (148); and the closed, lighted windows of the new private homes on Dropsie Avenue, after neighbors discuss how property values will drop given the recent "colorful" arrivals (172).

11   Not only do rings of cigar smoke prominently accompany the revelation of the city investigator's death (41), but Danny's gradual corruption is treated in similar fashion. The whirl of dollar bills that frames Danny's horse betting—Big Ed's attempt to indebt the young city planner to him—visually calls to mind the dispersing clouds of Big Ed's puffs (39).

12   At risk of applying fire imagery too freely, it is worth noting the number of times bright lights and streetlamps, perhaps reminiscent of fire, are prominently featured in the text—and the contexts in which they appear. They appear twice in the book's opening scene at the Van Dropsie's (4, 10), immediately before Coleen O'Brien is arrested for prostitution (21), the boxing match between Irish Mike and the Polo Palermo (69), the aforementioned scene in Berlin (83), Polo's attempts to sabotage Izzy Cash's buildings with acid (88), the beating of Rockie (an Italian) by a Hispanic gang (95), the boiler explosion at Svensen's building (117), the car bombing of Polo Palermo (141), and the demolition of the last building on Dropsie Avenue, this final instance featuring a streetlamp with a busted globe (159). What all of these visuals have in common is that they appear during episodes of violence.

13   Thus, another link to ethnic violence and the devastation of Berlin (83).

14   Eisner's rain drawing is reminiscent of the opening pages of *A Contract with God*, where Frimme Hirsch walks home in a downpour after burying his daughter, Rachele. Given the fact that *A Contract with God* is the first work in the 2005 collected trilogy, and *Dropsie Avenue* is its closing narrative, we can read this final

rain-drenched page as part of the trilogy's visual frame. It both begins and ends with gloomy, rainy weather. This is yet another way in which Eisner ties together, or even cycles, the various events in his text.

15   Significantly enough, when we first see Rowena she is a young, idealistic wheelchair-bound gardener. Later in life, when she comes back to attempt to save the neighborhood through her wealth—cultivate it, as one would a bed of flowers—one may wonder if her philanthropic efforts are crippled from the very beginning, doomed to the ethnic realities defining the community.

JEWS & SUPER HEROES

"ANOTHER EARNEST YET ULTIMATELY OFF-THE-MARK SURVEY OF AMERICA'S TWO FAVORITE OBSESSIONS."
BY ELI VALLEY

Part Two

Jewish Engagements with Comic Genres

The Servant: Marvel Comics and the Golem Legend

Robert G. Weiner

When I was woven together in the depths of the earth

Your eyes saw the Golem

Psalm 136: 15–16[1]

To say that the Jewish legend of the golem has securely placed itself in popular culture would be an understatement.[2] The golem can be thought of as the first superhero prototype. More recently, in his hit film *Inglourious Basterds*, Quentin Tarantino had the Hitler character make mention of his fear of the golem, and there are literally hundreds of golem stories and adaptations (including numerous children's books) in print and on the Internet. These stories range from traditional Jewish tales to horror stories. Even notable writer and Holocaust survivor Elie Wiesel wrote his own version of a golem tale. Michael Chabon's Pulitzer Prize-winning comic book-related novel, *The Amazing Adventures of Kavalier & Clay*, makes use of the golem legend. One installment in Terry Pratchett's *Discworld* novel series, *Feet of Clay*, deals with golems, and there are dozens of movies related to the golem dating all the way back to 1915 with the German *Der Golem*.[3]

Dan Bilefsky, in a May 10, 2009 *New York Times* article, argues that the world has gone more or less golem crazy. There are now golem-oriented hotels, toys, door-making companies, operas and musicals, and sandwiches. Even First Lady Michelle Obama has paid her respects to the golem legend. It is not surprising, then, that golem stories have turned up in sequential art narratives. There are a number of recent comics/graphic novels that use the golem as a metaphor for storytelling. Most notable of these are James Sturm's *The Golem's Mighty Swing*[4] and the Israeli graphic novel *HaGolem: Sipuro shel comics Israeli* (*The Golem: The Story of an Israeli Comic*) by Eli Eshed and Uri Fink, which at the time of this writing is not available as an English translation.[5] Other comics include Jaime Morgan Robert's *Golem*, in which the golem character actually confronts Hitler, who then commits suicide rather than die at the hands of a "Jewish Demon" (Roberts 5). There have also been numerous independent comics related to the golem,[6] and it should come as no surprise that the two big sequential art companies, Marvel and DC Comics, have put together their own versions of the golem in DC's various *Ragman* comics and recently in the 12-issue series *The Monolith*. This essay will look at the golem in Marvel Comics.

The golem legend

There are hundreds of stories related to the golem with as many incarnations.[7] But the basic story is that in 1580, the Jews of Prague were experiencing great difficulties and persecutions. It was rumored that their Passover Matzos, normally made of flour and water, were actually made with the blood of Christian children (known as blood libel). Because of this, Prague's Jews were forced into a ghetto with no rights of personal liberty, with the Czech emperor neither caring nor putting an end to the libel. Jews were then killed and victimized with alarming ferocity. It was in this environment that Rabbi Judah Löew ben Bezalel (c. 1520–1609), a great educator and lover of God (also known as the *Maharal* [teacher] of Prague), decided to act (Thieberger). Using the holy work of Jewish mysticism, the *Kabbalah*, Rabbi Löew and two rabbinical students formed a clay man-like figure (or homunculus) which in times of great trouble, would come to help the Jews out of their sorrows. The word "golem" appears once in the *Tanakh* in Psalm 139:16 as the Hebrew *Gol'mi*, which means (my) unshaped outline or "matter without form" (Scholem 351). The rabbi uttered a number of incantations to *Ha'Shem* and the spirits within, and inscribed into the clay of the golem's forehead the Hebrew word *Emet* or *Emeth*, (Scholem 352) which is both a name of God and the Hebrew word for "truth." The matter without form became alive, albeit without a soul, and the golem rose to obey the will of Rabbi Löew and save the Jews from libel and persecution. Other stories have the rabbi placing a scroll/*shem*[8] into the golem's mouth with the holy inscription on the scroll, while some stories have the rabbi naming the golem *Yosef* (Joseph). The golem did his job very well by destroying those who spread the blood libel against the Jews. Thus, by serving the Jews, the golem served God.

The golem also does chores, such as cleaning up and bringing water to the congregants of the synagogue. During services in the synagogue, the golem lights up, as though the spirit of God is instilling some kind of real feeling into the creature of stone-like clay. The golem creation story mimics that of God's creation of Adam out of dust. Eventually, however, the citizens of Prague complained to the emperor that the golem was out of hand. The golem's bringing down of anti-Semites made most of the Gentile citizens of Prague afraid to go out on the streets, afraid that something bad might happen to them. In response, the emperor decreed that no more persecution/pogroms against the Jews would be tolerated. With the *Ha'Shem*'s people safe, there was no need for the golem, so Rabbi Löew erased the letter *alef* from the golem's forehead, which then left the word *meth* (which means death) on the head of the golem. There are hundreds of variations to this tale. Some have the golem going berserk, while others have him continuing to serve the Jews and the synagogue. Other stories have Rabbi Löew's successors revive the golem when Jews were once again persecuted.

Of Hulks and golems

Marvel Comics roster of characters include many that have become well known including the Fantastic Four, X-Men, Dr. Doom, Iron Man, Spider-Man, and the Hulk.[9] Marvel Comics writer Roy Thomas was one of the first to bring the golem myth to light in *Hulk* #134 (December 1970) in the story "In the Shadow of the Golem." This makes sense as the Hulk himself is very golem-like. He does not have the most sophisticated reasoning powers, but his big, lumbering green figure looks like a golem. In fact, Thomas points out that the reason he chose to make the golem connection was "it's a great legend … and it appealed to me to have the Hulk BECOME the Golem, since some folks said he was a Golem type. Was it Stan [Lee] or I who first called him a 'green Golem'?" (Thomas) The Hulk is a "modern version" of the Jewish golem saga (Kaplin 109). Although Stan Lee and Jack Kirby created the Hulk with the monster of Frankenstein as the main inspiration, upon closer examination, Lee states: "When you think about it, he is a [golem] … Once you see the Hulk, he does seem to be like you'd imagine the Golem … but in the Modern World" (qtd. in Kaplin 109). The cover of *Hulk* #134 features the Hulk in the shadow of a much larger lumbering figure. The story takes place in the small village of Slavic Morvania, where some people are debating the existence of the Hulk, when a little girl actually meets him. This is very similar to a scene in the 1931 Universal Studios release of *Frankenstein*. The Hulk does not scare the little girl, but the rest of her family is horrified when they see him and they chase him away. The girl questions this and asks her papa whether "[h]e's the one you told me about. The Golem?" (Thomas 3). Her father, Isaac, still in disbelief, states that the golem is "only a story told to children," but he reevaluates his claim by stating it was an "old legend … and … dream … [he] … never dared believe until NOW!" Isaac then goes on to relate the actual Golem of Prague legend: "as the grim serpent of persecution reared its head … And our people hid in cellars … [Then] Rabbi Judah Low Ben Bezalel breathed life into a body without a soul." He goes onto relate how the golem freed the people of falsehoods and oppression until he was not needed, at which time the golem was nowhere to be found. What is interesting here is that there is no mention of the Jews, Israel, or Hebrews but rather "OUR People" (3). It is not as though the writer was trying to hide the fact that the golem is a Jewish story, as he does mention the rabbi's creation of the golem, and the reader knows that the family who has seen the Hulk is indeed Jewish. Obviously, Thomas was comfortable with a certain amount of Jewish customs and legends being related to the readers of the *Hulk*. One could see the Hulk story as a metaphor for the struggle for civil rights taking place at the time. The golem story itself is one of basic human rights to liberty and justice.

In a weird twist, Roy Thomas changes the story and says the golem fashioned an imperial amulet to be worn by royalty. The Jews of Morvania are in a situation similar to that of their forbearers in Prague; they are under the heel of the terrible dictator Draxon. Isaac wonders aloud to his family whether the Hulk could be the golem, to save the citizens from oppression. The Hulk does not want to get involved in this war of freedom, but as Isaac's little girl begs him to help, the reluctant Hulk realizes that he needs to act. It was the innocence and fear of the little child that so often in Hulk stories gets him to act on behalf of humanity, for which the Hulk does not care much. Like the golem, the Hulk obliterates Draxon's men, but Draxon himself is another story. The Hulk prevails against Draxon and his death ray tank machine. Later, Isaac tries to give the Hulk the golem's amulet and make him King of Morviania, but the Hulk admits he only helped the citizens "because of the girl." When the Hulk smashes the amulet,

Issac takes that as a sign, and says: "You **were** our Golem … No more kings no more **dictators**" (20, emphasis in original).

This story clearly uses the golem legend as an allegory for oppression by those who would seek to destroy the culture, livelihood, and political standing of "others," in this case, the Jewish peasants. The Hulk's questioning of the whole concept of a golem is also significant. In numerous golem tales, the "one without a soul," the golem, questions his own being. Golem is a powerful metaphor that would not go away and soon return in Marvel Comics.

The Golem proper in Marvel Comics

Editor-in-chief Roy Thomas and the staff at Marvel could not forget the legend of the golem. Several years after *Hulk* #134, Thomas finally suggested that they put a literal golem in the comics. He later stated: "I'm pretty sure it was my idea to create a Golem series, since we had so many monster comics. Hey, if we didn't do it, somebody else would … and then I'd be sorry." In *Strange Tales* #174 (June 1974), the Golem officially appeared as stated on the cover as the "thing that walks like a man" (Figure 7.1). The character lasted for only three issues of *Strange Tales* and one guest appearance in *Marvel Two-in-One*. *Strange Tales* first appeared in 1951 as a horror anthology published during Atlas Comics, one of Marvel Comics' earlier incarnations. The magazine went through a number of changes and was for many years home to the characters Dr. Strange, Nick Fury, and a host of creepy-crawly types. By the mid-1970s, Marvel was experimenting with its monster titles. At Thomas's urging, the Golem was born into the Marvel Universe.

The first Golem issue, *Strange Tales* #174, was written by Len Wein and illustrated by John Buscema, and the other two issues were written by Mike Friedrich with art by Tony DeZuniga. In these narratives, Professor Abraham Adamson and his nephew, niece, and the niece's boyfriend are searching in the desert for the mythical golem. The professor relates the story of Judah Löew and the creation of the golem, and the story of Prague is told; again, the Jews are referred to as "our people" (not Jews like in the Hulk story). Löew is called a "wise man" rather than a rabbi (2). In this incarnation, the creature is purple. The Golem is a tool for social justice, but in this version, the creature has left Prague, and fights autocracy wherever he finds it. Eventually, the Golem goes into the desert to die (3). Obviously, this is a modern representation of the traditional character. Although Judaism is not blatantly mentioned, Marvel was clearly not trying to hide the fact that they created a Jewish hero. In the letter column, under the "Special Bullpen Note" section, they printed a self-congratulatory remark: "It had to happen. Marvel was the first among comics publishers to feature black superheroes— and villains. Marvel was the first to recognize the women's movement in comics with characters like the Black Widow. And now in this issue of *Strange Tales*, we are proud to introduce the comic's first Jewish monster-hero" (18).

Later in this same issue, the professor found the golem of legend and dug him out of the sand. We learn that the barren region in which they are searched is a political battleground between two groups. The groups are never identified, but, as revealed

Figure 7.1 The first appearance of Marvel's Golem. Although the cover makes it seem like the character is only another monster, the story reveals elements taken from traditional Jewish stories (even though Judaism is never mentioned as such).

in a subsequent issue, the occupants and soldiers have names like Hassam, and they use phrases like "Great Allah" (Friedrich et al. 10). The assumption is that they are in Islamic territory, and as one letter writer pointed out, the fighting is a commentary on the Arab-Israeli war (Chomiak 32). The writer of *Strange Tales* #174, Len Wein, makes no judgment on this, asserting that the war is filled with "a territory of ideologies fought with great fervor but with little gain …" (7).

In this story, one of the army regiments commanded by Colonel Omar is caught stealing from Professor Adamson's supplies and is shot. Omar and his men take the professor's family hostage. As Adamson lies dying, he recites the divine Kabbalistic alphabets of the 221 gates and sheds a tear, which falls upon the Golem's foot. This spark of last life from the professor and his incantations bring the creature to life, and part of the professor's spirit goes into the Golem. This is a golem who is self-aware to a point and who becomes the protector of the people the professor loved most, his family. The Golem finds his "loved ones" and destroys their captors.

The Golem tale continued in *Strange Tales* #176, written and illustrated by Friedrich and DeZuniga. This time, however, the Golem has more than corrupt humans to deal with. We see the introduction of a supernatural wizard who is "pure evil" (11). In a perversion of the Holy Kabbalah, the wizard named Kaballa, "the unclean." The wizard wants the Golem's power as his own, and as guns don't hurt the creature, he is basically unstoppable. Kaballa sends air demons to capture the Golem as he is traveling to the United States. The Golem overtakes them by throwing them in the water; saving his "family." One aspect of this Golem, which is different from most tellings of the legend, is that he is self-aware, can make choices, and can even talk. When questioned about where his powerful strength comes from, he states: "I do not know. The land is my strength, [it is a] mystery, mystery!" (23). It is almost as if the Golem understands that his origins are mystical and sacred in nature. While self-aware, he does not fully understand who he is. He knows his purpose is to serve justice and protect his "family," but he knows that there is much about his existence that remains an enigma.

The third and last issue of the Golem, *Strange Tales* #177, begins with a prologue that is the most blatant statement about Judaism and Jewishness so far. The issue opens up with a golem story adapted from a sixteenth-century Jewish legend taken from Gersham Scholem's *Kabbalah* text. This time, Löew is mentioned as a Rabbi, though the story itself takes place well after Löew's time. In this legend, the Golem is a giant with the Star of David as his belt buckle and the holy word *Emeth* on his forehead. But the Golem keeps growing and growing until an unnamed rabbi fears the creature will become too colossal. He asks the Golem to take off his boots and bend over, and when the Golem does, the rabbi erases the first letter on the creature's forehead so that only *meth* (death) remains. However, when the Golem dies, it "fell on the Jew and crushed him" (1–2).

The professor's family takes the Golem to the University of San Pedro, off the coast of St. Petersburg, Florida, where they try to prove to a faculty member that this is indeed the mystical golem of legend. Meanwhile, Kaballa sends fire demons to the university, thinking that fire and earth (the Golem) do not mix, and the Golem realizes that he does indeed hurt and thinks to himself: "I am met with the essence of fire. I burn I burn" (15). Despite this, he extinguishes the demon's flames, and as he does the holy word *Emeth* reappears on the Golem's forehead. Since the Golem has an "emotional affinity with people," Kaballa then realizes that the way to control the Golem is to get at his "family" and use them (23). The story ends, unfinished, as the next issue of *Strange Tales* had the Adam Warlock as its feature character.

What happened? Was the comic book reading public not ready for a character like the golem to have his own series? Concerning the cancellation, Roy Thomas postulates, "[M]aybe it just wasn't different enough … or the word [Golem] wasn't well enough known … or something [else]" (e-mail) but as Richard Myer points out, "[T]he series was never really able to live up to that little bit of hype. In fact the book got off to such a rocky start and with such a lack of cohesiveness in its vision, that its creators just abandoned it …." It seems as though no one really knew what to do with it. It is not as though the world was unresponsive to the resurrection of the Jewish superhero, as golem stories had been a part of world culture for hundreds of years. The book did get off to a wavering start because the writers and artists changed just as the series started. Then Marvel skipped an issue because of deadline problems and filled *Strange Tales* #175 with reprints. It is not as though the Golem lacked a good storyline, far from it, Marvel simply did not know what to do with the character. The "Letters to the Golem" section indeed confirms this notion. They could not figure out how to characterize The Golem:

> [It was] a good idea that didn't work out … Our Golem strip just hasn't become what we hoped it would … we never quite found ourselves able to decide on the direction of for the strip. Was it a human-interest book like *Man-Thing*? A smasho-whammo-destructo book like the *Hulk*? A supernatural mystery thriller like *Werewolf by Night*? We couldn't make up our minds. ("Letters to the Golem" 32)

The character and the concept are indeed good ones, and the way Marvel recast the legend in contemporary times certainly worked. But one gets the feeling from reading the issues no one could agree on its direction. However, the purple Golem series was never really given a chance to grow and live up to its potential. Sometimes one has a winner with the first issue, but more often than not characters need a chance to grow and find their potential in the realm of sequential art storytelling. The material related to Judaism, while subtle, was certainly there, and a kid reading the series in the 1970s would certainly have received a cultural education. It could have been too culturally enlightening for the time; perhaps it was too specifically tied to a particular ethnic group.

The Golem meets the Thing: Two Jewish heroes trade blows

Roy Thomas could not let a story languish and go unfinished. It irked him to have things left undone; so nearly a year later, in the September 1975 issue of *Marvel Two-In-One* #11, the Golem tale continued. The Golem was paired up with the Jewish Ben Grimm, the Thing, from the Fantastic Four, in the Thing's solo series. The story was plotted by Thomas, scripted by Ben Mantlo, and drawn by Bob Brown; as with the later issues of *Strange Tales*, the story had a whole new team. Thomas appreciated the irony of having two Jewish heroes dueling: "irony, always … plus just an excuse for a good story that might bring a bit of attention to the Golem" (e-mail). In this story, Grimm is going with his girlfriend to Disney World when he hears that a great tidal wall of water has cut San Pedro University off from mainland St. Petersburg. He also hears about a monster going amok in the city. Apparently, Kaballa had figured out that separating the Golem from his loved ones will allow him to gain control of the hulking creature. While fighting Grimm, Golem musters up enough mystical power to make the holy word *Emeth* reappear on his forehead. Then, the Thing takes a terrible beating. Through telepathy, the Golem tells Grimm that he really does not want to fight him.[10] He also tells Grimm to get his "family" from the San Pedro University, who will know how to control him. After the Thing rescues Adamson's relatives, Kaballa's hold on the Golem dissipates; the *Emeth* burns brightly on the Golem's forehead, and the Golem stands immobile. Even though both the Thing (who is literally a walking pile of rocks) and the stone-like Golem are seen as monsters, each character's humanity is apparent. The story has a subtext about the difference between a monster and a human.

Jewish legends have always had an honesty tinged with real-life lessons that resonate with all of humankind (joy mixed with a bit of tragedy), and Marvel's golem tales were no exception. That was the last version of this particular golem seen in Marvel Comics, although, according to *Marvel Legacy: The 1960s–1990s Handbook*, he is now a member of the monster squad of Nick Fury's Howling Commandos. He can apparently be seen in 2006's *Nick Fury's Howling Commandos* #2 and #6 (Carycomix). A full reading of these issues give no real indication that this is the same Golem as the one in *Strange Tales* and *Marvel Two-in-One*, but it was meant to be this Golem in the original script written by Keith Giffen.

Roy Thomas: The Second World War, the Invaders, and a new golem

For Roy Thomas the golem was too powerful a metaphor to let it languish and fade away. Just a year later, in 1976, he took the golem legend one step further and created a creature that was a human/stone/clay hybrid for the Invaders series. The Invaders were patterned after the 1940s Golden Age team, the All-Winners Squad. They featured Captain America, the Human Torch, Sub-Mariner, Bucky, Toro, and occasionally others, and they fought the Nazis/Axis powers for the Allies during the Second World War. *The Invaders* comic books were written by Roy Thomas with inspired artwork by Frank Robbins (Figure 7.2). Since he was "dealing with WW II," Thomas knew that he had to address the persecution of the Jews, the Holocaust, and the Ghettos (e-mail). In *Invaders* #11, the team fights the Blue Bullet who is defeated but just barely. The Bullet suit was worn by the brilliant scientist Professor Gold, who was originally working on the side of the Allies, and nobody could figure out why Gold suddenly turned traitor. So in *Invaders* #12, the Human Torch has an idea as to why Gold became an agent for Hitler's Reich. When the Torch confronts Gold, the professor tells the Torch to go ahead and kill him, but the latter responds, "You're Jewish aren't you?"

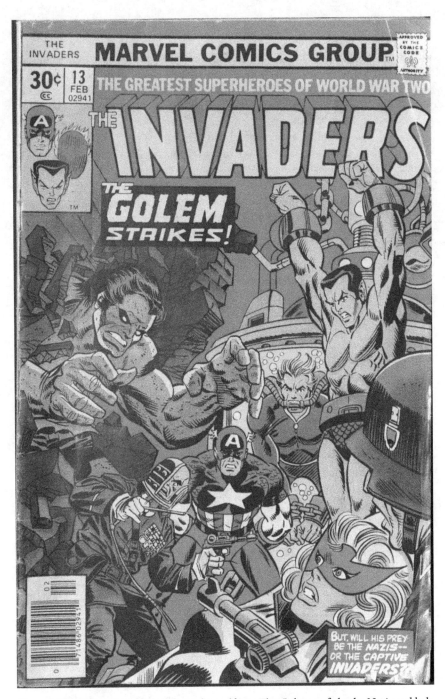

Figure 7.2 Jacob Goldstein transforms himself into The Golem to fight the Nazis and help rescue the Invaders within the Jewish ghetto.

With humility, Gold replies: "You've guessed my secret and shame … yes I am Jewish
…" (7). The scientist, whose real name is Johann Goldstein, relates how the Nazis
threatened to kill his brother, Jacob, back in the Polish Warsaw Ghetto if he did not
betray the allied cause and work for them. Johann fled, but his brother stayed behind.
Jacob was a devout student of *Torah*, Jewish mysticism, and rocks. The professor says
he would gladly work for the allied cause again if his brother were safe, as he "swore
to my dying mother that I'd never do anything to harm Jacob" (11). Johann's promise
to his mother is typical of Jewish culture and the ties to family. The Jewish mother's
dying wish is an important sacred vow that plays upon the sense of responsibility. The
Human Torch promises Goldstein that he will try to help and asks the Invaders to go
rescue Jacob. The Invaders go to the "oppressed Jewish ghetto of wartime Poland" (17),
where the heroes find Jacob Goldstein in his bookshop (which looks an awful lot like
a synagogue), studying the holy works with his *kippah* (*yarmulke* (head covering) or
a skullcap, the literal translation of which is "dome" (Hebrew word for skullcap). It is
a sign of respect toward God and all that is holy when praying, studying scriptures,
or preforming Jewish ritual) in place. The Invaders ask Jacob to go with them, but he
refuses to leave his "books and rare stones." To him, his devotional study is what is
most important, which is another Jewish characteristic written into the text. When
Captain America asks him: "Why don't you fight back?" Jacob responds: "With what?
No our only hope is patient submission to the will of God, and our persistent belief that
this too shall pass." This is another fine characteristic of Jewish identity: patience and
submission to the will of *Ha'Shem*. Jacob tells the Invaders about the golem legend, but
he is not hopeful that it could happen again. Here in Roy Thomas's writing is a blatant
attempt at addressing and acknowledging the Holocaust. If heroes like the Invaders
really existed during the 1940s, what would they do? Jacob just shrugs and puts his
head in his hands.

   All is not well, however, as the Nazis have found out the Allies' great heroes are
in the ghetto, and they come with their tanks. The Invaders seem to have the upper
hand against them, until the Nazis start using a typical Nazi ploy of intimidation and
threaten to destroy numerous innocent bystanders. Jacob responds with a sense of
chutzpah, saying, "our lives are our responsibility and no one else's" (30). The Invaders
surrender rather than let innocents get killed because of them. When Jacob asks the
Nazis to kill him instead of taking the Invaders hostage, they respond, "we should kill
you Jew," but they only take "the Allies' greatest heroes" into custody. The Jewish sense
of accountability is apparent here; Jacob cannot live with the fact that the Invaders are
most likely going to their deaths. He acknowledges that he has "known for some time
what I could do to fight against the wolves who ravage our land. And I have shrunk from
doing it" (31).

The golem walks again

In *Invaders* #13 (1977), the heroes have been neutralized by Colonel Eisen, a half-
faced, evil-looking Nazi, so that they can't use their powers. Eisen is the *gauleiter*
(paramilitary regional governor) of the Jewish ghetto and the city of Warsaw. The

colonel is distressed when a container of heavy water is stolen and hidden in Jacob's bookstore since "heavy water is the key to one type of reactor in which plutonium can be bred from natural uranium" (Federation of American Scientists). (Heavy water was instrumental in the creation of atomic power, and Germany experimented with it during the war. Here, Roy Thomas is mixing a little fact with fiction.) Jacob ponders over ancient holy *Kabbalistic* texts to find an answer to the problem. Seeking a way to rescue the Invaders, and help his people, he prepares a clay man and pours the heavy water over it. At that instant, a lightning bolt hits the bookshop/residence and the Star of David adorning the top. The building crumbles and the golem is born anew. A young girl yells: "It is a golem come to protect us!" as a Nazi soldier smashes her with the butt of his gun (7). The golem is not amused; he takes care of the soldiers and gives the girl back to her father (Figure 7.2).

Somehow, Jacob Goldstein's body has integrated with the clay to create a new golem—part a human and part a holy being but one with total free will. This golem still has the word *Emeth* (truth) etched into his forehead and wears a permanent *kippah*. The golem then rescues the Invaders from the Nazis and hits Colonel Eisen, who falls to his death in a pit. Then, when the golem erases the first letter to make the word *Meth*, he is transforms back into Jacob. The Invaders still want him to go back with them and help with the allied cause (especially now that he has supernatural abilities), but Jacob realizes that his responsibility is to his people in the ghetto and to stop the Nazi oppression. He tells the Invaders: "My people will revolt against the Nazi conqueror—perhaps successfully, perhaps not. And on that day, God willing, the Golem *may walk yet again* ... would you deny me and my people that moment Invaders?" (31, emphasis in original).

The golem returns

Roy Thomas brought the Golstein golem back for a four-issue *Invaders* mini series in 1993. This time, the Invaders contained a number of other Golden Age heroes, including the Whizzer (who gets captured by the Nazis), Miss America, and the inspired character of the Blazing Skull. In a twist of fate in this mini series, the golem is collaborating with the Nazis against the Invaders. A malevolent scientist, Dr. Death, has his own group of Nazi villains, the Battle Axis (many of whom are Americans-turned-collaborators). They plan to release deadly poison into the atmosphere and destroy the West Coast of the United States using a device known as the Oscillotron to create an earthquake and break the West Coast off from the United States. The plan is called Project Mojave, and the goal is to plunge the United States into a chaotic state, thus forcing it out of the war and giving Germany an upper edge against the rest of the Allies.

Ultimately, the Jewish ideal of being a *mensch* (one who does what is right)[11] prevails for both the Goldstein brothers. Captain America points out that Professor Johann Goldstein who "sacrificed himself to save his brother and the country he'd once betrayed; in the end he died a hero" (*Invaders #4* 30) Writer Roy Thomas believes that he did not feel any contradiction in using the golem as a Nazi collaborator because justice was served, saying: "I don't recall my motivations, except that the Golem was a good character and would bring a Jewish presence to the Invaders" (e-mail). In the end, the golem/Jacob Goldstein survived and goes back to the Warsaw Ghetto to serve the Hebrews against the Nazis.

Some of the readers of the first Invaders series were upset that Jacob Goldstein was not the traditional golem of legend, and they wondered if this was supposed to be the Golem of the *Strange Tales* stories. The editors acknowledged that this was an entirely new golem, not the purple-hued creature (*Okay Axis* 19). Goldstein, as the golem, was gray, and Thomas acknowledges that "this was of course a different Golem" (e-mail). This golem was part human and could change back and forth at will by erasing the first letter of the holy word on his forehead. The Goldstein golem had free will, but he also had a strong conviction of family and doing the correct *mitzvah* (the right thing).[12] The traditional legend was used as a starting point to create a totally new take on the golem. What if the golem had existed during the Second World War and could have fought against the Nazis? The golem stories in both of the *Invaders* series show a golem with the power of *Ha'Shem* but the frailties of a human.

A golem and the Thing meet again: The Yancy Street golem

A golem of sorts returned in the 2005 Fantastic Four title *Marvel Knights 4 #22* which was written by Roberto Aguirre-Sacasa. When people are getting hurt in Ben Grimm's old neighborhood on Yancy Street, reporters Ben Ulrich and Jessica Jones ask the Thing to investigate some tragic happenings. Apparently some type of lumbering being is dropping things (cinderblocks, bricks, etc.) on new residents of the neighborhood. The Thing is suspicious of Ulrich's motive (he thinks all the reporter wants is a story), but he agrees to check it out.

Meanwhile, Ben and Jessica interview a certain Ms. Loew, who tells them that she thinks a golem has been terrorizing the neighborhood. Her great grandfather "brought the Golem over from the old country where they used it against the people who persecuted us. Hurt us. Through pogroms and much worse" (Aguirre-Sacasa et al.). In this case, when the golem had done its duty, it was put to sleep, but eventually it awoke again in New York and started mimicking the actions of the old Yancy Street Gang by lashing out. This golem, with no Jewish persecutors to destroy, is trying to find a purpose. As a creature for good, it really does not understand that its actions are not appropriate now (in the tradition of some of the other golem stories). After fighting with this grayish, mud-like creature with blazing yellow eyes, the Thing tries to reason with it "monster to monster" and calls him Joseph (in the tradition of many of golem tales).[13] The Thing thinks about his run in with the original purple Golem and tells this golem: "—and sad to say this ain't the first golem I've mixed it up with." This is, however, the first time Marvel used the name Joseph for a golem. He cannot speak, but he can understand what is being told to him. This golem is much like a little child searching for something to do and looking for meaningful existence. But the Thing tells him that he just is "not needed here anymore." He tells Joseph to go back to the river to sleep as his time is over. Despite a different take on the golem, "The Yancy Street

Golem" is a heartfelt story that shows the creature trying to find a place in a world that no longer needs or wants him around. In this case, the golem is an anachronism whose time has passed. It is a genuine tragic tale as Ben Grimm also realizes that *his* time may be running out. The golem is not only a reminder of his Jewish identity but also of the fact that the Thing, like the Hulk, has golem-like characteristics. The golem goes into the river with a sad look on his clay face not really understanding why he must sleep, only that he must.

Conclusion

Marvel Comics had other golems, none of which really had any tie to Jewish traditions or concepts aside from the use of the name, Golem.[14] Given that the world has gone "Golem Crazy," perhaps it is time for Marvel to revisit the characters (the purple and the gray "Jacob"). The purple and Goldstein gray golems are powerful characters that deserve a revival in the comics. Even Superman has had the "golem treatment," being viewed as a golem figure and protector of Jews (Boganove and Simonson). And as Jewish comics historian Ari Kaplin points out: "The idea of a comic book embracing the Golem legend is now so mainstream that even Gumby has gotten in on the act. Heck he is made of clay …"(18).[15] When asked about the future of the golem in Marvel, Roy Thomas is hopeful that "he'll be back" (e-mail). The different versions of golems in Marvel Comics are varied and complex, though they all remain faithful in spirit to the original golem legend. The different interpretations are further developments of the multitude of versions of the legend, thus continuing the tradition of Jewish folklore and allegory, albeit in a new form—one with a strong Jewish history.

Notes

1   The Jewish Publication Society's 1985 translation of the *Tanakh* gives these verses as:

> 15: My frame was not concealed from You
> when I was shaped in a hidden place,
> knit together in the recesses of the earth.
> 16: Your eyes saw my unformed limbs;
> they were all recorded in Your book;
> in due time they were formed,
> to the very last one of them.

The Hebrew word translated as "my unformed limbs" is transliterated as *gol'mi*, which is the first person possessive form of *golem*, meaning "unshaped" or "without form."

2   According to Neil W. Levin: "the development of the Golem in Jewish Contexts derives from the magical exegesis of the mystical work *sefer y' tzira* (*Book of Creation*) and from the mystical ideas about the creative power of speech, of words, and even of particular letters of the Hebrew alphabet." He further states that the golem concept in Jewish lore can be traced back to the twelfth and thirteenth centuries among

the sect *hasidei ashkenaz* with the creation of the golem as a "mystical ritual" to understanding the work of God.

3   Released in the United States as *The Monster of Fate*. Paul Wegener directed this and two other Golem films (1917, 1920), the latter, the expressionistic *The Golem: How He Came into the World*, being the most famous.

4   Strum used Paul Wegener's version of the Golem from his 1920 film as a basis for his graphic novel. For a thorough analysis of this book, see Harde.

5   There had once been an online version of this comic translated into English, but that translation has since been removed. For a detailed look at this graphic novel, see Raab.

6   Such as the 1981 series, *Mendy and the Golem* by Leibel Estrin and Dovid Sears, published by Shevat/Adar, and the 2003 *Mendy and the Golem* series by Matt Brandstein and Ernie Colon, published by the Golem Factory.

7   See Ellstein and Leivick; Lee; Meyrink; Neugroschel; Singer & Shulevitz; and Wisniewski.

8   *Shem* is the Hebrew word for "name." In reference to the Golem legend, it may also be spelled *chem*. Orthodox and Conservative Jews commonly refer to God as "Ha'Shem," meaning "the name," which implies that the name of God appears not once but twice in the Golem's creation.

9   For more detailed information on the history and background of these characters, see Comtois; Daniels; Defalco; Sanderson; Steranko; and Weiner.

10   Apparently, the Golem can make other minds see its intent or the "truth of the situation" through telepathy. See McQuaid et al.

11   From the German *mensch*, meaning "man" or "human being."

12   *Mitzvah* is the Hebrew word for "work," and usually refers to a religious imperative deemed necessary to be a good person and a good Jew. There are 613 official mitzvot in traditional Judaism, though any appropriately good and charitable act may be called a mitzvah. Mitzvot are believed to be divinely sourced and inspired.

13   Grimm comments to himself "Speaking traditionally golems are named Joseph after a half-human, half-demon creature that uesta help the Jews out in ancient times … just cause I don't go to temple as much as I should don't mean I don't know my heritage and mythology."

14   These include a villain named Dennis Golembuski, called The Golem in issue #2 of the series, *The Hood*; a character called the Golem or the Golem Construct appeared in *Warheads* #2 and *Death's Head II* #13; a psychic investigator called Joseph Golem showed up in *Tomb of Dracula III* #4; agents of the sorcerer of Cagliostro are called golems, as seen in *Dr. Strange Annual* #2; and *Scarlet Witch* #1 had fighting warriors called Iron Golems.

15   See Burden.

"America Makes Strange Jews": Superheroes, Jewish Masculinity, and Howard Chaykin's *Dominic Fortune*

Brannon Costello

A key sequence in the 2009 Marvel Comics mini series *Dominic Fortune* finds the title character in Berlin in 1936, investigating a fascist conspiracy to overthrow the American government. Caught out after curfew in a Jewish ghetto by a Nazi patrol, Fortune skillfully dispatches his foes with a series of acrobatic leaps and well-placed pistol shots, all the while clad in a flamboyant brown and black costume. When members of the Jewish underground hiding nearby emerge to assist him, one of them marvels at Fortune's ruthless, efficient violence and professes surprise that Fortune is a fellow landsman. When a colleague explains that Fortune is American, he muses, "America makes strange Jews" (3.21).[1] His remark points to an implicit concern of Howard Chaykin's Dominic Fortune stories: the nature of Jewish masculinity in America.

Debuting in 1975, Fortune was among the earliest original characters created by Chaykin, a Jewish writer and artist whose four-decade career has been defined by his penchant for using mainstream genres as a platform to explore idiosyncratic and personal themes. The question of Jewish identity figures prominently among these themes—in particular, the representation of Jews in American comics. In a 1986 interview, he accounts for the increasingly personal nature of his work: "I'm no longer a Jew masquerading as a Gentile through comics" ("I Have a Hard Time with Vigilantes" 72). He expanded on this idea in a later interview, commenting:

> I like being Jewish, I get off on being Jewish, I use it as a manipulative tool. Most of the people who work in comics, a lot of the people who write comics, are Jewish too. And these people are obviously incapable of recognizing themselves. They write these comic-opera Jews whom I've never met—they write Jews the way gentiles write Jews. I can't do that. I won't do that. ("Howard Chaykin Puts It All Back Together Again" 90)

Appearing on a "Jewish Influences in Comics" panel in 2011, Chaykin cited his own life as the source for his interest in depicting the "contradictory nature" of Jewish experience in his comics (Chaykin and Morrison, "Jewish Influences in Comics: Panel with Bill Morrison and Howard Chaykin part 3/3").

Chaykin's insistence on complicating traditional representations of Jewish identity is evident in much of his work, perhaps most famously in his landmark *American Flagg!*, which Chaykin wrote and drew from its first issue in 1983 until he left the series in other hands in 1985. The protagonist, Reuben Flagg, is a Mars-born Jewish actor pressed into service as a police officer in a grim but dazzling future Chicago, where his misadventures include spending an amorous and ambivalent night with a beautiful Jewish doctor who is also a Nazi—or, to be precise, a "Gotterdammercrat" (*American Flagg!* 7.22–24)—and squaring off against a squad of "Shabbas Goys," gentile mercenaries who serve as "hired guns for the Militant Hassidim" (*American Flagg!* 2.11). As these examples make clear, ethnic and religious lines are blurry in the world of *Flagg!*, and Chaykin's characterization of Reuben Flagg defies traditional depictions of Jewish men. Arie Kaplan observes, "Reuben Flagg's status as a handsome James Bond-style leading man is important, because this non-stereotypical portrayal of a Jewish character—the polar opposite of the Woody Allen-style nebbish—was sorely lacking [in the] pop culture of the 1980s" (189). However, although Flagg's Jewish identity is frequently an issue in his adventures, *American Flagg!* is rarely *about* Jewish identity in the same way that Chaykin's stories involving Dominic Fortune often are. This loose collection of work, spanning almost the entirety of Chaykin's career, offers a wry commentary on questions of Jewish identity in general and Jewish masculinity in particular, with a particular emphasis on the popular notion of the superhero as a metaphor for Jewish experience.

As Derek Parker Royal has noted, the success of Michael Chabon's *The Amazing Adventures of Kavalier and Clay* (2000) sparked an intensification of interest in the foundational role of Jewish writers, artists, and publishers in the genesis of the American comic book (6–7). Writers such as Danny Fingeroth, Arie Kaplan, and Simcha Weinstein have in recent years offered valuable treatments of the biographies of Jewish creators and businessmen involved in the early days of the comics industry and explorations of the way that comics about costumed adventurers deliberately or unconsciously reflect aspects of Jewish experience. Fingeroth has argued that the centrality of Jewish writers and artists to the genesis of the superhero is no accident: "The creation of a legion of special beings, self-appointed to protect the weak, innocent, and victimized at a time when fascism was dominating the European continent from which the creators of the heroes hailed, seems like a task that Jews were uniquely positioned to take on" (17). Much of the work on Jewish identity in the context of superhero comics takes as its starting point Jules Feiffer's remark in "The Minsk Theory of Krypton" that Superman is the "ultimate assimilationist fantasy" (156). In this view, as Fingeroth puts it, Superman "was the immigrant who took all the best traits of his adopted country and used them to help the little guy, the abused wife, the exploited worker" (49). Fingeroth notes that Superman's alter ego as Clark Kent was just as important to this fantasy. He writes:

> For the immigrant, the dual identity becomes the way to either bridge to, or wall off from, the self we were in the old country. It holds out the possibility that we

can invent the new self we hope to become in this new world in which we have a reasonable amount of freedom to define who and what we are. (49)

Harry Brod describes the superhero/alter ego split in terms that point toward the significance of anxieties about Jewish masculinity: "The ridiculed personality that Clark Kent sheds when he casts off his street clothes is a gendered stereotype of Jewish inferiority. Superman exists to counter the notion that strength or manliness and Jewishness are incompatible" (10).

Chaykin himself has articulated his understanding of the Jewish roots of the superhero genre in similar terms, describing superheroes as originating in "Jewish guys putting on the mask of gentiles," and commenting, "Superman is the absolute epitome of what every Jewish guy wants to be perceived as" (Chaykin and Morrison, "Jewish Influences in Comics: Panel with Bill Morrison and Howard Chaykin part 1/3"). Yet in his hands, Dominic Fortune both enacts and troubles this narrative, embodying the possibilities and the limitations of the superhero ideal as metaphor for assimilation and transformation.[2] To be sure, the Fortune stories are not the only examples of Chaykin's interest in this topic. His 1994 superhero comedy *Power and Glory* satirized the Jewish creator/gentile hero split through its depiction of the antagonism between Allan Powell, a suave but cowardly costumed *ubermensch* who performs astounding feats of public relations for the American government, and Michael Gorski, the Jewish government agent charged with corralling Powell and carrying out the government's real dirty work. But the Fortune stories offer his richest and most sustained treatment of the theme. Of particular significance is the way in which Fortune offers an opportunity to extend and complicate the discussion of the Jewish nature of the superhero by connecting it to the long-running discourse about Jewish masculinity in twentieth- and twenty-first-century America.

Some readers might quibble over whether the term "superhero" quite fits a self-described mercenary with no superhuman abilities like Dominic Fortune. Peter Coogan has argued that the superhero is defined by his or her "pro-social mission," superpowers, and distinct identity as expressed in codename and costume (30). However, Coogan's enlightening discussion of the superhero genre's cross-pollination with other genres makes clear that "superhero" is an elastic term that is often used to refer to characters with and without superhuman powers, with and without costumes and secret identities, and whose altruism is inconsistent at best. While I admire the precision of Coogan's definition, I am not ultimately interested in proving that Dominic Fortune fits it perfectly. He may more accurately be, as Fingeroth puts it, a "superhero-style" character (131), but he is sufficiently grounded in the genre to make drawing on scholarly discussions of the relationship between superheroes and Jewish identity valuable. Although Fortune's roots lie as much in classic pulp fiction as they do in superhero comics, his adventures frequently take place in Marvel Comics' shared superhero universe, where he fights crime with characters such as Captain America and Spider-Man. Indeed, in 2011 the character appeared as a member of an early version of the Avengers, Marvel's premiere superhero team, in the pages of the *New Avengers* series (#9–#13) and in a Chaykin-written and -drawn mini series, *Avengers 1959* (2011–2012). More significantly, he makes explicit the connection between the superhero/secret identity dynamic and the new world/old country dynamic in that "Dominic Fortune" is actually the alter ego of David Fortunov, a Jewish adventurer for hire with a silver tongue and a gambling problem. Though Fortune's name-change is a strategy also favored by entertainers looking to make it big in Hollywood—one of Fortune's primary bases of operation—the fact that he dresses in a distinct costume when the time comes for derring-do grounds his transformation in the idiom of superheroism.

Fortune debuted in 1975, first appearing in the pages of *Marvel Preview* #2 in a tale co-written with Len Wein and then shortly thereafter in *Marvel Super Action* #1 in a piece written and drawn by Chaykin alone. In the latter story, "The Messiah in the Saddle Resolution," Fortune encounters an old foe who outs him as David Fortunov, but this passing reference is the only clue that Chaykin might be interested in exploring the question of the character's ethnicity. "Messiah in the Saddle" was also the last Fortune appearance until a handful of stories drawn by Chaykin and co-written with Dennis O'Neil that ran as back-up features in issues 21–25 of Marvel's *The Hulk!* magazine (June 1980–February 1981). In these stories, Fortune became a spokesperson for Ferdley's Milk—a position which frequently required him to slip into costume, to his paramour Sabbath Raven's exasperation and to his evident relief—and faced off against Nazis, zombies, and blimp-borne Irish assassins disguised as Santa Claus. The first of these stories, "All in Color for a Crime," is the most formally ambitious and immediately relevant to the question of Jewish identity. Set during the early days of the comic book boom in 1937, the story follows Fortune and his love interest Sabbath Raven from Los Angeles to Fortune's native New York, where Sabbath discovers Fortune's ethnic heritage and teases him that his "roots are showing" (51). Fortune is peeved to find that a new comic book sensation, the masked hero known as the Purple Slasher, is based on his exploits, and he intends to have a word with the publisher. Once in New York, he is troubled to discover that Jacob Weltman, the Purple Slasher's artist and the son of some old friends—and, Chaykin has noted, a stand-in for Jack Kirby ("An Afternoon with Howard Chaykin" 258)—has gone missing soon after taking a job as an artist for Acme Publications.

It soon emerges that Acme is really a Nazi front operation, and Weltman and his peers have been unwittingly drawing fascist propaganda. Early critics of the comics industry such as Fredric Wertham and Gershon Legman would no doubt have seen this twist coming miles away (if they considered it a twist at all) since they perceived in the comics' celebration of physical violence and the triumph of the powerful an ideology closely akin to Nazism. As Legman put it in a memorably indignant passage from *Love and War: A Study in Censorship* (1949), "comic-books have succeeded in giving every American child a complete course in paranoid megalomania such as no German child ever had, a total conviction of the morality of force such as no Nazi could even aspire to" (119). Sabbath Raven echoes Legman's reaction when she takes a closer look at the artwork of Weltman and his fellow Acme artists. Sabbath immediately detects something afoot at Acme more sinister than merely long hours, low pay, and a lack of intellectual property rights, exclaiming: "Dom, have you looked at this stuff? ... If I'm not staring at simon-pure Nazi propaganda, I'll eat Charlie McCarthy's top hat!" (53). Her analysis is seconded by a policeman who assists them later in their endeavor: "You played it straight with us, lady—cause unless I'm way off base, this is from the German high command!" (63). The content of the pages that Sabbath and the policeman are considering makes their remarks all the more significant: there is no evident pro-Nazi propaganda, no explicit celebration of Hitler or any other fascist leader. Rather, the roughly sketched pages we see look like nothing more than a classic 1930s comic book slugfest. The first page features a series of stylized explosions and impacts alongside a grimacing face, with sound effects reading "biff," "zap," "crack," "grunt"; the second page is a fight-and-chase sequence with one panel featuring a fist flying out at the reader (53). Another page later in the story depicts a rocket launched into the sky and a hero (or a villain) with a star emblazoned on his chest blasting or punching multiple foes at once. Of course, these pages are never shown in close-up, and Chaykin may simply not have drawn them with sufficient detail for the reader to discern what so horrifies Sabbath. On the other hand, the pages' lack of detail may suggest that, at their most fundamental level, the power fantasies of such comics share much in common with the power fantasies of fascism.

Fortune rescues Weltman from the Nazis, of course, but the story's happy resolution is complicated by Chaykin's use of layout and page design to highlight the potentially troubling implications of the model of heroic masculine agency that David Fortunov's "Dominic Fortune" alter ego represents. The first page of the story pairs and implicitly contrasts a photograph, ostensibly a documentary form, of Sabbath and Fortune in street clothes with a comic book page featuring the Purple Slasher (50). But Chaykin troubles the distinction between these two images by superimposing a drawing of Fortune in full costume running toward the foreground that violates the boundary between the images and suggests that by remaking himself as "Dominic Fortune," David Fortunov straddles the worlds of reality and fantasy. Although the ability to submerge one's ethnic identity beneath a surface of mainstream whiteness could be read as one version of an assimilationist ideal, the story's climactic fight scene develops this theme in a darker direction. As Fortune and his Nazi foe prepare to trade blows, Fortune first suggests that they should be "discussing [their] differences like civilized men" and then remarks, while dodging a punch: "You goose-steppers aren't much on civilized behavior, are you?" His opponent responds, "Poland learned that … as did Austria and Czechoslovakia!," prompting Fortune to retort as he delivers a punch: "Well, fine. I've been accused of a certain lack of civilization myself!" (61). Though typical of Fortune's wise-guy patter, his dialogue nonetheless suggests an equivalence between his own tendency to settle problems with his fists and the brutality of the Nazi regime.

The next page of the fight makes this connection even more explicit (Figure 8.1). Chaykin superimposes the action on a blown-up page of a Purple Slasher comic book story; Fortune's battle with his foe is set against a backdrop of the Purple Slasher battling his own. Notably, aside from a desk in the upper-left corner of the page, there are no background elements from the diegetic world of the main story, only three images of Fortune and his opponent trading blows in otherwise empty space. The only gutters on the page are the gutters of the Purple Slasher story, and, since the backdrop image is a full-page bleed, there are no other borders or margins. A series of captions reads: "Some say life imitates art … Others claim the opposite is true—that it is art which imitates life … Perhaps the truly wise man would observe that it makes no difference—not a

Figure 8.1 "All in Color for a Crime," *The Hulk* #21, page 62 (1980). © Marvel Entertainment, LLC and its subsidiaries.

damn bit of difference in the world" (62). The page layout and text dissolve the expected contrast between Dominic Fortune, Jewish hero, and the Purple Slasher, accidental fascist icon. The story thus raises the question of to what extent the costumed hero as an assimilationist fantasy for Jewish men may be compromised by the genre's oversimplified notion of violent might-makes-right masculinity.[3]

As various histories of the early days of the comic book industry suggest, superheroes offered a fantasy of powerful masculine agency which some Jewish men found appealing, and it is important to remember that superheroes did not emerge in a vacuum. Instead, as scholars working in the field of Jewish studies have well documented, traditional models of Jewish manhood underwent major revisions over the course of the twentieth century. Gregory Caplan notes that "in traditional Jewish culture, rabbinic authorities rejected the valorization of war making, dueling, and romantic love as *goyim naches*, or games of the gentiles," with the result that "Jewish principles and Christian stereotypes cast Jewish men as the foil for romantic imagery of male bravery, valor, and heroism well into the nineteenth century" (176). The growth of political Zionism catalyzed the revision of this traditional ideal in the late nineteenth and early twentieth century. According to Uta Klein, "the Zionists perceived the Diaspora Jew as passive and effeminate. The Zionist ideal of manliness was constructed as an antithesis of the Diaspora Jew. Physical strength and readiness to defend honor by means of fighting were the desired characteristics of the 'new Jew'" (193). Paul Breines argues that the emphasis on—to use Zionist pioneer Max Nordau's term—the development of a "muscle-Jewry" that could fight back against the forces of a pervasive and intense anti-Semitism in the west led to the elevation of the "tough Jew" (102). According to Breines, the

> tough Jews go so far as to create an ideal Jewish body imagery that closely resembles the classical Greek and Roman bodily ideals of the anti-Semites themselves. Jewish toughness, like the anti-Semitism it abhors, is literally a body politics, a politics of ideal bodily images and the moral virtues that supposedly inhere in them: courage, dedication to the national-racial cause, loyalty, self-discipline, readiness for self-sacrifice, robustness, manliness, and so on. (127)

In the early part of the twentieth century, Jewish gangsters and prize-fighters were among the most celebrated tough Jews in popular culture, and Breines cites a wave of pulp fiction in the 1970s and 1980s that featured "Rambowitz" protagonists—steadfastly loyal to Israel but rage-fueled and muscle-bound in the manner of Sylvester Stallone's Rambo—as a more recent iteration of the type. Writes Breines, "the new tough Jew is a child of Jewish fantasy and desire, but no less a child of Rambo, that is, of the contemporary American cult of violent masculinity" (172).

Not all critics share Breines's emphasis on the American nature of the model of violent Jewish masculinity that came to prominence in the twentieth century. Caplan demonstrates affinities between the German "tough Jews" of the early twentieth century and their gentile countrymen, and Daniel Boyarin puts it in terms of a more general Europeanization (Caplan 176–180, Boyarin 37). But whatever the basic similarities in the masculine ideal among various European nations and the United States, different cultures are bound to produce variations on a common theme, and thus Breines's argument that the tough Jew represents an "*Americanization* of Jewish political culture" (xii, emphasis his) is useful for thinking about superheroes—a genre with a US origin and often associated with US nationalism—and about Dominic Fortune. Warren Rosenberg argues that much twentieth-century American Jewish writing by men is preoccupied with an ambivalence about the role of violence in the construction of Jewish masculinity. Writes Rosenberg, "Jewish culture has always included a violent component, [but] for a variety of historically determined reasons [this component] has been repressed and transformed" (4). He finds in fiction by Norman Mailer, Philip Roth, and Bernard Malamud evidence that the relationship between traditional and modern versions of masculinity is always erratic and complex, and he insists that acknowledging the "messi[ness]" of this dynamic is crucial to understanding how Jewish American men have redefined manhood (3). Rosenberg does not discuss superhero comics—a genre dominated by the ostensibly righteous use of violence— but given the wealth of recent work on the role of Jewish culture in the genre, such comics would seem to be rich territory for investigating the ambivalence he describes.

Although Chaykin created Fortune, Marvel Comics owns the character, and Chaykin's falling-out with Marvel's then editor-in-chief Jim Shooter in the early 1980s meant that he did not chronicle Fortune's adventures again for many years. When he did return to the character, these issues of ethnicity, representation, and masculinity continued to be at the heart of the story. The four-issue 2009 mini series *Dominic Fortune* tracks its title character across the United States and Europe as he dodges deadly assassins, romances beautiful (and sometimes also deadly) women, and rubs shoulders with Depression-era Hollywood elite while trying to thwart a fascist takeover of the United States. In this series, Chaykin uses the character to satirize and explore a broad range of stereotypes about Jews in general and Jewish men in particular, and Chaykin is as interested here as ever in the blurry distinction between representation and reality, considering both the possibilities and the limitations of David Fortunov's heroic alter ego as an aspirational ideal of Americanized Jewish masculinity.

Setting Fortune's exploits in the 1930s places the character in an era when, according to Daniel Itzkovitz, anti-Semitism and American nationalism intersected in the figure of the Jewish male. Writes Itzkovitz:

America's massive influx of Jews at the turn of the century was perceived as a threat to the integrity of the 'national body' … and despite the efforts of Zionists in both the United States and Europe who attempted to combat this image of the Jew by calling for a 'Judaism with muscles,' in the popular imaginary 'the Jew' was a weak, nonproductive man, with shriveled body and atrophied hands. (188)

These imagined deviations from a supposed norm were part of an anxiety about the maintenance of racial difference. Itzkovitz notes that throughout the first half of the twentieth century, "the Jewish male was imagined to be a secret perversion of the genuine article," and he continues: "Jewish difference was … threatening because it was lurking somewhere behind an apparent bodily sameness, and anxieties concerning the troubled 'whiteness' of the Jew inform all discussions of the possibilities and impossibilities of Jewish American assimilation" (178, 181). Thus, while for Jewish men Superman might be a fantasy of powerful agency, for anti-Semites Clark Kent might be not a meek and unthreatening alter ego but instead a sinister disguise.

This tension is key to the 2009 *Dominic Fortune* mini series. Chaykin has characterized David Fortunov's transformation into Dominic Fortune as a version of the "think Yiddish, go British" philosophy associated with the work of Carl Reiner and Neil Simon—comedy writers who expressed their distinctly Jewish point of view through scripts voiced by gentile actors. In a 2010 interview, he commented, "it's a form of minstrelsy," and he continued, "playing with the layers of identity appeals to me enormously" ("Afternoon" 265). However, while the notion of handsome square-jawed (white) leading men who are really Jewish on the inside may seem a fairly innocuous form of masquerade, *Dominic Fortune* makes clear that such a performance could also be a matter of life or death. Published under Marvel's adult-readers MAX imprint, the series enjoyed fewer restrictions on the content Chaykin could depict than Marvel's general offerings. Chaykin took advantage of this new latitude by saturating the dialogue with ethnic slurs. Characters are constantly talking about each other's race or ethnicity and the associated stereotypes in terms appropriate for the historical setting, sometimes casually and sometimes with vicious seriousness. Chaykin thus highlights the pervasiveness of everyday racial discourse and its centrality to making meaning in the world.

Fortune's complicated position in this milieu is evident throughout the story. For instance, in the first issue, he accepts a job from Irwin Oppenheim, the Jewish head of a major Hollywood studio. Oppenheim needs Fortune to mind three aging Hollywood stars under contract to him: P. T. Oakley, Vaughn Lorillard, and Jock Madison (loosely disguised versions of W.C. Fields, John Barrymore, and John Carradine). The actors are in the midst of an epic bender, and Oppenheim is concerned that if the public learns that their beloved icons are actually racist, drunken lechers, it will ruin their bankability. When Fortune announces that Oppenheim has sent him to pry them free from an especially debauched party, Madison replies: "Fuck that Christ-killer and fuck you," while Lorillard cautions that Fortune will at least be "better ... than that dinge grappler from last time," and Oakley declares, "thank God and the bottle—a white man" (1.13). Fortune is thus identified as white by his charges, and he allows them to persist in this belief for most of the series—although by the final page they are cheerily saluting him as "Christ-killer" himself (4.23). Fortune's outing as Jewish is apparently of little consequence to the perpetually soused actors. But as a Jewish man who has changed his name and who takes no pains to advertise his ethnicity, Fortune inspires anxieties about the legibility of ethnic difference from a variety of characters. Most notable of these is Malcolm Upshaw, an American industrialist and the mastermind of the fascist plot. Upshaw means to enlist Fortune in his scheme, but when he is tipped off that Fortune is actually Jewish, he rails that Fortune is "but the latest example of a sinister masquerade—a masquerade eroding our great nation from within ... and threatening the very future of the white race itself" (2.6). Upshaw goes on to recite a familiar litany of anti-Semitic slurs, claiming that Fortune and other Jewish people must be respected for "their cunning, their wiles, their sexual depravity ... and their way with money" (2.7).

Chaykin complicates matters, however, by making his tough-as-nails, devil-may-care mercenary evoke some of these same qualities in his own self-presentation. The first page of the series features first-person narration by Fortune in which he reveals that he has been selling his services to both sides of the Chaco War between Bolivia and Paraguay, explaining, "I don't give a damn about politics, or religion, or nationalities

... Money's my god" (1.1). This claim to worship money is perhaps surprising for the hero of a book whose villains are defined partly by their anti-Semitism. However, it is important to remember that Fortune's remarks here are not merely internal dialogue but are also part of a retrospective record that he intends for a reading public: his narration appears in quotation marks in caption boxes, and he shares information that he would have no reason to think to himself as part of an interior monologue. It may be useful, then, to consider Fortune's narration as part of his performance of the role of an individualistic, hard-bitten, and cynical mercenary. His performance is good enough to persuade even one of Upshaw's allies and an occasional bedmate of Fortune's, Delatriz Betancourt—the descendant of Confederate officers who fled the American South for South America at the end of the Civil War—who errs in reassuring Upshaw that Fortune is such a nihilist he would little care about a fascist regime in the United States as long as he was well paid (1.23).

To be sure, Fortune *is* a mercenary, and I do not mean to suggest that his tough-guy act is *only* an act. Yet he evinces deeper allegiances with other Jews than his cynical manner would suggest. Delatriz's poor judgment is made plain in a handful of scenes in which Fortune demonstrates concern for the plight of German Jews and disdain for anti-Semites (1.6–7, 2.2). Fortune also displays an interest in the issue of Jewish stereotypes in the cultural imagination, most notably in a crucial scene in a Berlin cabaret. Fortune has gone there in order to make contact with someone who can provide information about a recent attempt on his life, but he finds that his ally is a comedian who dresses like a caricature of a rabbi, complete with oversized prosthetic rubber nose (Figure 8.2). Fortune, dressed in costume, towers over the smaller figure as he grabs him by his beard and interrogates him roughly. When he's gotten the information he needs, he tells him: "Thanks—and as for the outfit ... find a new line of work" (3.9). In his review of the series for *The Comics Journal*, R. C. Harvey found this scene deeply problematic, arguing that the comedian's "enormous hooked nose—the very personification of ethnic bigotry," along with the non-stop anti-Semitism of Upshaw and the trio of actors, has the "unintended consequence" of giving anti-Semites "something to applaud." (Harvey seems to miss that the comedian's nose is part of a costume—a reasonable error, given that colorist Edgar Delgado renders it the same shade as the rest of his face, making the seams easy to overlook.) I would argue, however, that in this scene Chaykin is wise to the implications of the stereotypes Harvey accuses him of passively transmitting. Here, Chaykin stages a confrontation between two images of Jewish identity, particularly of Jewish masculinity: a negative version of the scholarly, rabbinic ideal of Jewish masculinity that emphasizes physical weakness and even cowardice versus the new ideal that Fortune embodies, ruggedly masculine and powerful in the mold of a superhero, willing to use violence to achieve his goals. That even an ostensible friend of the Jews perpetuates the anti-Semitic caricature of the rabbi speaks to the sheer pervasiveness of the stereotype, and Fortune's angry warning indicates his desire to destroy it.

Although the scene might seem to endorse the replacement of an old image with a new one—to replace a model of Jewish masculinity perhaps irrevocably compromised by centuries of anti-Semitic stereotypes in favor of a muscular, violent, Americanized

Figure 8.2 *Dominic Fortune* #3, page 9 (2009). © Marvel Entertainment, LLC and its subsidiaries.

model—Chaykin complicates matters by probing the limitations of the ideal of heroic masculine agency that Fortune embodies. The series concludes with the expected and spectacular violent confrontation between Fortune and his fascist foes that seems to confirm his physical triumph over them. In one remarkable sequence, Fortune pilots a hijacked seaplane into a crowd of would-be storm troopers who are about to attack the White House, chopping them into what he describes as a "flesh, blood and bone jigsaw puzzle"; by contrast, he remarks: "I was still in one piece" (4.17). Chaykin's page layout resonates with Fortune's statement: the page depicting the dismemberment of the troops, sliced into five thin horizontal panels, is contrasted with a single full-page image of Fortune emerging intact from the wreckage and drawing his pistol, a formal strategy that emphasizes the coherence and integrity of his powerful male body (4.16–17). Fortune continues to display his physical prowess in a tense standoff situation with Malcolm Upshaw, who is holding Eleanor Roosevelt hostage in the Oval Office. Fortune surprises his foe by turning President Franklin Roosevelt into a projectile weapon, sending his wheelchair hurtling across the room and into Upshaw with a single mighty kick (4.20).

In these scenes, Fortune is the epitome of Breines's "tough Jew," flexing his muscles in a display of exaggerated heroic masculinity. Indeed, these sequences are so over-the-top as to verge on the parodic, and there are other troubling aspects as well. Earlier in the text, Delatriz suggests that Upshaw is homosexual, needling him that he made an apt choice by crossing the Atlantic on the "Queen Mary" and accusing him of "flirting … with every steward [he] could find" and "sneak[ing] down to the engine room for some rough trade" (2.23). To be sure, Malcolm's villainy is only ever ascribed to his fascism, never his sexuality, which is not mentioned again in the story. Yet the fact that Fortune's masculinity is spectacularly confirmed in a physical triumph over a gay man, a triumph effected by his reduction of a disabled man to the status of an object, suggest a potential dark side to this violent, Americanized notion of Jewish masculinity. To his credit, Fortune apologizes to Roosevelt, who jokingly absolves Fortune by telling him: "Not to worry, my boy … I've taken bigger spills before dinner" (4.21). Roosevelt's game, grinning attitude here may allay some of these concerns and suggest a certain winking lack of seriousness about the violence depicted.

Indeed, I would argue that Chaykin is here drawing a deliberate contrast between the outrageousness of the violence and its significance to the actual resolution of the tale. The story makes clear that the fascist plot against the United States was always doomed to failure: the plotters are poorly organized, their small band of soldiers ill trained and inept. Fortune and Roosevelt agree that Upshaw's plan had little chance of success (4.22). Roosevelt goes on to note, however, that had Fortune not arrived to save the day, he and the First Lady "would certainly have been hostages … which would have had a profoundly destabilizing effect on the nation" (4.22). In his daring raid on the White House, then, Fortune has primarily won a public relations battle—an important victory but perhaps not the most important one. In fact, the other victory that Fortune reveals at the end of the comic takes place outside the realm of manly, heroic violence, and suggests that the spectacle of such violence is most useful as a distraction. Using his job babysitting the Hollywood stars as cover for his investigation, Fortune steers the men to Germany for the Berlin Olympics, where he discovers that one of Upshaw's co-conspirators, another washed-up actor, has unbeknownst to the trio concealed a small fortune in bearer bonds in their luggage, intended as payment to his fascist counterparts in Europe. Fortune's solution is clever and satisfying: as he describes it to Upshaw while smashing his face into a wall, Fortune has had members of the Jewish underground pass counterfeit bearer bonds to European fascists while he used the real things to buy several hundred endangered Jews safe passage to the United States (4.21).

This scheme offers a key to reading Chaykin's treatment of the notion of costumed heroes as a metaphor for Jewish masculinity in particular and ethnic identity in general. The Hollywood icons are unwitting conveyors of a fascist message and fascist capital, and Fortune, through some swift thinking and clever counterfeiting, is able to take their message and money and transform it into something that helps Jews escape the Nazis. In this sense Fortune's strategy with the bearer bonds is a reflection of his approach to his own public identity: by adopting the cover of an Americanized persona so violently and aggressively masculine that other characters see it as an aberration from a Jewish norm and in some cases even as fascist-friendly, he is actually able to protect Jewish interests. It is telling that at the end of the story Fortune ends up not with Delatriz Betancourt, the fascist plotter whom he had earlier wooed, but with Hazel Fontaine, the Hollywood star. Hazel, whose real name is Hadassah Feinstein, is in fact a nice Jewish girl (at least to the extent that anyone in a Chaykin comic is ever nice). Their romance is sure to be short-lived: Hazel is married to Irwin Oppenheim, though Chaykin pre-empts any stuffy moralizing about her adultery in a comically lewd two-page sequence which depicts Fortune in bed with Hazel while on the phone with Oppenheim, who is being fellated by an unnamed woman. Not unlike Fortune, Hazel is savvy about the various ways in which her public image circulates. For instance, she flirts with Fortune by suggesting he bring his Tijuana Bibles featuring her to dinner. Thus, their fling at comic's end brings together a pair of individuals who have transformed themselves into fantasies from American popular culture, yet who have not completely lost touch with their Jewish roots.

When the *Dominic Fortune* mini series began its run in 2009, it joined a wave of contemporary, revisionary pop culture texts, including films such as Steven Spielberg's *Munich* (2005), Edward Zwick's *Defiance* (2008), and Quentin Tarantino's *Inglourious Basterds* (2009), that depicted Jewish men as violent, vengeful, aggressive tough guys— sometimes outrageously so, as in the case of Tarantino's film. Writing in the *Atlantic Monthly*, Jeffrey Goldberg worried that the glee these movies take in depicting violent Jewish revenge fantasies actually makes them fundamentally un-Jewish (76–77). One might argue that Goldberg's critique puts him solidly in the camp of Breines and Boyarin, scholars of Jewish masculinity who worry that the transformation toward a more Americanized model of manhood means leaving a crucially significant aspect of Jewish tradition behind. Chaykin's Dominic Fortune represents a thoughtful intervention into this debate—a complex model of Americanized Jewish masculinity, one that embraces many elements of the Americanized "tough Jew" but that, through its satiric focus on the excessive violence of the superhero genre, also calls both the ethics and the efficacy of such toughness into question. Fortune does not embody a full embrace of "tough" Jewishness or a complete rejection of traditional Jewish masculinity, but, rather, a flexible, strategic approach to the "layers of identity" (to use Chaykin's phrase). Ultimately, Chaykin's Dominic Fortune stories suggest that superhero narratives are not simply wish-fulfillment fantasies of Jewish masculinity but, rather, an opportunity to reconsider the complicated, multifaceted negotiation between ethnicity and nation, tradition and modernity, *mensch* and Superman.

Notes

1   Neither the series as originally published nor its eventual trade paperback collection featured page numbers, so I have determined them by counting from the first page of each issue—whether it's a story page or a recap of the story so far—as page one and disregarding advertisements and other non-story matter. Also, in all parenthetical citations where individual comic book issues are involved, such as *Dominic Fortune*, the issue number will precede the page number, separated by a period.

2   For a good discussion of the Jewish aspects of the Dominic Fortune adventures not written and drawn by Chaykin, see Fingeroth pages 131–133.

3   The 1937 setting of "All in Color for a Crime" may pose some complications for the notion of Acme Publications as a shop for fascist superhero comics, since Superman did not make his debut until 1938. There are a few possible explanations for this date. Among them is that there is really no complication at all: since there is no reason the birth of superhero comics in the Marvel Universe should conform precisely to real-world history (especially given the centrality of figures published by Marvel's chief rival to that early history), Chaykin and O'Neil were free to set the early days of superhero comics whenever they wanted within a rough historical period. Another may be that Chaykin and O'Neil perceive no significant difference between the costumed heroes who predated Superman in newspaper strips and comic books– such as The Phantom, Mandrake the Magician, and The Clock—and "superheroes" narrowly defined. Still another explanation may be that the story deliberately charts a *progression* from those earlier heroes to and those of the sort that emerged in the post-Superman boom and cites an increased fascist element in the later heroes. This may be the reason that Sabbath, looking at some of the yet-unpublished Acme work, tells Fortune, "the stories that bother you are nothing compared to these" (53). Although this last possibility may complicate a reading of the Purple Slasher as an accidental fascist icon, the fact that Weltman seems to perceive no distinction between the Slasher and any of the other comics he produces for Acme suggests that they are all ultimately of a piece, with differences perhaps of degree but not of kind. In any case, the Purple Slasher is still a Jewish artist's fantasy of masculine power, a fantasy that becomes co-opted by fascism.

Converting Schmaltz into Chicken Fat:
Will Elder and the Judaization
of American Comedy

Daniel M. Bronstein

For much of the twentieth century, Jews distinguished themselves as central players in the creation of a modern American popular culture. Whether or not this was consciously undertaken from a particular sense of Jewishness, American Jews have contributed to virtually every realm of American culture, from film to music, playing a foundational role in the crafting of modern American comedy. That Jewish comedic sensibilities came to permeate American comedy is significant because, to state the obvious, Jewish humor was not indigenous to mainline American culture. Likewise, American Jewish comedy has not solely been directed toward a Jewish audience, and even with its own peculiarities, it also appeals to a culturally broad audience (Bronstein 108). One such example of the Jewish contribution to American comedy, however obscure to some, was via *Mad* magazine's predecessors' *Mad* comics and its sister publication, *Panic*, launched respectively in 1952 and 1954. The creators of *Mad* were, like their type of humor, products of New York City, or at least Brooklyn and the Bronx. Jews might have arrived in New York in the mid-seventeenth century, but it took a long time for Jewish idiosyncrasies to infiltrate long-standing tradition of non-Jewish American humor. And it took artists like Will Elder who were first generation American Jews and consumers and creators of popular culture to do so.

Neither *Mad* nor *Panic* were conceived of as a Jewish publication but were rather intended for a mass audience. *Mad's* influence upon postwar American humor and popular culture is indisputable. Its distinct satirical style still resonates across the spectrum of modern American humor. But when did a distinctively "American" form of humor begin? Constance Rourke's landmark study, *American Humor*, traces its origins to the lampooning of certain cultural types: the Yankee, the backwoodsman, and African Americans (Rourke 89). "As a people the Americans are said to have had no childhood," she writes, but the Yankee type "stepped out of a darkness that seems antediluvian" (89). American Jewish comedy came to fruition in the country's adolescence. Built upon a foundation of self-parody, with frequent detours into satirizing the majority culture, Jewish humor offered a bifurcated worldview. Rather than emerging from the shadows, the Jews who wrote for *Mad* materialized under the bright lights of the great migration. The Yankee archetype may have been "indefatigably rural, sharp, uncouth, witty" but *Mad*'s Jews were thoroughly urban, although most certainly sharp and often uncouth, as well (25). The Yankee type began as a humorous foil to the British; Jews generally targeted the American WASP. The backwoodsman, a symbolic descendent of Davy Crockett, was later amalgamated with Yankee. But for Rourke, it was African Americans, the country's foremost "others," who set the bar for American humor. She writes, "The Blacks are the great humorists of the nation" (71). It was the Yankee who fought in the "initial revolt against the parent civilization, the backwoodsman in revolt against all civilization, the Negro in a revolt which was cryptic and submerged but which none the less made a perceptible outline" (86). *American Humor* was written in the early days of the Depression, and post-Second World War II African American humor can hardly be characterized as "cryptic" or "submerged." Jews shared with blacks the minority experience but unlike the latter could often "pass" in the majority culture, making American Jewish comedy a shotgun marriage of self-examination and broad social criticism.

This tension was all too real. One standard historical narrative contends that the newly civilized Jews were at once marginalized from majority culture because of their Jewishness and also divorced from the Jewish community because of their rejection of the tradition. "The [Jewish] problem of behavior," writes John Maury Cuddihy, "became strategic to the whole problematic of 'assimilation.' The modernization process, the civilizational process, and the assimilation process were experienced as one as the 'price of admission' to the bourgeois civil societies of the West as the end of the nineteenth century" (13). But the development of a particular type of American Jewish humor offers a somewhat different narrative.

Although Jewish humor may have been submerged in the 1930s and 1940s (Buhle), overt and consciously composed Jewish humor came into prominence after the Second World War via early television comedies like Sid Caesar's *Show of Shows*, with *Mad* eventually becoming a ascendant component in American comedy. Stated differently, Jews mingled their proverbial comedic *schmaltz* into the great melting pot of American humor. The Jews' ordeal was alleviated by means of Jewish comedy, as well as by the very act of Jews teaching the gentiles about what was, and how to be, funny. By the 1950s Jewish comedians were among American Jewry's greatest outreach experts, teaching gentiles about Jews and the United States about Jewish culture. Jewish humor provided a haven for preserving Jewishness parallel to the Americanization process. But instead of remaining ghettoized, Jewish comedy was, in addition to "acting out" in front of gentiles, a way to retain Jewish ties while also extending Jewish comedic sensibilities on a popular scale. Following earlier American humorists, twentieth-century American Jews played a noteworthy role in defining what was funny for the United States as a whole. The influence of *Mad*, especially through artists like Will Elder, offers a perfect example.

Now firmly ensconced in American popular culture, *Mad*'s mascot, Alfred E. Neumann, became as recognizable an icon as Mickey Mouse and Superman. As *Time* magazine's Richard Corliss writes, to say that the *Mad* approach to humor influenced American comedy is "to understate the case. Almost all American satire today follows a formula" generated by the creative father of *Mad*, Harvey Kurtzman (Corliss). As

Paul Buhle and Denis Kitchen write: "Without Harvey Kurtzman, there would have been no *Saturday Night Live* … [He] taught two, maybe three generations of postwar American kids, mainly boys, what to laugh at: politics, popular culture, authority figures" (Kitchen and Buhle xi).

In truth, *Mad* was spawned from several parents, including EC Comics and *Mad* publisher, William M. Gaines. But from the outset it should be acknowledged that founding editor Harvey Kurtzman was the overall architect of *Mad*, while his friend and colleague Will Elder played a key role in translating Kurtzman for the masses. Although a "silent partner," (Groth, Clowes, and Sadowski 50–52) Elder was "most widely known as Harvey Kurtzman's lifelong collaborator … he was in his own way, an autonomous artist" (Groth 253). Shorn of the contribution of his friend, artist Will Elder, Kurtzman's *Mad* work would not have packed the same punch. In fact, much like the work of Sid Caesar who assembled an extraordinary stable of writer for his television work, *Mad* was the product of a team effort. Nonetheless, if Kurtzman and "his *MAD* artists can be compared to another bunch of early-50s comic smarty-pantses the Sid Caesar writing staff," writes Corliss, then "Elder was Mel Brooks" (Corliss). As Kurtzman makes clear, Elder could "carry my stuff forward and enrich it by a multiple of five" (Benson n.p.) Even within an institution teeming with professional humorists, William M. Gaines declared Elder to be their "funniest artist" (Groth, Clowes, and Sadowski 51) and "unquestionably the nuttiest guy that ever walked in the doors here … [He] probably became the most popular artist in Mad," a position he maintained over the course of many years ("Will Elder").

Born Wolf Eisenberg in 1921 and raised in the Bronx, he was always a joker and called "Meshugganah Villy" (crazy Villy) by his family. Although twice rejected, first at age seventeen and later at nineteen, for a cartooning job at Walt Disney studios, Elder, along with several other *Mad* artists, was among the first graduates of New York's High School of Music and Art. He was also a combat veteran of the Second World War and among several other battles, participated in the liberation of Paris and the Battle of the Bulge, and he was among the first troops to cross the Rhine. Elder was likewise witness to the *Shoah*, although he appeared reluctant to discuss the topic for years (Groth, Clowes, and Sadowski 5, 8, 23, 30; Groth 86). It was only after the war that he legally changed his name from "Wolf William Eisenberg" to "Will Elder," in homage to the sixteenth-century Dutch artist Pieter Bruegel the Elder.

Together with his work on other EC comics, Elder contributed to *Mad* from its first incarnation as a comic book through its transition into a magazine, spanning the years 1952–1956. Known for his remarkable mimicry of almost any cartoon style, Elder meticulously aped other artists while still humorously eviscerating cultural luminaries, such as Donald Duck, Archie, Popeye, and Superman. Elder possessed a remarkable gift for replicating the design of almost any other cartoonist.

In "Mickey Rodent" (*Mad* #19, January, 1955) Kurtzman's Disney parody, Elder manages to show "Darnold Duck," obviously the Donald Duck stand-in, in a state of shock upon realization that he had been walking around without pants while also making the artwork appear to be the official product of Disney Studios. The Archie comics parody, "Starchie," (Mad #12, June, 1954) portrays Mr. Weatherby—here Mr. "Weathernot"—as sexually harassing the Betty and Veronica counterparts, Biddy and

Salonica. That spin on Archie would have been enough, but Elder added other details. The two coeds are shown as pockmarked, with Biddy packing a hypodermic needle in her purse along with unlabeled pills, hand rolled joints, and a deck of cards. As Elder noted, all of the "things that are wrong with people in society registered on those pages" of "Starchie" (Groth, "Will Elder" 96).[1]

But it was Elder's innovation rather than his skill in graphical impersonation that truly sealed his reputation as an original humorist. As Jack Davis, another (albeit non-Jewish) founding artist of *Mad*, later recounted, Elder "started the trend of putting in funny little things in the background" (Groth, Clowes, and Sadowski 50–52). Elder, he said, was "[k]ind of the original *Mad* artist. He'd put in crazy things that had never been done before" (Wochner 108). It was Elder's additional touches that became perhaps the most important part of his artistic legacy, a style of humor later christened as "chicken fat," that is, "schmaltz" in Yiddish. In Ashkenazi cuisine, rendered chicken fat was used to fry meats and also used in place of butter to season other foods. Later, "schmaltz" was transformed into a term for "excessively sentimental or florid music or art" or "maudlin sentimentality" (Webb 183–184). Jettisoning the Yiddish for literal English translation, Elder meant something different by the expression "chicken fat." More than one of Elder's acolytes has attempted to define what he meant and struggled to explain Elder's comedic technique, dubbing him the "Marx Brother in cartooning," an apt term for someone whose work resonated with Jewishness and held wide popular appeal.

For example, Terry Gilliam—animation artist, film director, and member of the Monty Python troupe—was among the many humorists who learned their craft via Elder and Kurtzman. He described the chicken fat format as the layering of "jokes on jokes on jokes" (Groth, Clowes, and Sadowski 48). Cartoonist Daniel Clowes also takes a crack at defining "chicken fat," writing that "Elder articulates his Milt Gross/Marx Brothers-Yiddish-vaudevillianism" that was in some manner a "descendent of Bosch and Bruegel … the backgrounds are literally cluttered with information about the artist himself and the very specific urban culture from which he has risen … the interplay of chaos and control is orchestrated … his crystal-clear vision of a world gone mad" (Groth, Clowes, and Sadowski 2–3). In fact, by "chicken fat" Elder meant the stuff that was "bad for you" but gave the stories extra flavor without advancing actual storylines. (Mad Mumblings Presents: Part II, A Conversation with Willy by Dr. Keith E Tubbs, a.k.a. Mad Doctor)

Kurtzman, a talented artist with a truly original style and a legion of disciples, wrote most of the scripts and laid out storyboards for every panel of the comic and seemingly all of the visual details of each story. As Gaines recounted, he was "like a conductor of an orchestra, made a pencil sketch, pretty tight pencil sketch, of every single panel of every single story and God help the artist who tried to change it!" (Decker and Groth 62). More than one of the artists, who worked with Kurtzman, whether at *Mad* or the other EC titles he edited, chafed under his tight editorship. Amid all of the creativity of the era were serious conflicts between Kurtzman and legendary comic artists like John Severin, Wally Wood, and others, some of whom remained resentful for decades. But the same rules did not seem to apply to Elder. His comedic appendages transcended Kurtzman's visual scripts for the *Mad* stories.

Kurtzman would "roughly set it down on paper in these little panels and written dialogue and sound effects," Elder recounted, and

> I would work with that as a base. Basically I would use that to start throwing things in. And he never said a word; because he figured whatever I did would only enhance the humor of what he did. And it was a good combination. It worked well. Before you know it, I was throwing in the kitchen sink and the dumbwaiter. Every blessed thing that came into my mind, which ended up in a hilarious clutter, as he put it. (Groth "Will Elder," 94)

Whether it was because Elder was a good friend or because Elder's additions worked better than those of other artists, Kurtzman affirmed: "Willy was much funnier than me" (Benson "A Conversation," Vol. II unnumbered page). As recounted by Elder in later interviews, Kurtzman was quite open to his adding supplementary material to the stories.[2]

> I elaborated on [Kurtzman's template] but also worked my way into situations where other people are doing other things. If it was a crowded scene, I have everybody doing the wrong thing. Instead of having just the concentration on the hero or heroine, it would be simultaneous action elsewhere, and something to do with the story—it was unrelated—it had something to do with the story … You've seen the Marx Brothers, of course. (Veri 118)

This is significant because Elder's flourishes created a new tier of humor for Kurtzman's already funny work. "Harvey would say, everybody will be reading Will's sight gags and not even my stories" (Groth, "Will Elder" 97).

Especially in his work for *Mad* Comics, Elder's work proves the adage that a picture is worth a thousand words. Full absorption of his work, such the splash page for stories like "Woman Wonder" (*Mad* # 10), requires familiarity with and understanding of the given cultural context, focused attention to the smallest details of the art, and repeated examination. For some, fully taking in Elder's artwork is a multi year process subject to many readings.

Like Bruegel's *Fight between Carnival and Lent* or *Triumph of Death* (1562), there is a multiplicity of individuals each requiring particular attention. Like Bosch's *Garden of Earthly Delights* (c. 1490–1510) there are a host of stories within stories, each requiring particular focus. Elder's scene of mass fright, like the splash page of "Woman Wonder" (*Mad* #10, April 1954), includes an aside of skeletal legs jutting out from a coffin running along with a fleeing mob. Similarly, "Ping Pong" (*Mad* #6, August–September, 1953) contains several scenes of crowds fleeing in terror. Elder's recurring trope of mass chaos almost suggests the painting, *Colossus*, or "Panic," attributed to Francisco De Goya (ca. 1812) *depicting* a mass of tiny figures fearfully scattering in every direction from a lumbering giant. Finally, throw in a bit of the untidiness and shock value of Paul Cadmus but with perhaps less cynicism—and Jewish comedy—and you have a Will Elder crowd scene. Along with such imagery, Elder's comedy also included word play. Elder clearly enjoyed affixing superfluous text onto background visuals. Following the precedent of cartoonist Bill Holman's *Smokey Stover* (syndicated from 1935 to 1973) and Roy Crane's *Wash Tubbs* (syndicated from 1924 to 1988), he deployed hosts of puns and other language-based humor and used panels breaking down the fourth wall separating the art from the reader (Veri 118).

The parody of the "Shadow" (Mad #4, May, 1953) offers several such examples. In one panel Elder throws in a sign saying: "Try the new breakfast cereal 'Hush'! Doesn't snap, pop or crackle!" Using a saloon scene from the same story, Elder inserts a sign on a wall saying "No drinks to Miners," illustrated, of course, with a picture of a miner. Elsewhere in the "Shadow," he uses the backdrop of a gas station to display a sign reading: "Eat and get gas." Despite the clear emphasis on visuals, "Ping Pong" includes a glimpse of a man reading a magazine with the same cover format as *Life* magazine but titled "Death." Elder also adds an image of stereotypical natives boiling a man alive in a large pot. A closer look shows an inscription on the pot: "Advice for thin people. Don't eat fast!!! Advice for fat people don't eat—fast!!"

The difference between Elder and say Bruegel, Bosch, or Goya is not simply that Elder was a twentieth-century American. The difference between Elder and the other great masters is not simply that his comics did not deal with Christian theology or the Bible. And the artistic distinction between Elder and the masters is not merely confined to the fact that his work unfolded in cheaply sold comic books rather than as paintings on permanent display in the Prado. Satirical as some of this work by classical artists may have been, the main difference between Elder and the others was that he was focused on making people laugh.

Larding Kurtzman's scripts with what seemed to be comedic ephemera, these generous dollops of "chicken fat" often employed the humor particular to the New York Jewish milieu of Elders' upbringing, explicated in Lenny Bruce's now-famous riff on what it meant to be a New Yorker: "If you're from New York and you're Catholic, you're still Jewish." Although Elder and Kurtzman later departed from *Mad* under less-than-happy circumstances, Elder's chicken fat style was nevertheless preserved by his artistic successors and it has endured in the pages of *Mad* for over a half century. Still, as his son-in-law and chief biographer, Gary Vandenberg, recently wrote: "Will and Kurtzman were hitting [the readers] over the head with Jewish humor … American humor had been set down a path where Yiddish sensibilities were never very far from the surface" (Vandenbergh, Gary "Will Elder: Mad Magazine's Yiddishe Kup," http://jstandard.com/index.php/content/item/will_elder/8233).

It is true that his Jewish material wasn't always easy to find in the mix, but the Jewish comedy was also never hidden. One such example dates back to his first *Mad* collaboration with Kurtzman, the story "Ganeffs" ("thieves" in Yiddish) from the very first issue of *Mad* comics (November, 1952). Unlike most of their other collaborations, "Ganeffs" was mostly an Elder creation (Groth and Sadowski 48). Although not a Jewish story per se, the use of the Yiddish word "ganeff" offered an explicit assertion of Jewishness, although they were aiming for a broad audience. Elder and Kurtzman used a peculiar Jewish New York dialect, and referenced New York culture. Relying on words like "fershlugginer" (an imaginary Yiddishism), they had their own satirical self-referencing system, something that no other satire magazine had or would choose to have. It was the Bronx counterpart to the sophistication of the *New Yorker* magazine" (Buhle and Kitchen 87).

For instance, interviewing Kurtzman in reference to his "Shadow" parody, *Mad* historian John Benson asked how he and Elder came to use the name "Shadowskeedeeboomboom" instead. "There was a comedian who did a record that went something like 'Cim-bedi-bim-bim, boom-bede-boom-boom, bim-bede-boom-bede-haskede-boom-boom,'" Kurtzman recalled. "I don't remember who he was. It might have been a guy by the name of Aaron Lebedaff [*sic*], who did some unusual Yiddish records. I remember he did a 'Romania' record ... It had a nice lilt ... I would pick up something ..." (Benson, Vol. I, unnumbered page). Other New York references abound in the Kurtzman–Elder collaborations. As related by *Mad* historian Maria Reidelbach, some New York Jewish specific material was foreign to some fans: "What in the world is 'borscht'?" demanded a reader .... "Please tell me what 'furshlugginer' means, pleaded another." "Ganeff," was coupled with words like "fasrhimmelt," and even references to "halavah" seemed "strange and exotic" to readers of the early *Mad* (Reidelbach 56).

The issue #7 of *Mad* included the Sherlock Holmes parody, "Shermlock Shomes," (October–November, 1953) with a recurring gag of the sleuth mistakenly kissing a hand that he believes to belong to a beautiful woman but really is that of "Mrs. Gowanus," an unkempt and unsightly cleaning woman, who always seems to enter the scene shortly after cleaning cesspools. As many New Yorkers knew, the Gowanus Canal was infamous for its pollution, filth, and malodorous condition. Given that *Mad* was sold throughout the country, this offered a glimpse into the distant and even exotic, multicultural city of New York. Benson himself offers the perfect example of a non-Jewish impacted by Elder's explicit Jewishness. "The first four [*Mad*] Elder stories were all city stories," he writes:

> Chicken fat, garbage can stories ... Elder brought out all of the unique aspects of New York, and Jewish New York culture, which were very strange to somebody from another part of the country; all these names and words that were unfamiliar, and that were used for comic effort. For example, I was fascinated by the name Gowanus Canal. I never knew it was a real place until I moved to New York." As Kurtzman explains: "these names come out of the artist's, the author's experiences." (Benson, "A Conversation," Vol. II, unnumbered page)

In other instances, Elder's Jewish points of reference were gastronomic. For example, issue #3 (February–March, 1953) included a parody of the radio show version of *Dragnet*, "Dragged Net." Searching through a cave for the bad guy, "Glotz," the two detectives are shown walking by what appear to be hanging hams, stamped both with "Swifts"—one of America's venerable meatpacking companies—and the word "kosher" in Hebrew as well as English. Another ongoing gag in the story revolved around borscht. The detectives interrogate Glotz in a restaurant while the latter gorges himself on an octopus, frog, what appear to be a human arm and hand bones together with prehistoric creatures, modern worms, and a chick coming out of Easter egg. In the midst of this gluttony and over the course of several panels, Elder shows a series of signs behind the characters proclaiming: "We got Borscht," "Borscht we got," "Borscht you bat!" "We're running low on Borscht," "Sorry! No more Borscht." References to Jewish food appear throughout Elder's marginalia.

Kurtzman and Elder's Popeye parody, "Poopeye," (*Mad* #21, March, 1955) includes a showdown with "Superduperman." In Elder's version of the "Man of Steel" the letter "S" on his chest is replaced in one instance with the label for "Fleischman's Yeast" and in another with the very words "Chicken Fat." Early in his tenure at *Mad*, Elder began putting visual representations of chicken fat in various stories. In the fifth issue, for example, a container labeled "Jar of Chicken Fat" is inserted in the story "Outer Sanctum" (*Mad* #5, June–July, 1953). The Mandrake the Magician parody, "Manduck the Magician" (*Mad* #14, August, 1954), includes a photo of bodybuilder Charles Atlas, another cultural icon, wearing trunks with the words: "I was raised with chicken fat." Elsewhere in the story, a woman is shown eating various foods from a box labeled "Manischewitz." Another example of Elder's gastronomically based humor is found in a 1954 *Mad* story, really a cultural study, titled "Restaurant," showing the ups and downs of having a family meal at a Chinese restaurant. (The splash page itself offers enough material to occupy one's attention for many years.) In yet another aside Elder adds a sign to a restaurant booth saying "Today's Special: Egg Foo Yong with Geflite Fish."

Somehow, the term chicken fat makes it into the work of two non-Jewish *Mad* artists as well. Chicken fat seems to appear in the John Severin story "Melvin" from issue #2 (December 1952–January 1953 and in Wally Wood's "Superduperman" from issue #4 (April–May, 1953). Finally, in a great mix of popular and elite culture from faux biographical sketch of Elder from *Mad* #22, young Elder is described as "shmearing chicken fat on towels, bald heads, visitor's dresses and convenient walls … Today those shmears … are hung in various museums and signed with Elder's various pen names such as 'Braque,' 'Matisse,' 'Picasso.'"

In fact, Elder's lack of self-consciousness as a Jew was notable. Paul Buhle relates that artists like Milt Gross can be seen as an early twentieth-century antecedent to Elder, although later, Jewishness "[was] purposefully hidden" in comics and cartoons. "That is, until Mad Comics ushered in something of a revival" (Buhle). The example of Milt Gross is instructive. Although his work dealt with the tensions between immigrant Jews and their American born children, "his work resonated with American audiences" (Kelman 1). They also covered some of the same territory, both artists reinterpreting the "Night before Christmas" and Edgar Allen Poe's "The Raven." Ari Kelman writes that "Gross fabricated a kind of unique English-Jewish speech for a general, largely non-Jewish audience," and although written in English, he utilized Yiddish grammar. "By relying on English vocabulary, Gross could still be understood no matter how foreign his sentence structure" (Kelman 11). Buhle argues: "[B]latant Jewish reference and Yinglish gags" gave "Yiddishkeit new life in postwar comics."

Elder's chicken fat was in part language-based, similar to Gross's text, but it was also visual.[3] Perhaps the most infamous display of Yiddishkeit, some of it inadvertent, was Elder's take on the poem "A Visit from St. Nicholas," popularly known as "The Night before Christmas," from the very first issue of *Mad*'s sister publication *Panic* (February–March, 1954).[4] Never as successful as its predecessor, *Panic* essentially drew from the same stable of artists but was edited—far less strictly—by Albert Feldstein, later editor of *Mad* magazine rather than Harvey Kurtzman. Although the "Night before Christmas" was not a result of collaboration with Kurtzman, its content would still have fit well in *Mad*. And *Panic* and *Mad* both had its detractors as well.

Mad's artists had provoked fury in the past. For example, the cover of issue #14 showed the classic Mona Lisa painting but with the painting's subject reading a copy of *Mad*. The cover art sparked great protest for the simple reason that some believed DaVinci's classic was a portrayal of the Virgin Mary. But Elder's "Night before Christmas" was actually banned in Massachusetts and also resulted in an uninvited visit from the New York Police Department to the *Mad* offices, resulting in the arrest of the non-Jewish, African-American receptionist on flimsy charges.[5]

For example, responding to the line "A bundle of toys he had flung on his back. And he looked like a peddler just opening his pack," Elder drew Santa Claus as what appeared to be an archetypal Lower East Side fish peddler (Figure 9. 1).[6] As refracted through the mind of Will Elder, another stanza about Santa being "dressed all in fur, from his head to his foot, And his clothes were all tarnished with ashes and soot," finds visual form in a black-faced Al Jolson singing "Mammy." But what most rankled was Elder's portrayal of Santa's sled as a car bearing the sign "Just Divorced" along with a YMCA bumper sticker (Figure 9.2).[7] The sign and bumper stickers were secondary jokes; Elder's visual interpretation of the stanza actually centered on literal portrayals

Figure 9.1 Santa Claus transformed into fish monger.

Figure 9.2 Santa as divorcee.

of the names of Santa's reindeers. Nonetheless, as Gaines recalled: "The trouble we had with the Santa Claus story was Bill Elder … Now how do a bunch of iconoclastic, atheist bastards like us know that Santa Claus is a saint and that he can't be divorced that this is going to offend Boston?" (Decker and Groth, 1983, 78). Although convened primarily in reaction to horror comic books, Elder's "Night before Christmas" was also referenced at a now infamous April of 1954 congressional hearing on the dangers of comic books chaired by Estes Kefauver and with testimony by Bill Gaines. Later reflecting on the controversy, Elder commented: "[E]verything is banned in Massachusetts" (Groth 94). But Gross's and Elder's versions of the poem, no matter how different, did perhaps share a certain outlook. Arguably, both artists' reinterpretation of the "Night before Christmas" served as a prophylactic against the "December Dilemma." Kelman writes that Gross had "reworked the classic holiday poem in Jewish dialect and recast the "American folk icon whose legend at once celebrated the myths of the Gilded Age and critiqued its realities." In comparing Santa Claus's nose to a pickle, Gross's version "drew out the dissonance between Jewish sentiment and the holiday season" (Kelman 18). Whether Elder's take on the poem was also an expression of the dissonance between Jewishness and the majority culture of the United States is debatable. What cannot be debated, however, is that Elder had reconstituted the "Night before Christmas" via the chicken fat method and had even Judaized a classic childhood character beloved to Christian America.

Even after Elder's departure from *Mad*, the chicken fat style was nevertheless retained and has persisted in *Mad* for over half a century. As Kurtzman was first to acknowledge, "Willie was the first of the sub-gag artists … Willie has an innate sense of humor that nobody can touch. He's a comedian, he was Sid Caesar, Danny Kaye, a Jewish comedian" (Benson, Vol. II, unnumbered page).

Elder's "layered, free-for-all approach," Daniel Clowes describes it, "influenced the cartoons of R. Crumb and films like *Airplane!* and the *Naked Gun* series" (Groth, Clowes, and Sadowski 2–3). One of his eulogists noted that while "earlier comic book artists like Joe Shuster and Bob Kane may have invented the superhero … Will Elder made possible [recent comedies like] *Superbad*" (Hajdu 28). Ultimately, as noted in his *New York Times* obituary, the chicken fat "approach to humor seeped into the rest of the magazine and the DNA of the contributors … It set the tone for the entire magazine and created a look that endures to this day" (Grimes). Kurtzman and Elder later became known for their periodic *Little Annie Fannie* stories for *Playboy* magazine. Many of their fans think that, despite the lush artwork, *Little Annie Fannie* was not all that funny, at least in part because of the absence of Elder's chicken fat. Elder's asides were generally edited out of the ongoing strip because, Elder reasons, the *Playboy* editors were aiming toward an audience of ostensibly sophisticated "younger executives. So I think they felt my shtick was unnecessary" (Kurtzman and Elder 203).

Elder-era *Mad* occupied the same world as those comedians designated at the time as "sick": Mort Sahl, Jules Feiffer, and of course the aforementioned Lenny Bruce. Through the course of their careers, Elder and Kurtzman collaborated with peers like Sid Caesar, Jackie Gleason (in the magazine *Help!*), and at *Panic* Elder they worked with writer Jack Mendelsohn who went on to write for *Laugh-In* and the *Carol Burnett Show*. But their work also laid the foundation for the 1960s counterculture. Alongside baby boomers like Monty Python members John Cleese and Terry Gilliam, San Francisco hippies like musician Jerry Garcia pointed to Elder as an important creative influence. Still others have linked Elder's chicken fat style to Louis Malle's film *Zazie* (1960) and to the Firesign Theater. Founding cartoonists of underground comix, Gilbert Shelton and Robert Crumb, also learned from Kurtzman and Elder at the short-lived magazine *Help!* and from growing up with *Mad* (Reidelbach 194). Crumb has said: "If you were growing up lonely and isolated in a small town, *Mad* was a revelation. Nothing I read anywhere else suggested there was any absurdity in the culture. *Mad* was like a shock, breaking you out" (Reidelbach 36). Elder's work continues to impact American comedy. Comedy animator David Wachtenheim, known best for his cartoons on *Saturday Night Live*, also credits Elder as a comedic inspiration and is a contributor to the yet to be completed documentary film on Elder, *Chicken Fat* (*Chicken Fat*).

"Will's boyhood antics exemplified what would later become known (and loved) as the quintessentially irreverent, offbeat and, plainly put, Jewish humor," Vandenberg notes, and what "started on the stage, screen, and radio of Fanny Brice, Burns and Allen, Eddie Cantor, and the Marx Brothers eventually found its way to the pages of *Mad, Humbug, Trump, Help!* and *Playboy*. The humor that grew out of the Bronx and Brooklyn ghettos has now become commonplace in the culture of modern America" (Vandenbergh, qtd. in Groth, Clowes, Sadowski 5).

Eddy Portnoy writes that "[w]hen one reflects on the history of Jews and cartoons, the central focus has typically been the Jew as victim of the cartoonist and not the Jew [as] producer of cartoons within the framework of his own culture" (Portnoy 286). The negative imagery of Jews in medieval art often revolved around pseudo events like host desecration. Such portrayals of Jews changed when they began drawing themselves in the Yiddish press. The difference with *Mad* was that it meant to appeal to a mass audience and was not produced solely for other Jews.

The schmaltz of Jewish humor was distilled into the chicken fat of American comedy. Departing from the humor of the Yankee, backwoodsman, and African American, Elder's chicken fat was, as so many observed, like "Marx Brothers on paper."

By instilling a distinctly Jewish comedic sensibility into *Mad*'s parodies of mainline American culture, Elder's work also exemplifies how the melting pot of American popular culture was laced with Jewish humor, and when digested became an essential ingredient of the humor consumed by Americans of every faith, creed, and stripe.

Notes

1   Archie was targeted by Kurtzman elsewhere. Issue 18 (1954) contains a parody of the film *Stalag 17*. Titled "Stalag 18," Nazi spy "Price"—played by Peter Graves—was illustrated as Archie (wearing a swastika over a Riverdale High sweater) rather than as Graves. In this instance, Wally Wood illustrates the story. Second, Kurtzman and Elder renewed their attack on Archie in the February 1962 issue of *Help!* (one of Kurtzman's post-*Mad* creations). In a story titled "Goodman Goes Playboy," Archie serves as a stand in for Hugh Hefner. In this incarnation of Archie, the character is portrayed as a lascivious, greedy, and disturbed figure who making a pact with the Devil ultimately fiddles away like Nero as his mansion burns down. Although Hefner found it amusing the publisher of Archie took legal action and forbade the story from being reprinted in full. Decades later after the Archie people forgot to renew the copyright; "Goodman Goes Playboy" was reprinted in full in *TCJ* no. 262.

2   See discussions found in Groth, *TCJ*, 2003, pp. 94, 100–102, 106–107; Veri, *TCJ*, 1995, 110, 112.

3   As one critic wrote, "[i]f you are able to read the peculiar dialect of Milt Gross aloud (it cannot be read any other way), you will enjoy his 'De night in front from Chreesmas,'" although another contemporary observer wrote that
Gross' work had the "high merit of being almost impossible to read aloud unless one is born on Grand Street," on the Lower East side of New York Coty. Regardless, Elder's work is devoid of the aurality that made Gross so unique. See Kelman, 26.

4   Milt Gross also took on the poem and actually rewrote the text while Elder's retained the text while reimagining the visuals. Even so, Gross did compare Santa Claus' nose to a pickle.

5   Fred von Bernewitz and Grant Geissman, Interview with Albert Feldstein, *Tales of Terror: The EC Companion*.

6   Will Elder, "The Night before Christmas," *Panic* no. 1, 27. Copyright © (1953) William M. Gaines Agent, Inc., reprinted with permission. All rights reserved.

7   Will Elder, "The Night before Christmas," *Panic* no. 1, 25. Copyright © (1953) William M. Gaines Agent, Inc., reprinted with permission. All rights reserved reprinted with permission. All rights reserved.

The Third Temple: Alternative Realities' Depiction of Israel in Israeli Comics and What it Tells Us about Political Consensus in Israeli Society

Ofer Berenstein

In Israel, the medium of comics is generally associated with fringe culture. During the first decades following the establishment of the State of Israel, short comic strips and single-page stories were frequent fixtures in children's magazines and in the young reader's sections of newspapers. This led to a public perception that here was a medium intended for children and as such was inferior, immature, and inherently lacking in depth (Gaon 12). This attitude, which held steady for many years, has diminished in the past few decades, as the medium was embraced by Israeli illustrators and multimedia creators, as well as by literary critics and journalists.

Despite, or maybe because of critics' and artists' interest in it, the medium came to be associated with avant-garde and alternative sub cultures. Those, oftentimes subversive, counter cultures were either opposed to the values of Zionism or at the very least unsupportive of them (Raab 215–216). Thus, comics came to be perceived as a form of expression that glorified values of individualism and self-expression (Gaon 12). With this in mind, one would expect that the narratives in these comics would portray Israeli reality in a way that would suggest alternative viewpoints and novel ways of looking at the state of Israel, its relationship to its surroundings, and solutions to the internal and external challenges it faced.

However, an examination of Israeli comics from a variety of literary genres disproves this assumption. Under closer scrutiny we find that identification with the values of mainstream Israeli Zionism is commonplace both among artists who are associated with the counterculture and among those attempting to appeal to a mass audience. This can be seen in attitudes toward Jewish-Israeli nationalism, the concept of the cultural melting pot and the ideal of reclaiming sacred land. In light

In the spirit of full disclosure the author would like to note that he served as editor and professional adviser for a number of the works discussed here but that at no point was he involved in constructing or writing the plots.

of this, I argue that Israeli comics can be seen as a further reflection of the dogmatic rigidity that characterizes much of Israeli society in its attitudes toward the internal and external conflicts it faces.

Perception of reality in works of science fiction in international and Israeli comics

Although comics can deal with any variety of issues through any number of genres, it is most often associated with those of soft science fiction and urban fantasy. This assertion also holds true for Israeli comics, although in recent years they show signs of becoming more reminiscent of European personal comics. A review of Israeli fantasy and science fiction literature shows that, by and large, it tends to identify with the concept of the social "melting pot" and the ideals of the Zionist movement. In this regard, Israeli literature is unusual compared to the rest of the world, where the tendency is to espouse alternative, non-conformist approaches to viewing reality (Yanai 7).[1] While being so, it differs much from foreign science fiction and fantasy comics, particularly the American kind. These cultures often adopt a non-conformist stance and distance themselves from the underlying assumptions of its contemporary society.

Like other comics traditions, Hebrew language Israeli comics frequently embrace plot structures that make use of alternate realities and parallel dimensions to challenge accepted notions regarding existence and the human condition. However, unlike other comics traditions, which often tend to distance themselves from the underlying assumptions and norms of their contemporary societies, Israeli comics literature maintains a strong adherence to the Israeli reality of the here and now, with few narratives straying from it to any meaningful degree. This adherence creates a situation where, rather than act as a liberal, creative, nonconformist socialization agent (Merlock-Jackson and Arnold 25–27), the science fiction genre in Israeli comics becomes yet another means for institutional socialization, which perpetuates the ideals of the Zionist movement and the societal arrangement it seeks to establish.

In order to evaluate this claim, I analyze the implementation of the alternative realities concept in a number of different Hebrew language comics that deal with Zionist-Jewish life in territorial Israel, from the days of the British mandate up until the last decade.[2] Narratives are divided into three categories that distinguish between different implementations of the idea: parallel universes, alternate realities, and "what if" narratives.

Parallel universe narratives in Israeli comics

Parallel universes are actualities where some of the chemical, physical, and biological elements are retained while others are altered: for example, a planet that appears identical to earth but where intelligent life forms evolved from dolphins rather than humans. In this hypothetical scenario the basic physical properties, such as the atmospheric makeup, gravity, geography, and climate systems are the same. Therefore, if humans were to land on this imaginary planet, they could go about their lives as though they were on our own earth.

The parallel universe genre is divided into two sub categories of actualities based on the distinction between models that are close to the human actuality and those that are removed from it. The example mentioned above is removed from the human actuality because it is based on an ahuman reality that denies the status of humans as the most intelligent life form on earth. In contrast, narratives of the superhero genre are basically ones that take place in a world parallel to ours (one that is remarkably similar) and in which the laws of physics allow for the development of super powers. That the laws of physics permit the existence of super powers meets the basic definition of a parallel universe—retaining some of the central aspects of reality as we know it, while replacing other, equally central, aspects with fictitious ones.

Despite the superhero genre's limited popularity in Israeli culture (Hareven 52),[3] there are several examples of such narratives in Israeli comics. These works—for example, *Azure Giants* by Ofer Zanzuri or *Profile 107* by Uri Fink, Koren Shadmi, and Michael Netzer—perpetuate both the concept of the social melting pot and the accepted institutional positions regarding the territorial conflict with the Arab world.

Azure Giants, published since 2004, by writer-artist Ofer Zanzuri draws much inspiration from the American superhero genre. Yet, it is characterized by a sober, realistic view of Israeli society and Jewish history in the modern age. The storyline in the series revolves around the struggles of several stereotypical Israeli characters who have to deal with their newfound super powers. These they received as a result of exposure to radiation released into the environment during an accident at Nahal Sorek nuclear research facility.[4] One of the central characters is Professor Ariel Fidelman, AKA Professor Lahat (Hebrew for heat), a nuclear scientist and Holocaust survivor, whose experimental work was one of the principal causes of the radiation's releasing (#0:21; #3:5–7). Another central character is Atzum (Ofer Muklabi). Atzum (Hebrew for gigantic) is the son of Georgian immigrants, who is orphaned from mother and a sole caregiver of his disabled father (#1:1–3; #4: 20–21). The central female character, Hadar (Keren Abutbul), also brings pronounced contemporary Israeli color to the title. The daughter of divorced parents of North African origin, Hadar (Glory in Hebrew) is an average student growing up in meager circumstances. Her mother is an alcoholic and her newly religious (Ba'al Teshuvah) father is a taxi driver who lives separately from them and holds custody over her two younger brothers (#1:5; #4:11–12).

Most of the characters in the series live in the peripheral cities of the coastal plain, such as Ashdod, Ness-Ziona, and Yavne. This allows for a comprehensive examination of the melting pot reality of Israeli society. This setting also represents a significant break from the Yuppie, Tel Aviv-centric atmosphere that dominates contemporary Israeli comics, according to the series creator (O. Zanzuri Public Talk). While the action centers on heroic battles against criminal elements and terrorist groups, the series also deals with various day-to-day social and economic struggles and common teenage anxieties faced by typical Israelis.

The dominant underlying theme of the series is that the national character and very existence of the state of Israel is threatened by both internal-social and external-national threats. For example, while the narrative deals with the Arab-Israeli conflict, it also asks ethical questions about the use of violent and borderline criminal acts as legitimate courses of action in the war on terror (#2:10). When dealing with the struggle against organized crime, various background scenes portray an Israel that seeks to embrace new immigrants by replacing their culture of origin with a new Israeli identity (#1:3–4; #4:8–9; #6:4) and frequent use of nationalist imagery and symbols such as the Israeli flag and characters' naming (e.g., #5:17–19). As a result, the dominant ideas found in the series mirror those of the standard Zionist discourse.

In contrast to the serious tone that characterizes *Azure Giants, Profile 107* by Uri Fink, Koren Shadmi, and Michael Netzer (1998) provides some light comic relief. It tells the story of Lt. Colonel Dan (Bar-On) Baranes, an Israeli superhero serving in the Israeli Defense Forces (IDF), where he acts primarily as a deterrent against external threats to the state. However, his super powers are never brought to bear, since Israel is a signatory to a convention that prohibits the use of super-soldiers in war (41). Moreover, in contrast to his high rank and supposedly elevated position, Bar-On ("super-strong" in Hebrew) is primarily preoccupied with avoiding responsibility, receiving medical exemptions, and being excused from actual operational activity, as though he were the least of the enlisted men on base (8). In the end, when Bar-On is finally required to make use of his super powers, he does so against an Islamic Palestinian super-villain while under the watchful eye of an American supervisor, Liberty, a super-heroine CIA agent (Figure 10.1).

Figure 10.1 Bar-On called to arms. *Profile 107* by Uri Fink, Koren Shadmi, and Michael Netzer (1998).

Note: Word of the terrorist attack and the international treaty in the panel to the right and word of the CIA observer in the middle panel.

Like *Azure Giants*, this story does not question the possibility of individuals who possess super powers nor does it call into question the accepted Israeli attitudes toward national and territorial concerns. These attitudes hold that Israel, the state of the Jewish people, is under a real multidimensional threat from its Arab neighbors, the occupied Palestinian population in the West Bank, and that the western governments and institutions fail to appreciate this situation (46). Moreover, the story hints at the existential threat facing Israel as the Jewish-Israeli population develops attitudes of apathy and lack of concern with national responsibility, and where self-seeking and laziness have become the norm.

In this regard, some might view *Profile 107* as an example of anti-establishment criticism seeking to warn against the trends in the moral development of Israeli society. However, while the title does present a critical discourse regarding internal societal concerns and seeks to present the authors' view of the desirable situation (through negation of the one depicted in the story), in national-territorial matters it is not only lacking in any alternative statements or criticism, it actually identifies and perpetuates the current state of affairs.

As mentioned earlier, the superhero is but one comics genre that employs the setting of a parallel universe. Yet, examples of this narrative type using other genres' settings proved to be most unfruitful. One title, "The mystery of the space children" by author and poet Yizhak Sade (writing under the pseudonym Yariv Amatzia) and illustrated by Elisheva Nadel, which appeared in the newspaper *Ha'aretz Shelanu*[5] in 1962, stands out as the only such example.

Set in the distant future, this classic sci-fi story depicts an alternate Israel that is free from threats by the Arab world and even lives harmoniously alongside it. Readers learn this as the protagonist child and his alien companion arrive at unified Jerusalem, the Israeli capital. This thriving advanced city has succeeded in bridging the conflicts of the present and achieving social and territorial stability. However, the manner in which this state of affairs was brought about is never described, and despite the apparent coexistence in this alternate depiction, it is entirely consistent with every accepted institutional Zionist doctrine as stated in numerous sources from the Declaration of Independence onward. Therefore, it is impossible to view this portrayal as a thought experiment of political, economic, or international alternatives.

As a coda to the discussion of this genre, it is significant to note that in it one finds a clear identification with national Zionist values. In this context, it is necessary to keep in mind that this is the least common genre among contemporary Israeli creators, and in some respects, it is perceived (at least artistically) as the most subversive and least mainstream choice in present-day Israeli reality (Fink 66; Giri Berenstein qtd. in Morag 5). This is also the place to mention that despite their insignificant weight within the corpus of Israeli output, narratives of the near-actuality type fare much better than narratives associated with the distant-actuality type (i.e., non-human reality). The latter are missing entirely from Israeli comics as of this writing. Some would argue that stories in the *Zoo'la* series by Erez Tzadok, which portray anthropomorphic creatures living in a Disneyesque universe, should be counted as belonging at least partially to the distant-actuality genre. However, the anchoring of the story in the national Israeli reality is marginal if not nonexistent.

Alternate reality

Alternate reality occurs when the narrative takes a divergent path from some recognizable historical event or development: for example, Catholic Christianity did not stop the Mongol invasion from Asia and was obliterated by the armies of Genghis Khan. It stands to reason that in such a world many cultures would have developed in unexpected directions, and it would be difficult if not impossible to gauge the state of human culture in the twenty-first century. Conceivably, it is possible that by that stage the human race would already be traveling out to the stars, or conversely, still living in the dark ages. Yet, in any case, the historical split occurs after the human race (and more importantly some of its cultures) has already achieved a level of dominance over other life forms on earth.

In these narratives, too, it is necessary to distinguish between two sub genres: small change—big difference and big change—small difference. It is noteworthy to mention that the definitions of small and large are made on a case-by-case basis for any given story might be made in a non-objective or culturally influenced manner.

The title, *Revolt* by Moshik Gulst, which I will turn to later, develops along lines that suggest a small change—big difference type. In contrast, the works of Dov Zigelman and Giora Rothman in the newspaper *Ha'aretz Shelanu*, most notably "Yoskeh Mayor" (1972), are associated with the big change—small difference type.

"Yoskeh Mayor" was published in serialized form in *Ha'aretz Shelanu*. Initially, Yoskeh, the hero and title character, belonged to the Palmach, and later, with the establishment of the State of Israel he joined the IDF. One of the strengths that made this series so popular was the emphasis the creators placed on maintaining high believability and accuracy, both in historical-narrative terms and also in visual-artistic terms. The decision to maintain this veracity stemmed from a number of reasons. First, there was the creators' desire to impart knowledge to their young readers. Second, the creators understood that many members of the 1948 generation were exposed to these comics, whether as parents of children or by other means, and that inaccuracies in detail would result in complaints by these readers (Dov Zigelman and Giora Rothman in Eshed, "Yoske Mayor: The Israeli Comics as a Historical Epos"). This might even have led to loss of artistic freedom if it were to result in greater oversight from the paper's editors (Rothman, "Meet the Creators").

Still, Zigelman and Rothman allowed themselves to rewrite reality somewhat, mostly by inventing fictional plots that wove together nicely with the factual historical details. In most instances, the plots of the comics revolved around notably influential events such as large military operations and declarations of leaders. The stories portrayed the big picture of these events rather than the minutiae of the battles. Oftentimes historical events, such as terrorist or Fadayoun attacks, were referenced as source material that contextualized the era. However, in a small number of instances the creators allowed themselves some artistic freedom and incorporated Yoskeh's character into minor actions that turned out to be major historical events. One such example is the story of the "Burma road" and Yoskeh's role in it (*Ha'aretz Shelanu* #50-#53).

The Burma Road, which bypassed Latrun garrison that overlooked the approach to Jerusalem, was a trail constructed by the Harel brigade, workers from Solel Boneh (a major construction company at the time), and the army core of engineers. It was used as an alternative route to bring ammunition and supplies to Jerusalem. Interestingly, the circumstances that led to the initial discovery of that trail and the identity of the discoverers remains unclear to this day. It is commonly accepted that three Palmachniks[6] from the Harel brigade discovered it while traveling outward from within the besieged Jerusalem area, and only a few days later, in light of their success in circumventing the blockade, did the brigade commanders attempt to move vehicles along the route.[7]

The murkiness surrounding the identities of the soldiers gave the authors a convenient platform, and by rewriting some of the verified, accepted historical facts, they contrived a tale where it is Yoskeh himself, along with two of his friends, Avi and Yair, who undertakes the journey in an attempt to resolve the problem of the siege of Jerusalem (Rothman and Zigelman, *Ha'aretz Shelanu* #50—August 13, 1973).

The Burma Road was immensely important in Jerusalem's success in withstanding the siege and many researchers have attempted to uncover all the relevant details surrounding the events that led to its construction. However, despite the clear differences between the known historical details and the fictional details outlined in the "Yoskeh Mayor" story, the end result remained the same; the credit that was given to Yoskeh and his friends is in essence a credit that was given to the hero Palmachniks at large. In terms of cultural values, the end result of the story is to commemorate and glorify the fighters of the Palmach in the Jerusalem campaign and the war of independence.

This title, like the comics in the superhero genre, treats the Zionist ethic and ideals in the accepted, institutional manner. The comics of Zigelman and Rothman are intended to be educational and impart values (i.e., the values of Zionist Judaism), therefore, it is unsurprising that the messages they contain, as well as the reality they are based on and to which they return time and time again, are consistent with the common Zionist-Israeli perceptions (Rothman in Eshed, "Yoske Mayor: The Israeli Comics as a Historical Epos;" Rothman, "Meet the Creators").

However, when he wanted to, Rothman was capable of expressing messages that, to some extent, stood in contrast to those of the Zionist establishment. One such example is the title "The ghost from Hirbet-el-Jath," which he published in *Ha'aretz Shelanu* in 1975 without his frequent collaborator Zigelman. In this title, which takes place around the time of the first wave of Jewish immigration to Palestine (around the early 1910s), the Jewish settlers in a southern settlement and their Bedouin neighbors come under attack by a mysterious ghost of an unknown attacker. This leads to each side blaming the other. After investigating the situation, the warden[8] of the Jewish settlement discovers that the mysterious ghost is actually a wealthy Arab landowner who wants to rebuy the land he sold to the Jews but to do so without being labeled a traitor by either side. Although this narrative's point of departure lies in the same values of Zionist land reclamation, its distinction lies in its sober treatment of the problematic relations between Jews and Arabs that were already evident at that early date, as well as its pointing to possible solutions of coexistence that could relieve the tensions between the two groups. All the same, this title, too, cannot break free from the Zionist paradigm and offer an alternative course of action to that of Jewish development and settlement of the land at the expense of its Arab and Bedouin occupants.

Contrary to that, small change—big difference narratives seek to distance themselves from our familiar reality in a particularly explicit manner. It is therefore unsurprising that it is difficult to find many examples of such narratives in Israeli comics, neither contemporary nor in the past, considering Israeli creators' particular attachment to the accepted historical narrative and familiar reality. A single exception to this is the relatively new title, *Revolt*, by Moshik Gulst (2010). *Revolt* follows the premise that the kingdom of Judea overcame its internal divisions and successfully broke free from the Roman Empire during the Great Revolt. Furthermore, the Judean kingdom managed to maintain its independence even against the Arab-Mamluk assault and was left standing to face the crusades that came a thousand years or so after the revolt. While this historical development diverges widely from the course of actual history, the change is not quite so great when it is examined in terms of the culture depicted in the comics and its various sources of influence. In that sense, according to his own testimony, Gulst spent a great deal of thought trying to anticipate the character of such a culture ("Meet the Creators"). For example, the dress styles, forms of worship, and weaponry of the second Judean kingdom are reminiscent of the Persian aesthetic that was prevalent in the area during earlier times. On the other hand, some of the more modern weapons, as well as styles of building and decorative motifs are indicative of early Roman and Byzantine influences (Figure 10.2). All the same, the elements that

Figure 10.2 The king's hall. *Revolt*, by Moshik Gulst (2010). Note the Roman statues, Persian Wings as well as the walls' reminiscing look to the Hasmonean era's '*Beit-Guvrin*' caves system.

stand out the most in jewelry, mosaics, and other artifacts, are those that are associated with the art of the Second Temple and the Hasmoneans.

When examining the narrative, one of the main assumptions Gulst makes is that in order to maintain its independence the second Judean kingdom would have had to be well fortified and maintain a well-trained, professional army in order to guard it from conquest by other powerful kingdoms in the region, which were constantly seeking to gain control over the sea lanes and the spice trade routes. Another assumption is that the divisions between the Sadducees, Pharisees, and other various sects within Judaism would continue to exist and that the differences between them would even increase over time. However, in Gulst's title, the corrupting influences of power led to a situation where even the descendants of the great fanatics who led the rebellion eventually became reprobates who lived off the common people (#1:10). This is evident in, among other things, the relationship between the two brothers Dror and Netzer, commoners who rose to prominence as military commanders, and the corrupt king whom they served. As can be seen, despite the radically divergent historical paths, the actual change is relatively minor in terms of its effect on the way of life and the development of the country's cities and culture. The main question left open is how would this affect the future Israel(-ite) state.

Given Gulst's assumption that Judea withstood the Mamluk onslaughts and the rise of Islam, the picture that emerges is that the eventual alternate solution to contemporary problems would be the non-existence of the Arab nation, at least as we know it today. True, this is not a particularly comforting method for disentanglement from the accepted Zionist-national worldview. However it does stand as an almost singular example of outside the box thinking in a contemporary Israeli comics work.

"What if" narratives

"What if" narratives are those that deal with a specific, concrete issue while raising questions regarding the way in which it could impact contemporary human existence and reality. An example of this would be President Truman deciding not to bomb Hiroshima or Nagasaki. Some view these narratives as a subgroup within the alternate reality type. However, the fundamental difference between the two lies in the tendency of "What if" narratives to stick to a historical narrative or course of events right up to a particular moment when the divergence occurs, as opposed to alternate reality narratives which does not tend to be constrained by any specific historical event.

Many "What if" narratives contain some element of humor since at the outset they are conducted as lighthearted thought experiments by which to examine the meaning of life and existence. A minority of these works is of a contemplative nature and includes a strong social commentary. In the Israeli creative arena, humor comics hold a place of honor and even more so in the "What if" genre. Among the examples of this type are short comics strips such as the "Topsy-Turvy World" that was published in 1938, and "Little Soldier Ktina" published in 1941, both by Leah Goldberg (writer) and Arieh Navon (story and art) which appeared in *Davar Le'yeladim*.[9] These strips, as well as others by this creative team, were devoted to serving the Zionist ideal, as might be expected of any column appearing in the Israeli press during the time of the mandate. So, for example, Ktina helps the British forces defeat the Nazis at the battle of El Alamein by creating a sandstorm using a simple household fan. In all of Goldberg and Navon's stories, there is an obvious devotion to the Zionist cause and to education by combining names and concepts lifted directly from the pages of the newspapers but with an emphasis on an elevated Hebrew style, along with rhyme and meter, as though these strips were being published in the pages of the literary supplement rather than in the children's section.

However, the duo's comics appeared in the form of short strips no longer than four frames each and therefore could not establish a depth of nuance and layers of meaning in the manner of other works previously mentioned. Consequently, they provided their young readers with only a skeletal outline of a plot using the common and accepted stereotypes of the time as "shorthand" to express the creators' ideas. Nonetheless, it was precisely these stereotypes that conveyed the institutional Zionist messages in the most direct and forceful manner: the Americans were rich and soft but not truly "Zionist"; Arabs were stupid, greedy, and violent; while the British were full of self-importance and did not really understand what was going on around them. Only the Zionist Jews, and even more so, the Israeli-born Sabras, were clever and resourceful and capable of resolving predicaments.

In contrast, Matan Kohn's 2002 book, *Angels*, is almost the sole representative of the contemplative type of narrative. This work ask the question: "What if Yizhak Rabin had not been killed by an assassin?" In the title, an angel intervenes in the events of the rally and uses his body to stop the assassin's bullets from hitting the prime minister. The narrative does not end there but rather starts from that point. In the following year the angel keeps preventing other violent events from taking place. He stops a bombing on a Jerusalem bus and in the entrance to the Dizengoff Center in Tel Aviv, intervenes in the Grapes of Wrath operation in Lebanon, and prevents the murder of a teenager.

By itself, this title does not contain many noticeable political or ideological messages. It is a simple exercise in storytelling that expresses a yearning for the cessation of violent and painful acts. However, a critical examination of the plot shows that the author does not conceive a reality different to our familiar one. This is evidenced by the fact that although the Rabin assassination is averted, all the subsequent events that followed it in real life appear in the narrative too. The mysterious angel's intervention did not prevent tragedies from happening, it only blunted their effects. Operation Grapes of Wrath takes place regardless (presumably under the direction of Prime Minister Rabin, rather than of Shimon Peres, as actually happened), the wave of terrorist attacks continued and with it the mounting difficulties in the Israeli-Palestinian peace process and violence continued to run rampant within Israeli society. While some might argue that the title should be classified as a big change—small difference type of narrative, in light of its fidelity in tracking real-life events through their chronological order fundamentally make it a "What if" narrative.

In conclusion, works identified with this narrative type perpetuates the accepted Zionist notions of good (secular, Israeli, Zionist) beating evil (Arab, diasporic, religious-mystic) too. Be it Ktina the soldier or Uri the angel, the essence remains the same and the fictional elements, which in foreign comics have often led to a reexamination through alternative viewpoints, do not have a meaningful impact of that kind in the Israeli corpus.

Zionist messages in Israeli comics: What do they tell us about Israeli society?

I do not presume to provide a full explanation in this article for the phenomenon in some Israeli comics of fixation on Zionist paradigms to the exclusion of other alternative forms of discourse, post- or anti-Zionist, which are becoming more widespread within Israeli society. I would, however, offer my explanation for what this phenomenon means to the wider Israeli society.

If one wishes to accept the suggestion that fictional writing serves as a "sandbox" of sorts where thinkers can play with different ideas and imagine their effect on human society; fictional writing, unbound by political and moral constraints, can lead to the development of new societal insights and their dissemination among a wider audience, which in turn can lead to long-term transformations of values as new ideas migrate from the fringe into the mainstream. This is particularly true when content is being consumed by a younger audience whose perceptions and stances have not yet been fully formed, which for many decades has been the case for comics readers in Israel and the rest of the world.

The failure, or unwillingness, of Israeli comics authors to create narratives with a national, political, or moral alternative to our reality could point to an additional impediment to Israeli society's breaking free from the self-perpetuating cycles of ideological fixation in which it is stuck. The sense that there is no possible substitute for the ideas of Jewish Zionism is what political scientists such as Sami Samooha call the "limits of the Zionist paradigm" (23–24). By its very nature, this perpetual cycle feeds off the behavior of these creators, who in turn create a perception among the public, and so the cause becomes the effect, ad infinitum.

This statement should not be taken as the author taking sides in the ideological debate between the Zionist paradigm and the post- and anti-Zionist paradigms. It is merely intended to shed light on the apparent lack of diversity in voices and opinions regarding political and social reality. It seems reasonable to expect that voicing alternative views could have some positive impact on promoting new solutions to the Israeli-Palestinian conflict and to healing the internal rifts within Israeli society. This receives further support from studies concerning conflict resolution and reconciliation processes, which stress the importance of changing the narrative, or at least acknowledging other possible narratives, as a precondition for reconciliation (Landman 136–137). Some of these studies also highlight the central role popular culture plays in broadcasting and amplifying the familiar narrative and affixing it in the collective mind (Auerbach 109).

The case before us illustrates how in spite of the decline in prominence of the values of the collective and the ascendance of individualistic and pluralistic attitudes within

Israeli society, Jewish-Israeli comics authors continue to create science fiction and fantasy narratives that remain within the confines of the Israeli-Zionist consensus. This is the case not only in these genres specifically, but is true for other Israeli comics genres such as personal memoirs, slice of life comics, and humoristic works (Sandi; Raab 215). As mentioned previously, the reasons for this are self-perpetuating and self-reinforcing. Israeli comics creators, especially the older ones, were raised and educated in a society based upon the values of national Jewish-Israeli Zionism. In their role as creators, many of them feel the need to pass these values on to the next generation (Rothman, "Meet the Creators").

Furthermore, Israeli creators who might wish to depart from traditional Zionist conventions, or to criticize social injustices, are occasionally condemned as belonging to the extreme fringe, outside of the bounds of acceptability (Gulst, "Meet the Creators"). It is possible that artists' fears of various forms of social and economic sanctions lead them to avoid being labeled as fringe, anti-establishment, or subversive. The perceived economic risk entailed in producing material that would run afoul of public tastes could be enough to reduce artists' willingness to go beyond the limits of the consensus and to increase their desire to appeal to the widest possible common denominator.

One of the methods Israeli comics creators have chosen to ensure a minimal level of commercial success and to recoup publishing costs is to avoid discussing issues that are politically controversial. Alon Raab (219) points to Eli Eshed and Uri Fink's book *The Golem* as a fine example of such a decision. Another way is to present criticism in an understated, sophisticated manner that neither throws sand in the public's eyes nor rubs salt in their wounds. This is the method chosen by Ofer Zanzuri in the *Azure Giants* series. Another option available to creators who wish to express criticism but not be targeted as anti-establishmentarian critics is to pick civic, non-political topics to criticize, ones that enjoy wider public acceptance; topics such as fighting corruption and organized crime, such as in the title *Uzi* by Nimrod Reshef.

The state of affairs discussed here leads to the conclusion that in Israeli comics, as in other fields of Israeli commercial entertainment and culture, creators face a certain amount of political-social pressure. Even if this system of pressure is not intentional, institutionalized, or persistent, it is still there and serves first and foremost as further evidence of Israeli society's inability to alter its pattern of thought and behavior. No true change can come in the Israeli-Palestinian conflict, and the internal conflicts of Israeli society, until it is possible to rise above its rigidity and start imagine itself in new circumstances and situations. Let us hope that these changes will come sooner rather than later.

Notes

1   See also Eshed (From Tarzan to Zbeng); Bartana; Duvdevani; Manheim.
2   The most recent example, *Revolt* by Moshik Gulst was published in 2010.
3   See also Eshed (From Tarzan to Zbeng).
4   Nahal Sorek Nuclear Research Facility is a real-life nuclear research facility in the Israeli southern coastal area.

5   *Ha'aretz Shelanu* (*Our Country*) was the weekly children's supplement of the daily newspaper *Ha'aretz*. *Ha'aretz* is a privately owned newspaper, usually affiliated with Liberal, left-wing leaning political agenda. The weekly supplement's publication had been terminated at the early 1980s.

6   Historians, Palmach members, and others have identified them as Arieh Topper, Yair Mondlek, and Shlomo Ben Shalom—but this has never been officially confirmed.

7   See Shamir, 1994

8   The term Warden in this instance stands for the historical term, Shomer (Sentinel or Guard in Hebrew) as demonstrated by the HaShomer movement.

9   *DavarLe'Yeladim* (*Words for Kids*) was the weekly kids' magazine published by the General Federation of Laborers in the Land of Israel (Ha'Histadrut), Israel's biggest workers' union since 1931. In 1985 it united with the two other left-wing leaning kids magazines in Israel—*Ha'aretz Shelanu* and *Mishmar Le'Yeladim* (*Kids on Guard*) to form *Kulanu* (*All of Us*) a magazine that is still published to this day. As a union-owned magazine, it was not only highly socialist in character, but also highly Zionist in nature.

Part Three

Jewish Comics, the Holocaust, and Trauma

The Search: A Graphic Narrative for Beginning to Teach about the Holocaust

Wendy Stallard Flory

Esther Hecht, the main character of *The Search*,[1] has survived the Holocaust in hiding, in the Netherlands, as a child. The book's second page shows her at the Bar Mitzvah of her grandson, Daniel. In the first panel he is reading aloud from the *Torah*, a passage from *Deuteronomy*, 6: 6–7 and his speech balloon gives this verse in Hebrew. Its English translation is included in an inset box as "You shall teach these words to your children and speak of them always." Like so many of the details in this graphic narrative, this specific verse has been very carefully chosen. "These words" from verse 7 refer, most immediately, to the first two commandments given to Moses. Verses 20 to 22 expand the frame of reference:

20. When your child asks you on the morrow, saying, What (mean) the precepts, the laws, and the regulations that YHWH our God has commanded you?

21. Then you are to say to your child:
Serfs were we to Pharaoh in Egypt,
and YHWH took us out of Egypt with a strong hand;
...

24 ... to keep-us-alive, as (is) this day. (883)

This injunction to pass on to the children the story of Pesach is later elaborated in the section of the *Haggadah* on the instruction of the four sons. The four particularized answers to their questions recognize how, in teaching the significance of the Passover story, it is necessary to take into account the different capacities for response of individual children according to their temperaments, aptitudes, and attitudes. As Jews have the religious duty to teach this story to the next generation, so both Jews and Gentiles now have the responsibility to make sure that the story of the *Shoah* is passed on. To have survived the Holocaust as Esther did, in hiding but with the loss of her family, is to have experienced a latter-day Passover but of the most bitter kind. *The Search* is an attempt to pass on the story of the *Shoah* to children of several countries and in a way that will be adaptable to many different degrees of receptiveness.

The Search is a unique graphic narrative in various ways, some of them determined by its subject, some by its intended readership, and some by the collaborative nature of its creation. Drawn by the Dutch artist Eric Heuvel and with text by Lies Schippers and Ruud van der Rol of the Anne Frank House in Amsterdam, it has been created to teach the subject of the Holocaust to students from the ages of thirteen to sixteen. Published initially in Dutch, in 2007, it has now been translated (with accompanying teaching materials) for use in German, Polish, and Hungarian schools. An English version was initially available from the Anne Frank Center in New York and, after October 2009, from Farrar, Straus and Giroux.

Given its subject and its purpose, this project needed to be—and has been—handled with the utmost care. The website of the Anne Frank Center in Amsterdam tells how "historians from the Netherlands and abroad evaluated and advised on the project at all phases of its development, and many teachers and pupils also collaborated in the production of the book." "Before its adoption abroad, *The Search* was tested by over 3,000 students in Germany, Poland, and Hungary."[2] Beginning in March of 2008, the International Center for Education about Auschwitz and the Holocaust, whose offices are in the Auschwitz-Birkenau State Museum, joined a pilot program connected to *The Search*. This involved about 1,000 pupils from all over Poland who worked with the book and, together with their teachers, sent their comments to the Center.

Shoah, Maus, and The Search

As different as the book is in most respects from Claude Lanzmann's documentary film *Shoah*, or Art Spiegelman's *Maus* volumes, it does share with them the ability to open up space for an imaginatively engaged and strongly affective response to some details of the enormity of the Holocaust. Of these three works, it is *Shoah* whose affective impact is the most immediately full. It occurs as the film is being watched for the first time. In the case of *The Search*, the strongest responses will come *after* the book is read, once the student begins to explore the documentary material—such as *Shoah*—that the episodes in *The Search* point toward. This makes the book's title doubly appropriate. While the focus of the story is Esther's search for information about her parents' fate, the purpose of the book's creation is the search of its child readers for knowledge about and insights into the overarching historical catastrophe.

To the end of intensifying the reader's or viewer's affective engagement, there are definite advantages to approaching the historical record of the Holocaust through indirection. Documentary footage or photographs of the camps are an essential part of the record but not the best material to begin with in teaching the subject to children. They can even have a counterproductive effect for the adult viewer in cases where they trigger a voyeuristic or an alienating response. Lanzmann's film is, for me, the preeminent cinematic treatment of the Holocaust, primarily because he has chosen to have events described rather than shown. The camera focuses on those involved who give their testimonies, many years after the events they are recalling, sometimes doing so in the places where the atrocities occurred. These speakers include survivors, perpetrators, bystanders, and, in the case of Jan Karski

(Jan Kozielewski), an intervener and horrified witness of conditions in the Warsaw Ghetto in August 1942 (167–175). As viewers are being told rather than shown, they must participate actively throughout in supplying for themselves the mental images of the scenes being described and in responding emotionally to the intimations of the unspeakable suffering of the victims.

Spiegelman's *Maus* depicts the experience of his parents, Vladek and Anja, both Auschwitz survivors. Several kinds of indirection create distance between this experience and the artist's representations of it, tacitly acknowledging that *Maus* is necessarily a very incomplete rendering of the actuality to which it refers. The choice of the graphic narrative genre obviously has a distancing effect, as does the use of black and white rather than color. Spiegelman also keeps his illustrated version of his parents' Holocaust story at one more remove by beginning and ending each chapter with his interactions with his father in the present. This is the framing story of how Art elicits Vladek's oral account; deals, often impatiently, with his father's foibles; and periodically wrestles with doubts about his right to be representing experiences so devastating and so remote from anything in his own life. Paradoxically, it is the intimately personal nature of this framing story that makes possible Spiegelman's most surprising use of indirection—his decision to draw his Jewish characters with the heads of mice. A further surprise is the discovery of how undistracting the mouse-heads prove to be. The dialogue gives such a detailed sense of the people presented that, although they have the heads of mice, we think of them as human and, specifically, as the author's parents, relatives, and family friends, and acquaintances. As the Jewish characters are the heroes of the book, the reader identifies with them and, seeing them as the norm, barely registers their mouseness. In contrast, the other animal heads—those of the German "cats," Polish "pigs," American "dogs," and French "frogs"—are more obtrusive. Only three photographs of human faces are included. The first volume contains a 1958 photo of Anja and Art (100); *Maus II* has as a frontispiece a photo of Vladek and Anja's first child, Richieu; and, on its third-to-last page, a studio photo of Vladek in Auschwitz uniform, taken after liberation, as a souvenir (134). All three family members are dead by the time that *Maus* was published in 1986. Richieu died when his aunt poisoned him, her children, and herself to save them all from transportation to a death camp. Anja committed suicide twenty-three years after liberation. Vladek died of illness and old age in 1982.

The Search is, of course, a very different kind of Holocaust project from *Shoah* or *Maus*. In comparison to them, it will seem relatively flat to the adult reader and even to those children of thirteen and older who have already made some study of the subject. As its aim is to bring in as many as possible of the particulars of the Holocaust, all in sixty-one pages, it necessarily appears rather rushed or forced. This is because it has been created to be a teaching text. It serves only as a first step toward the strongly affective experiences that come when some of the very wide range of Holocaust specifics that it presents or refers to are explored in depth. As a teaching text it has many strengths. It deals with this painful material very sensitively but also, with a few deliberate exceptions, directly. It is also impressively extensive in its coverage of so many aspects of the Nazi persecution of the Jews of Europe from 1933 to 1945. (It does refer briefly to the murder of the Roma and Sinti and of political prisoners but not of homosexuals, the mentally impaired, or Jehovah's Witnesses.) As it covers so many aspects of the persecution and murder of the Jews, a teacher can use topics that the book addresses only in quick succession, as points of departure for detailed study of the widest possible range of Holocaust materials in libraries, museums, or on the web in written, photographic, filmed, or audio formats. Where the following commentary is descriptive only, rather than analytical, this is to identify the many topics introduced in the course of the story.

The structure and design of *The Search*

Sonia Phalnikar, in a February 1, 2008, article for *Deutsche Welle* about the reception of *The Search*, quotes Maatje Mostart, head of communications at the Anne Frank Center in Amsterdam, as saying that "Teachers have told us that students are surprisingly quiet when reading [*The Search*] in class. Many are really moved by it and get really interested in the subject." Of course, teaching the Holocaust in the Netherlands, with its history of Nazi occupation, is going to be a less fraught undertaking than teaching the subject in Germany. Phalnikar then refers to recent studies that show that "Germans under twenty know exceedingly little about twentieth-century history. While Hitler is recognized by all, only one in three was aware of the meaning of the word, 'Holocaust.' Less than one in ten students could identify Nazi Propaganda Minister Joseph Göbbels." One 16-year-old was quoted as saying on a German TV station: "I think it's about time that schools realized that graphic novels are here to stay and that they can teach a dry subject better than some dumb textbook," but another teenager described comic books as "way uncool," and Phalnikar notes that such "skepticism is shared by others who question whether students, who aren't interested in history anyway, could critically read a Holocaust comic book."

An article by Caroline Lagnado in *The Jewish Week* of July 25, 2005, quotes Maureen McNeil, director of education at the Anne Frank Center USA, who says that the book is "particularly popular ... with teachers who are interested in teaching to a span of educational levels" and also with "students who speak English as a second language, those with learning disabilities, and students who have not yet learned to enjoy reading." The more advanced student might well be encouraged to do as this essay does—consider the book from the point of view of its creators. This is an invitation to reflect on the decisions that the authors made in constructing the book—to think seriously about what is involved in trying to find ways of treating this emotionally overwhelming subject in a graphic narrative of sixty-one pages, intended for children. A particular challenge for the authors has been to include such a range of topics in a coherent narrative, and their inventiveness in doing this has been impressive. Before giving a sense of this by outlining the first part of the story, I will make a few points about Heuvel's artistic choices. His style of drawing in *The Search* is, in part, an homage to the *ligne claire* style of the Belgian cartoonist Hergé (Georges Remi)—for example, in his Tintin stories. This choice is appropriate to the time period of the events that are recounted in the book. It is also possible to see it as a respectfully self-effacing gesture on Heuvel's part—a way of giving the maximum prominence to the book's subject by forgoing an entirely original, signature style, such as Spiegelman's in *Maus*, that would have drawn more attention to the artist (although Spiegelman's different choice is appropriate to his highly personal undertaking of writing about his own father's Holocaust experience).

Heuvel has been very deliberate and inventive in how he uses color in *The Search*. The choice of black-and-white, as in *Maus*—or in Steven Spielberg's *Schindler's List*—works well for an adult reader or viewer. It is fitting for this dark subject. Also, by creating a distancing effect, it is a tacit acknowledgment on the part of these artists of their necessarily imperfect attempts at representing the unrepresentable. (In his unreasonably strong objections to *Schindler's List*, as in a *Village Voice* group debate of March 1994, Spiegelman overlooks the deliberateness of a further distancing strategy of Spielberg's.[3] The decision to let the specific and anomalous case of the outsider, Schindler, determine and constrain the film's focus and scope is a clear signal that the filmmaker is presuming to present no more than an approximation of just one dimension of this inherently unpresentable subject—and that at several removes.) Heuvel's decision to use color rather than black and white makes his book more appealing to children. It both allows him to create additional levels of significance and makes it easier for his student-readers to follow a narrative that is constantly moving back and forth between events of the story's past and its present. Heuvel distinguishes between the story's two time periods by using vivid colors for the scenes from the present and muted colors for scenes from the past. For example, as a girl, Esther Hecht, the story's main character and a Holocaust survivor, is shown in a dress that is dull pink in color, but the Esther of the present, now a grandmother, wears a suit that is bright pink. The different orders of text are distinguished by color also. When characters in the scene depicted are speaking, their speech balloons are white. In the many panels that depict past events that are *showing* the story that Esther is *telling* in the present, her head is drawn in, in one of the top corners of the frame and her words are given in speech-boxes that are bluish gray. The authors occasionally include brief explanatory comments such as "A few weeks later …" or "The arrival at Westerbork …," and these are in beige boxes.

There is one extended "history-book" sequence of almost two pages, and this too is handled very skillfully. It shows how many topics can be conveyed within the constraints of the graphic-narrative genre despite its requirement of maximum economy of presentation. At this point in the book, Esther is retelling for her family the story told to her by Bob Canter, a childhood friend and Auschwitz survivor. (Bob's story forms the book's second half.) We have just been shown how he and his parents were crammed into the boxcar and how some people managed to write brief letters that they threw from the train, some of which were mailed by local people who found them. We are also shown guards robbing the prisoners, taking their money and jewelry at gunpoint. The page ends with a black panel with the words, in white: "They were on their way to Auschwitz, a Nazi death camp in occupied Poland. The reality of what had gone on in Eastern Europe only became clear after the war" (39). Overleaf is the documentary sequence. These two facing pages (40 and 41) include panels illustrating the following: the Wannsee conference, with Hitler, Heydrich, and Eichmann identified; the establishing of the ghettos in "occupied Poland [where] more than 100,000 Jews lived locked away" (40); the German invasion of the Soviet Union; the *Einsatzgruppen* massacres; the location of the death camps on a map; the decision to enforce secrecy about the camps; and a final map showing the train routes to these camps from cities all across Europe. Then Bob's story resumes with a distance shot of the transport and Esther's inset comment that of the 107,000 Jews deported from the Netherlands, only 5,000 survived. The next two pages show scenes of the arrival of the transport at Auschwitz and the selection—the separation of those fit to work from those sent immediately to the gas chambers. These scenes, like several others in the book, are based on well-known archival photographs.

Further contrasting uses of color are very effective also, for example, in the book's endpapers. Immediately following the title page, and on the left page and in grayscale, are the names and images of the seven main characters as they were before the Nazi takeover. These are Esther as a child with her parents, her childhood friend Helena, and Bob and his parents. On the facing page, in full color, are the surviving family members in the present: Esther and her grandson, Daniel; Helena and her grandson, Jeroen; and Bob, who is looking at an album of photos of his present family. On page 60, Heuvel has included two panels in sepia tones to suggest old photographs. They show Esther's parents pushing her in a baby carriage and her mother photographing Esther sitting on her father's knee. On page 9, the present-day Esther is saying "My mother absolutely loved taking pictures." This theme of family photographs provides the ending for the book. After Esther has told Bob's story, she says, "like Bob, I've spent my entire life missing my parents terribly … I have nothing to remind me of them … I can barely remember their faces" (57–58). This jogs Helena's memory and she goes up to the attic to find the album that she managed to salvage as a keepsake from Esther's parents' house, before the Germans emptied it. The back endpapers of *The Search* show two pages of the open album with their sepia photographs of Esther with her grandparents, with her parents, with Helena, and with Bob. There is also one photo of the two families—of Esther and Bob, who survived, together with the four young parents, who did not.

Before *The Search*, Heuvel had already produced the graphic narrative, *A Family Secret*, published in 2003 and widely and successfully used in Dutch schools since then for teaching about the Netherlands during the Second World War. That book ends with Esther, now a grandmother, back again in Amsterdam, from the United States where she lives, to search out more information about the fate of her parents. When she speaks at a public memorial ceremony, Jeroen, Helena's grandson, hears her and goes to tell his grandmother about this. *The Search* picks up directly where *A Family Secret* ends with Jeroen serving as a bridge between the two books. *The Search* begins with him, on his bike, thinking to himself: "I'm glad they asked me to go!" He has been invited to travel with Esther, her son Paul, and her grandson, Daniel, to visit Barend, the son of the man who hid Esther for six months at his farm and paid for this with his life. When Jeroen meets Daniel, the topic of Daniel's recent Bar Mitzvah comes up, allowing information about that ceremony to be presented. Here it is Daniel's head inset in the upper corner of the pictures, explaining the scenes in which he appears, including the one in which he is shown reading his chosen passage from the *Torah* (8).

Esther's story of surviving in hiding

The trip by car to Barend's farm is the occasion for Esther's narration that the reader is seeing unfold in pictures. The decision to make the Hechts a German family that flees to the Netherlands for safety after *Kristallnacht* expands the scope of the narrative. In the car, Esther tells Daniel, Paul, and Jeroen about her childhood, first in Karlsruhe and then in Amsterdam. Then Holland is invaded and, a few days before her parents had planned (like Anne Frank's parents) to go into hiding, they are rounded up while Esther is still at school. Her friend Helena's father is a policeman for the German occupiers and this is part of the "family secret" of *A Family Secret*. Rather than arresting Esther also, however, he relents and gives her the choice of being deported with her parents or going into hiding with Professor Bouwer, a friend of her father's. The professor arranges for her to move from house to house until she is taken in by Barend's father who is already hiding a mother with two children and Jacques, a young teacher. When they are betrayed, Esther sees the German soldiers approaching. While the others are arrested, Jacques tries to escape and is shot, and the distraction allows Esther to run away unobserved. Barend's father is also arrested and dies in Vught concentration camp. In this way, the topic of the dangers of helping to save Jews is highlighted. When Esther is on the run, we are shown one family driving her away when she asks for shelter but another family allowing her to stay until the liberation. She then goes to Amsterdam in search of news about her parents. Her childhood friend Bob, now an Auschwitz survivor, sees her newspaper advertisement asking for any information about her parents and he is able to contact her and tell her that both of them died in the camp. She is so distraught that she blocks out the details he is giving her and he goes away.

Esther ends her story by telling how she emigrated to America, married and had two children and then, feeling the need to find out more about the past, contacted Barend. After the drive back from Barend's farm, Esther says how bitterly she regrets not having listened to all that Bob could have told her and having lost contact with him completely. Then it dawns on her grandson, Daniel, that he can use the Internet to try and trace Bob. His post on a Canter family website is answered by Bob's granddaughter in Israel. Heuvel uses a variant of the old comic-book icon of the "bright idea" light bulb in the frame in which Daniel realizes he can use Google to try and contact Bob (29). When the email response comes, in the middle of the night, Heuvel uses an icon to which the schoolchild reader can readily relate—an envelope with rays and the words, "Bleep! You have mail!" (30). Esther phones Bob and then flies to Israel with her son, Paul, and hears Bob's story in detail. After having spent a week in Israel with Bob, Esther returns and phones Helena to ask when she can come over and tell Helena what she has learned from Bob. This is the lead-in to Bob's story. As Jeroen, Daniel, and Helena listen to Esther transmit Bob's Auschwitz narrative, the reader sees it unfold on the page.

Bob's story of surviving Auschwitz

Bob's story that makes up the second half of the book begins with the day on which his family as well as Esther's parents were rounded up and taken to the Amsterdam

Theater Hall, prior to transport to the Westerbork transit camp and, from there, to Auschwitz. It follows Bob from then until, on the forced march from Auschwitz into Germany, he escapes during a bombing raid and makes contact with American GIs. His story also includes his emigration to Israel and his trip, many years later, with his wife, children, and grandchildren to Auschwitz. Both survivors' stories, Esther's about the early days of the Nazi takeover in Germany and the Netherlands, as seen from the point of view of a fugitive, and Bob's about the later, death-camp period, as told by a prisoner, are very skillfully designed so that they work well as both personal stories and historical accounts. As accounts of the historical specifics of the Holocaust period, they provide a strong incentive for further study. As personal stories, they engage and hold the attention of their primary readership of schoolchildren. Both Esther and Bob have to take complete responsibility for making a very difficult choice about their parents. Their respective situations provide teachers with an excellent opportunity to encourage their students to put themselves in the place of these characters, to identify the competing considerations affecting their choice under these circumstances, and to imagine the emotions involved. Esther's decision to go into hiding rather than joining her parents on the transport may seem to be conveying an opposite message from Bob's decision to stay with his parents. Yet Esther knew that her parents were committed to avoiding deportation. They had first tried, unsuccessfully, to escape to England. As, at the time of her parents' arrest, the arrangements for going into hiding had already been made, Esther knew that she would be following her parents' wishes by choosing to hide. Bob, on the other hand, was rounded up with his somewhat older parents, and his mother was already having trouble coping physically with the situation. For him to escape at that point seems to him to be abandoning them when they need him. Neither set of parents survives Auschwitz, yet Esther's father and Bob were able to help each other in the camp. When Mr. Hecht's strength finally gave out on the forced march from Auschwitz so that he was shot, Bob was still trying to help him. Mr. Hecht's support of Bob had a positive outcome in that it contributed to Bob's survival.

The children of the Holocaust

The authors' decision to have these two main child characters survive, against overwhelming odds, is deliberate and effective, given the primary readers of the book and how it is intended to engage them. The topic of the children of the Holocaust is addressed further, elsewhere in *The Search*, and in ways that make clear how atypical Esther's and Ben's survival was. The selection upon arrival at Auschwitz is shown with the women and children sent to the left. One panel shows a Kanada Kommando prisoner telling Ben to claim to be sixteen and the next shows Esther, in the present, explaining to her grandson: "Anyone younger was gassed immediately" (42). Inset in this episode is a set of three panels on the situation of the children of the Auschwitz Commandant, Rudolf Höss. The middle one, telling how he "lived with his wife and five children right next to the camp," is a brightly painted scene from a birthday party of one of his three daughters who is receiving a present from the son of another officer. The final panel shows Höss saying to the boy's father, the next day: "Kids grow up fast." The color here is predominantly gray; they are walking beside the cattle cars of a transport; and, as a finishing touch to the bitter irony of this sequence, the officer is saying: "Let's have a drink, shall we?" (43). Under such circumstances, alcohol is most valuable for its anaesthetizing properties, and this theme has been obliquely introduced (together with the theme of choice) in the three panels on the *Einsatzgruppen* massacres on page 40. The middle panel shows a family group right before the machine-gunning (Figure 11.1). A young boy and girl are shown in close-up with their parents and grandfather. The final panel has the rubric: "In just over a year, 1.5 million Jewish men, women and children were shot dead." (The dead are not shown, only the pile of the clothing left when they were forced to undress.) This panel shows three soldiers with three different reactions. One says: "Yesterday 3,000 Jews, today twice as many. We can be proud!" An officer is saying: "Dirty job. But we've got our orders." The soldier in the foreground is thinking to himself: "All these women and children … I can't stomach it. I need to get out of here!" (40). His response is a link to information first supplied in detail by Christopher Browning in *Ordinary Men: Reserve Police Battalion 101 and the Final Solution in Poland,* who found that, even though these men would not face serious repercussions were they to ask to be assigned away from this work, most stayed with their units, largely because of peer pressure. The distressed soldier in *The Search* is shown as on the point of drinking from an army-issue bottle when he is interrupted by his impulse to request reassignment. Even the detail of the bottle is allusive. Does it contain water or, rather, the alcohol that that the men of these killing units were given

Figure 11.1 Reprinted from *The Search.* 19 © 2009 by Erich Heuvel, Ruud van der Rol, Lies Schippers, used with permission of Farrar Straus Giroux Books for Young Readers.

in large amounts in an attempt to deaden the psychological trauma of murdering at close range men, women and, hardest of all, children? If it contains alcohol (and it is a different shape from a typical water-canteen), then his hesitation to drink would be a further telling detail.

A child is made the focus of the sequence depicting the fate of the women and children at Auschwitz, after the selection. The first of the nine panels on page 45 shows a close-up of Bob's mother and behind her, another woman with a child of six or seven who is saying to the doll tucked under her coat: "Don't be afraid …" Next is a distance view of the line of women, walking toward the gas chambers with a crematorium chimney, with flames, behind. Here a guard is telling them that they must take a shower. Then, in a closer frame, the women are being told to remember the number of the hook when they hang up their clothing. Next is an undressing scene in which the child is laying down the doll and saying "see you later …" Two more panels show the closing of the gas chamber from the outside and then the soldiers on the roof, dropping in the Zyklon-B crystals. For these two panels, Esther's head is inset, explaining: "They thought it was a shower," and "But poison gas pellets were dropped through the ceiling. In 15 minutes everyone was dead." Here, as in the *Einsatzgruppe* massacre panel, the dead are not pictured, only their discarded clothes. We see a guard keeping an eye on the Kanada Kommando prisoners who are searching this clothing for valuables. In the next picture his foot is shown kicking the child's doll (Figure 11.2). In the final panel on page 45 we are back in the present, and Esther is saying: "My mother was gassed and her body burned in the crematorium …"

Judith's mother's choice and the rescue of Dutch children

The guard's kicking of the doll is drawn according to traditional comic-book convention. It is a close-up of a violent blow and the impact is represented by the traditional splatter-shape with two red stars. This panel is, however, particularly effective because of its simultaneous levels of significance. Most immediately, the wider significances of the SS boot are very evident and also the way in which the doll represents obliquely the fate not just of the girl to whom she belongs but of all the child-victims of the Holocaust. The comic-book representation of the blow is a well-conceived deliberate touch that makes the doll seem like a person. The doll also serves as a reminder of a previous scene involving a doll. Early in Bob's story, when, in the Dutch Theater Hall with his parents, he is trying to sleep, he overhears one of the staff attempting to persuade the parents of a five-month-old to leave her behind in the hope that she can be got to safety. This woman is in touch with the Resistance and they are sometimes able to smuggle children out of the day nursery across from the Hall. She tells the mother: "When you're put on the transport we'll give you a doll … so the count is correct" (35). Three subsequent panels show a girl and a boy being smuggled out from the nursery, and Esther's text tells that around 600 children were saved in this way. The child's name, Judith, is given, but the mother remains unnamed, and we do not learn what she finally decides at this agonizing moment when she must choose whether or not to give away her infant to a stranger. The last words we hear from her

Figure 11.2 Reprinted from *The Search*. 19 © 2009 by Erich Heuvel, Ruud van der Rol, Lies Schippers, used with permission of Farrar Straus Giroux Books for Young Readers.

are "I don't know if I can do this" (35). To recall this scene while looking at the doll in the changing room (45) allows us to consider how some of the dolls left behind with the clothing in the undressing rooms would have been carried there by women who *did* leave their infants behind, some of whom would have been saved.

Some opinions of *The Search* are bound to be negative. Some people will be automatically dismissive, others more thoughtful in their reservations. The more we can think of the book as a teaching tool, the more we are likely to focus on its constructive potential rather than on how its simplifications fail to do justice to its subject. For thirteen- to sixteen-year-olds, whatever their degree of interest or attention span, every page of the book provides provocations engaging enough to be points of departure for venturing into a study of this daunting subject. People with various kinds of qualification to assess the value of this project have had positive reactions. Annette Insdorf, Columbia University Professor *Emerita*, prize-winning filmmaker, and author of the widely acclaimed book *Indelible Shadows: Film and the Holocaust* (2002), is particularly well-qualified. In the *Village Voice* debate about *Schindler's List*, Insdorf defends it against Art Spiegelman's scathing attack on both Spielberg and his film, in part by recalling her mother's reaction when they watched the film together. Insdorf's mother Cecile, a professor of literature and cinema at Hunter College, survived Płaszów, Auschwitz, and Bergen-Belsen. In the Płaszów camp, a key setting in Spielberg's film, she had been able to get the names of three relatives onto the list— although not her own name. Noting that her mother was a far from aesthetically naïve viewer, having "seen just about every Holocaust film and [being] conversant with the imagery as well as the conventions," Insdorf says of her mother that "After seeing *Schindler's List* she was grateful. She was grateful that the story was told by a popular filmmaker who could get the audience into the theater. She was happy that it was going to be commemorated" (29). For Lagnado's article on *The Search*, Insdorf says that her "gut feeling was positive" and that "As evidenced by Art Spiegelman's *Maus*, even a medium like the comic strip can introduce readers—especially younger ones—to aspects of the Holocaust which they might ignore or resist in more traditional formats." This recalls the four sons (or four children) of the *Haggadah* and how each is to be taught about Pesach according to the child's ability to be receptive. And then there is the fifth child, sometimes added to the traditional four to represent the children of the *Shoah* who did not survive to ask their Seder question. Lagnado's article ends with the response to *The Search* of Rosa Sternlicht from Forest Hills, Queens. She, like Esther, was born in Germany and raised in Holland, but she survived the Holocaust by making an illegal aliyah to Israel. Before reading *The Search*, at the age of 84, her question was: "What does a comic book have to do with the Holocaust?" But her final verdict was positive. It is "very, very well written [and] it tells the story exactly like it was."

Notes

1   *The Search*, original title *De Zoektocht*, was published in English in 2007 by the Anne Frank House in cooperation with the Jewish Historical Museum, Amsterdam, the Netherlands. The 2009 Farrar, Straus and Giroux edition includes some minor textual

changes. *The Search* is a sequel to Heuvel's *De Ontdekking* [The Discovery] translated
as *A Family Secret*.

2 Website of the Anne Frank House and Museum, Amsterdam, the Netherlands. http://
   www.annefrank.org. Web. September 17, 2009.

3 "*Schindler's List*: Myth, Movie, and Memory: A Debate," *The Village Voice*, March 29,
   1994, pp. 24–31. J. Hoberman moderated the discussion. The participants were James
   Young, Annette Insdorf, Ken Jacobs, Art Spiegelman, Wanda Bershen, Gertrud Koch,
   and Richard Goldstein. Spiegelman's comment, "The main dream image the movie
   evokes for me is an image of 6 million emaciated Oscar award statuettes hovering like
   angels in the sky, all wearing striped uniforms" (29), is revealing about the spirit of
   his critique.

Picturing "The Holiest Thing": Joe Kubert's Children of the Warsaw Ghetto

Samantha Baskind

The most fearful sight is that of freezing children. Little children with bare feet, bare knees, and torn clothing, stand dumbly in the street weeping. Tonight, the 14th, I heard a tot of three or four yammering. The child will probably be found frozen to death tomorrow morning, a few hours off. Early October, when the first snows fell, some seventy children were found frozen to death on the steps of ruined houses. Frozen children are becoming a general phenomenon ... Children's bodies and crying serve as a persistent backdrop. People cover the dead bodies of frozen children with the handsome posters designed for Children's Month, bearing the legend, "Our Children, Our Children Must Live—A Child Is the Holiest Thing."

—Emanuel Ringelblum, *Notes From the Warsaw Ghetto,*
November 14, 1941 (233–234)

Some of the most heartrending stories entwined in the history of the Warsaw Ghetto concern children. First, Judenrat (Jewish Council) head Adam Czerniakow killed himself by swallowing a cyanide pill on July 23, 1942, the day after the SS asked him to compile a list of 6,000 people, including children, to be transported to Treblinka; at that time Czerniakow realized his stance of working with the Nazis was futile and the childrens' extermination was imminent. Allegedly, he left a note referring to this calamity: "The SS wants me to kill children with my own hands. There is no other way out and I must die" (qtd. in Gutman 136). Soon thereafter, yet another tragic event occurred, underlined by the untenable choice of Janusz Korczak (born Henryk Goldszmidt), a highly esteemed author, educator, and pediatrician whose dedication to the orphans in his care in the ghetto was so unwavering that he accompanied two hundred of them from Warsaw to Treblinka on August 5, 1942. There he perished with his beloved children, even when the Nazis offered him a chance to be free. Knowing, of course, the children's final destination, Korczak still dressed them in their Shabbat best and led them, all singing in an orderly line, to a freight car by telling them that they were going on a picnic. Looking at the larger, numbing picture—the plight of innocent, bewildered, and terrified Jewish youth during the Holocaust in Warsaw as well as throughout Europe, and their torture and then brutal extinction, which thus obliterates the continuation of future generations—resonates deeply. By war's end, the death of an estimated one-and-a-half million Jewish children effectively wiped out innumerable future Jewish generations.

This essay examines representations of children from the Warsaw Ghetto in American comics, focusing especially on work by the legendary Joe Kubert, aiming to illuminate how and why some comics highlighted this material over that which has typically been more popular in literature, film, and fine art: the valorous actions of the armed band of Jewish militants who staged the now iconic Warsaw Ghetto Uprising. In short, notwithstanding their modest numbers and meager weapons, a number of Jews in the Warsaw Ghetto valiantly held off the German army for nearly four weeks beginning on Passover eve, April 19, 1943. Since that time the Warsaw Ghetto, and especially the Uprising, have captured the American imagination. To be sure, one of the most repeated, discussed, and remembered moments from the Holocaust, this seminal affair has since provided a potent symbol of Jewish life, suffering, and heroism during the Nazi Genocide. Yet, as the following pages will demonstrate, comic imagery and stories about the ghetto hold some surprises and are more nuanced than typically understood.

Joe Kubert, of Hawkman and Sgt. Rock fame and the founder of The Joe Kubert School of Cartoon and Graphic Art, most consistently addressed the Warsaw Ghetto in his work. An early project to engage this subject is the disturbing cover of the *Unknown Soldier* #247 (January 1981). A DC Comics character that Kubert co-created in 1966, the Unknown Soldier initially appeared in *Sgt. Rock* stories until he received his own series in 1970. The Unknown Soldier suffered such devastating injuries to his face by a grenade explosion during the initial years of the Second World War that heavy white bandages or masks must cover him from the neck up. This motif allows the soldier to assume a disguised superhero persona that includes latex masks and make-up when his missions as a secret US agent call for such. Primarily occurring during the Second World War, the Unknown Soldier's assignments include suppressing Nazis across borders, including saving General Eisenhower from an assassination attempt during the Battle of the Bulge (*Star-Spangled War Stories* #163, "Kill the General!," June–July 1972), and in the end killing Adolf Hitler while making it appear as if he took the cowardly way out by committing suicide (*The Unknown Soldier* #268, "A Farewell to War," October 1982). It is no surprise, then, that at some point the Unknown Soldier would make his way into the Warsaw Ghetto.[1]

Just a year before the first edition of the series ended (it has since been reprised twice), the Unknown Soldier infiltrated the Warsaw Ghetto in the aforementioned issue, dubbed "A Season in Hell," detailing Nazi violence toward Polish Jews. To the left of the title headline for the story, on the first page of the issue, the Unknown Soldier's quest is laid out (emphasis in original): "In every war there is a man who *no one knows*, yet who is known by *everyone*! He wears a *thousand faces*—fights countless battles—and *proves* that one man, in the right place at the right time, *can* make difference!" With just his bandaged head depicted, the soldier surveys the ghetto immediately under this headline, a witness to Nazi cruelty; the full-page image shows a Nazi slamming the butt of his gun into a Jewish pushcart peddler's head with nearby SS men smiling and mocking the "Polish schweine." The Unknown Soldier responds to this viciousness, beckoning the reader: "Come with me now on my most harrowing adventure, as I fight my greatest battle." The weight given by the Unknown Soldier to his forthcoming mission as his "greatest battle" implies the significance of the Second World War and especially life and the events in the Warsaw Ghetto for the writers and artists of *The Unknown Soldier*, in addition to the implications of the ghetto in American culture. Naturally, readers would anticipate a story about the Uprising, but instead a tale of a young child's miraculous escape unfolds with the Resistance as merely the backdrop.

Part one of the story introduces common archetypes: Nazi savagery; trucks filled with heaps of dead bodies; a bent, wizened Jew wearing a kepah; the younger generation prepared to fight; and escape through the sewers. A twist occurs when the Unknown Soldier (first disguised as Stanislaus the peddler and then as Abraham the Rabbi) is entrusted to save a learned professor's granddaughter named Tovah. Translated as "good" in Hebrew, Tovah's name is obviously meant to combat metaphorically the Nazi characterization of Jews as bad—and Tovah's kindness and strength of character reinforces that notion (the Resistance fighters later call her "one of God's angels"). In Part two, as more of a side note rather than the focus of the issue, readers encounter fighters who militantly and resolutely assert that the following day they will rise against their oppressors: "We stand up like men … or die! Tomorrow!" This material—expected although not explored in depth because the story centers around Tovah rather than the Uprising—adds a precise historical bent to the issue, typical of Unknown Soldier comics. Part three, titled "Only the dead can hope," chronicles the Unknown Soldier's transport of Tovah out of the ghetto. This section recalls earlier, mocking words from a Nazi soldier as he smashed in the peddler's head with his gun on the initial full-page panel: "Ja! Only the dead leave the ghetto! Ha! Ha! Hah!"[2] The Unknown Soldier remembers this taunt and realizes the only way to escape is for him and the girl to hide in a truck full of corpses that will soon exit the ghetto, pretending they too are dead. Before they can execute this plan, the Unknown Soldier scales a building with Tovah on his back and he coaxes her into the truck by explaining that "as horrible as it may seem, what the S.S. promises is more terrible." The brave girl replies: "Yes, solider." In a small panel, their faces peer out of the SS truck, replete with a swastika underneath their diminutive forms. This pivotal scene receives much larger treatment as the cover of the issue.

Indeed, Kubert's cover imparts a much more explicit rendering of the frightening episode than that inside the comic. The cover conveys the harrowing moment in the story when the Unknown Soldier transports Tovah out of the ghetto in a wagon piled high with dead, skeletal bodies. The soldier places his hand over Tovah's mouth to keep her from shouting out in terror; her tiny head peaks out of the side of the wagon, blue eyes wide with fear. One of Tovah's hands clasp the Soldier's arm, the other hangs out of the wagon. A reader cannot help but notice how little her fingers are and by extension how sad that this sweet, diminutive girl has suffered so profoundly. Tovah and the Unknown Soldier's ruddy, peachy flesh contrasts with the rotting, brownish-gray toned, loose-limbed corpses haphazardly surrounding them, albeit the pair's placement at the front of the picture, noticeably in the viewer's space, brings them into focus as much as the hues in which they are rendered.

Although Kubert portrays just one appalling incident, the cover really brings home the kinds of horror to which children were exposed. In the many diaries kept chronicling life in the Warsaw Ghetto, children and adults share excruciating particulars. Emanuel Ringelblum's famous journal supplies the epigraph to this essay, which offered some gruesome observations. Two other frequently read diaries from the ghetto—that of Janusz Korczak and Mary Berg—afford similar commentary. In a few simple sentences, Korczak relays the direness of the children's existence and their resilience, or at least forced indifference: "A dead boy is lying on the sidewalk. Nearby three boys are fixing something with some rope. At a certain moment they glanced at the body and moved away a few steps, not interrupting their game" (43).[3] Berg's famous diary, smuggled out of Warsaw by Berg herself, recounts the devastation and distressing conditions in the ghetto—the bitter cold, the loss of possessions, the mass graves, and the despair of parents cradling their dead children. Started by Berg, a child herself, at the age of fifteen, the diary testifies to a young person's fear and reveals her mature and sensitive reactions. On July 10, 1941, Berg wrote: "I am full of dire forebodings. During the last few nights, I have had terrible nightmares. I saw Warsaw drowning in blood; together with my sisters and my parents, I walked over prostrate corpses. I wanted to flee, but could not, and awoke in a cold sweat, terrified and exhausted" (73).[4] Visuals conveying such troubling circumstances and elements of the war appear in Kubert's imagery but the Unknown Soldier's exploit ends on an optimistic and unexpectedly emotional note.

After exiting the ghetto, with Tovah standing by his side, the Soldier poignantly reads the Kaddish, the ancient Jewish prayer for the dead, as Jewish militants prepare to stage their Uprising. The final two pages submit one more fearful scene in which the Nazis threaten Tovah's life again just outside the ghetto walls. Happily, the pair escapes and share an affecting conversation. With their backs to the reader and holding hands, the Unknown Soldier and Tovah walk toward a new life. Tovah says: "You mean, soldier, I can have all I want to eat now …?!? Grandfather would be so happy!" To which the soldier responds: "Yes, little Tovah! You're safe now … Forever!" Tovah's strength, amid her escape and the loss of her grandfather, surely murdered in the ghetto, along with her simple need—enough to eat—purposefully tugs at the heartstrings.

Award-winning comic writer Bob Haney, who worked with Kubert for years, conceived the story with his longtime partner, with whom he shared an interest in Jewish topics and a predilection for the plight of children. The pair also collaborated on "Totentanz" (*Star-Spangled War Stories* #158, August–September 1971), the German word for "Dance of Death" and the name of the death camp at the center of the story. This early issue depicts the Unknown Soldier entering a concentration camp, disguised as a Jew, to rescue an underground leader who provided crucial aid to Jewish refugees. The cover features inmates, including three children at front—the most vividly colored—staring despairingly out of a barbed wire fence.

"A Season in Hell" does end hopefully with little Tovah's survival but it then circles back, briefly, to the defiant Jews left in the ghetto. An epilogue written underneath the final panel extols the epic actions of the Jewish Resistance while noting their grim end: "The Warsaw Ghetto was ultimately doomed to failure—but the story of those valiant people and their glorious courage is immortal!" Even with these final words about the

Resistance, what makes this comic so remarkable is that an avenging fantasy could be so easily drawn and shared here. Yet the story concentrates on one life, a life that will help ensure future Jewish survival. It is worth noting that here the child, Tovah, is saved, unlike Yossel, the child-hero of Kubert's most sustained excursion into the story of the Warsaw Ghetto, described later.

Little known is Kubert's work for a monthly children's magazine, *The Moshiach Times*, published by the Chabad. After persistent requests from Rabbi David Shalom Pape, editor of the Lubavitcher magazine *Moshiach Times*, in 1984 Kubert initiated the series, *The Adventures of Yaakov and Isaac*, which relayed two-page stories in comic book form about two brothers studying at a yeshiva.[5] The stories, engaging biblical material, biographies of Chabad leaders, and Jewish history, provide life lessons rooted in Judaism for readers, often by looking to the past to make modern Jewish life relevant.[6] As Kubert put it, he aimed "to compose and illustrate stories that would be of interest to contemporary readers … Stories that would evoke thought and emotion today, based on concepts that have existed for thousands of years" (Kubert, *Adventures* 4). In a compilation of these comics published in 2004, Kubert's thoughtful reflections precede each story, which include "The Importance of Torah" (1985) addressing the magnitude of faith; "The Jewish Heart" (1985), delineating the significance of helping fellow Jews; and "An Act of Resistance" (1985), relaying the Uprising to demonstrate dedication to, and the significance of learning Torah no matter how exacting the circumstances. Throughout the series, Kubert manages to overcome the limitations of a two-page spread to convey details and ideas, often by adapting lessons learned in his earlier secular comics to appeal to Chabad youth. For example, in "The Jewish Heart," a French soldier crouches in the trenches and then engages in hand-to-hand combat akin to Kubert's many war comics. Too, in "An Act of Kindness" (1984) the influence of Kubert's prehistoric character Tor manifests with renderings of a jungle-like atmosphere, employed to share a message about kindness to animals.

"An Act of Resistance" begins by superimposing a rectangular horizontal box containing Yaakov and Isaac's modern-day existence atop a vertical, full-page illustration delineating the much darker and bleaker life of oppressed Jews in the Warsaw Ghetto (Figure 12.1). Yaakov tells his younger brother Isaac, playing baseball, that the time has come to return to yeshiva. Having fun, Isaac indicates his disappointment that the game will end. In a second box, laid atop both the first modern-day exchange and covering part of the ghetto story, Yaakov explains that the pair must go to school because learning Torah is "VERY IMPORTANT," penned in bold letters, and then to make his point he asks Isaac if he knows about the Warsaw Ghetto. Yaakov proceeds to share with Isaac what happened there during the War, first describing Jewish oppression, accompanied by a bird's-eye view of ghetto Jews herded by Nazis aiming guns at their backs. This haunting yet easily read scene communicates many details, including Jews wearing yellow badges to indicate their Jewishness, a Nazi commander with a swastika around his bicep, and a truck portentously looming in the background with a group of nameless Jews filing into it, soon to be transported to a death camp.

The first panel on the second page, made up of nine total panels about the ghetto with one superimposed of contemporary life, supplies the only image chronicling

Figure 12.1 Joe Kubert, "An Act of Resistance," 1985. Reproduced with permission of the Joe Kubert Estate.

Nazi fear tactics. To emphasize both Jewish fear and Nazi brutality, the stark white background highlights the ominous shadows cast by the SS oppressors standing before a terrified trio of Jews, a family about to be transported out the ghetto and who cast

Figure 12.1 (*Continued*)

the longest, most haunting, shadow.[7] Similarly, a shadowing motif was used very effectively by Bernice Eisenstein in her graphic memoir, *I Was a Child of Holocaust Survivors* (2006), which relays the author's second-generation experience. The book's cover vividly demonstrates the extent to which her parents' ordeal informs her identity. Against a blood-red background, a black-and-white rendering of Eisenstein as a child does not cast a shadow; instead, the dark figures of Eisenstein's parents metaphorically provide the shadows behind her tiny body.

In "An Act of Resistance," Kubert adeptly juxtaposes two very different times, indicated especially through divergent color schemes—the sun shines in the contemporary scenes, and a gray-green pallor of war and cold pervades the Warsaw Ghetto—and then, of course, also the subject matter. Just as expertly, Kubert shares the story of Jewish resistance, deportation, and study in only two pages. Opening remarks by Kubert provide his perspective on the Warsaw Ghetto Uprising, which, he asserts,

> must and will be told over and over again. How a small vestige of young Jewish survivors fought side by side against the Nazi horde despite the knowledge that their deaths were inevitable ... But, another important aspect of this story is the continued faith displayed under extraordinary circumstances ... People held in the Warsaw Ghetto knew that the Nazis intended to kill them all, men, women and children. No one would survive. Yet, they continued to teach the children Torah. Above all else, parents believed the children must learn Torah. How else would the heritage survive? And the heritage does survive ... As the character in the story expressed, " ... learning Torah is our supreme act of resistance." (*Adventures* 21)

Note Kubert's focus on children in his commentary, emphasizing the lengths to which adults went to teach children and to keep Judaism alive for them even in the bleakest of circumstances. A long panel in the middle of page two portrays three children and three adults covertly studying "[i]n a dark corner of the ghetto, in an old crumbling building." Significantly, the main child studying is named Yussele, Joseph Kubert's name in Yiddish and the title—spelled just a bit differently—of his haunting full-length graphic novel about a child in the Holocaust.

Yossel: April 19, 1943 (2003) depicts an alternate universe, a very personal *Sliding Doors*-like story in which Kubert imagines himself not as an immigrant in Brooklyn but rather as a child remaining in Poland during the Second World War.[8] Kubert's tale revolves around Yossel's life if the artist's family had not immigrated to the United States in 1926 when he was two months old. Highly researched, Kubert explored his "'what-if' thoughts ... [in] a work of fiction, based on a nightmare that was a fact" (*Yossel*, unpaged introduction).[9] Deeply effected by the Holocaust, Kubert reflects that "if my parents had not come to America, we would have been caught in that maelstrom, sucked in and pulled down with the millions of others who were lost ... The experience [of researching and making the graphic novel] was very personal, a little scary, and sort of cleansing. It was something I felt I had to do."[10]

Yossel begins with the title character, at age sixteen, recounting the actions of the Uprising, noting that the partisans "have lived a hundred years of hell in the Warsaw Ghetto" (4). Each of the introductory pages features a collage of sketchy pencil images rendered in black-and-white as if Yossel himself made them, often hurriedly as the events occurred. Kubert's choice to delineate the story only in pencil, forgoing ink entirely, provides a perfect confluence of form following function; not only does the colorlessness evoke the immediacy of the moment but also the cold, emotional darkness of the time in addition to the frequently severe, gloomy climate. Moreover, the collaged images are not constrained by panels but rather sprawl, undefined, across the book's pages.

For Yossel, drawing affords an escape from a life of fear and desperation. On several occasions Yossel notes that he "could create [his] own world" (7) and "drawing seemed to cleanse my mind, drive my fears into little corners and crevices" (13). By page eight, Yossel flashes back to early Nazis tyranny, recalling Kristallnacht, school restrictions, and the rape of Jewish property. His memories include ones that very well could have been those of his alter ego, Joe Kubert, considering the fictional Yossel describes an early, failed attempt by the family to immigrate to the United States when his mother was pregnant with him—a true story that happened to the Kubert family. Yossel also records his origins as an artist and interest in recreating the prehistoric world and American comic strips. The young Pole draws heroes and superheroes but unlike the Golem-like Superman that saves the Warsaw Ghetto inhabitants in *Superman: The Man of Steel* #82 (August 1998, drawn by Jon Bogdanove and co-written by Bogdanove and Louise Simonson), in the end Yossel is doomed. Yet, those same superheroes keep Yossel alive for a longer period than many other Warsaw Jews—including his parents and sister who were killed at Auschwitz—because Nazis capitalize on his talent for their own enjoyment. Shockingly, though, Kubert does kill his surrogate in the book's final pages.

With the Resistance in full effect, in part initiated by Yossel's brave actions, the young artist recounts being hit by a bullet with pressure akin to his rabbi "jabbing me with his finger to make a point in learning Torah" (118). After Yossel is shot, the final three pages depict his death. Kubert allots a full page to Yossel's loss of consciousness (Figure 12.2). He draws Yossel's head five times, lolling backward with his eyes losing focus as he slowly fades away. The final page of the book does not show a prostrate or bloody Yossel—but instead a full page piece of sketch paper. Poignantly, it is not covered with Yossel's drawings; it is empty, devoid of imagery, just as Yossel is now devoid of breath.[11]

Clearly geared for mature teenage readers as well as adults, *Yossel* subverts strategies typically found in books and movies about the Holocaust aimed for a younger audience. As Lawrence Baron observes in relation to Holocaust films for children, such representations follow a "classic disruption-resolution narrative structure" (174).[12] By this Baron means that while a disruption occurs in Holocaust cinema geared toward children—Nazis oppress, restrict, and murder Jews—these films still end on a relatively happy note. In relation to the aforementioned *Unknown Soldier* comic book, even though the reader encounters difficult circumstances, Tovah survives.[13] Movies commonly follow this type of pattern, with endings including rescue scenarios and also positioning the film to convey the events as a test of faith—and that faith does endure. Kubert's *Yossel*, though, pictures a very different and surprising ending. Why?

Kubert's unique position as a Polish immigrant who could easily have been a victim of Nazi genocide certainly helps to account for his personal and sustained foray into Holocaust subjects. That he was able to imagine, if not explicitly draw, his surrogate dead does confound but then again, how can anything surrounding the Nazi's gruesome killing program really make sense? Certainly, much has been written about the children of Holocaust survivors and such experiences have been explored,

Figure 12.2 Joe Kubert, *Yossel: April 19, 1943*, 2003. Reproduced with permission of the Joe Kubert Estate.

for instance, in Eisenstein's aforementioned *I Was a Child of Holocaust Survivors* and in Art Spiegelman's seminal *Maus* (1986, 1991), a graphic novel that became one of the most distinguished artworks to address the Holocaust and also triggered interest in graphic narratives on Jewish themes.[14] Interspersed with his father Vladek Spiegelman's experiences in Polish ghettos and camps are present-day images of him narrating the story to his son along with Art Spiegelman's thoughts about creating the graphic narrative. Spiegelman's attempt to share his father's tale and make sense of the legacy of the story for his own life, a generation removed from the tragedy, exemplifies the concept of postmemory. According to Marianne Hirsch, who originally developed the principle while reading *Maus*, postmemory "characterizes the experience of those who grew up dominated by narratives that preceded their birth, whose own belated stories are evacuated by the stories of the previous generation shaped by traumatic events that can be neither understood nor recreated" (23). As a child who just barely escaped Nazi tyranny, Kubert occupies a unique position—not a Holocaust survivor nor a second-generation witness but still closely attuned to the War's disastrous consequences. As such, akin to Spiegelman, the trauma and fate of the Jewish people has become an enduring concern for Kubert, who has taken the burden of the Holocaust on as his own.

Because of space limitations I have confined this article on children in Warsaw Ghetto-themed comics to those made by Joe Kubert. Worthy of mention, however, are two other important instances in comics about children and the Warsaw Ghetto. Trina Robbins's understated and moving *Zog Nit Keyn Mol (The Partisans Song)* (1985) presents a black-and-white two-page intergenerational story in which a teenage granddaughter prepares to go to a demonstration to stand up for what is right. She gets ready in the company of her immigrant grandmother who, it is implied, taught her such values and to that end the granddaughter carries on a legacy of Jewish resilience and also embodies the continuation of the Jewish people. The Warsaw Ghetto Partisan's Song underscores the short story as it unfolds, and when the grandmother waves goodbye, the reader sees a concentration camp tattoo etched into the elderly woman's forearm. Mentioned cursorily above, *Superman: The Man of Steel* #82, an historical retelling of the good versus evil paradigm often found in traditional superhero comics, sends Clark Kent/Superman and Lois Lane back to the Warsaw Ghetto. After the reader is confronted by numerous atrocities, the story ends with the kind of "disruption-resolution narrative structure" that *Yossel* eschews. To be sure, in the final frame, Superman, with Lois Lane at his side, marches out of the ghetto with dozens of dazed Jews behind him. Superman himself cradles a sleeping, rescued child in his arms.

Over the years, in history and the arts, the Warsaw Ghetto has metamorphosed into an emblem of the War akin to Auschwitz. The Ghetto, though, provides and incites stories beyond suffering, and as such offers artists malleable material for their work. In comics, the ideal of the muscular Jew who boldly withstood the Nazis during the Resistance, to subvert the common trope that Jews went to the gas chambers like lambs to slaughter, did not take precedence as it did in literature, film, and more traditional fine art.[15] Take for example Leon Uris's *Mila 18* (1961), which appropriated the Uprising after the fact as an icon of Jewish pride. Anchored by the passionate Jewish hero Andrei Androfski who mobilizes the Resistance, Uris tells a tale based on the actual establishment and ultimate liquidation of the Warsaw Ghetto—and of course the Resistance. As the dust jacket announces: "The hero of *Mila 18*, however, is the Jewish people as represented by this handful of doomed men and women. It was fortitude and heroism like theirs that led to the creation of the state of Israel and the fulfillment of a two-thousand-year destiny. It was a proud moment in the history of Jews." Similarly, films capitalize on the Resistance and the tough Jew persona. Jon Avnet's nearly three-hour NBC miniseries *Uprising* (2001) concentrates on empowered Jews, and Claude Lanzmann's award-winning nine-and-a-half-hour documentary *Shoah* (1985) conspicuously ends with an interview with one of the few survivors of the Resistance following hours of interviews detailing Jewish victimization.

The extermination of children, the next generation, provided a major focus of the Nazi plan to remove Jews from the face of the earth. Most of those children that lived—either because of the Kindertransport, in hiding as Gentiles, or by luck—were orphans who suffered unfathomable emotional trauma after the War. Nevertheless, their unlikely survival provided a much-needed legacy of hope for the Jewish people. Symbols of innocence and redemption, children no doubt provided hope for regeneration. All of the comics described in this essay exploit this notion with the exception of Kubert's anomalous *Yossel*. There, it seems, we have an artist struggling to come to terms with his existence by virtue of his family's felicitous immigration prior to the rise of Nazism. Not a child survivor, Yossel instead becomes a model of sacrifice, a child hero—an active, valorous Jew—who helps set into motion the Resistance, a moment that provided its own sign of hope to both oppressed European Jews caught in the "maelstrom," to use Kubert's words, and concerned American Jews across the ocean. Looking at Yossel's actions and reactions in the longest sustained comic story about a child in the Holocaust described here, a reader can see that despite his demise, for Kubert and the other artists and writers noted in this essay, a child, indeed, is the holiest thing.

Notes

1   The first thirty-eight stories featuring the Unknown Soldier in the *Star-Spangled War Stories* (#151–190, June 1970–June 1975), before the character received his own title, can be found collected in Kubert, *Showcase Presents*.
2   This fact, "only the dead leave the ghetto," indicates the depth of research the makers of the comic must have done; Chaim Kaplan's Warsaw Ghetto diary includes a very similar passage from October 9, 1941: "No one enters or leaves the overcrowded ghetto ... Only the Jewish dead are the exceptions" (266).
3   Like so many figures from the ghetto, Korszak also produced a diary, although only chronicling a short period, May to August 1942, four days before he went willingly to Treblinka death camp with the children.
4   For a compilation of excerpts from children's diaries see Holliday, *Children in the Holocaust and World War II: Their Secret Diaries*.
5   Of interest, Rabbi Pape's first visit to the Kubert's New Jersey home helped initiate the artist's renewed interest in Judaism. Kubert recalls that when Pape and his entourage arrived they brought mezuzahs and hung them. Author's Introduction

(*Adventures* 4). Subsequently, the Rabbi and Kubert regularly discussed different story possibilities and their meanings, thereby also providing lessons about Judaism for the artist as well as his young Chabad readers.

6   The stories were later collected in Kubert, *The Adventures of Yaakov and Isaac*. Al Jaffe of *Mad* magazine fame has contributed a comic adventurer named Shpy, replete with various gadgets to assist him in maintaining Jewish traditions and values, to the *Moshiach Times* since May 1984. *Mad* artist Dave Berg also made comics for the Jewish periodical before his death in 2002.

7   An earlier comic in the Yaakov and Isaac series, "Into the Shadows" (1984) employs the Holocaust to convey a message about pride in one's Jewish heritage even though it differs from the mainstream and, consequently, danger may ensure. Here Kubert also treads delicately, eschewing much graphic material, although one panel portrays Jews in concentration camp barracks (the first panel about the war provides a bird's-eye view of fearful Jews horded by Nazis similar to that found in "An Act of Resistance"). All scenes from the War are rendered in black-and-white, contrasting sharply with color used for the present day.

8   For an extended discussion of *Yossel*, paying particular attention to the author's choice to render his illustrations in pencil rather than ink, explaining how this technique works on a number of levels, see Prager, "The Holocaust without Ink."

9   Schelly's *Man of Rock: A Biography of Joe Kubert* provides many details about Kubert's life and work, mentioning, at times, Kubert's interest in Jewish themes.

10   Kubert, *Yossel*, unpaged introduction.

11   In short, there are other important points made in *Yossel* especially, for example, about faith, but space does not permit elaboration. Miriam Katin's personal, first-hand account of her experience with her mother as the pair faked identities and left their hometown of Budapest after Nazis occupied the city, *We Are on Our Own* (2006), also adopts pseudonyms and addresses the young protagonist's struggle with faith and God. Understandably shaken as a young child on the run amid atrocity, Katin's alter ego—named Lisa in the book—aches for a solid connection to, and belief in, God. Like Kubert's "Into the Shadows" (see footnote 7), this compelling dilemma, with some exceptions, juxtaposes color for scenes in the present day with black-and-white pencil for panels describing Lisa's experience in Europe.

12   For more on this structure and children's films see Wojcik-Andrews, *Children's Films*.

13   An excellent example of disruption-resolution in a children's picture book can be found in *Child of the Warsaw Ghetto* (1995), wherein author David Adler and artist Karen Ritz chronicle the life and resiliency of Froim Baum, one of seven children and a true-life survivor who shared his story with the author. Baum lived in Korczak's orphanage both outside and inside the ghetto when his mother could no longer provide for him after his father died. Told in muted tones with some underscores of color to convey the despondency of Baum's situation, and briefly describing the Uprising, the book ends with Baum's survival; Baum survived when Dachau was liberated by American soldiers and ultimately reunited with his two surviving brothers in 1947. Earlier Adler and Ritz collaborated on two other picture books about the children of the Holocaust: *Hilde and Eli: Children of the Holocaust* (1994) and *A Picture Book of Anne Frank* (1993).

14   On *Maus* see, for example, Geis, ed., *Considering Maus*. On Jewish graphic novels, see Baskind and Omer-Sherman, eds., *The Jewish Graphic Novel*. A special issue of

Shofar—on which this current book is partly based—titled "Jewish Comics" and edited by Derek Royal, focuses on this matter as well.

15   In his second graphic novel with a Jewish theme, *Jew Gangster*, Kubert portrayed muscular Jews through the lens of the Jewish mobster. Drawn in a distinctive film noir visual style with more traditional frames than that found in Yossel's sketches sprawling across pages, several of the characters in *Jew Gangster* actively participate in the perpetuation of the "tough Jew" stereotype. Not only do they perform brutal acts, but the toughest of them, Monk, is literally depicted as physically (if not morally) superior; in one scene Monk wears a "wife beater" and has a five o'clock shadow, preternaturally square jaw, and bulging muscles. A fight scene at the end capitalizes on the artist's experience drawing superheroes (Batman) and war comics like *The Unknown Soldier* and *Sgt. Rock*, among others. Neil Kleid's and Jake Allen's *Brownsville*, also rendered in a noir style, similarly takes up the subject of Jewish gangsters, in this case a true story of "Good Jewish Boys" who became "The Most Dangerous Men in America," as the two halves of the book are divided and titled. Allen attended the Joe Kubert School of Cartoon and Graphic Arts for two years.

Trauma in Gaza: The Israeli-Palestinian Conflict through the Eyes of the Graphic Novelist

Ellen Rosner Feig

For a while, Israel and Palestine were engaged in a peaceful co-existence, albeit a tenuous one. That all changed on June 12, 2014, when Israeli teenagers—Naftali Fraenkel, Gilad Shaer, and Eyal Yifrach—were kidnapped as they hitchhiked to their homes (*Times*). This event ended any peace in the area when the Israeli Defense Forces (IDF) moved into the West Bank in an attempt to arrest those involved. When the boys were found dead, Prime Minister Benjamin Netanyahu identified the killers as members of Hamas, the current (and controversial) political party in Gaza. By August 21, 2014, Israeli and Palestinian officials had agreed to at least four major ceasefires with all of them broken by one of the parties (*Times*). This is not the first time the world has seen an escalation of this conflict due to the murder of civilians.

In March 2012, ABC News highlighted the murder of five Israeli settlers while sleeping in their West Bank home. Days later, in retaliation, the Israeli government bombed militant groups within the Gaza Strip even though there was no indication that a Palestinian was responsible for the initial attack. The Palestinian reaction to the bombing was renewed use of missiles to hit major Israeli towns eerily familiar to the situation the Israelis and Palestinians find themselves engaged in now, in 2014. Such attacks serve as reminders of the age-old conflict between these groups; a conflict over land, over political power, and over history defined by others. Israelis, a majority of whom are Jews, live with the specter of the Holocaust over their shoulders. They are a people who have been victimized, and they continue to see themselves as victims who must be prepared to fight the bully at any provocation. Palestinians are a people who once stood as proud landowners but now stand, shoulder to shoulder, in the densest place on earth without a home to call their own, without an identity. The stories of these two warring factions are rarely told objectively. In fact, recent and ongoing mergers within the global mass media has created less diverse opinion within the news organizations; the "value of reporting is determined by how valuable a country is to the economic and political global superpowers and mass media moguls like those in America" (Scanlon 4). One could easily discern that due to the importance of America's relationship with Israel, the news (at least those organizations in the west) showcases only the Israeli side of any issue—a life lived in constant fear of random violence. As Joe Sacco argues in his work, the world rarely sees the Palestinian side of the conflict. Rather, they are portrayed as terrorists who act without context, who kill without reason. How can one tell the story of the silent in a way that allows the viewer/reader to see the multitude of perspective? How can one use alternative forms of storytelling to bring a conflict alive to a viewer/ reader? How can one create "alternative discourse of both international conflict and journalistic practices?" (4).

Using image and text to relate a specific event, to freeze a moment, or to confront a traumatic experience, graphic novels allow the reader to produce meaning as they move through the work. By deliberately placing images and text in a defined sequence, the graphic novelist creates a sense of time moving, a sense of transformation and change. For Will Eisner, this "juxtaposition of unrelated images or conflicting images and words convey mood or tone" in a way that standard novels do not (Eisner 1985). He goes on: "The art then [of the graphic novel] is that of deploying images and words, each in exquisitely balanced proportion, within the limitations of the medium and in the face of the still unresolved ambivalence of the audience toward it" (Eisner 171). Accordingly, the graphic novel can be considered an excellent medium in which to explore complicated, difficult issues including those surrounding the Israeli-Palestinian conflict.

Graphic novelists like Sacco and *Waltz with Bashir* author and filmmaker, Ari Folman, have created a new form of journalism: "comic journalism, a blend of the comic form of visual storytelling and the rhetorical aims of new journalism" (Eisner 4). Graphic novels focusing on the Israeli-Palestinian conflict tend to apply this "blend" to the work while incorporating narrative storytelling to create a hybrid of non-fiction and fiction. The reader is left to determine what constitutes truth and what constitutes fiction. Throughout these works, characters use various tools to detach from the conflict around them (a type of psychic numbing): they are promiscuous, moving from bed to bed without emotion; they live day to day on the edge with a seeming lack of concern for the opinion of others; they are hardened to the facts and unable to remember their past; and they close their ears and eyes unwilling to hear yet another horrendous story or witness another traumatic experience. While the narratives in which we meet these complicated individuals are contemporary, the characters are nonetheless defined by their reaction to the past, including the Holocaust, and the present, the Palestinian conflict. The graphic novelist is both a visual and a narrative witness to the moral, political, and historical issues that surround these lands and their citizens. They are witnesses who keep their eyes open to the trauma in Gaza.

This chapter will review recent graphic novels, written by Jews, Israelis, and non-Israelis that focus on the experience of those in either Israel or the occupied territories of the West Bank and/or Gaza. By reviewing the work of artists such as Joe Sacco, Rutu Modan, and Ari Folman, one may gain a better understanding of perspective, thereby acting as a more objective witness to the events, the conflict, and the price of such.

Jewish Americans

Many of the recent graphic novels focusing on the Israeli-Palestinian conflict have been written by Jewish Americans, particularly those who visit Israel through a program called Birthright. Birthright allows every young Jew, anywhere outside of Israel, to travel there for a two-week period during which they travel through the country visiting important landmarks and meeting young Israelis. The program has been very successful as many of its participants return to Israel to make "aliyah," or the homecoming trip to Eretz Yisrael.

In *How to Understand Israel in 60 Days or Less* (2010), Sarah Glidden relates her actual journey through Israel. Her trip is an attempt to understand, through the eyes of a skeptic, the context of the conflict going on in Israel. As she says goodbye to her Arab boyfriend she states: "Okay Jamil, I'm ready to go there and discover the truth behind this whole mess once and for all. It'll be crystal clear by the time I come back!" (Glidden 6). This will not be the case for Glidden as she embarks on her birthright trip (an Israeli paid trip for young Jews) with Israeli experts in an attempt to discern the truth versus the propaganda.

Sarah finds herself surprised at how "plain" Israel looks until she comes to the wall and questions its significance. Gil, the guide, begins his explanation of the fence with a neutral, and rather unbiased, account of why it exists. However, soon enough, his tone changes and he relates: "So the fence definitely causes problems, but the Palestinians take these day to day issues and turn them into very harsh propaganda" (25). As she and her group tour the Golan Heights, they are brought to an IMAX-type theater called "Golan Magic," where they are shown a film that delivers the Israeli point of view concerning the territory complete with a "ghostly Yitzhak Rabin" floating over a visual of the area stating that any withdrawal would compromise Israeli security (40). When the group moves to Kinneret and visits the original kibbutz, Deganya, Sarah explores the dilemma she finds herself in with Nadan, a young man on her tour:

> I'm Jewish so that means I'm supposed to support Israel no matter what, right? But according to a lot of people any support for the Palestinians means that you don't support Israel. At the same time, when it comes to politics, I'm left-wing and progressive, and if you're progressive, you're supposed to be anti-Israel ... any sympathy with Israel means that you don't support the Palestinians, so see? I'm stuck! (77)

She visits Independence Hall and hears a speech by a young female tour guide who explains the creation of the country. The speaker, after delivering the historical portion, states: "Everyone thinks that Israelis are so tough. But you don't get used to terrorism, guys. We get into our cars in the morning and we turn on the radio to hear what kind of song is playing. You know, they don't play a happy song if there has been an attack" (98). This, and seeing the youth of the soldiers, creates anxiety in Sarah; she thought she knew that Israel was bad, had done horrible things to the Palestinians, and yet she questions her own reestablished beliefs. Her transformation continues as she meets members of the Bereaved Family Forum in Jerusalem, a group made up of Arabs, Palestinians, and

Israelis who have lost a loved one due to the violence. Maha, a young Arab woman, tells the story of her brother Fadi's death at the hands of an Israeli. She begs Sarah's birthright group: "We ask only one thing of you and that is not to be pro-Israel or pro-Palestine, but to be pro-peace and when you go back to your country explain to your friends about what we do here and help them be pro-peace, too" (152). By the time her journey is over, Sarah realizes that the conflict is not cut and dry, that the Israel she experienced was not the Israel she imagined.

In *Jobnik* (2008), Miriam Libicki, an American, relates her experience serving in the IDF as a non-combat soldier (or "jobnik"). Through simplistic black-and-white drawings in linear form, Libicki delivers an autobiographical look at her job as a secretary in the infirmary section of an IDF base. Depressed that she has not been chosen to serve in the actual army (Figure 13.1), her anxiety is heightened by the confusion around her. She simply has no clue what any of her superiors want with the exception of one clearly defined job: to place "Hamas" (the Israeli code word for secret documents) in a fire chamber and to dispose of the ashes afterward. The visuals of a plump, disheveled Miriam versus the well-groomed upper echelon of the IDF showcase the fear of our narrator within this land of constant civil unrest (Figure 13.2)

When Ariel Sharon's visit to Temple Mount triggers confrontations with Fatah youth gathered to protect the site—thirty Israeli policemen and four Palestinians were injured—Miriam finds herself in the middle of the chaos that is present-day Israel. As she celebrates Jewish New Year with her sister, Naomi, in Jerusalem, violence erupts (Libicki 48). Soldiers, including the lowly Miriam, are told they are at particular risk for harm: "I don't need to tell you the kind of danger we all face right now. Our tanks are preparing to mobilize at any moment and even on leave, you as soldiers make very tempting targets" (48). To deny her walking target status, she attempts to continue on with life's tasks including having a meaningless sexual relationship with Shahar, an Israeli soldier, who can't understand Miriam's need to call and check on his safety (50). Miriam handles her fear through sexual promiscuity, something that seems to run rampant among the soldiers. This consistent need to be held, to be loved, to feel safe in the arms of another is a form of numbing; she simply cannot handle the violence around her or the potential for death and so she engages in casual sex as a means of detachment.

Without forethought or intent, Miriam inevitably takes on the viewpoint of her Israeli colleagues as she experiences detachment and disdain for the plight of the Palestinians. As she sits reading the newspaper at breakfast, she contemplates: "The terror attacks and the horrible stories and pictures from the Palestinian side have been so constant in the last few weeks that they fade into the background. I hear how many killed, I am sad for a second, then I go numb again. On the news they call it 'the current situation' or just 'the situation'" (52). Once she recognizes that violence is part of her life and becomes immune to it, her transformation to true Israeli citizen is complete (63).

After the brass tells the soldiers that the IDF will no longer simply react but will actually "initiate actions against the Palestinian gunmen," Miriam decides it is time to take a leave of absence and return home to New York (75). Before she leaves, she is given instructions to never identify herself as Israeli soldier, to not participate in Israeli-themed events, and to display no Israeli items (115). Being an Israeli soldier

Figure 13.1 *Jobnik* by Miriam Libicki with following: Illustration 1. Courtesy of Miriam Libicki, 2012.

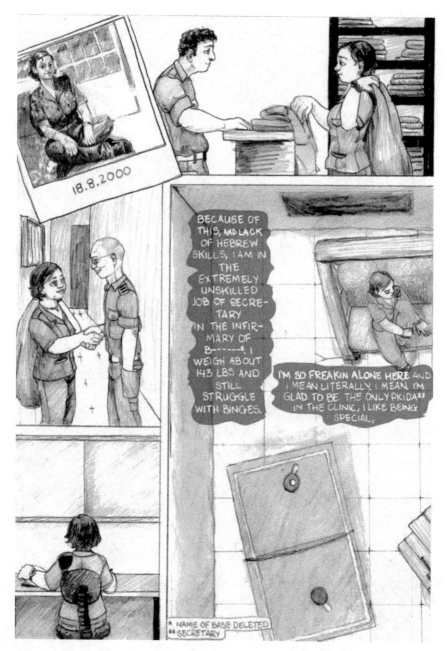

Figure 13.2 *Jobnik* by Miriam Libicki with following: Illustration 2. Pages 14–15; Courtesy of Miriam Libicki, 2012.

means living with an identity crisis: who are you, and how does the world perceive you? Are you a colonizer who pushes paper across her desk? Or are you a patriot who has volunteered to serve?

The Israeli-Palestinian perspective

While Libicki and Glidden are American with a unique perspective on the conflict, what is the perspective of those who live with the violence, with the fear, with the anger, day in and day out? One of the most well-known graphic novels to be created by an Israeli, *Waltz with Bashir* (2009), is a visual wonder with images akin to landscape paintings in black/gray scale and muted colors. According to the creators, "*Waltz with Bashir* has a frame/tale construction; the current-day episodes are largely indicated by white margins and the flashback events by black margins as well as sepia tints" (Folman, Foreward). Boaz, our narrator and protagonist, relates a recurring dream which references his experience as an IDF soldier in Lebanon. Part of a team that searched for Palestinians, Boaz was told to shoot the dogs of the village first, a warm-up for the eventual shooting of men. Twenty years later, he continues to struggle with dreams of this experience in the Sabra and Shatila refugee camps and is unable to define reality versus fiction (Folman 24). He has forgotten the Lebanese war and his role in it. When he visits his friend Carmi, someone who served with him in the IDF, Carmi responds that the "massacre's not in my system" (27). This response symbolizes a society that refuses to recognize their actions concerning Palestinians, a reaction, or denial, that is remarkable in that it emanates from a people who have experienced hate and annihilation on an enormous scope.

As Boaz leaves Carmi, his memory returns: "So I find myself going back the way we came. Me, who in my whole life has hardly seen a drop of blood, let alone an open wound, suddenly I'm commanding an APC full of injured soldiers and dead men, looking for a bright light" (31). The reader is taken back in time to the event: men hanging out on the beach where there had previously been fighting, as if it was any other day, unaware of the war around them, swimming, smoking, and having fun. These visuals change to those of Israeli soldiers being attacked by a rocket launched by a young Palestinian boy. Although his friends tell him he was there on the beach, Boaz has forgotten the event as a means of coping with the terror (57).

Unable to understand his memory loss, Boaz visits Professor Zehava Solomon, an expert on combat trauma, in an attempt to understand how he has forgotten so much of his experience. Solomon explains it is a "dissociative event," where someone is in a situation but feels like they are not part of it (58). Much like Libicki uses sex to forget the terror around her, to dissociate, Boaz uses his memory loss as an excuse. Solomon illuminates this dissociation with the example of a photographer who enters Beirut and finds a stable of horses killed. This sight makes him snap, finally unable to handle the conflict around him. Solomon relates the photographer's statement: "War is bad enough, the things people do to each other ... But what had these lovely horses done, what sin had they committed, that they had to suffer this way?" (Folman 60).

It is here that the novel moves back in time to the story from which the dream emanates. On leave, Boaz is amazed that life continues around him, but soon he is called back to duty in Beirut (71). When he arrives, he walks through the airport as if in a dream, believing he could easily get on an international flight out of the area. He awakes from his repose and realizes that the airport is destroyed, the planes bombed by shells. As he moves down the main roadway in Beirut, snipers shoot at him as civilians stand on their balconies watching in silence (83) His comrade, Frenkel, moves into the street and dances as the snipers shoot above him, "a waltz among their bullets" (83).

Boaz enrages his friends who swear they do not know what he is remembering. Ori, a friend who served with him, believes that his hallucinations come from a memory of Auschwitz and tells him: "Your only way out is to learn what really happened in Sabra and Shatila. Talk to people, find out how it happened, who was where. Get the details. They might lead you to remember where you were and how you're connected to it" (95). These images appear to be visually aglow, brilliantly filled with color, while those of the massacre are in shades of burnt yellow (amber), brown/black, and whitish, and filled with dirt and fog of war. The graphics of the novel move to a place of horror as if seen through the lens of a binocular; the reader/viewer is shown an image of Phalangists (who served side-by-side with Israelis) shooting people lined against a wall. Boaz clearly remembers being at the massacre and standing in the circle of soldiers watching and sending up flares so Phalangists could kill by light: "Against your will, you were cast in the role of Nazi. It's not that you weren't there, you were. You fired the flares. But you didn't carry out the massacre" (107). The Jew, a member of a race annihilated by the Nazis, has now become the mass murderer. The final pages of the novel transform from graphic images into actual photographic images of the massacre. There is no text, no dialogue, only silence so we, the reader, may recognize the tragedy for what it is.

Tiny text appears in script under small black line drawings that seem to be without boundary in the work of brother–sister team Galit and Gilad Seliktar in *Farm 54* (2011). Based upon their own experience growing up on a communal farm in Israel, the Seliktars relate the uncertainty faced by young children in a country that is perpetually in conflict. From the very first page of the novel, the authors push the reader to discomfort when they relate how the narrator is so engaged in flirting with a young man that she fails to see her brother, Amnon, the baby of the family, drown in the pool. This death serves as a metaphor for the lives of Israelis, evidenced when the father calls the narrator and her boyfriend "murderers" (Seliktar 30). What the father fails to realize is that he will soon be called upon to murder when he leaves the family to serve in the army and his first experience includes storming Arab villages while insuring that the men (Arab and Israeli) don't touch Arab women. Explaining this experience, the father relates how the Arabs are "willing participants in their destruction," moving items from their homes without argument. It is this experience, the uncertainty of war, the fear of the group that is captured by the Seliktars (30).

Not all works by Israeli graphic novelists directly reference the Israeli-Palestinian conflict; many use normal activities, emotions, and lifestyles as metaphorical allusions, as indirect statements on the world they live in. Actus Comics, one of the largest comic book cooperatives in Israel, published a multi authored work titled *How to Love* in

2007. These emotional stories, told through the eyes of Israeli graphic novelists, include Mira Friedmann's "Independence Day," a story of the celebration of Yom Ha'atzmaut, Israel's independence day. In Friedmann's Jerusalem, the city is divided down the middle much like a sheet that divides the bedroom of two warring siblings. As one walks through the streets and alleyways, one must always be aware of the route taken (or not taken); the sound of gunshots ringing out aid in plotting one's route (Actus Comics 50). In the midst of celebration, a young Israeli girl decides to leave and unwittingly ends up in Arab territory. The visuals create a sense of fear in the reader: will our young heroine be captured? Will she be tortured? Will she be killed? Playing on our emotions, and turning the stereotype of Arab as terrorist on its head, the young girl is treated cordially by an Arab man, and she is brought to the local police station so that she can return home. Even as she sits at the station, her thoughts lead her to wonder what will occur. Ultimately, she is turned over to the United Nations and released to her family. A metaphor for the conflict, upon her return she is met with media who immediately identify her as yet another victim of the Palestinian "terrorist." Her story, a hopeful one where she is helped and saved by the "dreaded Palestinian," will never be told to Israelis; rather, the never-ending story of hatred and "the other" will be the one aired on the evening news.

Modan's *Exit Wounds* (2010) is one of the most critically acclaimed Israeli graphic novels in the last ten years. Using the traditional clean-lines reminiscent of the work of Belgian cartoonist Hergé in *The Adventures of Tintin*, Modan relates the story of Koby Franco, a young Israeli taxi driver in search for the truth behind the disappearance of his father, Gabriel. Numi, a female soldier and ex-lover of Gabriel, believes his father died in a Hadera suicide bombing. "One of the ... bodies was so badly burned that they still don't know who it was," Numi relates to Koby, advising him that she saw the scarf she made for Gabriel on television and is sure it is his body (Modan 38). At its heart, the story is a mystery—a journey to discover the identity of the victim of the bombing—but it must also be considered a search for the identity of young Israelis in a world of conflict and uncertainty.

Numi knows a side of Gabriel that Koby never saw, and it angers him; there is resentment that fills the space between them (79). What makes matters more tense is that no one who was at the scene of the bombing remembers seeing Gabriel. Eventually, they find Atara Dayan, another of Gabriel's girlfriends, who was waiting for him at the bus station. She tells them of her secret affair with Gabriel and how she waited for him, but he never showed; after the bombing, she left the hospital so no one would find out she was there. Numi is enraged and soon finds herself in the arms of Koby. Their sex is passionless, wrought with tension and leading Numi to sarcastically state: "Like father, like son" (139).

As the story proceeds, it is clear that the unidentified body was that of another man. When Koby receives a large check from the sale of Gabriel's apartment, he becomes determined to find his father without the assistance of Numi. He eventually discovers that his father is living in an Orthodox neighborhood with a new wife. Koby goes to the location and waits hours for his father to return, but he never does. This recognition of who his father has become, or always was, leads Koby to return to Numi and beg her to be with him. In doing so, he searches for some form of redemption.

When interviewed by Joe Sacco, Rutu Modan expressed the thought behind the work: "Reality provides wonderful materials. In fact, it is much more extreme and peculiar than anything I could imagine. On the other hand, I never stick to reality; it is just a starting point for the story. The problem with reality is that it is too chaotic. Too coincidental. Art is supposed to make some order in this chaos we call life." For an Israeli, it is normal for a person to die in a suicide bombing. It is not out of the ordinary for a body to remain unidentified, and it is comforting to lie in the arms of someone you barely know in order to retain some semblance of humanity. "Modan's visual style is laconic, evocative at times of Daniel Clowes; faces are deliberately rendered in a minimalistic fashion, and textures barely shaded. Sometimes this works; other times, it makes it hard to get a read on the characters" (Modan 2). His is a reflection of the reality of a society split in two: them versus us leads to an inevitable detachment. One cannot care too deeply for another as that other may not exist tomorrow. The fragility of life becomes the reality of life.

The Palestinian perspective in *Palestine* and *Footnotes in Gaza*

In *Palestine* (2001), Joe Sacco's graphic novel on his experiences in the West Bank and Gaza Strip, he delivers a first-person chronological narrative of the area from December 1991 to January 1992. The book was controversial from its initial publication in 2001, with many reading the work as antagonistic toward Israel. Sacco's follow up, *Footnotes in Gaza* (2009), furthered his critique. In December of 2009, the *Los Angeles Times* wrote: "The knock, of course, is that Sacco is in with the very people about whom he's reporting, which colors his perspective in unsettling ways. That's true, in one sense, but the take-away is more important than any bias, and regardless, his sympathies are not so easily categorized. Yes, he is on the side of the colonized over the colonizers" (Weiland 2).

In order to write and draw *Palestine*, Sacco lived among Palestinians for a period of two months in an attempt to experience their lives, their disillusion, and their view of Israelis. He gives both voice and visual narrative to a forgotten people. A series of vignettes of Palestinian life in gray scale images of Arabs, offset with faceless images of Israeli soldiers, the work showcases the harsh life of those living in the occupied territory and consistently questions why the Jews, who have survived genocide, treat the Palestinians in such an abhorrent way. There is a pervading sense of a parallel universe (much like in Modan's work): on one side of the wall "traffic, couples in love, falafel-to-go, tourists in jogging suits licking stamps for postcards ... And over the wall behind closed doors: other things—people strapped to chairs, sleep deprivation, the smell of piss" (Sacco, *Palestine* 102).

In one section of *Palestine* titled "Blind Date," Sacco begins to question the media representation of the Palestinian as a terrorist who kills randomly. Initially, Sacco cannot bypass what he has been told by the media, and he cannot connect to Palestinians. However, once he establishes a human connection, his view changes: "The real-life adaptation of all those affidavits I've been reading! The flesh and blood stuff!" (*Palestine* 10). Much as Jews equal Israel in Sacco's view, Palestinians equal the Gaza

Strip and the West Bank. In other words, land defines these groups. Visuals, including Hebron settlers as gun-toting vigilantes determined to protect their settlements even if faced with killing another; a visit to a Nablus hospital where Palestinians suffer without adequate medical care; a trip to a UN Relief and Works Agency school in Balata that has no electricity, heat, or indoor plumbing, attack the reader. These showcase the characters' sense of fear, hopelessness, and the dream of leaving that pervades the occupied territories (28).

Sacco relates, in the chapter titled "Remind Me," the historical context to the current situation from his view in Balata, the biggest refugee camp in the West Bank. Sacco seems to lose his journalistic objectivity as he relates the beliefs of those he interviews, opinions that Israelis have ignored the events of 1948 when Ben-Gurion made it clear that Palestinians must be spirited or induced to leave. There is a sense of life in chaos—even when one attempts to live in calm, to avoid trouble, one finds conflict and violence. Sacco is overwhelmed when taken on a tour of homes destroyed by the occupation, hearing the story of a villager shot by a settler during an altercation dying when unable to get to a hospital (70). However, he recognizes his role in the process: "[I]t's not like I'm here to meditate … and let's face it, my comics blockbuster depends on conflict; peace won't pay the rent" (76).

Sacco chooses to focus the middle of the work on the prison experience, including the notorious Ansar III Prison. Most of those placed in Ansar find themselves on administrative detention, six months in prison without trial and without being charged. Through Sacco's images of black/white and gray, the reader can feel the hell that is prison: buckets of shit, tiny rooms filled with men, images of pain and bewilderment, cages used as isolation for group leaders, and stones and pieces of bread used to communicate. To drive home the sense of displacement, fear of the unknown, humiliation, and the breakdown of identity, Sacco relates the story of Ghassan, a Palestinian man removed from his home and tortured by Israeli police. Sacco utilizes small images arranged in rows of four—repetitive, quick flashes into the mind of a prisoner. The reader enters his experience which includes interrogation, starvation, sleep deprivation, and placement in a cell filled with urine: "After four days without sleep, I began to have hallucinations" (109). Once the prisoners are released and return to their homes, the images change to those of normal society going about their business.

The problem with Sacco's journalist work is the fine line between subjective and objective reportage. Although Sacco is a trained journalist, how can we be sure his work is not biased by his close interaction with those he meets? When he is relating the story of the massacre in Khan Younis, the author delivers a panel that is visually chaotic in an attempt to replicate the chaos of the event and the difficulty in discovering the truth behind it: "I want to show things from my point of view because I think it's more honest in a way to be subjective. Admit your prejudices; just admit it. I would rather be honest about what's going on. Which means the oppressed aren't all angels—but the fact would remain that they are oppressed" (Weiland 2). While Sacco recognizes that his "perspective has been limited, perhaps even compromised, by his immersion into Palestinian life," Sacco does not shy away from but rather immerses himself in the experience (Williams 43–60). Rather, he shows the view through his perspective and allows readers to make their own decisions. The constant presence of Sacco's cartoon image—long face, round eyeglasses, slight build—always reminds us who is narrating and suggests a subjective human being who feels rather than an objective reporter who ignores emotions (Bowe 26–27). As Janice Morris points out: "By feigning neither neutrality nor moral authority, Sacco instead makes obvious his apprehension and ambivalence, constantly questioning his own motives (and that of his hosts for whom he holds no delusions of totalized victimhood) and acknowledging a perception that is always already subjective and unavoidably fallible" (Morris 187–88). The reader is a fly on the wall, looking over Sacco's shoulder and experiencing what he experiences, hearing what he hears, seeing what he sees. Indeed, Sacco says in one interview, "You have to put yourself in everyone's shoes that you draw, whether it's a soldier or a civilian. You have to think about what it's like: what are they thinking? What are they feeling? The truth be told, that's part of the reason I don't show Israeli soldier's faces. I couldn't understand it" (Sacco, "English Interview").

Sacco returned to Gaza in November 2002 and March 2005 to investigate the alleged massacres of Palestinians in Khan Younis and in Rafah. Again, he attempts in his work *Footnotes in Gaza* (2009) to objectivity when telling the story of the Palestinian by living among them and listening to as many versions of a story as feasible. The blending of text with visual allows for a new way of representing an old conflict through the eyes of those who tend to remain invisible in western media, the Palestinians. Quoting scholars Isaac Kamola and Tristam Walker, Sacco gives the reader "immediacy and material reality of the lived experience of war" (Scanlon 5).

By approaching the conflict on the ground, Sacco is able to present (visually and narratively) the story as witnessed. When confronted with retelling events, Sacco will present the witness' version of the story in the upper panel and will then present the newspaper version in the bottom panel. Rocco Versaci "points to this [page] as a demonstration of juxtaposition, a way for Sacco to visually present these two narratives in order to highlight the differences" (Versaci 6). In his bird's-eye landscapes, Sacco is able to show the reader the trauma of the violence, how such an experience affects actual human beings and gives face and voice to the citizens of Palestine. A perfect example of this is when Sacco relates the Muslim celebration of El Eid-Adha where the village men slaughter a bull for food. As Molly Scanlon points out: "The feast scene in [*Footnotes in Gaza*] provides readers a visceral, striking aspect to the narrative that allows Sacco to parallel the slaughter of the bull with the perceived slaughter of the Palestinian people" (7).

Although time has passed, there is a sense that nothing has changed. *Footnotes* acts as a metaphor for the experience of Palestinians, a history that drops to the bottom of a page and is forgotten. However, Sacco wants the reader to take notice via visuals of destruction, violence, and dysfunction. The most painful images of the work surround events on November 12, 1956, or "The Day of School," a section of *Footnotes*. A loudspeaker calls all the men of army age to go to the official school in Rafah. As men left homes, they met soldiers firing, and they began to run out of fear, as one of the men relates to Sacco: "They were many soldiers. Some of them standing and some of them lying down with their machine guns, shooting at each group that passed in front of them" (Sacco, *Footnotes in Gaza* 215). To show scale, Sacco uses his art to create a high angle visual perspective of those running with their arms over their heads versus the soldiers with their guns and batons. A low angle perspective shows bodies lying in the street and people walking on those who are still alive. Sacco makes the decision to tell each man's story using small boxes that contain the headshots of those who have witnessed the events, text bubbles coming out of visual box (238). These visual elements, these creative decisions made by Sacco insure that the reader is there with these men and experiences the humiliation of Palestinians (265).

In *Footnotes in Gaza*, the pictures of what happened in Khan Younis and Rafah in 1956 alternate with the present scene of crowded cities bursting at the seams with restless energy and seething rage. Sacco depicts the grinding desperation of families attempting to make ends meet under forced resettlement and occupation. He reports on the late-night gatherings of aging, exhausted freedom fighters, and unemployed young men. And, always, there are the memories of dispossession, humiliation, loss, and the ineradicable hope of return to the land itself and to a condition of dignity and visibility (22).

Conclusion

The Israeli-Palestinian conflict frustrates and confounds. Many have tried to bring peace to the region only to be stuck in the muck of age-old political, social, and cultural differences. In order to bring some sense to the world around them, graphic novelists have become comic journalists, narrative and visual artists who bear witness to the conflict. Jewish American cartoonists such as Libicki and Glidden use the graphic novel as a means of relating their own personal story of being an American in Israel whereas Israeli artists like Folman and Modan, use the medium to immerse the reader in the experience of those on the ground. Finally, Sacco relies on his journalist background to tell the other side of the story—the side of the Palestinians. While each author enters their journey identifying their subjectivity as omnipresent, their experience will drastically and irreparably alter their ability to deliver same. In fact, as their characters move through the events, they become detached from the constant war around them, able to move easily from bed to bed, able to numb their psyche from the actions of their neighbors, able to forget the past in order to be able to live with the present. Artists like Sacco (and to some degree Glidden), on the other hand, enter the conflict with the intent to present the other side, to showcase the view of the underdog, and accordingly, their objectivity is constantly in question. Are they journalists or are they simply narrators voicing the stories of those on the ground? While the truth lies somewhere in between black and white, in the shade of gray, these authors take the risk to tell stories filled with complexities. They bear witness to the past, the present, and the unknown future as it relates to the trauma in Gaza.

"To Night the Ensilenced Word": Intervocality and Postmemorial Representation in the Graphic Novel about the Holocaust

Jean-Philippe Marcoux

Primo Levi, in *If This Is a Man* (1947), argues that the irreconcilable "divide" between survivors and secondhand witnesses is rooted in the absence of referential "language" (129–131). Elie Wiesel concurs in his famous essay "Holocaust as Literary Inspiration," speaking of a specific codification of language that only firsthand witnesses of the Holocaust can decipher (7). Robert Eaglestone argues that combined, Levi's emphasis on the fallibility of language and Wiesel's survivor's code point to the "impossibility of identification" to firsthand witnesses of Holocaust horrors, an impossibility primarily renegotiated by second generations (33). In his essay, Wiesel confirms that those "who did not live through the event will never know it [for] between our memory and its reflection there stands a wall that cannot be pierced" (7). Despite this impenetrable "wall" of memorial trauma, Wiesel notes that his generation of survivors "invented a new literature, that of testimony" (9). This inherent problem of identification with survivor stories underlies the complexities of testimonial literature of the Holocaust. More precisely, the conditions under which testimony occurs require (re-)definitions. If the narratives of testimony are, as Levi and Wiesel affirm, ungraspable for secondhand witnesses because of a lack of lived experiences and of memorial references, then what is the ontological purpose in retelling the stories?

In this chapter, I shall discuss how Jewish authors of graphic novels about the Holocaust—second-generation graphic novelists drawing from the collective and fluxional memory—develop a poetics of intervocality as a way to navigate between memory and fictionalization of collective memory. What I am interested in are the authors' negotiations and narratological performances of postmemory that study the translation of the witness's transmissible voice—real, imagined, or reconstructed—in the narrative structure of the graphic novel.[1] To this end, I will study graphic novels by second-generation authors, namely Art Spiegelman's *Maus* (1986), Miriam Katin's *We Are on Our Own* (2006), Martin Lemelman's *Mendel's Daughter: A Memoir* (2006), and Bernice Eisenstein's *I Was a Child of Holocaust Survivors* (2007), in order to show the multi functions of intervocality in secondhand witnessing and postmemory in narrative of the "abject past" (Roth 7).[2] Each of these graphic novels shows the difficulties of representing and integrating the survivor's voice in their own work.

Because *Maus* has received significant critical attention and is continuously invoked when discussing postmemorial work, I will use its seminality as point of entry into a larger study of the generational crisis of intervocalic representation. In *Maus*, this crisis of representation—representing his father's experience, representing the creative process of reimaging, re-constitutively, the experience— functions dialogically; that is, because Art has not lived through the death camps experience, the experiential trauma remains fundamentally inaccessible except through his father's narrative voice. Because he cannot, initially, perform intervocalic representation—that is, he cannot integrate his father's narrative of trauma in his own narrative/creative voice unless he sublimates both sources of trauma—he remains alienated from his identity as second-generation witness and also from any portal to identification to the collective experience of Holocaust survivors. In different yet intersecting and complementary ways, Katin's, Lemelman's, and Eisenstein's graphic novelizations of intervocality all deal with such crisis. Whereas Katin carefully unpacks her double-voicedness as both first and secondhand witness to her story, Lemelman and Eisenstein combine the genres of the graphic novel and the memoir in ways that suggest the polyvocality of testimonial literature. Lemelman's graphic novel is a near-perfect example of intervocality, for his drawings are faithful to the received history; he never allows the subjectivity of reconstruction and testimonial reconstitution to enter the panels. Eisenstein intermixes memorialization in the form of long prose passages with drawings meant to evoke the serpentine process of postmemorial refigurations.

In "Ash-Aureole,"[3] poet-survivor Paul Celan writes: "No one/ bears witness for the/ witness" (p. 261, lines 24–26). While this verse seems to stand alongside Adorno's seminal line about post-Holocaust poetry, it also gestures toward the incommunicability of witnessing and testifying to Holocaust trauma. Shoshana Felman, citing Celan's poem, adds that, "[t]o bear witness is to *bear the solitude* of a responsibility, and to *bear the responsibility*, precisely, of that solitude" (3). Using Celan's verse as template, Felman clarifies her statement:

> Celan's verse … is in effect so charged with absolute responsibility and utter solitude, so burdened with the uniqueness of the witnessing that it becomes itself not a simple statement but an act of speech which repeats, performs its own meaning in resisting our grasp, in resisting our replicating or recuperative witnessing. It thus performs its own solitude: it puts into effect what cannot be understood, transmitted, in the mission of transmission of the witness. (3, n4)

The "solitude" with which Celan's verse is imbued resonates in many canonical firsthand witnesses whose own witnessing of the indescribable resulted in a crisis of recuperation, one that widened the generational gap with second-generation Holocaust authors, especially in terms of the very act of narrating Auschwitz.[4]

For Dori Laub, coauthor of *Testimony* (1992) with Felman, the process of "bearing witness" (70) requires a listener. In turn, the listener "has to be at the same time a witness to the trauma and a witness to himself" (58) for " [t]estimonies are not monologue; they cannot take place in solitude" (70). Laub's assertion that testimonies cannot "take place in solitude" seems to wrestle with Celan's position; however, it is clear that the reciprocal relation of "bearing witness" conveys an individual processing of the testimony.[5] As Victoria A. Elmwood correctly states, bearing witness "is a matter of finding a way not just to acknowledge the distance between [second-generation children] and their parents' traumatic experiences, but to make that distance central somehow to the process of plotting an identity" (718).

In their narratives, second-generation witnesses must negotiate the integration of their parents' voice into their narrative and creative voice, in a creative performance of *intervocality*.[6] In the context of second-generation literature, intervocality refers to the navigation of narratological gaps between levels of witnessing. Through representation of narrative cross-fertilizations, second-generation witnesses struggle to create dialogic intersections, revealing the tensions in illustrating the problems of secondhand witnessing and postmemory.[7] Intervocality, therefore, attempts to resolve the creative tensions of "intergenerational acts of transfer" (104) at the level of postmemorial representation.

In "The Generation of Postmemory," Marianne Hirsh provides an extended definition of postmemory that it worth quoting at length. She writes:

> Postmemory describes the relationship that the generation after those who witnesses cultural or collective trauma bears to the experience of those who came before, experiences that they "remember" only by means of the stories, images, and behaviors among which they grew up. But these experiences were transmitted to them so deeply and affectively as to *seem* to constitute memories in their own right. Postmemory's connection to the past is thus not actually mediated by recall but by imaginative investment, projection, and creation. To grow up with such overwhelming inherited memories … is to be shaped, however indirectly, by traumatic events that still defy narrative reconstruction. (106–107)

Those "imaginative investment, projection, and creation" account for the multi-functionality of intervocality in the graphic novel about the Holocaust. Intervocality, in the case of graphic novels written by Jewish authors, allows for a reinvestigation of postmemory as more than an "inter- of trans-generational transmission of traumatic knowledge and experience" (106),[8] it also allows for an extension of the narrative possibilities to all Jewish men and women who must cope with the Holocaust as history shared, as collective memory.

In this sense, intervocality becomes a potentially adaptable term, encompassing the narrative voices of second-generation authors as well as those of graphic novelists who must negotiate the trauma of the Holocaust by means of their Jewish identity and identification to the collective history of the Jewish experience. What this means— but it is not the focus of this essay—is that Jewish authors *write* or *imagine* what the Holocaust experience might have been, not only from the testimonial tradition of generational witnessing but also from the flux of archival memory. By proposing intervocality as a new aesthetic paradigm for studying the Jewish graphic novel about the Holocaust, I wish to contest Ernst van Alphen's argument that transmission of trauma in postmemorial work is improbable.[9] He writes:

The normal trajectory of memory is fundamentally indexical. Memories, partial, idealized, fragmented, or distorted as they can be, are traces of the events of which they are the memories. There is continuity between the event and its memory. And this continuity has an unambiguous direction: the event is the beginning, the memory is the result ... In the case of the children of the survivor, the indexical relationship that defines memory has never existed. (485–486)

What van Alphen does not consider is that memory, in cases where trauma is transmitted or requires narrative mediation, is fluxional. And it is this flux of memory, which is comprised of testimonies, memorializations, images, pictures, stories, reports, data, official documents, and journalistic efforts to investigate the Holocaust, that forms the archive readily available to both second-generation witnesses, and to other Jewish authors, whose generational, geographical, or circumstantial distance from the Holocaust experience prevent them from accessing the intimacy of first-hand witnessing. Moreover, it is this flux of memory, what Eva Hoffman calls an "inner storehouse" (193) of fragmented remembrances to remember, that allows for intervocality to exist. It is from this familial or cultural legacy *and* in this psychological and ontological framework, which James E. Young appropriately terms "received history" (669), that graphic novelists draw their inspiration for conceptualizing the survivor's voice and language.

Art Spiegelman's *Maus* is an autobiographical graphic novel that exemplifies second-generational struggles to "bear witness" to the trauma of their parents' survival of the Holocaust. His identity as second-generation witness to the testimony of his father's experience is contingent upon his own struggles to claim identification to postmemory. As a creative artist, Art is initially unable to negotiate his father's story, thereby making it very difficult to represent it creatively. Accordingly, Art tells Françoise, "I can't even make sense out of my relationship with my father ... How am I supposed to make any sense out of Auschwitz? ... Of the Holocaust?" (*Maus II* page 14, panel 6). Later, he admits his emotional, and artistic, impotence: "I feel inadequate trying to reconstruct a reality that was worse than my dreams" (*II* 16, 4). These passages suggest that one of the loci of Art's guilt is his relationship to his father's past; however, this subsequent avowal conveys another layer of his guilt-ridden postmemory that results in an inability to perform intervocalic representation.[10]

Revealingly, Art affirms that "I somehow wish I had been with Auschwitz *with* my parents so I could really know what they lived through! ... I guess it's some kind of guilt about having an easier life than they did" (*II* 16, 3). Spiegelman's interesting choice to have "with" in bold letters conveys a sense of ontological detachment, a sense of a child "without" a shared familial past, but that still requires remembering. It is correct, then, to note that intervocality, in Art's case, is contingent upon the necessity "to write himself into a family from whose founding trauma he was absent" (Elmwood 691). Still, to repurpose Art's self within the familial portrait depends primarily upon his acknowledgment of his own postmemorial trauma. As Dora Apel aptly notes, "[e]xperience that has not been processed cannot be narrated, constituting trauma, not memory" (qtd. in Elmwood 709). The inability to identify with the meaning of his trauma thus parallels Art's struggle to mediate his father's experience of the Holocaust and results in the fragmentation of his intervocalic potential.

Misidentification with his father's past experiences also prevents the protagonist/ narrator from drawing meaning from the present. Art, whose second-generation identity is interlocked with his integration with his father's voice and trauma as survivor, is unable to recognize the cultural and personal signifiers that constitute his father's story. Failing to grasp the "problems of interviewing and representation" (LaCapra 86), Art is forced to refigure the archival meaning of signifiers as a way to reconstruct the link to his father's testimonial voice. He has still not come to terms with his role as listener, witness, and mediator to the "eyewitness." Art has no "desire to repair" his father's fragmented past (Hirsch 112).

For instance, the intermeshing of Art's cigarette smoke and the Auschwitz chimneys (*II* 69, 6, 9) does not point to an understanding of testimony but, more accurately, to the consummation and gradual processing of postmemory.[11] This channeling of history, while not entirely connected to the linearity and temporality of its process, underpins the inevitable reidentification with the father's story and, ultimately, with the collective memory of his Jewish ancestry. Later, when Art mocks the "curfew" (*II* 69, 6, 9) imposed by his father, he further denotes his failure to grasp the evocative meaning of the "curfew" in the traumatic story; missing curfew in the death camp meant to be killed or taken as prisoner to be killed later. Metaphorically, Art's mockery underscores the negation of his own imprisonment within the survivor's story as well as his problematic negotiation of postmemory. Similarly, Art misunderstands the intentions of his father when he throws out his coat (*I* 68, 6) to replace it with a warmer (*I* 69, 2) one. Focusing only on the materiality of the coat instead of its memorial significance, Art unpacks his miscomprehension of the importance of warm clothes for Auschwitz prisoners. Again failing to grasp the personal and cultural implications of signifiers for Holocaust survivors, Art denounces Vladek's emphasis on the value of food (*I* 43, 3) and dedication to pick up of a piece of wire (*I* 116, 3–6). The rationing and economy of food do not only evoke Vladek's starvation in Auschwitz but also underlie, again, his paranoia about the potential for repetition of history. Likewise, the wire that Vladek picks up on the street (3) recalls the barbed wire that surrounded the prisoners' camps; to pick it up is another attempt to prevent the future from reenacting the past.

Similarly, Art does not reciprocate the urgency with which Vladek repairs the drainpipes and gutters; he prefers to have coffee instead (*I* 96, 7). In deferring his answer, Art fails to understand the evocations of the trenches and "cremation pits" (*II* 72, 2) contained in the symbols of drainpipes and gutters. In repairing the holed drainpipes and gutters, Vladek gestures toward a repairing of history so that those scenes of the "big" (3) "graves" (4) are never reenacted. The very graphic final panel of the page (5)—the panel in which bodies of mice are piled while other mice await genocide—symbolizes the penultimate dehumanization and agony that Vladek wants his son to avoid experiencing.

More importantly, the tears in the intertextual and intervocalic fabric show that "the tense relation between procedures of objective reconstruction of the past and emphatic response, especially in the case of victims and survivors" (LaCapra 87) is the crux of the testimonial dilemma in *Maus*. Art must recognize in the actions and words of the father the grounds for the transmission of fragments of history, which he must remember intervocalicly by narrating what has, up to then, resisted mediation.

Finally, by integrating Vladek's experiential voice into his own, Art, in an intervocalic performance of representation, addresses, at the end of the second volume, the tensions that define second-generation literature; that is, the two volumes map the creative process that led to the final acknowledgment of the second generation's "obligations to [the parents'] past" (Hoffman 29). Through its creation of a grand narrative, which conflates the metanarratives of the two volumes, *Maus* reassesses Art's postmemorial identity within the lineage of trauma victims.[12] Spiegelman—and his protagonist, Art—provides an ontological, representational, and self-reflexive *mise-en-abîme* that attempts to affirm, by means of intervocality, Art's conceptualization of selfhood amid his father's metonymical "story." Essentially, through intervocalic performativity—the integration of the witness's voice into the narrative voice—Spiegelman (and Artie) comes to terms with the postmemorial reality of having been defined by "the force of the internalized past" (Hoffman 27).

The second generation's initial problems of identification often reside in their inability to perform "the act of belated witnessing," thereby preventing them from "witness[ing] the *delayed impact* of the Holocaust" (Levine 68) on their own processes of postmemory. Such is certainly the case for Miriam Katin in *We Are on Our Own*. While *Maus* is mostly concerned with negotiations of postmemory, Katin engages with the intertwinings between postmemory and rememory, which, in Hirsch's reading of Toni Morrison's term, suggests "traumatic reenactment and repetition" (*Generation* 82–83). The idea of reenactment is particularly pertinent when dealing with *We Are on Our Own*. In her graphic novel, Katin conceptualizes intervocality at two intrinsic testimonies: as both survivor and second-generation author, she must revisit, and as such, reenact, a history she has lived through but which meaning she could not grasp because of her young age. At the same time, she must integrate her mother's voice, and later her father's narrative voice, into her own narrative voice as a way to reconstruct, and thus, a repeat, a past that defines her. It is in the liminal narrative space—a figurative memorial gutter—that multiple levels of narration create that Katin's intervocalic performance of reenactment finds its most telling expression.

Indeed, *We Are on Our Own* takes the reader into uncharted postmemorial territory by presenting the author, not as the mediator of her parents' experience, not as translator of the witnesses' testimonial voices but as a passive and innocent firsthand witness of the trauma of experience.[13] About the origin of the graphic novel, she tells Samantha Baskind, "it was years of 'narration,' within, that took the form of the book" (241).[14] Katin's narrative depends on her ability to integrate her parents' voices—which, interestingly, come from her mother's own intervocal reenactment of history—into her own in order to reconstitute an experience she misunderstood and to perform historical[s] redress.[15] For instance, when the mother cries on the bed, a young Miriam wonders, "Why is Mommy crying every time the nice man goes away?" (Katin page 43, panel 5). In the previous panel that spills over to the next, a German "commandante" gives the mother "silk. From Paris" (4). What the daughter fails to understand at the time is that the mother is not crying because the man left but because he forced himself on her, reducing the mother's body to a site of sexual violence she has no control over. While the daughter tries to reassure her mother that "[H]e will come back Mommy. Don't cry" (5), Miriam, under the guise of the artist, highlights the generational schism in the mediation of experience.[16] For Miriam, the "commandante" is nice because he brings her chocolates she will feed to the dog—which works as a surrogate for the initial loss of the dog abandoned earlier. However, the gift is deceitful as it is a gateway to raping the mother. It is only through the graphic novelization of her mother's mediated experience that Katin can understand the violence of the act performed on her mother.

It is from the mother's testimony—one of the narrative voices from "within"— of what *really* happened that Katin is able to correct the misinterpretations of her firsthand witnessing. When planes bomb the town, the refugees wonder if they are "next" (48, 2). As they gradually realize that the planes are not German, young Miriam exclaims, "Look! It is snowing" (2). This misunderstanding of the event foreshadows the narration of their escape from the wine cellar during a snowstorm. The escape, remembered primarily because it led to the abandonment of another dog, is drawn using a technique of scribbling (62, 1, 3–4) supposed to suggest the strong winds of the storm. The scribbling is also an indication of the diffusive memory of the event that Miriam harbors. In turn, this rememory of reaching the orchards and the small barn leads to the second instance in the graphic novel where Katin sets her narrative in the present, and in color.[17] The silent panels show Miriam, as a mother, playing with her child and racking the leaves in what seems to be an analog to the orchard. As the child asks, "I am hiding Mom! Find me! Find me!" the mother answers, "There you are" (63, 6–7), which sets the narrative back to the past and to an imagined rememory of what happened to the dog that Miriam cared for. Again, this reenactment is tainted by the mediation of loss, renegotiated through the imagery of the storm affecting both visual clarity and memory. Therefore, the child's demand to "find me" becomes an invitation to revisit unresolved traumatic experiences, which only the intervocalic performativity of the mother can achieve. To "find" is to remember what Miriam, the child, could not fathom. The parallelism of intervocalic transmission is unmistakable: from Miriam's child to Miriam *as* a child, "the testimonial chain" (Levine 64) is kept alive through the mother's authenticating and corrective witnessing.

Recuperating the symbol of the snow as a signifier for memory, the mother, now in the present—and in color—calls Miriam and tells her: "It is snowing" (70, 2). Interestingly, Miriam, despite having lived through the experience of escape during the snowstorm, cannot identify with the signifier. When the mother asks, "Do you remember any of that?" Miriam answers, "I don't think so" (70, 9). Later in the graphic novel, Miriam, in the colored present, opens a bottle of wine (84, 6), which brings the reader to perform what Katin does with the graphic novel; that is, the opening of the bottle invites the reader to go back, in a gesture reminiscent of rememory, and remember the moment when the mother gave wine to little Miriam to calm her down after her dog was chased out of the cellar. The wine is re-semiotized as the agential signifier via which Miriam will address the trauma of loss (of the dog, of the experience she cannot remember, of her childhood innocence).

The ruptures in the testimonial chain can only be attended to by writing and drawing the graphic novel, which becomes the new map, replacing the "tattered old map with mysterious pencil marks."[18] The new map becomes an analog of the father's testimony. Like the "map [Katin's] father carried around while tracing our steps trying to find [his wife and daughter],"[19] the graphic novel's intervocality is the map "tracing" the journey back to rememory. By integrating the narrative of her father's quest to remember his family, Katin fills the interstices in the grand narrative of her family's survival and therefore addresses the ruptures that prevented her from understanding the reverberated meanings of familial trauma.[20] Her conclusion certainly gestures toward such a conceptualization of the work. She writes,

> This book is the story of our escape and life in hiding ... I could somehow imagine the places and the people my mother told me about, but a real sense of myself as a small child and the reality of the fear and confusion of those times I could understand only by reading the last few letter and postcards my mother had written to my father.[21]

In this sense, the graphic novel is Katin's contribution to the "storehouse" of familial memory. The appropriation of the experience ("our") remediated through testimonies and subsequent intervocalic reenactments allow for a rehistoricization of a past marred ("imagine") in the "fear and confusion" of childhood subjectivity. In the end, her graphic novel—which she calls a memoir—performs its *devoir de mémoire*, or memory as duty.

Martin Lemelman's graphic novel *Mendel's Daughter: A Memoir* elaborates a poetics of representation that remains intimately connected to the aesthetics of the memoir. More precisely, Lemelman draws his panels so that they function not as creative extrapolations but as visual analog to the text, itself a literalization of the recorded voices of his mother and family members. Working from a compositional template borrowed from portraiture for his characters, Lemelman similarly illustrates the events his mother narrate so they remain as faithful as possible to the reality of the horrors that resisted mediation. The graphic novel is filled with real photographs, especially of family members and friends that authenticate the visual content.[22] The inclusion of these photographs further affects the way Lemelman conceptualizes his panels as authentic representations of the testimony of his mother; the photographs often replace drawings, thereby evoking Levi's contention that there is no referential (graphic) language available to second-generation witnesses. Lemelman prefers the photographs to his creative reimagination of his family members.

The graphic novel opens with Lemelman drawing himself into the narrative to address the reader about the veracity of his mother's tale (Lemelman 1). His expressed skepticism is the point of departure for his negotiation of intervocality. On the following illustrated page, Lemelman reveals that before his mother died, "She spoke to me" (3). The words are boxed and stand outside the illustrated panel in which a hand, Lemelman's, touches his dead mother's face. Here, Lemelman suggests that the end of her testimony—her narrative death—is the beginning of his intervocalic performance of postmemory. In fact, images of hands that work as metonymies for the intervocalic performativity of the illustrator traverse the entire narrative. The graphic novel is a composite of testimonies that Lemelman, as second-generation witness, repurposes. For that matter, the inside cover page features a drawn portrait of the mother that the creative hand holds under the title header crediting the graphic novel to both mother and son, thereby suggesting that this is a work of postmemorial intervocality.

In the pages that follow, one can see Lemelman's hand touching his mother's grave on which she appears to her son and says, "Listen to me ... Sometimes your memories are not your own" (4, 2). What is interesting here is that the mother's words, her transmission of her traumatic experience, trigger the narration of the process of the graphic novel's production. Thus, it is Lemelman's same creative hand that takes the videotape of the mother's testimony (5, 1) and puts it in the video player (2), leading to another illustration of his face (3), reflecting in a mirror, an obvious symbol for how the trauma of the first-generation witnesses is reflected in the postmemorial predicament of the second generation that has to cope with this immutable heritage. The transmission of the mother's memories onto his narrative voice finds its crystallization in the final panel of that page in which the text, isolated in a box, says, "This is her story. It's all TRUE" (3). In isolating the image from the text, Lemelman provides an aesthetic representation of his intervocalicic function: as illustrator of his mother's "received history," he must infuse his novel with his mother's and families' testimonies of trauma for which there is no document.

Here again, the drawing hand appears at various times to punctuate the narrative with reaffirmations of the intervocalic undertaking of the second-generation graphic novelist. However, what the reader comes to realize is that the drawing hand of the illustrator is the intervocalic extension of the providential hand that saved the mother (124, 1–2), and therefore, it is the expansion of the agential hand that protected the story so that it could be transmitted. The hand of the "Angel" (1) is part of a narrative that Lemelman did not initially believe—his skepticism is counter balanced by the unspeakable horrors of the Holocaust experience. Transmuted in the creative hand of the illustrator, the "magical" hand becomes the intervocalic conduit for the second-generation narrative, which will reconstitute the testimonial chain and metaphorically rebuild the family tree (131, 1). By remembering the fragmented narratives of survivors, Lemelman proposes a counter narrative to "the story of how [Nazis] killed our family" (1). In this case, intervocality empowers Lemelman to organize the narrative fragments and create a grand narrative of familial trauma. To this end, Lemelman draws his fictional hand sorting through real portrait of family members (p. 189). The one-page panel is a striking example of intervocalic potential: these photographs are silent testimonies to these people's existences. The creative hand will give them back their narrative voices and re-map the geography of their survival stories.

The same re-constitutive attention to details can be found in the reconstruction of the spaces that the family members narrate. While the organization of the space on the page is evocative of the compartmentalization of their memories, the preciseness in the drawing recalls the very structured existence they needed to maintain in order to survive (e.g., 47–49). At the same time, the vast majority of the panels are silent; family members do not speak through/in balloons. The testimony is usually boxed above, below, and on the sides of the illustrated panels; elsewhere, the text is floating in the image. This technique of isolating the text from the image undergirds the intermeshing of memoir and graphic novel in an intervocalic framework.

The passage from one genre to the other—a passage that shows the process of de-fictionalizing the myth of the "hand of the Angel," integrating its intervocalic potential and narrating the many voices of survivors—culminate in an affirmation of the graphic novel format as the symbolical map that, like Katin's map, will preserve the memories. In one of the last pages (217), Lemelman creates four panels, with each one imagining the final testimonial words of lost family members. Interestingly, the creative hand covers the eyes of each person, thereby prefiguring how the graphic novel, as an intervocalic work of postmemory, will lift the veil from their silenced and traumatic deaths and make them meaningful for the familial narrative. As palliative narrative of both rememory and postmemory, *Mendel's Daughter: A Memoir* is a crucial contribution to the polyvocalic genre of the Holocaust graphic novel. As a "child of survivors," Lemelman, accepting the transmutability of the imaginary/creative hand, becomes a "parent to the interpretation of [his family's] survival" (Sucher qtd. in Berger 2).

Like Lemelman, Bernice Eisenstein's *I Was a Child of Holocaust Survivors* conflates the memoir and the graphic novel. However, whereas *Mendel's Daughter* paid great attention to restructuring the testimonies as events were chronologically remembered, Eisenstein has very little care for narrative linearity. Miriam Harris pertinently observes that, "[t]raditional chronologies, in their linear sequencing of time, possess a rational logic that seems unsuited for the expression of incomprehensible horror" (130). In fact, the structure of her graphic novel, or "illustrated memoir" (129), develops an aesthetic of representative spontaneity that underlines the post traumatic disorder of memorial remembrances. Events, drawn or narrated, are conjured up by the recognition of particular semiotic or philological signifiers. This narratological choice is interconnected with how Eisenstein defines her postmemory: "Like a dusty book in a reference library, memory gets pulled off the shelf and riffled through to find a familiar passage to look at once more" (Eisenstein 48).

The temporal and spatial dislocations that characterize the graphic novel are also indicative of the difficulties of the second generation to negotiate the burden of memories they do not share. She admits, "I am lost in memory. It is not a place that has been mapped, fixed by coordinates of longitude and latitude, whereby I can retrace a step and come to the same place again" (19). Lacking referents, she cannot mediate her parents' witnessing: "I had no chronology, no laid-out sequence of events in order for me to hold a newly found fragment and place it where it belonged" (29). The representational difficulties also extend to semantics, to the need to find the language to write the "incomprehensible": "It's difficult enough to discover the right words for what is to be remembered, but even harder when each word longs to shelter and sustain the memory of a generation aged and dying" (55–56). In many ways, the graphic novel, the result of a mediation of fragments, works in a similar way. She grafts fragments of memories with a chronological imprecision that matches the shadowed delineations of her identity's contours found in many illustrations of a young Bernice (e.g., 52, 66).[23] She later confesses, "I have this problem—growing up in the household of my parents was not tragic, but their past was. My life was not cursed, theirs was. They were born under an unfavorable star and forced to sew it onto their clothing. Yet here I am … pushing history and memory uphill, wondering what I'm supposed to be" (53). In a very telling moment of postmemorial tensions, Eisenstein draws a young Bernice holding an apple while standing next to her father. In this panel that fills the page, the father bestows this dictum onto his daughter: "'A' is for epel, and it doesn't fall far from the tree" (66). It is clear, however, that the memorial distance, symbolized by their dissociative shadows, contradicts the dictum: Bernice cannot identify with her father's firsthand witnessing of trauma and, therefore, cannot define herself through filial heritage. This troubling absence of portals to filial and cultural identification leads to a panel in which Bernice spirals down amid fragments of blank pages and of pages with family members asking her to remember and memorialize ("gedenk!") the testimonies (68). Forced to use "resurrection" as narrative technique, "Eisenstein is able to confront a past that has affected her very core but which she never experienced, and that continues to haunt her through its very lack of embodiment" (130).

Confronted with her parents' silence, Bernice lacks the cultural literacy that would allow her to engage with her postmemorial challenges.[24] What Bernice needs is to find her way back to archival memory comprised of "narratives about the Holocaust, narratives in books, images, and films" (Harris 132). In a panel that reinvokes Art drawing on a pile of dead—and silenced—mice, Eisenstein draws a naked Bernice sitting on a pyramid of seminal works on the Holocaust experience (Eisenstein 88).[25] The child's nakedness indicate that, unlike her parents and unlike these survivors-authors, she is, at that point, devoid of *a* narrative about her identity as second-generation witness.

Indeed, she will find meaning, identitive and cultural, through the intertextuality of these works: "I have always been moved when one book speaks to another, expanding what I had first understood" (98). Next to this text in the book, Eisenstein draws a young Bernice writing, and not reading. The inherent meaning of this panel lies in the transference of intertextuality into intervocality; it is through the dialogic dimension of texts that speak of a shared experience that she will find the narrative path back to her parents' stories and voices. In the same way that Shoshana Felman and Dori Laub's *Testimony: Crises of Witnessing in Literature, Psychoanalysis, and History* and Eva Hoffman's *After Such Knowledge* revisit and respond to Elie Wiesel's *Night*, or Primo Levi's *The Drowned and the Saved*—all works Bernice is "sitting" on—Bernice will develop her intervocality by reestablishing and renegotiating the dialogic potential between first and second generations of the Holocaust experience. Harris rightfully believes that "these authors can be viewed as a bridge between the living and the shadows of the past" (137). Eisenstein's graphic novel therefore "speaks" to her parents, to their experience, and to their role in the trauma Bernice now feels by proxy. She "expands" on this intergenerational dialogue by formulating the aesthetic terms of her understanding and mediation of trauma, both familial and personal.

It is only by coming to terms with "the importance of remembrance" (167) as well as with her intervocalic responsibility to her parents' story that Bernice Eisenstein will claim her identity as a "child of Holocaust survivors." Eisenstein concludes, "I think in some way I have always been able to step into the presence of absence. It is something that I have needed to do ... Without my family's knowledge or even their understanding, their past has shaped my loneliness and anger, and sculpted the meaning of loss and love" (167). This newfound intervocality will lead her to other victims (her aunt and uncle, their circle of friends), to other testimonies: "While envisioning the journey of two brothers, my own takes me to the parallel past of two sisters" (134). The intervocality retheorized and deployed throughout "the journey" to voice, to self-generated narrative, to the parents' stored trauma, shapes the graphic novel. Working as a surrogate "Hall of Remembrance," as a substitute "place for silent contemplation" with "concrete walls ... engraved" with words and images (178), *I Was a Child of Holocaust Survivors* is the intervocalic "inscription" of memorial preservation and of postmemorial commemoration.

In essence, intervocality, as shown through this analysis of Jewish graphic novels of the Holocaust, encompasses many dialogic possibilities. As a narratological companion to intertextuality, intervocalic performance in the graphic format includes the ways in which the second-generation author integrates, speaks to, responds to, engages with, reenact, repeat, and iteratively transcribes the voice of first generation witnesses in a narrative expansion of the initial trauma, a spilling over of their story into his or hers.

Notes

1   For an elaborated study of the performative in *Maus*, see Costello, 22–42.
2   I chose these works out of a desire to expand on Laurence Roth's brief, but pertinent, discussion of these Jewish graphic novels of the Holocaust.
3   Entitled "Aschenglorie" in its original version. Also often titled "Ashes-Glory."
4   I use the Victoria A. Elmwood quote on pp. 3–4 to specify my meaning of "distancing."
5   One can further assert that the problematic secondhand witnessing—which plagues Laub's listener—also finds its most vibrant expression in the literature produced by second generation of survivors who must come to terms with the burdening limitations of their mediated experience of Holocaust trauma. As survivors realized that it was time to "pass on their experience as a 'legacy'" and "children of survivors began to participate ... in the process of bearing witness," (Levine 63) the centripetal problem remained one of identification and, consequently, of delineation of identity. Levine avers that

> [f]or this second generation it was a question not only to elicit their parents' stories, of persuading them to write, speak, or agree to be interviewed, but also of coming to terms with their own implication in their parents' experiences. Indeed, many of these children had reached a point in their own lives where they were discovering that the first generation's stories had in a sense *already* been passed down to them, that they had themselves become the unwitting bearers of a legacy of pain, of a trauma that had, in [Art] Spiegelman's words, inadvertently "spilled over" from one generation to the next. (63)

Moreover, this "spilling over" of history, which finds its echo in the title of the first *Maus* volume, "My Father Bleeds History," underlines Art's struggle to identify with his survivor/father Vladek.
6   My definition of intervocality stems mostly from existing theories on vocality, especially those found in jazz studies. While the term "intervocality" already exists and is often associated with intertextuality, I wish to resituate in the musical realm and evoke Steven Feld's theorization.
7   To this end, this writer agrees with Victoria A. Elmwood who notes that,

> [s]uch is the predicament of the second-generation offspring of the traumatized ... They must find ways to include their parents' trauma

within their own story in a way that neither appropriates nor subsumes the parents' experience into their own. Not having lived through these experiences, the second generation cannot lay claim to these, but only to their aftereffects, having experienced those by virtue of prolonged intimate contact with the first generation. (703)

8   Evoking Hirsch's definition, Eaglestone adds that "[s]earching for an identity, 'those born after' attempt to relocate themselves by forging 'an aesthetics of postmemory'" (81).

9   See Hirsch, "The Generation of Postmemory," 109.

10 Spiegelman locates the three sources of Art's trauma: Vladek's experience of suffering in the Holocaust that sublimates his own, his guilt about his mother's suicide, and the guilt of creating from witnessing. These three sources of trauma constantly overlap and intersect in *Maus*, and, ultimately, become symmetrical with the "three strands of narrative" that Erin McGlothlin develops in her essay. McGlothlin writes,

> [t]he three narrative levels can be viewed as forming a sort of continuum, by which the inner narrative (story or Vladek's Holocaust experience) gradually makes its way through the medium of witnessing (discourse or Vladek's testimony) to the outer narrative (narrating or Art's memory and representation ... In *Maus*, the movement between diegetic levels occurs with the absorption of the father's trauma into the son's memory through the very agency of narrative, the act of storytelling. (184)

The "narrative continuum" McGlothlin alludes to parallels the process of re-inscribing Art within the "cultural continuum" of familial trauma (Young 674).

11 Levine concurs that the intertwined smokes of the chimney and cigarette suggest that, "Auschwitz is the very air [Art] breathes," 92. See also Ole Frahm, 68–70.

12 Young highlights Art's centrality in the testimonial process of *Maus*. He writes,

> [B]y weaving back into his narrative the constant reflection on his own role in extracting this story from his father, Spiegelman graphically highlights not only the ways that testimony is an event in its own right but also the central he plays in it ... That is, what is generated in the interaction between father and son in this case is not a revelation of a story already existing, waiting to be told, but a new story unique to their experience together. (676)

13 Katin "clarify[ies] the personal account issue" in her interview with Samantha Baskind, 237.

14 Actually, Baskind's interview is not only perceptive but also insightfully constructed. In it, Katin also discusses *Maus*, her aesthetics, and provides a thoughtful definition of the Jewish graphic novel, 237–243.

15 Katin tells Baskind that her mother told her the stories when she was thirty years old, 237.

16 Even though the narrative is autobiographical, Katin tells Baskind that the names of her family members and the name of her "alter ego Lisa" were all changed to respect her grandmother's wishes, 241.

17 In her interview with Baskind, Katin reveals that "the past comes to me as black and white and grey," 240.

18 This panel is found on the second to last page of the graphic novel. It is not assigned a page number.

19 Because of its placement in the appendix, this panel is not assigned a page.

20   This narrative can found on pp. 94–100 and pp. 104–114.
21   This panel exists independently from the text in the same appendix as those
     described in n56–57. It is not assigned a page number.
22   Laurence Roth notes that Lemelman's graphic novel "employs photographs … to
     establish an interpretive space that visually distinguishes … Lemelman's mother and
     her testimony" (11).
23   For more on the trope of the shadow, see Miriam Harris, 129–143.
24   Harris contends that, "[b]ecause her parents were silent about their experiences,
     Eisenstein turned to a variety of narratives about the Holocaust … to expand
     her knowledge" (132). See also pages 134, 137 for more examples of intertextual
     knowledge.
25   See also figure 8.5 in Harris, 138. For an analysis of this page, see 137.

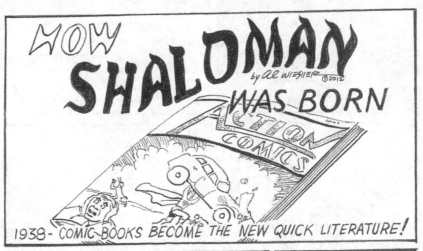

NOW SHALOMAN WAS BORN
by al wiesner © 2012

1938- COMIC BOOKS BECOME THE NEW QUICK LITERATURE!

ALONG WITH ALL OTHER CHILDREN ALBERT TAKES TO THE NEW MEDIA FOR FUN AND ENTERTAINMENT!

HE READS AND READS AND NOTICES SIEGEL AND SHUSTER (TWO JEWISH GUYS) CREATED SUPERMAN!

SUPERMAN IS POPULAR! HE IS FROM ANOTHER PLANET AND IS NOT ANY RELIGION!

BEING RAISED IN AN OBSERVANT FAMILY, AL HOPES TO FIND SOME CONNECTION WITH THE STORY, THE CHARACTER AND HIS RELIGION ... NONE!

STILL LOOKING, HE TRIES SPIDERMAN (CREATED BY STANLEY LIEBER)! AGAIN; THE WRITER IS JEWISH BUT NOT THE CHARACTER! EVERYBODY DRAWS ON THEIR T-SHIRT! FOR AL, THERE'S NO JEWISH CHARACTER!

© 2012 AL WIESNER

1.

MORE BOOKS WERE PUBLISHED AND AL (NOW TEN) IS ATTRACTED TO THE ART OF EISNER, OF SHELLY MOLDOFF AND MILTON CANIFF TOO IN THIS NEW FORM OF ART THAT HAS CAPTURED HIS IMAGINATION!

The SPIRIT

HE COPIES THE ARTISTS AND THEIR STYLES! THE STORIES ARE INTERESTING BUT NONE HAVE ANY CONNECTION TO JUDAISM! HE IS DISAPPOINTED, BUT KEEPS ON COPYING!

JACOB KURTZBERG, BOB KAHN...MAX FINKELSTEIN...JEWISH ARTISTS, BUT NO JEWISH STORIES OR SUPERHEROES!

IF SUPERMAN CAME TO AMERICA FROM EUROPE, HE MIGHT BE MORE JEWISH! HE DIDN'T COME OUT OF CLOSET—HE CAME OUT OF A PHONE BOOTH! HMM THE SHIP HE WAS IN, DID LOOK LIKE THE ONE MOSES WAS IN IN THE BIBLE!

THERE DON'T SEEM TO BE ANY SUPERHEROES THAT ARE JEWISH! WHAT DO THEY THINK—IT WON'T SELL? ALL MY JEWISH FRIENDS BUY COMICS! WELL, I CAN ONLY KEEP ON COPYING THE ART AND BECOME PROFICIENT AN ARTIST! MAYBE SOMEDAY....HMMM!

YRS. GO BY AND AL HAS JOINED THE US AIR FORCE DURING THE KOREAN WAR!

I KNOW I CAN USE MY ART ABILITY IN THE AIR FORCE FOR THE NEXT EIGHT YEARS!

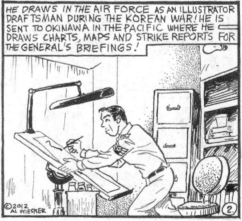

HE DRAWS IN THE AIR FORCE AS AN ILLUSTRATOR DRAFTSMAN DURING THE KOREAN WAR! HE IS SENT TO OKINAWA IN THE PACIFIC WHERE HE DRAWS CHARTS, MAPS AND STRIKE REPORTS FOR THE GENERAL'S BRIEFINGS!

©2012 AL WIESNER

2.

AFTER HIS TIME IN OKINAWA IS OVER, AL WITH OVER 620 OTHER AIRMAN, COME HOME! HE IS NOW DECIDING HIS FUTURE!

WHEN HE WAS SEPARATED FROM ACTIVE DUTY AL DECIDED TO DRAW A BOOK OF GAGS ABOUT A JEWISH BOY IN SERVICE CALLED "G. ISAAC"!

WITH THE WAR OVER, INTEREST IN JEWISH BOYS GOING INTO SERVICE WANES MAKING THE PUBLISHERS LOSE INTEREST!

AL GOT A JOB DOING ART FOR A FREE LANCE WINDOW DECO-RATER PART TIME WHEN THE PUBLISHER REFUSED!

HIS MOTHER TOLD HIM HE NEEDED A FULL-TIME JOB IF HE WANTED TO MARRY AND RAISE A FAMILY!

USE YOUR G.I. BILL TO GET A NEW CAREER; A STEADY JOB! YOU COULD BECOME A HAIR-DRESSER LIKE YOUR BROTHER!

BUT, MOM I NEVER CARED ABOUT HAIR!

TRY IT!

OK!

HE TRIED, WENT TO SCHOOL AND THEN ENTERED THE FIELD! YRS. WENT BY! HE WAS SUCCESSFUL!

HMM....THERE'S STILL NO ISRAELI SUPERHERO!

©2012 AL WIESNER

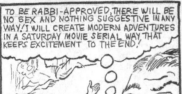

Part Four

Representation of Israel, Biblical Text, and Legend

The Art of Persuasion and Propaganda: The Israeli-Palestinian Conflict in Comic Books and Graphic Novels

Chantal Catherine Michel

The Palestinian-Israeli conflict[1] is one of the most significant confrontations in the world since the Second World War, if not the most prominent. After over sixty years since the declaration of independence of the Israeli state in 1948, the two opposing sides are still not able (or willing) to overcome this conflict and make peace, and the two are more opposed than ever. Because both sides keep up their own collective narratives[2] of the conflict, these "prime devices for providing the backbone of a group's sense of *shared identity*" (Salomon 275, italics in original) are transmitted to the children, for whom it is, in turn, impossible to develop an understanding for the other side, since the two narratives "delegitimize" one another (277).

Israeli and Palestinian art, literature, theater, and film contribute to the development of these collective narratives. Palestinian filmmakers, for instance, appear to use their art mostly as a "weapon of culture" (Massad 32). Their fellow writers, on the other hand, seem only to have just started giving the Palestinian narrative a voice in their literature. On the Israeli side, the artistic community contributes to the Jewish-Zionist narrative, but some members also happen to be more critical toward it and consequently more open to the Palestinian narrative.[3] This repartition more or less also applies to comic books and graphic novels. A number of Jewish and/or Israeli authors, like Dov Zigelman and Giora Rotman, Al Wiesner, Yaakov Kirschen, Marv Wolfman, and Miriam Libicki are supportive of and thereby contributing to the dominating Jewish-Zionist narrative. Others, such as Batia Kolton and Rutu Modan, both members of the Actus Tragicus group, communicate through their work their personal, Israeli perspective without really supporting the Jewish-Zionist narrative. Modan, together with Igal Sarna, approaches the subject more critically and can thus be counted, as well Sarah Glidden, Uri Fink, and Galit and Gilad Seliktar, among those comics authors

This chapter is based on the paper "The Power of the Image: Taking Sides in Comic Books and Graphic Novels on the Israeli-Palestinian Conflict" presented at the Comics and Conflicts Conference of Roehampton University, August 19–20, 2011, at the Imperial War Museum in London. I would like to thank Philipp Hickey for his valuable comments and proofreading.

who are torn between the two narratives. Their approaches of the conflict can be seen as contributing to peace, especially in the case of the Seliktars and Fink (Michel, "Panels for Peace"). On the Palestinian side, the works of amateur comic author Samir Harb can be considered as contributions to peace. Ammar Saliman, Mohamed Mazari, Haider Mahfud, Mahi Ad Dih Allabad, and Said Ali Maluah, on the other hand, are solely contributing to the Palestinian narrative. Perhaps the best-known Palestinian artist underscoring the Palestinian narrative, however, is Naji al-Ali, especially through his Handala-figure, famous throughout the Arab world.

To these authors, who are all involved culturally and by means of their identity in the conflict, can be added a surprisingly high—and still increasing—number of "onlookers" who have chosen to focus on this subject. The best known of them is probably the emblematic figure of comics journalism, Joe Sacco, who wrote and drew several works on the Palestinian-Israeli conflict: *Palestine* (2003) and *Footnotes in Gaza* (2009), as well as a section on "The Palestinian Territories" published in *Journalism* (2012). Mainly because of his intriguing way of combining journalistic techniques and the art of comics, he has, so far, received the most academic attention when writing comics about the Israeli-Palestinian conflict.[4] But besides Sacco, there are numerous other outside-standing or "onlooking" comics authors. The style, intensity, and range of subgenres chosen by them to approach the topic is wide, including action/spy (such as the work of Pierre Boisserie and Frédéric Ploquin, as well as Jean-Claude Bartoll and Pierpaolo Rovero), romance (Bernar Yslaire and Kim Bo-huyn), and humor and satire (Farid Boudjellal and Jean-Marc Reiser). However, the majority has selected the documentary style (e.g., Ferra, Baloup, Maximilien Le Roy, Soulman and Le Roy), also combining it with the autobiographical subgenre (Philippe Squarzoni, Roannie and Oko, Guy Delisle, and Analële and Delphine Hermans).

Being culturally involved in the Palestinian-Israeli conflict means for most people the impossibility of adopting a neutral position. This could, hypothetically, only be possible for those who aren't culturally involved. The choosing of the documentary subgenre by many of the "outsider" authors makes exactly this suggestion: that they watch the conflict from the sidelines and are therefore able to recount objectively. Of course, to "recount objectively" is a paradox, because everybody has a unique perception of the surrounding world. "Reality" and the act of retelling also implies the introduction of this personal point of view by selecting certain aspects, omitting others, and so forth, even if the image is recorded through an ostensibly objective lens. This is an issue that has been extensively discussed in documentary film theory.[5] A documentary comic book makes this personal perception of the artist even more evident, of course, since it consists of unique drawings. On the other hand, it is possible to visualize scenes in comics which cannot be recorded with a camera. In situations, for instance, where permissions to film are declined, a comics artist is still able to make sketches. Furthermore, the comics medium allows choosing angles that are impossible to render with a camera in such "documentary" situations; it enables the artist to emphasize certain aspects by excluding certain elements in an image or varying the shape and size of the panels, thus changing the way an image is framed.

Within these artistic and stylistic liberties that make the language of comics so fascinating lies the power of comics' images. But when it comes to politically and/

or ideologically motivated comic books, this power can also be used by the artists, knowingly or unknowingly, for purposes of persuasion and propaganda, attempting to convince the reader of a specific political conviction (Duncan and Smith, chapter 11, and Michel, "Bericht Oder Propoganda?" 195–196). These propaganda and persuasion techniques consist, among others, of the use of stereotypical renderings, denigrating descriptions and denominations, emphasis and/or omission of information through framing, and also of the specific association of images and/or text (Michel, "Bericht Oder Propoganda?" 196–202). Comics are a very efficient medium for propaganda purposes, since the reader is, most of the time, not aware of this manipulation (Duncan and Smith 249). This is especially the case when applied to documentary comics, because the reader more or less assumes the story to be real, and therefore, the truth (Woo 169).

In the following sections of this essay, I demonstrate the effectiveness of these persuasion and propaganda techniques on the basis of the analysis of a chapter of Joe Sacco's *Footnotes in Gaza: A Graphic Novel* and Maurice Rajsfus and Jacques Demiguel's *Moussa et David—Deux Enfants D'un Même Pays* (2007).

Subtle persuasion techniques: *Footnotes in Gaza*

In *Footnotes in Gaza*, Joe Sacco tries to reveal what happened at the beginning of the Suez Crisis in November 1956 in two towns of the Gaza Strip, Khan Younis and Rafah, where hundreds of Palestinians died. For this book of 389 pages the "graphic journalist" made two research trips to Gaza, each a duration of several weeks, during which he interviewed dozens of Palestinians and a few Israelis. As in *Palestine* (2003), whose nine chapters had been published for the first time separately over a decade earlier (1993–1995), Sacco uses the journalistic method of authentication of including himself in his account by narrating the story in the first person and by drawing the figure representing himself in at least one panel on almost every page. While he depicts, at least in *Footnotes*, his interviewees in a fairly realistic style—his drawings are, as he states himself, mostly based on photographs (417)—he chooses a much more caricatured, self-ironic style for himself, omitting his eyes behind his round spectacles. Dirk Vanderbeke sees in this self-depiction a parallel with Marc-Antoine Mathieu's hero *Julius Corentin Acquefacques, Prisonnier Des Rêves* (2004) of his nightmarish-claustrophobic world, which possibly emphasizes the dystopian character of Sacco's depiction of the conflict (79). But most of all, as Vanderbeke points out, Sacco's art calls to mind McCloud's theory in *Understanding Comics* (1994), according to which a simple drawing style permits the reader to identify with the figure depicted, thereby encouraging the reader to become part of the comic itself (36–37). In *Footnotes in Gaza*, this method thus allows the reader to look at the Israeli-Palestinian conflict through Sacco's eyes. In contrast to *Palestine*, Sacco forefronts his approach and research methods in *Footnotes in Gaza* (203) and demonstrates a critical distance from his interviewees by broaching the inconsistencies in their accounts. He not only makes sure to mention this issue in his foreword (x), but he even dedicates an entire chapter to the problem, "Memory and the Essential Truth" (112–116). The last panel of the penultimate page of the chapter—the *mise en image* of the question, "What are we to make of this?" (115), which is squeezed in a small, scalene caption floating in pitch-blackness—vividly illustrates the holes in the memories. It also suggests Sacco's (and our) doubt and confusion about contradictory witness accounts. In addition to the filter of memories the story had to go through, Sacco mentions "another filter, namely my [Sacco's] own visual interpretation" (x).

Even though the reader should be cautioned against these multiple layers of subjectivity, he may be inclined to accept the presented facts as "essential truth" (116), since Sacco thoroughly corroborates the accounts with U.N. reports and other official documents.

When it comes to pictorial renditions of his research trips, this strategy helps the reader to accept the visualizations of the present as reliable depictions of reality as well, even though they are also Sacco's very personal interpretations of reality. The outcome of this method results in a manipulation of the reader. A striking example for Sacco's persuasion technique is the two-page chapter "Let's Blow Up Everything" (290–291). Here, we see Sacco and his interpreter, Abed, sitting in a taxi on the way to Rafah. The taxi driver is raging, demanding more suicide bombings against the Israelis since he can no longer stand the ongoing demolition of Palestinian houses by Israel Defense Forces. Sacco, sitting in the back of the taxi, doesn't comment on this outburst. Instead, an older Palestinian who sits besides the journalist asks the taxi driver to keep quiet; not because he is wrong but to remind him the risk of arrest. The taxi driver has the final say in this conversation. He is dominating the last panel, in which the violence of his proposal is underlined with a close up of his face, with flashlight-like ideograms around him that represent his anger. The chapter continues on the next page (Figure 15.1).

Three days have passed. Sacco informs the reader—in a small caption in the upper left of the page, framed with an eye-catching 0.5 cm black line—about a suicide bombing that had killed "17 Israelis, mostly students, in Haifa" (291). In this text, Sacco is referring to a bus bombing that actually occurred on March 5, 2003 (Israel Ministry of Foreign Affairs). The caption slightly overlaps a large panel covering about two-fifths of the page and which depicts a market scene. Sacco and Abed stand in its center, their backs are turned to the reader. Before them stands a man, framed visually by the journalist and his interpreter who look at him. Their gazes guide the reader to the man's face: he is smiling while holding his cell phone to his ear. Left and right of the trio can be seen other men who also seem to talk on cell phones or to each other. They, too, are smiling. Two additional captions, one above the head of the man in the center, the other spread over Sacco's and Abed's backs, inform about the quick circulation of this news and even imitate the very act of spreading it. According to McCloud's theory of scene-to-scene transition (71), the reader cannot but make the connection with what the taxi driver just said on the page before: a suicide bombing has occurred and nobody in Rafah or elsewhere in Gaza or the West Bank is sorry about that. Rather, people seem to be content. This reading is confined at the bottom of the panel by the smoke arising from a bus in flames, framed in medium long shot with nobody in or around it. But even if there were people included in this image, they would be quite small due to the size of the framing. Psychologically, it is very hard for the reader to

Figure 15.1 Joe Sacco, *Footnotes in Gaza*, Metropolitan Books, Henry Holt & Co, p. 291.
© 2009 by Joe Sacco.

feel compassion looking at this type of depiction, since the distance is too great and one cannot see anybody suffering (Schwender 41–56). In addition, the bus in this frameless panel is almost completely blurred by the smoke and, compared to the figures talking and laughing in the panel above it, it looks quite surreal.

On the lower part of the page, which takes up the last two-fifths, the *mise en scène* changes completely. Only another thickly framed caption in the upper left part of the sequence is similar to the top of the page. It informs about an Israeli operation, which took place the day after the suicide attack on the bus. Eleven Palestinians had been killed in the Jabaliya refugee camp during this operation (McGreal). But in addition to this fairly neutral information given in text form, Sacco chose to add five other captions that are spread like the fingers of a hand over the sequence. In them, he gives further details: "Eight are killed in one spot ... where firemen are trying to put out a blaze .... We watch the footage over and over on the Arab stations .... Israeli shells explode amongst the firemen and onlookers," and finally, "All of them are non-combatants" (291). These added details suggest that the Israeli operation was an insidious act of cruelty, as the Israeli army seems to have struck twice in order to cause even more victims. The scarce information about the bus bombing in Haifa creates, on the other hand, the opposite effect on the reader: it isn't made clear that the majority of the "students" were underage pupils returning from school. Furthermore, the information is omitted that the suicide bomber chose to add metal shrapnel, probably in order to cause the maximum possible injuries (Israel Ministry of Foreign Affairs). As a result, the reader is made to sympathize with the Palestinians rather than with the Israelis.

This strategy is considerably reinforced by the visualization of the attack: the sequence is divided into four panels that are partly covered by the aforementioned captions. Two of these panels are lightly tilted. In the left one are two firemen presented from their knees up. They direct a jet of water onto a car and a house in flames. In the one to the right, three wounded, probably dead, men are visible, a trail of smoke drifting above them. Compared to the firemen, the man in the foreground is framed even closer, in medium close-up, so that his face, as well as the wound in his chest, is plainly visible. Between these two panels is positioned a frameless panel which represents the blasting of a shell. Although the two framed panels are overlapping the drawing on both sides, the violence of the blast is tangible, since jets from the blast are partly concealing the drawing of the bus above in the middle of the page. Finally, positioned on the lower left corner of the page, can be seen Abed's and Sacco's black, more or less silhouetted heads, in half profile, from the back. Their gaze is directed to the right, to the blast, the five captions and the dead bodies. Their faces are lit by the light of the TV—as it is said that they are watching the scene on TV—but, as none of the other panels include a television set, it looks like if their faces were lit directly by the explosion, which underscores it's violence.

This *mise en scène* of overlapping panels—which gives the entire scene a visual complexity that forces the reader to slow down his reading rate in order to take in all the information—brilliantly retraces the timeline of the events: the Haifa bus bombing, followed by the Israeli army's operation in Jabaliya, both of them watched later on TV by Sacco and his friend. But the framing and the content of the drawings themselves also reveal a clear strategy of persuasion. To retell the bus bombing, Sacco opted, as a reference, for a photograph like that taken by Nir Elias of Reuters, which is shot in a wider angle (Israel Ministry of Foreign Affairs). He also chose not to show any injured or dead, but rather happy Palestinians rejoicing over the news. For the "answer" of the Israel Defense Forces, on the other hand, he provokes compassion by splitting the event in several panels (and captions) forcing his readers to slow down their reading speed thereby allowing the information more time to "sink in." Most important, however, is that he chose to depict not only living, but also wounded, (and probably dead) people, and that in much closer angles (referencing, en passant, the prize-winning photograph taken by Ahmed Jadallah of Reuters). The outcome of this skillful example of persuasion-technique is that there is no sympathy for the Israelis, yet it allows for compassion for the Palestinians.

Propaganda for children: *Moussa et David*

Compared to Sacco's subtle techniques of persuasion, those displayed in Rajsfus and Demiguel's *Moussa et David* are a lot less complex and much easier to detect. The comic explains the Palestinian-Israeli conflict by telling the story of two ten-year-old boys, one Palestinian and one Israeli. They live, respectively, in a refugee camp in the West Bank and a mansion with a garden in Jerusalem. They only meet thanks to their shared passion for soccer, as a game is organized between an Israeli and Palestinian team. The story first shows Moussa and David in their respective environments, thereby explaining the two different Palestinian and Israeli/Zionist narratives. It terminates with the two boys sympathizing during the soccer game that ends in a draw, two goals for both sides. Therefore, it could certainly be a valuable pedagogical tool to explain the conflict to children, if the *mise en scène* did not clearly valuate the Palestinian side over the Israelis'.

To begin with, this favoritism is quantitatively countable in terms of panels and pages dedicated to the illustration of the two characters' lives: While Moussa's story is retold on twenty (out of forty-six) pages and a total of sixty-five (out of two-hundred and three) panels, David's comprises only eight pages and twenty-seven panels.[6] As to the recount of the historical background, thirty-two panels are devoted to the rendition of the Palestinian side, compared to ten for the Israeli's. Even the depiction of the match is unequal, since Moussa appears in a third more panels than David.

This privileging of the Palestinian narrative also continues on the level of the visualization of the story, which is drawn in a semirealistic, clear-line style, very rich in icons and symbols. For instance, the Israelis are dominantly shown as menacing, villainous soldiers who bully the Palestinians, even the children (e.g., 11, 20, 27–28, 36, 38). The Palestinians, on the other hand, are depicted as gentle people who manage to bear their fate with dignity, and keep smiling (18, 22). According to Annette Matton, this different form of portrayal is a widely used propaganda technique in caricature and comics. Furthermore, brown-greenish monsters with sharp teeth are present in the panels, to symbolize "the hatred in every context" and situation, as the artist explained in an interview (Demiguel). However, these monsters, which even cling sometimes to the figure's shoulders (e.g., Rajsfus and Demiguel 27), are more present in panels where Israelis, mostly soldiers, are depicted: nineteen times, to be exact, thus visualizing the Jewish hatred, whereas the same applies only eleven times to the Palestinians'.[7] Following the logic of Demiguel's explanation of these renderings, the comic thereby suggests that the Jews must hate the Palestinians much more than the other way

around. This insinuation becomes even more powerful as it is enhanced by the fact that
the Palestinian narrative is already favored quantitatively.

On countless occasions, Demiguel also includes national icons, such as the
Palestinian or the Israeli flags (e.g., 24, 31, 39, *passim*). In many cases, the use of the
colors and designs of the two flags merely represent the two different groups so that
even children that do not know about the flags should be able to easily distinguish
between the two groups. In a couple of panels, however, the blue-colored Star of David
is visualized independently from its flag-context, changing into a monstrous creature
(37), stone monsters with eyes that have pupils in the shape of the Star of David
(20) or a missile, causing a severe bomb crater (36). In another panel (Figure 15.2)
this national (Israelis) symbol becomes a kind of six-fold yoke that imprisons one
Palestinian in every of the six triangles (25). In the center of it can be seen a wickedly
smiling figure that, considering the hairdo, resembles David Ben-Gurion. Around the
Star are displayed blue, Hebrew letters. The drawing takes up the text in the caption

Figure 15.2 Maurice Rajsfus (text) and Jacques Demiguel (drawings), *Moussa et David—
Deux enfants d'un même pays*, Tartamudo Éditions, p. 14. © 2007 by LISEZ-MOI. Used
with permission.

of the same panel, which states that some of Moussa's family members had learned to speak Hebrew in Israeli prisons, but it reflects very badly on Israel in the same time. The Palestinian flag and its colors, on the other hand, are never used in a comparable way in the comic book.

This kind of anti-Israeli, pro-Palestinian propaganda can be found in many other drawings of this comic, as well. According to its editor, some of the drawings even had to be modified by Demiguel to attenuate their anti-Israel perspective: the gun barrel in panel 6 of page 11, for instance, was initially pointing at Moussa's head (Jover).

The propaganda is not limited to the visual level, but can be detected on the textual level as well, even though Rajsfus manages to keep a fairly neutral tone and chooses not to use direct speech but only a commentary that accompanies the pictures. When it comes to the description of the preparation of the football game, for example, the text ridicules the anxiety of the Israeli security regarding the possibility of suicide attacks. By means of ironic half sentences—for example, "One never takes too many precautions …"[8] (45) or "That in itself was a small victory!" (44)—the fear of the Israelis in the book, that the Palestinians could hide explosives in the studs of the soccer boots or the soccer ball itself, is denoted to be nothing else but absurd. Just as absurd is their anxiety, that the two Palestinian coaches could be dangerous. In other captions, the word "terrorists" is put into quotation marks (20) and it is associated with the "horrible separation wall" (40). While the quotation marks added to the word "terrorists" put into question the perception of terrorism in the context of the Israeli-Palestinian conflict, the adjective "horrible" is judgmental and the "separation wall" could also be perceived as a critique of the Israeli politics. Both are therefore rhetorical choices, by which the Israeli narrative is put into question.

These seldom, but nevertheless existing, textual passages that suggest a more pro-Palestinian perception of the conflict are particularly astonishing, since Holocaust survivor and acclaimed historian Maurice Rajsfus wanted to be as "neutral as possible" (Issartel) in his attempt to explain the history of the Palestinian-Israeli conflict to children, even though he adopted a very critical attitude toward Zionism in other publications.[9] What is more bewildering is that the pro-Palestinian propaganda of this work seems to have gone unnoticed by the critics (e.g., Marie and Histoire d'en Lire). The comic even won the Sid Ali Melouha-prize of the *Carrefour Européen du 9ème Art et de l'Image* in Aubenas in 2008, honoring its defense of human rights (Rédaction Carrefour Européen du 9e Art et de l'Image).

In the respect of their intention of creating a comic book for juvenile readers that neutrally explains the Israeli-Palestinian conflict, Maurice Rajsfus and, especially, his illustrator Jacques Demiguel have come up short. On the other hand, this work, as well as that of Sacco's, demonstrates that comics are just as suitable as the other media to treat such a serious topic as the Palestinian-Israeli conflict. But just as with other media, comics can easily serve as an effective tool of persuasion and propaganda, especially while treating a subject as explosive. The rhetorical power that lies within comics, therefore, has to be handled with care, not only when addressing younger readers who may be unaware of any ideological manipulation, but also when written for adults. This is especially important when the topic is purported to be handled journalistically or through a documentary lens.

Notes

1   For the sake of neutrality, I will use the terms "Israeli-Palestinian conflict" and "Palestinian-Israeli conflict" alternately.

2   Collective narratives are social constructions in the form of histories, beliefs, stories, aspirations, and current explanations that a group holds about its surroundings and itself and thereby part of the collective's shared identity (Salomon 274).

3   On Palestinian writers, see Mahmud Ghanayim, as well as Nurith Gertz and George Khleifi. On Israeli artist giving voice to Palestinian concerns, see Jacob Feldt, Ella Shohat, and Françoise Saquer-Sabin.

4   For example, see the scholarship of Mary Layoun; Thomas Juneau and Mira Sucharov; Dirk Vanderbeke; Benjamin Woo; and Bridget Maher.

5   See, for example, the work of Bill Nichols and Eva Hohenberger.

6   Every panel including a drawing of Moussa and/or his name or reference to his family has been counted as Moussa's. The same method has been applied to David.

7   Israeli hatred: see page 26, panels 2–3; 27, panels 1–5; 28, panels 1, 3 and 5; 34, panel 4; 36, panel 3; 38, panel 4; 47, panel 2; 50, panel 4. Palestinian hatred: see page 17, panel 4; 25, panel 4; 26, panels 5, 7 and 9; 36, panel 1. In four more panels the monsters symbolize the hatred of both sides: page 31, panel 7; 39, panel 1; 40, panel 3; 41, panel 1; 46, panel 1.

8   This and the following are my translations.

9   See, for example, *Israel-Palestine: L'ennemi Intérieur* and *Palestine: Chronique Des Événements Courants, 1988–1989*.

Strange Encounters in Rutu Modan's
Exit Wounds and "Jamilti"

Stephen E. Tabachnick

Rutu Modan's *Exit Wounds* (2007) and "Jamilti" (2008) offer a uniquely individual reflection on the suicide bombings of the Second Intifada period in Israel. While the negative effects of these bombings on the Israeli psyche are apparent in these works, Modan surprisingly shows that the bombings can result in completely unexpected and even positive outcomes. Via Hergé's clear line style, she brings a startling, new, and even encouraging clarity to these horrible events.

In an interview with Steve Korver, she has stated that when a boyfriend stopped phoning her, she thought he might be dead. This reminds us of Wordsworth's "Strange Fits of Passion I Have Known," in which the speaker fears for a moment that his beloved Lucy might be dead, simply because the moon has gone down behind her house as he approaches it. The title of the poem contains Wordsworth's admission that people in love often feel strange, exaggerated, and unfounded emotions. But behind Modan's statement, the ever-present and real possibility of a suicide bombing as the cause of her fear of her boyfriend's possible death gives that fear more of a basis in reality than Wordsworth's "strange" (as he puts it) and relatively baseless feeling. That personal phone incident and the Israeli documentary film *No. 17* by Dan Ofek about a suicide bombing on a bus, after which no relative or friend comes to claim a particular victim, were the inspiration for *Exit Wounds*, according to Modan. Modan's use of the real people's names Koby Franco and Moran Palmoni in her story, as stated in her acknowledgments, further anchors *Exit Wounds* in reality, however fictional the actual characters and events depicted are. While we read the colorful panels and follow the fanciful plot twists in her work, we can never forget their solid historical basis in the phenomenon of suicide bombing.

Also, despite the absence of religious topics in Modan's interview with Korver, her graphic novel centers around a quest for belief in God's benevolence despite all reasons to believe the contrary. In fact, Modan discusses without overtly seeming to do so the problem of how a good God can co-exist with evil, in this case with the evil of suicide bombings, and comes to perhaps surprising conclusions.

Modan's drawing style defines the issues and characters very clearly. She does not use cross-hatching or shadows. She is also skillful enough for us to read the expressions on the characters' faces, although sometimes faces change too much like that of the Abu Kebir woman (46, 47), where the nose in the profile and the full facial expression don't seem to fit together well. Also, Numi's tears do not look natural (130). And Koby's body sometimes seems distorted (17). Despite these lapses, the colors are always good, the faces and gestures are expressive and convincing, and Israel (except perhaps for Numi's house, which would be exceptionally luxurious in any country) looks much like Israel actually does.

Briefly, the story of *Exit Wounds* is told from the point of view of a Tel Aviv cabdriver, Koby Franco, who lives with his aunt and uncle Ruthie and Aryeh, because his mother is dead and he does not get along with his father. He is contacted one day by a female soldier who tells him that his father may have been killed in a suicide bombing that took place in the Hadera central bus station. The soldier, Numi, wants Koby to provide DNA to establish if one of the bodies found after the blast was indeed his father's. Koby thinks it highly unlikely but agrees to help in her quest, which is based on her having seen a scarf which she made for his father appearing in a newspaper photograph showing the aftermath of the blast. In the course of their investigation, Koby comes to understand that she had an affair with his father, and he himself begins to like her despite her lack of any special physical attractiveness. After some ups and downs in their search for his father and in their own relationship, leading to a break, Koby discovers that his father is indeed alive and has married an ultra-Orthodox woman. This fits his father's mode of operation—"exit wounds" in one sense refers to his father's absence from the lives of Koby and his sister, as well as to his habit of doing things and appearing and disappearing without notice. Koby visits the woman, but as usual his father is nowhere to be found when he wants him, and he seems to have disappeared from that woman's life as well as from his son's. Koby feels that he must tell Numi about this important result of their search despite their estrangement. This is when the final, climactic scene takes place, after he is turned away from Numi's door by her sister.

In that final scene, Koby leaps from a high tree branch ostensibly into the arms of Numi, who has come into her backyard to see why her dogs are making a fuss. He first asks her for a ladder, which she doesn't have, because he is afraid that he will break his neck if he jumps from that height, as she advises him to do. She tells him that she will catch him. When he jumps, Modan is giving us a metaphorical rather than a realistic ending, because he could not jump from that height without indeed breaking something, and Numi could not catch him without getting seriously injured (172). The idea, however, is that Koby has learned to trust Numi, and that both of them are now ready to risk being hurt in order to be with each other. They have both gained confidence through their relationship. The mental exit wounds first caused by the suicide bombing in Hadera and the thought that Koby's father is dead, and then again by Koby's father's seeming abandonment of both Koby and Numi, are healed or at least overcome when Koby and Numi finally learn to trust one another.

Because Koby's father Gabriel seems to have been a non-presence in his life— disappearing during important moments, not showing any steady concern for him, and even revealing ignorance of his preferences to the point of getting him a birthday T-shirt for the wrong soccer team (77)—Koby has lacked belief in everything. When he tells Numi that "I'm happy as I am," she sardonically comments, "Yeah, I can see that" with a knowing look on her face (86). And when his sister Orly seems to indicate that he is obsessing about his relationship with his father, he hangs up on her (156), indicating the depth of his Gabriel-inflicted wound.

Most of all, he can't get over the idea that Numi has had a relationship with Gabriel. She is tall and awkward, and in a country where there is a chronic shortage of men because of the wars, she is at a disadvantage because of her mediocre looks. So she has had a relationship with a man in his sixties. Numi contacts Koby only because she is concerned that Gabriel may have been killed in the suicide bombing in Hadera. In the course of their search for his father at the Abu Kebir forensics institute (and at the cemetery where he is supposedly buried, and at the site of the bombing), Koby finds that he has something in common with this ungainly woman, who is taller than he is and not particularly attractive physically. And when Numi gives Koby a signed T-shirt from the team he actually likes (116)—as if making up for his father's mistaken gift of the wrong shirt years ago—he understands her inherent goodness, and their relationship moves to a new level. One might think that part of her attractiveness to Koby is that she is from a very rich family (her father owns the team that signed Koby's shirt), with a house that would look expensive in the United States, let alone near Tel Aviv; but nowhere does Koby ever refer to her money or even seem to care about it.

So far, the romance seems a bit unusual. Super-rich girls do not usually go with poor boys. Sons do not usually date girls who have gone with their fathers. But Numi is hurt when she realizes that Gabriel has been two-timing her with an old (quite literally) flame closer to his own age, Atara Dayan, and that propels her relationship with Koby forward (127). And Gabriel seems never to have been around when Koby needed him. They both now have the feeling of abandonment—the true exit wound—by Gabriel in common. But Numi's comment, "Like father, like son," which is uttered at precisely the wrong moment (when she and Koby are first making love, 137) exacerbates an already fragile situation, and leads to a break. However, the romance between Koby and Numi becomes even more unusual and achieves a biblical resonance, when we examine the religious clues within the story. If Gabriel is an absent father, God as a father has not abandoned Israel or indeed humanity, including Koby and Numi.

When speaking to his aunt about his father's possible death, Koby recalls what he takes to be his father's over-emotional reaction to his Bar Mitzvah ceremony (57). Koby's aunt Ruthie does not believe in Gabriel's possible death, and states that Gabriel will probably "show up out of nowhere," as he apparently did during Koby's Bar Mitzvah (56). But then she cries as she remembers the Bar Mitzvah of her son Tulik, who was killed during a war or action in Lebanon—yet another "exit wound" the family has suffered. Surprisingly, inscribed right behind her on a wall, most probably that of a synagogue, as she cries, in Hebrew with no English translation, is the phrase: "I will place my Sanctuary among them forever" (57). This phrase, from Ezekiel 37:26, refers to God's statement in that chapter that He will bring the people of Israel together and make them into a single nation. Following on a discussion of the possible death of Gabriel, Tulik's actual death, and Koby's Bar Mitzvah ritual—all religious in their import—this phrase is strangely resonant. Modan makes no comment on the phrase via Koby or Aunt Ruthie, and does not call attention to it in any way. In fact, printed in black ink on a purple wall partially obscured by Koby's speech balloon, it is very easy to miss, even for a reader of Hebrew. This phrase appears again in a panel on the top of page 58, but it is even more obscured by Koby's head in that panel. This shows Modan's subtlety and yet persistence in getting her views across—the reader must work a bit to discern her message, which is there for those who can find (and understand) it. The phrase's appearance only in Hebrew in this English-language edition might be seen in terms of realistic probability, that is, as a usual Orthodox synagogue wall inscription, which very well might be printed only in Hebrew, with no English translation, whether in Israel or the United States. But its effect on English-only readers is truly to make it into a coded message.

In this phrase, once it is translated, we have a clear application to Koby and Numi, even at a relatively early point in the story when their eventual coming together is far from realization: like the people of Israel under God's influence, Koby and Numi will indeed be brought together and united. Without their knowing it in their secularity (they give no indication of being religious), God is indeed watching over Israel and all humanity, including them, and even possibly has plans for them. This phrase in Hebrew with no translation in the English edition reminds us that, especially for Israeli writers, the Bible usually stands in some relation to all events that take place in Israel, even a seemingly casual love affair, whether or not the participants acknowledge that. Readers who do not know Hebrew—or who do but may have missed the single phrase from Ezekiel inserted in the background of this panel and the second, even more obscured statement of this phrase (58)—may not realize that Modan, over and above any character's voice, seems to be making a statement that God stands behind all events in this book. And that proves to be the case, especially given the positive outcome.

When we look at the names of the major characters, Modan's biblical symbolism is again clear. Gabriel means "man of God" in Hebrew, and the archangel Gabriel was sent to explain Daniel's visions in the Book of Daniel. Koby mentions that his father Gabriel cried at his Bar Mitzvah, and Numi says he cried when the soccer team Maccabi won, so he seems to be unusually sensitive, a sign again possibly aligning him with an angel. Also, Numi mentions that he went trampoline jumping with her, not something one associates with someone nearly seventy years old. While Gabriel in *Exit Wounds* is an absent father, he does send both Koby and his sister Orly the proceeds from the sale of his apartment instead of keeping this considerable sum of money himself (149–150). Gabriel therefore, while distant, is a caring messenger, and it is because of him that Koby meets Numi. In particular, it is through his absence—his exit—that Koby meets Numi. At first, this is the imagined absence caused by Numi's fear that Gabriel has died in the suicide bombing; later, the absence consists of Gabriel's moving on to other women, as well as his failure to appear at any point in the graphic novel. He is absent from our eyes as well as from Koby's and Numi's during the duration of the story recounted in *Exit Wounds*. His absence causes wounds which are healed only when Koby and Numi finally come together as a couple at the very end of the book. Gabriel's possible disappearance has led Numi to Koby, and as improbable as their romance is, it seems to have been ordained by heaven or fate to give comfort to two wounded people.

This idea receives further support when we look at the name "Koby," which is short for Jacob, or the supplanter. Koby supplants Gabriel in the affections of Numi. The name "Numi" means sleep in its imperative form, and like sleep, she gives Koby comfort in the form of a release from holding a grudge against his father and finally by placing her trust and love in Koby. Both Numi and Koby have reasons to be angry with Gabriel, and he will always be present in their relationship to some degree, but when they are together they are able to find comfort and happiness. Ariel Kahn points out that the scarf that Numi originally gave Gabriel as a present, and which he then gave to his old flame Atara Dayan, and which she lost during the explosion in Hadera (leading Numi to think Gabriel had died there), was used by Numi to try to tie Gabriel to her (210). While Numi's attempt to bind Gabriel fails, she ends up binding Koby to her, even without a scarf. Thus, a suicide bombing and Gabriel's possible death (as well as the death of innocent people) have resulted in a binding of the living to the living, rather than the dead to the living, as in the Bible's use of the term *Akedah*, or binding, as Kahn tells us.

During their search for Gabriel, Koby and Numi get to Hadera's central bus station, where the bombing occurred, and they see a sign in Hebrew—again, not translated into English—saying, "The Corner of Chaim" (65). Chaim is the man who owns a small kiosk and who currently has the scarf that was found in the bus station after the bombing—the same scarf which, previously, Numi made for Gabriel, and which he later gave to Atara Dayan. In Hebrew, "Chaim" means "life," and the sign is right over a makeshift memorial for the bombing victims. So the sign can be read as "The Corner of Life" meaning that the memory of the victims lives on. On the other hand, Chaim the kiosk owner, who was fortunately kicked out of the café fifteen minutes before the blast, sells Numi flowers to put on the memorial. He also wants her to donate to his cause of keeping the small business stalls at the central bus station, stalls which the city apparently wants to replace with fancier shops. Later he extracts even more money from them for this cause and at first refuses to give up the scarf to Numi—he calls the scarf a souvenir of the blast. Similarly, a customer in the café complains that Yossi, the owner of the café where the blast occurred, always used to give him free tea. And this causes Yossi's bereaved wife, who now runs the restaurant alone and who has refused to give him free tea, to scream, "There is no Yossi! Yossi's dead!" (71), to which he responds that she is a "tightwad." This shows the insensitivity to the deaths of those not directly affected by the bombing and the uncaring background against which Koby and Numi continue their quest. This same customer is also insensitive to the foreign workers at the station, and he confuses the Filipino woman Del with Nora, the new cleaning woman who has replaced her. Clearly, says Modan via this incident, there is a need for people to come together, and to realize that God has, indeed, placed His sanctuary among them forever. The woman at the desk of the Abu Kebir forensic institute, is similarly insensitive, as are the doctors there, to the plight of the relatives seeking their dead loved ones. It is as if the death of someone else, even as the result of a suicide bombing, is not important to anyone outside of their former families and friends, and even sympathy is lacking. Since no one seems to care about anyone else, something of which Numi accuses Koby at one point (82), it is good for Numi and Koby, finally, to care about one another. That is the positive thing that comes out of all of this death and the insensitivity it generates.

The exit wounds left by Gabriel's repeated absences are healed as Numi and Koby come together. Even though Gabriel has again disappeared, this time apparently leaving the Orthodox wife he has married, his being alive is a blessing, and we come to realize that we can never see him because he is a heaven-sent body whose supposed death was the occasion for Numi's first contact with Koby. Even if he does not come home to his new wife on time (or ever) and we never see him, he remains an important presence in the book—ever-present in his absence, like a messenger of God who works in mysterious ways to bring people together. Koby compliments Gabriel's new wife on her food, and she gets to meet Gabriel's son, so something positive results even from their relatively brief encounter.

The theme of bringing people together continues throughout the story. When she thinks that Gabriel might be dead and buried, Numi comments on how non-Jews are buried apart from Jews in Israeli cemeteries, and she says that should not be so. As Koby and Numi walk into the cemetery, they ignore a man asking for charity. Yet they, too, need charity—both are hurting, both lack faith. Numi is distraught after she discovers that Gabriel was two-timing her and after she makes Koby angry with her because of the love-making incident when she mentioned his father. Koby is hurting because he is estranged from Gabriel and from his sister Orly, and his mother is dead. When Numi and Koby gain faith in each other and in God, who (Modan strongly implies) will not allow Koby to break his neck or to harm Numi when he falls into her arms from the tree, all is well. The final chapter, in which many of these events take place, is appropriately entitled "Resurrection." Not only is Gabriel found to be alive, but Koby sees himself in the young Palmoni child now living in his family's old apartment (152), especially when he finds an old present that he and Orly gave to his dead mother. And Koby and Numi's love affair begins anew. Whether or not Koby would admit it, their improbable romance has been put in place by an absent, ethereal figure who seems to be everywhere and nowhere. They are brought together because God, through an unlikely angel named Gabriel, is watching over them.

If Numi had not made the scarf for Gabriel, he could not have given it to Atara Dayan, who would not have lost it in Hadera during the suicide bombing, and Numi would not then have thought that Gabriel might have died in the blast, causing her to seek out Koby. And if Chaim, who has the scarf, had not insisted that they support his petition about shops in the Hadera bus station, and if he not had a list of people who supported his petition, and who must also have been present around the time of the blast, they would not have found Atara Dayan. And finding her, and having her recognize the scarf, causes Numi to get angry at Gabriel for jilting her with an older woman; and that in turn opens her up to Koby's advances. And if Gabriel had not sent Koby a check through his lawyer after he sold his apartment, and if Koby had not found the Orthodox wife of Gabriel and hurried to tell Numi that he had traced him, and that he was alive, Koby and Numi would never have come together again. These seeming coincidences indicate a force working behind the scenes—and here we again recall God's statement in Ezekiel, part of which is on the wall early in the graphic novel, that He will bring his people together.

The idea of togetherness also affects the economic disparity between Koby and Numi. This disparity never seems to influence events in a negative or positive way, and that is surprising, again indicating a larger force working behind the scenes to bring them together. Numi's mother is a famous model, and her father is a millionaire. In

Israeli terms, they are living in almost untold luxury. As we have seen, Numi's father even owns the soccer team that Koby likes, so Numi is able to give him a birthday present of a signed shirt from the team. Koby is only a cabdriver. But nowhere does any of this seem to influence Koby's thinking; he never mentions Numi's money and does not even seem overly impressed with her house. Numi seems spiritually estranged from her elegant mother and sister, and she is not a Savyon snob who would not even look at a cabdriver for a boyfriend. She never seems to think, and certainly never says, that Koby is interested in her because of her money. Once again, a force larger than both of them seems to be operating here, bringing together at least some of the people of Israel regardless of social status and wealth. And all this is the result of a suicide bombing. Although Modan never presents suicide bombing as a constructive act, she does show the unexpected positive outcome of such destruction.

Modan's story, "Jamilti," in *Jamilti and Other Stories*, is another reflection on the strange and unexpected consequences of a suicide bombing and again reminds us that Israeli artists are in a position to see things from a unique angle because of the difficulties with which their country has been surrounded since its beginning. Some Arab countries, too, such as Iraq, have suffered suicide bombings, but in those cases one group of Arabs is attacking another. In Israel, suicide bombings are inevitably Arab attacks on Jews and therefore involve tensions between two distinct peoples. And they represent only the latest method used by hostile Arabs to cause harm to the Jewish state. But despite that very real harm, Modan's unique imagination in "Jamilti," as in *Exit Wounds*, shows how a suicide bombing can have unexpected and possibly positive results across national lines.

In this story, a Jewish nurse who is about to be married argues with her husband-to-be and a cabdriver about politics, because she is more liberal than they are and refuses to agree with them that all Arabs are bad. When she angrily gets out of the cab as a result of this argument, she happens to stand next to the Café Noir, or Black Café, which unfortunately becomes red because of an explosion inside. Rama, the nurse, rushes in, sees an individual with his legs blown off and applies a tourniquet and mouth-to-mouth resuscitation. After she does so, he calls her "Jamilti" as he looks into her eyes (14). Later as she watches the aftermath of the explosion on television news with her fiancé, it transpires that the only person who was injured in the blast was the suicide bomber himself (16), and it was therefore he who called her "Jamilti," or "my beautiful one," in Arabic. The police speculate that he set the bomb off accidentally because no one else was in the café at the time. She says nothing about this to her fiancé, who has been relieved to find her safe outside the cafe after the blast, but she reflects to herself on the meaning of this event. In essence, she has kissed a suicide bomber who might have killed many innocent people, including her, and he has called her his beautiful one, as if he has been in love with her. It is almost as if she has been disloyal to her fiancé by making love to a suicide bomber, who is now dead.

There are many dimensions to this story seen from both the bomber's and Rama's individual perspectives. When she finds him, Zuheir al-Aziz is unconscious and moaning and has his legs blown off at the knees. When she applies a tourniquet made from her hair ribbon and attempts mouth-to-mouth resuscitation, he awakens and looks at her. Does he think that she is one of the seventy-two virgins promised by

Allah to martyrs? Or in his pain and confusion, is he confusing her with an Arab girl of whom he is fond? He calls her "Jamilti," "my beautiful one" before he hears her speak. But then she says "What?" in Hebrew and he still continues to call her "Jamilti" (14). So does he know that she is Jewish and still calls her "Jamilti" despite the fact that he was out to kill Jews? Or is it that he understands that she is a nurse (she is dressed in her white Magen David uniform with a Star of David above her heart), and simply thanks her for her attempt to save his life? Or is this simply a last gasp at life, an expression of love from a dying young person, albeit a suicide bomber? We cannot know which of these perceptions—or a combination of these perceptions— on the part of the suicide bomber is correct, and Rama cannot know. But there is the possibility that he did know that she is Jewish, and in his dying moment, seeing that she is trying to help him and has even "kissed" him as it were, found her to be a beautiful person. So, in his last moments, did Zuheir cross the Arab-Jewish divide between hate and love? The question remains open because we do not hear from him again, and, because he is evacuated to a hospital for treatment, we do not know if he dies or not.

From Rama's perspective, the story is a bit different. She was blown back by a blast and then rushed into the café to help, asking if anyone is in there. She hears Zuheir moaning and instantly takes off her hair ribbon to use as a tourniquet, begging him to "hold on" (although his eyes are closed at that point, indicating unconsciousness, and he undoubtedly does not hear her). She then administers mouth-to-mouth resuscitation. At this point he awakens and looks in her eyes with a loving, fervent look, calling her "Jamilti" (14). She asks what he said, not knowing Arabic—and even possibly not knowing in which language he is speaking (although Israelis know at least the sound of Arabic, this one word might not be a clear clue to the language)—at which point the medics come in and take him away as he again repeats "Jamilti." Only later, after her boyfriend runs to her aid and they are home watching the television news, does she understand that she was trying to save the suicide bomber. The announcer's statement, "No one was wounded in the attack" (16), is questioned twice by Rama, who knows she tried to help someone wounded. She comes to understand that this is the announcer's way of putting things—no innocent civilian was wounded, and the suicide bomber was the only casualty—as if the suicide bomber was not human. This is something like Numi's comment in *Exit Wounds* on the separation between the graves of Jews and non-Jews in Israeli cemeteries. Zuheir, whatever his motive and the disaster he intended to create, is still human. And Rama has, via her mouth-to-mouth resuscitation, made him think that he was kissing her, perhaps. Or perhaps not. Maybe he only praised her as a beautiful person for trying to save his life. She cannot know, but she does not tell her boyfriend about what happened in the café. She understands that she tried to save the life of a suicide bomber who called her by an endearing name and then she even learns his name from the broadcast, giving him an identity. Is she sorry that she has helped save a suicide bomber who might have killed her, too, had she gone into the café before the blast? Or does she feel that, owing to his uttering "Jamilti," she has proven her point that Arabs are people too even though the cabdriver's comment that "they bring up their children to be killers too" (10) seems to be borne out in the case of Zuheir, who might have managed to kill innocent civilians had his bomb not accidentally gone off? Or, because she is a nurse who therefore rushed into the café when others might have run away from it as the narrator says, does she feel that she has given some comfort to a dying man, regardless of who he is and what his deeds?—Or, finally, does she feel that she has somehow been unfaithful to Guri, her boyfriend, who would be furious if he thought that a suicide bomber might have thought that he had kissed Rama and that that had given him comfort before he died? Modan does not answer these questions. Rama never tells Guri anything, saying that she asked about the meaning of "Jamilti" for "nothing" (17). She simply agrees with Guri about the day's events and listens as he talks about contacting the disc jockey concerning the music for their upcoming wedding. Clearly, it has been quite a day, and Rama has been permanently affected by it. How will she come to terms with this semi-infidelity caused by her nurse's desire to help save a life?

The third important character in this story is Rama's boyfriend. Guri is initially portrayed as callous, in that he cares more about playing a game of soccer with his friends than helping Rama select a wedding dress or make the seating arrangements at the wedding hall. Rama even calls him a "fascist" (10) when he agrees with their cab-driver that the Arabs can't be trusted and says that Rama does not know what she is talking about. To her jibe at him, he answers that he is just being rational. Rama, also incensed at Guri's agreement with the cabdriver that peacenik girls are promiscuous (10), gets out of the cab, and that is when the suicide bombing occurs. Guri runs up to her and embraces her when he sees her emerge from the café, and they seem to be at peace when at home watching the news. But Rama never tells him what happened, and the story closes as she seems to acquiesce in his wanting to call the DJ about the wedding music. What would Guri think if he knew that Rama had saved the life of a suicide bomber who then called her a "beautiful one"? Maybe nothing, but perhaps it's better not to know because he might perceive it as a form of semi-infidelity, or at best a misguided attempt to apply benign peacenik principles to an Arab who attempted to murder Jews. So it all remains unsaid.

The reader is the remaining party to the story, and the question is what he or she should think about this. Has Rama's nurse's training simply prevailed and molded her behavior without involving any thought about morality or consequences? That may have been the case in her initial reaction to the blast, but her failure to inform Guri about what transpired and her thoughtfulness after hearing the television report indicate that more than unconscious nurse's training is involved.

So is Modan suggesting that even a suicide bombing can have a positive effect if it results in a positive connection between Arabs and Jews, however strange? That is, did Zuheir knowingly call a Jew a "beautiful one" and realize the mistaken nature of suicide bombing after having been wounded by it? Did Rama think that it is a good thing that she gave a wounded man, no matter how heinous his attempted deed, a feeling of love and kindness? Did she think because of his calling her a "beautiful one" that Zuheir realized his error in wanting to kill Jews and tried somehow to take back his action? How has her feeling about the relationship between Arabs and Jews changed after this encounter? Is she even more of a peacenik than she was before? Or does she reflect that had she gone into the café a few moments earlier, she might have been injured or killed in the blast, and that Zuheir like all suicide bombers is fanatic and crazy despite his use of a term of endearment to her? Maybe she is silent about these events because she has become less of a believer in peace and human goodness, and she does not want to admit an error in her earlier conversation with the cabdriver and Guri? We simply cannot know; this is a story that asks a cascade of unanswerable questions. But her wedding will proceed, and she has become a more thoughtful person as a result of this encounter. Certainly she will value her own life and that of Guri more than she might have done otherwise.

If we take *Exit Wounds* and "Jamilti" together, what is Modan trying to tell us? That difficult situations, including suicide bombings, have unexpected consequences, some of them positive. Koby and Numi come together because Gabriel may have died in a suicide bombing. Fortunately, that is not the case, and he exists only in his role as a messenger. Although he may leave exit wounds all around him, the biggest exit wound is when Koby and Numi seem to break up, and that wound is healed when they come together and trust one another. In "Jamilti," Rama and Zuheir come together in an unexpected way. Their encounter leaves her with a lifetime of thought about her beliefs, including her willingness to believe in the goodness of all people. Certainly Rama will value life more as a result of this encounter, but will she also reevaluate her view of the Arabs and the political situation in Israel? Will she believe even more in the necessity of fighting for peace, or regard that as a lost cause? Or will she view what happened as a clandestine love affair, however brief? Modan does not tell us what to think, only to expect the unexpected to emerge from strange encounters. But what is clear is that in her work, sometimes evil can produce good results, showing that despite man's failures God's benevolence may still be operating and may bring us—all of us, regardless of nationality—together in strange and unexpected ways.

The "Outsider": Neil Gaiman and the Old Testament

Cyril Camus

Neil Gaiman, the Minnesota-based former Englishman who wrote the world-acclaimed DC Comics series *Sandman*, is a prominent Jewish comics writer, although his experience of Jewishness is very distinctive. In Robert K. Elder's interview "Gods and Other Monsters: A Sandman Exit Interview and Philosophical Omnibus," as Gaiman tries to articulate a description of his childhood, in regard to the issue of Jewishness, he states:

> I was brought up Jewish. But I was Jewish and attended High Church of England schools, which is everything you get in Catholic education, without nuns. It was a lovely way of receiving all the religion one ever needed, as an outsider. It was very odd. I was the kid scoring the top marks in religious studies despite the fact that the religious studies would be on the *Book of Matthew* or whatever and I wasn't even a Christian, which was a lovely position to be in. One got everything as an outsider. (Schweitzer 71)

His Jewish identity certainly made him an "outsider" in his Anglican educational environment but being half immersed in another belief system than his family's, from an early age on, actually allowed him to put both systems in perspective. As he puts it, "in a sense, it made [him] view *everything* as myth" (Bender 105). So his situation made him more or less an "outsider" as to Jewish faith too. Nowadays he describes himself as a believer, but he is unable to name a particular dogma to which he adheres. His comics and other writings often feature pagan gods and mythological beings from many different traditions, interacting with one another. As for "believ[ing] in a biblical god," he claims: "sometimes I do and sometimes I don't" (Elder 70). It is as if the spiritual stance he had decided to adopt was the same as Samantha Black Crow's in his novel *American Gods*—"I can believe … anything" (Gaiman, *American Gods* 421)—or the child protagonist's in his semiautobiographical short story "One Life, Furnished in Early Moorcock": "a magnificent anarchy of belief" (Gaiman, *Smoke* 284). This is, at least, Bethany Alexander's reading of his works, in her article "No Need to Choose: A Magnificent Anarchy of Belief" (Schweitzer 135–139). Gaiman certainly retains a fond but detached outlook on his Jewish roots, which he seems to deal with, in interviews, in the same half respectful, half tongue-in-cheek idiom that he uses, in his fictions, for any religion or myth: "I don't think I've particularly practiced since my bar mitzvah. Then again, I take a certain amount of comfort in the fact that if ever anywhere they institute the camps and they want to start sticking Jews in them again, I'd go in and fry. I don't think it's something one particularly stops being because you've stopped practicing" (Elder 71).[1]

Being a believer, and having, at the same time, an outsider's outlook on the belief systems most familiar to him, could easily qualify him, making due allowances, as a sort of modern-day Kafka,[2] if it were not for his being absolutely not melancholy about his condition. Quite on the contrary, he states: "I actually love feeling like an outsider. For example, I really enjoyed the first six years I spent in the U.S. because everything was so alien. I'm starting to get used to America now, which makes me think it may be time to move somewhere else" (Bender 106). This cheerful embrace of the privileged position of the "alien" often shows on a close analysis of his writings. "Part of *Sandman*'s dynamic stemmed from Neil's discovery and fascination, as both a European and an Englishman, with America," if we are to believe Mike Dringenberg, one of *Sandman*'s pencilers, inkers, and co-creators (McCabe 80). It is even truer with *American Gods*, as the meditation on American culture is more explicit (hence, the title), and as Gaiman emphasizes the importance of his outlook as an outsider when discussing the book with Stephen Bissette: "I don't think *American Gods* could have been written by someone who was American. A lot of that is because, if you're a goldfish in the water, you don't go, 'This water tastes odd.' You go, 'This is what water tastes like'" (Wagner, Golden, and Bissette 493).[3] Similarly, instances of Gaiman enjoying the feeling of being an outsider can easily be traced as far as religion is concerned. A reader who is trying to understand Gaiman's relationship to the one fundamental text of Jewish faith and culture—the Old Testament—might find two of such instances very telling. And these instances are, namely, the intertextual borrowings from, and rewritings of, the sacred book contained, on the one hand, in *Sandman*, and on the other hand, in *Outrageous Tales from the Old Testament*.

The latter (and, chronologically speaking, the first) is an anthology of short, black-and-white graphic narratives that was released in 1987 by the British publishing house Knockabout Comics.[4] As the title suggests, all of these narratives are adapted from the Old Testament. Nearly all the contributors are British comics writers and comics artists: for example, Alan Moore wrote "Leviticus," which was illustrated by Hunt Emerson, and Dave Gibbons wrote and illustrated "Sodom and Gomorrah." Kim Deitch, who wrote and illustrated "The Story of Job," is the only American contributor. Gaiman, who still lived in England at the time, contributed not one (as the other writers did) but *six* different scripts. That might be a good measure of his interest in the project. But what, exactly, was this project about? Obviously, from the title again, it can easily be inferred that it did not consist in faithful and graphically neutral remakes of the biblical texts, of the kind one could have found in *Classics Illustrated* comics.[5] On the contrary, these works of ruthless theological satire take their inspiration, both iconographic and thematic, from the two traditions, in the history of comics, which defined themselves by their offensiveness: underground "comix" and EC Comics horror anthologies. The "iconic"[6] visual style that is used in most narratives in *Outrageous Tales from* the Old Testament, as well as their humorous, cynical emphasis on violence and sex, are pervasive clues of the comix inspiration of the anthology. As for the debt to EC Comics, it appears more clearly in one particular story (one of Gaiman's), and we will come back to it a little later.

To understand what *Outrageous Tales from the Old Testament* is all about, it seems particularly relevant to stress that various theoretical works have shown that violence and fear are important aspects of the religious experience. Theologian Rudolf Otto has identified the "*tremendum*," that is, "awe," inspired by the power of the deity, as a primordial part of the "numinous," the irrational feeling that lies at the core of the rational concept of the "holy" (for the respective definitions of the "numinous" and the "*tremendum*," see Otto 5–7 and 13–19). Philosopher René Girard has touched on this idea of awe at strange, inhuman power, but his interest was not so much in religious psychology as in religious sociology. Therefore, such considerations are meant, above all, to lead him to his point, that is, how the deep-seated fear of *human* aggression bears on the founding of a religious community:

> The sacred consists of all those forces whose dominance over man increases or seems to increase in proportion to man's effort to master them. Tempests, forest fires, and plagues, among other phenomena, may be classified as sacred. Far outranking these, however, though in a far less obvious manner, stands human violence—violence seen as something exterior to man and henceforth as a part of all the other outside forces that threaten mankind. Violence is the heart and secret soul of the sacred. (Girard, *Violence* 31)

Girard understands ritual murder and other sacrificial practices in primitive and ancient religious communities as an implicit model for the way *any* human community, especially a religious one, builds the integrity and harmony that it needs to preserve in order to thrive. In Girard's terms, "the sacrificial process prevents the spread of violence" by "polariz[ing] the community's aggressive impulses" (18) through the ritualizing of a "unanimous act of violence directed against [a] surrogate victim" (280) that symbolizes any antagonist whom individual members of the community might have wanted to kill or injure. Instead of "reciprocal violence, the violence that really hurts, setting man against man and threatening the total destruction of the community" (124–125), this process allows the community to "unite against" (102) a "scapegoat" (79), and, by casting it out through ritual assault, "to keep violence *outside* the community" (92). These reflections on the mechanisms of social unity allow him to conclude: "The failure of modern man to grasp the nature of religion has served to perpetuate its effects. Our lack of belief serves the same function in our society that religion serves in societies more directly exposed to essential violence. We persist in disregarding the power of violence in human societies; that is why we are reluctant to admit that *violence and the sacred are one and the same thing*" (262, emphasis mine).

It is that essential link between violence, terror, and religion that the writers and artists of *Outrageous Tales from the Old Testament* deal with. And the way they chose to deal with it is a peculiar kind of "caricature"—the technique, "in a verbal description" or "in graphic art," that consists in "exaggerat[ing] or distort[ing], for comic effect, a person's distinctive physical features or personality traits" (Abrams 28). Here, the word can be applied both to narrative aspects of the rewritings and to the graphic style and devices employed by the artists. And the target of the caricature is not so much a person as a *mood*, the one that can be found in the Old Testament. Caricature is, fundamentally, a humorous emphasis on one single aspect of a reality which is, as all realities, multifaceted. The trait which is emphasized at the expense of any other is, of course, the essential violence of the Old Testament.[7] And this emphasis is made humorous by the way it systematically *trivializes* Otto's dramatic notion of "*tremendum*," or Girard's almost lyrical styling of violence as "the heart and secret soul of the sacred." This trivializing is operated thanks to a variety of choices of cultural hypotexts that downplay the "*mysterium*" and the "*majestas*" attached to the "holy," or the sacred, leaving only a grotesque bloodbath.[8] For instance, *tremendum*-related phrases such as "Wrath of God"[9] and "Enormous Boils" or signifiers linked to Girardian violence such as "Human Sacrifice" and "Murder" are listed on the cover, ironically suggesting that those bleak topics are to be considered as exciting thematic assets of the narratives contained in the anthology, in a way that is deliberately reminiscent of exploitation movies' posters (Figure 17.1).[10]

Among Gaiman's six stories for the anthology, five are adapted from the Book of Judges, the second of the Historical Books occurring after the Pentateuch. The first chapters of this Book depict Yahweh's recurrent punishments against the Israelites, because, as an angel explains:

> And ye shall make no league with the inhabitants of this land; ye shall throw down their altars: but ye have not obeyed my voice: why have ye done this? Wherefore I also said, I will not drive them out from before you; but they shall be *as thorns* in your sides, and their gods shall be a snare unto you. (Carroll and Prickett, Judges 2:2–3)

After that, time and again, Yahweh's Jewish followers, caught worshiping "strange gods," are enslaved by other Semitic people with Yahweh's consent, and then he sends "Judges" to free them. Thus is the reader confronted with an almost iterative passage, peppered with variants of this phrase: "and the anger of the LORD was hot against Israel and he sold them into the hand of ..." (Judges 2:14, 3:8, 4:2, and 6:1). Gaiman and Mike Matthews's rendering of those chapters is typical of the general desacralizing tactics of the anthology. First, of course, it compresses the "plot" and simplifies its expression, in order to make as clear as possible the tyrannous absurdity, from the point of view of a modern outsider, of Yahweh's behavior. Gaiman even puts, in the mouth of one of the Jewish hearers of the angel's message, the anachronistic comment: "Sounds like divine fascist crap to me" (Gaiman et al. *Outrageous Tales* 23).[11] Then, Matthews visually emphasizes the gory aspects of every massacre that he and Gaiman selected. The penultimate panel, notably, shows Shamgar, one of the Judges, standing on top of a mountain of corpses. The panel would look very much like one from a warlike heroic-fantasy comics series such as Marvel Comics' *Savage Sword of Conan*, if it were not for the iconic style in which it is drawn, and the anachronistic and misspelled colloquialisms printed in Shamgar's speech balloon, which make him sound like a lampoon of a dumb action hero. That hypotextually rich depiction satirically suggests

Figure 17.1 Gaiman et al. *Outrageous Tales from the Old Testament*, cover. © Knockabout Comics. All Rights Reserved.

a purposeful likening of the Old Testament wars to the blood and combat trances of Conan and other comic-book barbarian heroes. The funniest adaptation, though, is probably the aforementioned reference to EC Comics: Gaiman has given to this biblical passage a visually embodied narrator who is typical of the horror-host tradition launched by EC Comics in the late 1940s and early 1950s (Figure 17.2). The character is even named "the Bible Keeper" in an obvious allusion to the Crypt Keeper, who was the host of EC's *Tales from the Crypt* and probably the most famous comic-book horror-host ever. By this narrative conceit, Gaiman suggests that, not only is the Book of Judges a typical barbarian fantasy but also, in a way, a collection of gruesome horror tales of the kind Dr. Fredric Wertham would have strongly disapproved of.

Many other examples of the graphic or verbal desacralization that constitutes the agenda of the anthology could be cited. In Gaiman's "Journey to Bethlehem," which corresponds to chapter 19 of the Book of Judges, something which is expressed with only one short sentence in the Old Testament—"And [the Levite's] concubine played the whore against him, and went away from him unto her father's house" (Judges 19:2)—is fully developed in a six-panel scene (spread through a whole page) in the

Figure 17.2 Gaiman et al. *Outrageous Tales from the Old Testament*, p. 23. ©Knockabout Comics. All Rights Reserved.

graphic adaptation. The style used by artist Steve Gibson is even more iconic than Matthews's, and the crude sex panel that results from the expansion of the passage is typical of the unapologetic obscenity and of the grotesque caricature style usually employed by comix creators. The hyperbolic size of the concubine's bottom and the depiction of the Levite as a scraggy weakling are particularly reminiscent of some of Robert Crumb's well-known stylistic quirks and efficiently contribute to strip the story of any semblance of spiritual dignity. Later in the same story, Gibson's cartoony art gives a very striking, terrifying, expressionistic edge to the horrible scene where the Benjamites gang rape the Levite's concubine. The same can be said of the representation of the Levite's cold rage, the morning after, while he "divide[s] her, *together* with her bones, into twelve pieces, and sen[ds] her into all the coasts of Israel" (Judges 19:29)[12] to raise all the other Israelite tribes against the Benjamites.

English artist Dave McKean's work, in Gaiman's "The Prophet Who Came to Dinner," is far from cartoony, although there is some abstractness to it. In fact, it resembles the art McKean has provided for such early Gaiman graphic novels as *Violent Cases* or *Black Orchid*: alternating impressionistic panels depicting landscapes or sheer movement and hyperrealistic close-ups on human characters. The difference, with those other Gaiman/McKean collaborations, is that this comic is neither painted nor even inked. It is only pencils, which makes it look like a set of very elaborate sketches. The visual mood clearly stands out from the comix mood that predominates in the anthology. This adaptation of chapter 13 of the First Book of Kings (more precisely: 1 Kings 13:1–32) does not look satiric. It looks haunted, in a way which is quite typical of Dave McKean's visual works and which does not seem quite devoid of aesthetic equivalents of Rudolf Otto's *majestas* and *mysterium*. Therefore, the necessary impertinence—or, to put it in a more Jewish manner, the "chutzpah"—of that story lies mostly in the contrast between that visual ambience (which is rather adequate for a serious adaptation of a biblical narrative) and the ambience suggested by Gaiman's verbal work. The captions and speech balloons throughout the first pages contain mostly excerpts from the original text, and, when Gaiman's text departs from it, at least the style looks biblical (see Gaiman et al. *Outrageous Tales* 48–49). But at the bottom of page 49, when the prophet from Beth-El is introduced, the language register becomes less historically accurate, as can be seen in the following dialogue:

Hello.
Hello.
I hear you're a prophet.
Yup. You?
Yer. Business good?
Mustn't grumble. You?
Neh! It's a living. (50)

The effect of this incongruousness is quite funny, in a way that clearly pertains to desacralization (especially as the condition of a prophet is referred to very casually, as if it were no more than a common trade). Yet, it is, just as clearly, far less offensive than the humor in the rest of the anthology. The conclusion of the story displays the same mild iconoclasm, the same "thrusting downward from the exalted to the workaday,"[13] as the captions show the narrator (an impersonal narrative voice, this time, not the "Bible Keeper") trying and failing to find a moral interpretation to this sad tale of God's inscrutable ways: "And the moral of this story is … *never* listen to anyone who says God told *him* what *you* ought to be doing. Not even a *prophet*. Or you'll get eaten by a lion on your way home, or something. *Damn*. No, *that* can't be right" (Gaiman, *Outrageous Tales* 52).

Gaiman's contributions to *Outrageous Tales from the Old Testament* would probably not be as interesting if they could not be contrasted with his very different approach to the biblical hypotext in *Sandman*. Those British short comix would merely be a funny study in blasphemous wry, a very extreme version of the "ironic or playful domestication of myth" that Robert Alter finds in most Jewish humor.[14] They become a clue to Gaiman's delight in being a perpetual cultural outsider, as soon as you compare them to *Sandman*. If Gaiman, as a Jewish writer who understands his own native faith as an outsider, enthusiastically helped to give some cachet to the Knockabout systematic desacralization of the Old Testament's *tremendum* and violence, it is a work of *resacralization* that can be enjoyed, as to the Old Testament characters, in *Sandman*. And that is one of the many ways in which Gaiman, in what is usually considered as his *magnum opus*, approaches American mainstream comics, and therefore American popular culture, as an outsider.

Contrary to *Outrageous Tales from the Old Testament*, *Sandman* is a mainstream comics work, which means that it was created under the supervision of (and then published by) a big company whose editorial concerns are resolutely about popular entertainment, and mostly about superheroes. This company is DC Comics, and it is best-known for publishing in monthly comic books the adventures of Superman, Batman, and Wonder Woman. Apart from those emblematic figures, it owns the rights of many superheroes and other fictional characters and employs many writers and artists to run their multiple, interconnected, perpetually ongoing series. *Sandman* is one such monthly series. But Gaiman was not hired to write a storyline in the endless adventures of a previously existing DC-property hero. Instead, he created the concept and many of the main characters. He wrote every single issue of the series (from 1988 to 1996). And, contrary to the commercial philosophy of mainstream comics series, he killed the protagonist at the end of his run and ensured that DC would not try to clumsily resurrect the character under the auspices of another writer.

Sandman has an extremely complex plot, which melts together horror/fantasy, historical fiction, tragedy, intertextuality-based experimental narrative, and mythopoeia. However, it can be roughly summarized by way of two statements. First, it is the story of the Endless, seven siblings who are more than gods; actually, they are the reason why there are gods. Indeed, the seven of them (Destiny, Death, Dream, Destruction, Desire, Despair and Delirium) are anthropomorphic embodiments of "eternal human traits."[15] Their very existence is the cosmic framework that shapes human imagination, thought, beliefs, and condition. Second, the protagonist is one of the Endless: Dream (also known as Morpheus, the Sandman, the Dream-King, the Prince of Stories, or the Lord-Shaper). The Endless have very distinct personalities, and Dream is one of the most cheerless. He is a Byronic, brooding, romantically self-centered character. More importantly, he has a very impersonal, detached, and "professional" perception of the humans over whose dreams, hopes, inspiration, and nightmares he presides. Defining himself only by his cosmic responsibilities (contrary to his sister Death, who is a very sympathetic and lively character), he is, most of all, pathologically reluctant to change. The series delineates the way he is forced, by circumstances, to learn human feelings, to change, and how that leads him to the tragic decision to die, leaving his kingdom—the Dreaming—to the rule of a new, less misfit embodiment of the idea of Dream.

Throughout the millennia-encompassing plot, the Endless interact with Norse, Egyptian, Greek, and other gods and mythological beings, with fairy folk, angels and demons, with historical figures such as William Shakespeare, Augustus Caesar, Robespierre or Joshua Norton, and with ordinary human characters created by Gaiman. But as *Sandman* is a DC series, it must be noted that it is also part of this fictional microcosm that is referred to as "the DC Universe." That means that all the DC characters (superheroes and otherwise) exist inside *Sandman*'s diegesis, and they are therefore likely to be involved in the plot. Characters from *Batman, Superman*, or members of the Justice League of America (notably the Martian Manhunter) make cameo appearances. However, just as Alan Moore had done a few years earlier in his DC series *Swamp Thing*, Gaiman preferred to use mostly, in *Sandman*, less famous DC characters.

Cain, Abel, and Eve are such characters. The three of them first appeared as horror-hosts in DC Comics horror anthology series in the EC Comics vein. As Hy Bender explains in his chapter on the "Secret Origins" of *Sandman* characters, "Cain and Abel were respectively hosts of two highly popular titles [in the 1970s], *The House of Mystery* and *The House of Secrets*" (Bender 244). From mere heterodiegetic narrators, the two characters had already been made homodiegetic (albeit with a mostly choral function) in Alan Moore's *Swamp Thing*. In *Sandman*, they are much more involved in the action, as they are identified as dwellers of the Dreaming, and faithful assistants to the Dream-King. So is Eve, a woman who is sometimes young and beautiful, sometimes old, and who spends most of her time in a cave in the Dreaming, alone with a raven. In a piece of interview with Bender in the "Secret Origins" chapter, Gaiman explains where this character comes from:

> Tom [Peyer]'s research [in the DC archives] unearthed another obscure 1975 series, *Dark Mansion of Forbidden Love*, that was hosted by a beautiful unnamed woman with a raven. That made me remember a mad crone named Eve who had a raven, and who appeared in several other short-lived DC titles, such as *Secrets of Sinister House, Secrets of Haunted House* and *Plop!* It occurred to me that the beautiful woman with a raven and the crazy crone with a raven were aspects of the same character, who was named Eve. (244–245)

Of course, Cain and Abel, who were already presented as brothers in *The House of Mystery* and *The House of Secrets*, were clearly inspired by the eponymous brothers in Genesis. And as for Eve, even if the connection is less obvious, her name, given to such a forlorn and ageless character, cannot but evoke the Eve from Genesis. Yet, the obviously intertextual nature of the characters was never much exploited by the writers who used them before Gaiman. In *The House of Mystery*, Cain is the caretaker of a Gothic mansion adjoining a cemetery, and he spends his time telling horror stories to the reader. In *The House of Secrets*, Abel does exactly the same thing, in a house at the other side of the cemetery, and his bully brother Cain sometimes visits him, mostly to scare him or mock him for his supposed silliness and cowardliness. In Moore's *Swamp Thing*, the characters' houses appear to be located in some nonphysical piece of land, overlooking Hell, and which can be visited in dreams. Moore first introduces a vague but identifiable reference to the brothers' biblical models, in the form of a horror/slapstick routine, consisting in Cain recurrently killing Abel, who resuscitates every day, so that he can be killed over again, in a perfect illustration of Henri Bergson's description of the comic, in his 1900 essay *Laughter*, as "something mechanical in something living" (Bergson 405).[16]

In *Sandman*, the brothers are very similar to the depiction that is made of them in *Swamp Thing*, except that the reader encounters them much more often—they appeared only in two issues in *Swamp Thing*, "Abandoned Houses" (Moore et al. *Swamp Thing*, vol. 2 164–183) and "The End" (Moore et al. *Swamp Thing*, vol. 4 165–203). That allows Gaiman to develop their relationships, giving some poignancy to it, by suggesting that Abel hopes beyond hope that he and his brother will make peace some day, or that, secretly, Cain could actually not live without his much-reviled and often-murdered brother. More importantly, those Gothic/slapstick characters are resacralized inasmuch as some passages make very clear that the DC Cain, Abel, and Eve, and the Old Testament Cain, Abel, and Eve, are indeed the same.

The first of these passages occurs in the issue that serves as "Chapter 1" in the storyline entitled "Season of Mists." Dream needs to go to Hell and to negotiate something with Lucifer, but the latter bears a grudge to the Dream King, and a strong sense of diplomacy is required. Before going, Dream decides to send one of his servants to announce his visit, but as Hell is a very dangerous place for anybody who ventures there, Dream chooses to send Cain. When they meet, Lucifer greets Cain as "the first man born of woman" (Gaiman et al. *Absolute Sandman*, vol. 2 44). And then, when some demons offer to destroy Cain after he has delivered his message, Lucifer explains Dream's choice, partly by quoting from the Old Testament:

> You cannot hurt him. We may not give you our permission. Cain is under protection of one far greater than the Lord of Dreams. "And the Lord said unto him, therefore whosoever slayeth Cain, vengeance shall be taken on him sevenfold, and the Lord set a mark upon Cain, lest any finding him should kill him …." … You're under his protection. Dream was sensible to send you as his messenger—any other envoy would have been returned with his liver in his mouth (45).[17]

A few pages later, Gaiman continues weaving the explicit link between the DC character and his Old Testament prototype, still through Lucifer's speech balloons. The Lord of Hell entreats Cain of the existence, in the second century BCE, of a Gnostic sect named the Cainites, who believed that "Yahweh was positively evil," who "rever[ed] such rejected figures as Cain …, Esau and the Sodomites," and who thought that "salvation … c[ame] only by breaking all the laws of the Old Testament" (see "Cainite"). The information given by Lucifer is more or less that, the main difference being his use of the deictic "you" instead of the name "Cain": "they believed that you were the persecuted party in that unfortunate affair with your brother" (Gaiman et al. *Absolute Sandman,* vol. 2 46). Referring to an obscure group in the history of religions helps giving back to the DC character the *mysterium* that belongs to his biblical roots; such information is not necessarily well-known to the reading public of *Sandman*. So it can be considered as "esoteric," in a very literal sense. Some *majestas* is conferred to the character as well; a few people actually used to *revere* him. The fact that Gaiman and artist Kelley Jones included the text from Genesis inside a panel actually showing the mark of Cain also has an effect of that kind, both thanks to the natural fascination exerted by graphic symbols whose meaning is unclear, and to the suggestion that we are looking at a physical trace of Yahweh's *majestas*, a mere circle on Cain's flesh, that suffices to prevent anybody from harming him.

Such numinous features can also be found in the issue "A Parliament of Rooks" (part of "Convergence," a triptych of stories marginal to the main plot). In this narrative pause in Dream's story, Cain, Abel, and Eve are to be found having a "tea party" at Abel's House of Secrets, with a baby dreamer from the waking world, who is to become, later, Dream's successor. Cain suggests that as "old storytellers" (an intertextual allusion to their editorial past as horror-hosts), they should tell stories to their guest (Gaiman et al. *Absolute Sandman,* vol. 3 28). Eve and Abel successively narrate their origin stories, which are easily identifiable as similar to their Genesis counterparts'. Eve's story is recognizable but strangely different from the best-known Genesis tale. Instead of Adam being made of dust, and having only one wife, Eve, made from his rib while he sleeps, the story starts with a hermaphrodite Adam, whose female part is divided from the male to make Adam's first wife, Lilith (33). As she behaves as Adam's equal, she is "expelled from Eden," and a new wife is made. But as Adam could see her creation, "bones first, then internal organs, then flesh" and so on, Adam can't bear her sight, sees her as "full of secretions and blood" (34–35). So she is also expelled, or destroyed, without even being given a name, and finally God makes Eve, in the aforementioned manner. Actually, this version of the story is not from the Old Testament proper; a caption claims that "that's what the Midrash states" (35).[18] Besides, Gaiman explains in an interview: "That's a story which has haunted me since age twelve, when Cantor Meir Lev taught it to me during my bar mitzvah lessons. The cantor happened to be an expert on Jewish Talmudic, Mishnaic and midrashic apocrypha, and I found it all fascinating and pumped him for information; so by the age of thirteen, I knew more arcane Jewish lore than most adults" (Bender 154).

And here again, the "esoteric" nature, for most readers, of that Jewish lore, and its use in the embedded story, efficiently confers *mysterium* to the comic-book character of Eve, while such striking images as the hermaphrodite Adam, or the revealed process of creation of the second wife (quite realistically depicted by artist Jill Thompson) have effects that pertain to *majestas* and *tremendum*. Eve's story should be contrasted with Abel's, in which he tells their infant guest of his biblical troubles with Cain, and then of Dream's (non-biblical) decision to give asylum to the brothers in the Dreaming. Abel's version of the story takes the form of an upbeat nursery tale, where all the characters (Dream, Death, Cain, and Abel) are depicted as little children, and where the brothers end up "hugg[ing] each other joyfully" (Gaiman et al. *Absolute Sandman*, vol. 3 40). Thompson adapts her style to Abel's idiosyncratic storytelling. In the panels that reflect Abel's fantasizing, the characters are drawn in a very "cute" and childlike style, with "enormous heads and large eyes, but tiny noses and mouths that appear close to their chins" (Bender 153). Gaiman wanted them to look roughly like Sugar and Spike (two baby characters from a DC comics series for children, created in 1956 by Sheldon Mayer). As Thompson points out, they eventually look a lot like "little Japanese manga figures" (Bender 153). The point of this funny rewriting of the Genesis story in the form of a nursery tale is to stress the excessive sweetness and innocence of the *Sandman* version of Abel. The character's craving for brotherly love gives a deep poignancy to many of the passages in which he is murdered by Cain. In a way, *Sandman* takes sides in favor of the sacrificial victim, just as the Old Testament does according to René Girard. Thus, Gaiman adds a very empathetic, human, dimension to the slapstick routine introduced by Moore in *Swamp Thing*. That does not prevent the sadness below this wishful story to be as gripping as that which explicitly pervades Eve's tale. But Abel's surely has nothing numinous to it. One of the great emotional strengths of the *Sandman* characters is precisely the way Gaiman alternates depictions of them either as "wholly other" (Otto 25), and therefore creating aesthetic echoes of what the numinous may feel like, or as wholly *human*, and eliciting the reader's sympathy.

In his essay on the history of Jewish comics creators in America, Danny Fingeroth reveals that, when he personally asked him, in an e-mail, about Jewish content in his writings, Gaiman answered: "I think the stuff in my work that's definably Jewish is probably the stuff that's Jewish on the surface—the midrashic ... stories that crept into *Sandman*, for example. Beyond that (shrug) it's anyone's guess" (Fingeroth 144). Unlike Fingeroth's book, this paper is not dedicated to a psychoanalytic search for implicitly Jewish aspects, or hidden Jewish themes, in superhero or fantasy comics. So it is not meant to go "beyond" what "is Jewish on the surface." But Gaiman's approach to explicitly Jewish content is interesting, just as his oblique way of dealing with much of world culture always is. His intimate yet detached knowledge of the Jewish sacred texts and of the Judeo-Christian religious history gave him assets to create some powerful details in his syncretic *Sandman* mythos. Anybody Christian could have linked Cain, Abel, or Eve to their biblical types, but the idea of including midrashic content probably contributed a lot to the successful aura of *mysterium* and *majestas* of Eve's tale in "A Parliament of Rooks." Even if his ambivalent religious education "made [him] see *everything* as myth," he is thoroughly aware of the value of myths. As to *Outrageous Tales from the Old Testament*, it is obvious that the main difference between Gaiman and the other writers, apart from the number of scripts he contributed, is that most of the others wrote about very famous stories: Creation, the Garden of Eden, Sodom and Gomorrah, Samson, and Job. Gaiman was one of the few who chose books that are known mostly to people who actually read or studied the Old Testament. Filmmakers like Mel Brooks or the Monty Python have often shown, in their careers, that there is no better parody than a parody by someone who actually knows the original work fairly well. Gaiman's "outrageous tales" certainly convey that impression.

Fingeroth also wrote about the "Golden Age" of the comic books in the late 1930s and early 1940s: "As recently deceased Jewish comics writer, Arnold Drake ..., told me: 'There was an extraordinary representation of Jews and Italians. The Jews were primarily writers, the Italians were primarily artists, and I saw it being an extension of the two cultures. *Jews had always been involved in storytelling going back to the Old Testament*. The Italians had been involved with art for centuries and centuries'" (24, emphasis mine). As a writer whose works are characterized by recurrent explicit intertextuality, Gaiman always overtly pays his hypertextual debts to his hypotextual creditors. Both as a Jewish author and as a Western popular culture author, he could not have ignored the founding text of the rich Jewish storytelling tradition of which he is part, especially if this text happens to be a founding text for the whole Judeo-Christian western culture as well. However, as an author who also has the passion of creative retelling, of ever-changing and ever-updating universal narratives—in a nutshell, as someone who believes that "we have the right, or the obligation, to tell old stories in our own ways, because they are our stories, and they must be told" (Gaiman, *Adventures* 68)—he sometimes pays his debts in quite unexpected ways. Ways that are sideways: an outsider's ways.

Notes

1   Gaiman is probably at his most Jewish when he displays such a wry sense of humor, as when referring to a hypothetical new Holocaust by incongruously claiming to take "a certain amount of comfort" at the idea, trivially expressed, that "[he]'d go in and fry." Indeed, "Jewish humor" is often construed as "disturbing and upsetting, its phrases dipped in tragedy," according to Irving Howe's 1951 essay "The Nature of Jewish laughter" in (Cohen 19). And yet, as Gaiman's phrasing illustrates, it does not consist in "imagining that it would be appropriate to seek fulfillment through suffering, to create a mythology out of suffering," and it is rather used "as much to shrug at adversity as to bear it," as Robert Alter puts it in his article "Jewish Humor and the Domestication of Myth" (Cohen 26).

2   Franz Kafka is usually depicted as the archetypal outsider. His personal friend and first biographer, Max Brod, quotes from Kafka's diary: "I am often seized with a sad but calm astonishment at my lack of feeling. I am separated from everything by a space to whose limits I can't even force my way out" (Brod 96). American playwright and essayist David Zane Mairowitz wrote a comic-book biography (illustrated by Robert Crumb), in which he states that "Kafka was alienated from his country, his surroundings, his family," and that "he was also a stranger in his own body" (Mairowitz and Crumb 37). As for the late Pierre Desproges, a French satirist who admired Kafka's writings very much, he had this comment about the Jewish-Czech author: "he had life the way someone has cancer" (Desproges 102–103; translation mine).

3   This theory of Gaiman's concerning the advantages of being an *English* immigrant is very interesting as Danny Fingeroth, a comics scholar, teacher, and a former editor and writer for Marvel Comics, has exactly the same theory about being a *Jewish* immigrant. And it explains, to him, the historical predominant presence of scions of Eastern European Jews in the American comics industry, as well as in Hollywood:

> It can be argued that the reason immigrants in general, and Jews in particular, thrive in open societies like the United States is because they bring a unique outlook to the party, seeing insight and opportunity where others can't or don't, because the values and vagaries of a society are so familiar to its natives as to be invisible. Add to that the feelings of persecution and alienation ... and you have a perfect group of outsiders ready to reflect a culture back on itself. (Fingeroth 101)

4   Knockabout publications are considered as "alternative" as the firm does not publish straightforwardly entertaining materials such as superhero or adventure/fantasy comics (usually called "mainstream" comics). Instead, they concentrate on intellectual, experimental, and/or satirical comics, in the tradition of underground "comix" from the 1960s and 1970s. They distribute the works of American underground legends such as Robert Crumb in the UK, and they publish many works by British creators as well. Their best-known and most emblematic publication by locals is probably *From Hell*, the historical and sociological graphic novel about Jack the Ripper and the Victorian era, by English writer Alan Moore and Scottish artist Eddie Campbell.

5   This famous American line of didactic comics for children used to adapt (in a very stately species of graphic narrative) historical events, tales from the Bible, and great literary classics such as those by Homer, Melville, Shakespeare, and so on. It ran discontinuously from 1941 to 1971 and was successively owned by two publishing companies, Gilberton Company and Frawley Corporation. Gilberton publications are discussed and analyzed in Witek's book (14–17 and 20–36).

6   I use this adjective in the same meaning as Scott McCloud, who often uses it as a synonym for an "abstract," or "simple" visual style, and who once parenthetically equates it with "cartoony" (McCloud 37).

7   René Girard wrote specifically about the Bible in his book *Things Hidden since the Foundation of the World*. He observes that the Old Testament more than often illustrates the theory developed in *Violence and the Sacred*: "[I]n all the great scenes of Genesis and Exodus, there is a motif, or a quasi-motif, of expulsion and the founding murder" (Girard, *Des Choses* 166; translation mine). However, Girard sees a striking difference between the sacrificial *ethos* of primitive and ancient religions and that of the Jewish text: in the latter, the innocence of the surrogate victim, and therefore the arbitrariness and injustice of the founding murder, are systematically proclaimed and denounced, in a way that Girard reads as a foreshadowing of the non-violent, "non-sacrificial" God of the Christian New Testament. Yet, he notes that "a conception of the deity which would be thoroughly foreign to violence is never actually reached in the Old Testament" (Girard, *Des Choses* 180, translation mine). And, later, he contrasts the deity as described in the "synoptic Gospels" with the "vengeful and retributive conception of which traces remain until the end of the Old Testament" (206, translation mine).

8   "*Mysterium*" and "*majestas*" are Otto's concepts. They are, like "*tremendum*," aspects of the numinous. The "*majestas*" or "absolute overpoweringness" of a numinous object (Otto 19–23), combined to its "*mysterium*," that is, completely alien and incomprehensible nature (25–30), are the reasons why it inspires awe.

9   To Otto, the very notion of " the 'wrath of Yahweh' ... is nothing but the *tremendum* itself, apprehended and expressed by the aid of a naïve analogy from the domain of natural experience, in this case from the ordinary passional life of men" (18).

10   An exploitation film is "a cheaply made film which relies on explicit displays of sex …, graphic passages of violence or sordid or sensationalist subject matter to reach an audience" (Jackson 86). The promotion of such movies usually relies on various ways of boasting their *outré* character, including sensationalist taglines on the posters or in the trailers, and more generally, as Eric Schaefer has it in his study on early exploitation cinema, "bombastic promises about shocking truths and fearless frankness" (Schaefer 3). The very title of the Knockabout anthology, "*Outrageous Tales from*," partakes of that paratextual pastiche of exploitation films' promotional techniques.

11   The comment is not only anachronistic but also highly ironic, as the God of the Hebrews is not accused only of tyranny, but of "fascism," a historical form of tyranny most famously characterized by anti-Semitic violence.

12   Those scenes, in Gaiman and Gibson's story, are to be found in Gaiman, *Outrageous Tales* 43–45. In his previously quoted essay *Understanding Comics*, Scott McCloud suggests an explanation to the often-noted expressive power of abstract, cartoony drawings: "the cartoon is a vacuum into which our identity and awareness are pulled" (36). Such a process of identification comes from the fact that detailed realism gives individual concreteness to a drawn character, creating a distance from the reader, whereas a cartoon character looks less like a particular human (other than the reader), and more like the vague, universal idea of a human (which includes any reader). "By de-emphasizing the appearance of the physical world, in favor of the idea of form," McCloud argues, "the cartoon places itself in the world of concepts. Through traditional realism, the comics artist can portray the world without, and through the cartoon, the world within" (41).

13   The phrase is borrowed from Mark Shechner, "Dear Mr Einstein: Jewish Humor and the Contradictions of Culture" (Cohen 148).

14   See his article "Jewish Humor and the Domestication of Myth" (Cohen 209).

15   Marilyn Brahen, "The Thin Line Between" (Schweitzer 140).

16   The translation is mine, but it corresponds to a usual translation of Bergson's formula "*du mécanique plaqué sur du vivant*".

17   Lucifer's quotation comes from Genesis 4:15.

18   The three adjuncts or interpretations actually come from different texts. Lilith comes from *The Alphabet of Ben Sira*, a medieval compilation of lists of proverbs with haggadic commentary. The unnamed wife and the hermaphrodite Adam come from *Genesis Rabbah*, a midrashic text from the third century that is "haggadic in character" (Mills 733). In rabbinic literature, *haggadah* refers to "nonprescriptive … descriptions of historical events, aphorisms, parables, proverbs, legends of biblical or post-biblical heroes, folklore, and other materials … used by the rabbis to illustrate moral and ethical duties," as opposed to *halakah* which is a "prescription," "the definition of the precise way in which a commandment of the Torah (Law) was to be performed" (732).

Jewish Giants: Nephilim, Rephaim, and the IDF

Tof Eklund

The Nephilim and Rephaim of the Pentetuch (and the rest of the Tanakh) are mysterious: usually translated in Christian Bibles as "giants," the words themselves are archaic and of uncertain meaning, thus they are untranslated in the JPS English Tanakh. The uncertainty comes not out of their giant stature, which is established contextually, but what else those words might mean. These towering figures are, at best, morally ambivalent and are associated with war, power, and destruction. Moreover, the all-consuming and cannibalistic appetite of the Nephilim is a terrifying thing to be associated with, especially for a contemporary Jewish audience for whom it may evoke everything from the Shylock stereotype to the blood libel. The "giant" has its place in the grand scheme of Jewish identity, but that place is one of profound isolation, at the margins.

Yet it is Jewish giants that a number of contemporary Jewish comics creators reference, from "the Giraffe" in Rutu Modan's *Exit Wounds* (2007) to the literal giants Joan Sfar's *The Rabbi's Cat 2* (2008). Jewish giants also appear in works by gentile creators such as James Sturm's *The Golem's Mighty Swing* (2001) and Tom Gauld's *Goliath* (2012). They even come to life in videogames, such as Blizzard's *Diablo* series (1996) and the indie strategy/world mythology game *Dominions 3* (2006). In Sfar and Modan's work in particular, there is an ambivalence toward gianthood that combines with story elements about Israel and Palestine, raising questions about the price of power. The Nephilim and Rephaim of old can be traced through Sfar's "lost tribe" of African, Jewish giants to Modan's Giraffe and are connected with the Israeli Defense Force (IDF) through these narratives they question what it means to be "giants in the land." In the end, these works are not anti-Zionist but nuanced, human, and ambivalent, like the "giants" themselves.

A crucial piece of the puzzle in understanding the importance of the "Jewish giant" as a trope may be in the need modern Israel had to fashion an image of Jewish power and potency to counter old, internalized narratives of impotence and ineffectualness. Miriam Libicki, creator of *Jobnik!* (2008), considers this problem in her illustrated essay "Towards a Hot Jew: The Israeli Soldier as Fetish Object" (n.d.). She details the "stereotypes which cast men as weak and neurotic and women as coldly materialistic," and the way that the IDF's success in the 1967 war was instrumental in creating a new self-image, one that was powerful and, equally important, virile (2). She notes that "Jewish organizations fund youth trips to Israel and they explicitly state that one of their aims is to try to prevent youth from 'marrying out' of Judaism" (6). Libicki argues that the appeal is made, as it so often is, though a combination of sex and (potential for) violence: "The soldiers are young ... at the peak of the Western standard of sexual attractiveness. And they have big guns" (8).

The media-enabled image of the IDF soldier as militarily and sexually potent, a fetish object perhaps in the ritual as well as libidinal sense, has withstood the ugly history of the Israeli-Palestinian conflict, perhaps even been strengthened by the already fetishized power relationships in it. Libicki cites Joe Sacco himself mooning over an IDF soldier in *Palestine* (2001) as evidence of this. One of the differences between them is that Libicki is very aware of the way that the IDF represents Jewish youth in a general capacity. Unlike the "all volunteer" US Army, the Defense Service Law, and the pattern of late-teenage Jews, especially Americans like Libicki, traveling to Israel to serve in the IDF makes it very diverse and broadly representative of an entire people. This is why it is so urgent to consider whether, as, Libicki concludes with seeming reluctance, "the New Jew" represented by the IDF soldier is indeed "an adorable oppressor for every persuasion" (11) (Figure 18.1). The mythic Nephilim connects this "New Jew" with older images of Jewish power but also with some of the most hateful stereotypes of and slanders against the Jewish people.

Johan Karlsson and Kristoffer Osterman's *Dominions 3: The Awakening* is an epic computer strategy game with nations based on world mythology. One of these nations is based on the mythic Nephilim and Rephaim and their interaction with "lesser" humans. Osterman assumes that the Rephaim are descendants of the Nephilim, a conceit that works well for the game but has no textual basis beyond the presumptive genetic compatibility of giants and humans, as the Nephilim themselves are half-human and half-divine.

This is clearly the jumping off point for Blizzard's cosmologically Manichean *Diablo* series of games, where the "Nephalem" are the offspring of angels who interbred with demons and all humankind are the descendants of the unruly Nephalem. In these games, it is cannon that the Nephalem were greater in strength than their supernatural parents. This original and very modern conceit suits those action RPGs, wherein the player's human protagonist gradually grows in power until even the "prime evils" are easily trod underfoot.

Dominions 3 is deeper and much more faithful in its use of the Nephilim myth. Osterman's "Late Era" faction Gath is one of the most dynamic in the game, and presents a compelling narrative fictionalization of the "giants" based on the scattered religious texts (including Christian and Manichean as well as Jewish sources). At first glance, this faction's presentation of pseudo-Judaic giants is disturbing: the Rephaim of Gath, descendants of the Nephilim of old, are horned giants who practice Blood Sacrifice and Blood Magic (use of either in-game requires the player to first assign units to hunt for sacrificial victims). The most powerful priest unit that a Gath player can recruit is a Rephaim Kohen Gadol.

The Kohen Gadol, Hebrew for "high priest," is a historical, rather than mythical, role of great importance: the Kohen Gadol was responsible for going into the Holy of Holies in the Temple once a year to perform the most important rituals. In *Dominions 3*,

By the quirks of history, propaganda, and the
voyeuristic urge, we have arrived
at the New Jew: an adorable oppressor
for every persuasion.

Figure 18.1 Guns and charity, the modern "Jewish Giant." Image ©Miriam Libicki (11).

the "Kohen Gadol" unit is depicted as an old man with a long white beard, dressed traditionally, complete with what appears to be a pixilated Choshen, the ceremonial bejeweled breastplate worn by the historical Kohen Gadol: "You shall make a breastplate of decision (or 'judgment') ... Set in it mounted stones, in four rows of stones ... The stones shall correspond (in number) to the names of the sons of Israel: twelve, corresponding to their names. They shall be engraved like seals, each with its name,

Figure 18.2 Left, the "Kohen Gadol," high priest of Gath; middle, the "Kohen"; and right, the "Abba" in *Dominions 3. Dominions 3* ©Shrapnel Games, 2006.

for the twelve tribes" (Exod. 28:15a, 17a, 21).[1] This unit can perform "Blood Sacrifices" and "Blood Magic." The sprite for this unit is nearly identical to artists' depictions of the historical Kohen Gadol, except of course for the horns (Figure 18.2).

This monstrous figure bears unpleasant echoes of the medieval European myth of the old Jew as diabolist. The word "cabal" for a sinister, secret group or cult comes from a corruption of Kabbalah, Jewish mysticism. Some versions of the Faust myth claim that an old Jew introduces Faust to or teaches Faust how to summon the demon Mephistopheles. In George Sand's (first-wave suffragette) feminist Faust-inspired play *The Seven Strings of the Lyre* (1838), Mephistopheles takes the form of an "old Jew," to literally bedevil Helen, the heroine of this version of the story—she finds him to be "a disgusting old man!"—and shortly thereafter he nearly drives her to suicide: "I will kill myself. It is necessary. This wicked Jew has shown me all my miseries" (58–59, 65). A contemporary comment on this demonization can be seen in the "running of the Jew" sequence from Sacha Baron Cohen's *Borat* (2006), with its grotesque, green, horned masks.

Perhaps the most uncomfortable association is of the Kohen Gadol with Blood Magic and human sacrifice, evoking the old anti-Semitic "blood libel" (the myth that Jews kidnap and sacrifice Gentile children). Second only in infamy to the Czarist propaganda piece, *The Protocols of the Elders of Zion* (1903), the blood libel is still often reported as true in the Middle East, especially in combination with the *Protocols*.

It would be easy to condemn *Dominions 3* and its creators for perpetuating this image. Osterman is clearly aware of the possibility of such an interpretation and says so in his online development diary for the giants: "I have long waited with Gath, since I'm very fond of ancient near eastern myth. I have always felt a bit worried that they would not become what I imagined, so I've waited." Gath is, indeed, complex, as are its sources. Osterman's "nation of giants" resonates not only with the canonical religious texts of Genesis and Ezekiel but also the apocryphal Ethiopic Book of Enoch (1 Enoch) and the *Zohar*, the most famous work on Kabbalah, both of which are mentioned in Osterman's development diary. The Book of Giants, a lost Manichean text revealed by the Dead Sea Scrolls to have been a Jewish text first, and the *Sepher Ha-Razim*, a Kabbalistic spellbook that predates the *Zohar*, seem to be outside the scope of

Osterman's research, but their relationship to and influence on the final versions of the aforementioned texts are relevant here.

An exploration of the history of the myth of the Nephilim and Rephaim is prerequisite to an analysis of their role in Modan and Sfar's comics and of how they are presented in Osterman's *Gath*. Gath is a historical city of the Philistines, as is Ashdod, from which the Middle Era nation of giants in *Dominions 3* takes its name. Gath is the Biblical home of Goliath: "His name was Goliath of Gath, and he was six cubits and a span tall" (1 Sam. 17:4b). Paradoxically, not long after David kills Goliath, he and his army seek refuge from King Saul in Gath: "So David and the six hundred men with him went and crossed over to King Achish son of Maoch of Gath" (1 Sam. 27:2). Gath is, therefore, home to both Goliath and David, if not simultaneously.

The same might be said of Gath in *Dominions 3*, as most of its troops are modeled on the tribes of Israel, including Benjaminite Slingers, who get a bonus to Pillage ("Benjamin is a ravenous wolf … in the evening he divides the spoil"), well-equipped Asherite Soldiers ("Asher's bread shall be rich,/And he shall yield royal dainties"), and Levite Zealots and Priests (Gen. 49:27, 20). At the same time, it has Goliath-like giant soldiers and its most powerful leaders are Rephaim giants. Osterman's Gath, with its subtitle "Last of the Giants," suggests a subsequent age in which the human tribes make their way alone, and the last Rephaim Kohen Gadol would be succeeded by a Levite High Priest.

A parallel is created in the game to the emergence of Judaism as we know it in the form of the Abbas (Hebrew "fathers"), giant units who reject human sacrifice and the superiority of giants to humans, as it is said in *Dominions 3* that they "find the bloody cult of the Kohanim despicable and have sworn their [lives] to aid the meek. They tend to the human population of Gath." These patriarchs are Gittites, lesser giants more removed from the bloodline of the Nephilim, and so lack the horns of the Rephaim.[2] The Abba's simple robe, unkempt white hair, and beard are congruent with the western art tradition's depictions of Abraham preparing to sacrifice Isaac. This is coherent with one historical and Rabbinical interpretation of the importance of the binding of Issac. In this interpretation, it is not Abraham's willingness to kill his son that is emphasized but his reluctance, carrying with it the rejection of human sacrifice as it was (presumably) practiced by established Semitic cultures.

Abraham is often painted wearing a blue robe or sash belt. A blue sash belt is one of the standout details in the image of *Dominions 3*'s Abba, contrasting with the red sash belts of the Kohenim. Though a red sash is part of the traditional garb of the historical Kohenim, the game's incorporation of kabbalistic themes and Merkavah mysticism suggest a different reading: in the kabbalistic Sephirot, red is the color of Geburah, the sphere of wrath, whereas blue is the color of its "opposite," Chesed, the sphere of mercy or "loving-kindness." Chesed also bears the meaning of going beyond the minimum requirement of a/the covenant, being *chasid*, and as such is the theological and semantic root of the Hasidic movement. From this, we may hypothesize a transition from the fictionalized myth of Gath to the historical practice of Judaism, led by an Abrahamic figure, a "father of a multitude of nations" (Gen. 17:5), who exceeds the minimum terms of the previous covenant (between giants and humans) and bans the practice of human sacrifice.

Such a giant would be a messianic figure, but also an exception, and functions in *Dominions 3* as a reversal of the process of becoming-giant that connects the mythic giants to modern power. So far, we have redeemed "Israel" at the expense of the giants, but they are not the Biblical boogeymen they may at first seem.

Mention of giants in Genesis is brief and equivocal. Genesis 6:2&4 states that

> the divine beings (or 'sons of God') saw how beautiful the daughters of men were and took wives from among those that pleased them ... It was then, and later too, that the Nephilim appeared on earth—when the divine beings cohabitated with the daughters of men, who bore them offspring. They were the heroes of old, the men of renown.

This passage has historically been interpreted as the mating of angels and humans, producing giant offspring, partially because elsewhere the word "Nephilim" is associated with great strength and size.

The "divine beings" or "sons of God" it mentions have also been interpreted as noblemen and their children as larger than life in deeds ("the heroes of old") rather than physical size. This interpretation is reasonable in itself and informs a social perspective on the pride and isolation of the Nephilim, understanding them as isolated by virtue of being exceptional rather than monstrous. There are, however, extended and much less ambiguous versions of this story in 1 Enoch and the Book of Giants.

The Qumran fragments, better known as the Dead Sea Scrolls, establish the historical context of 1 Enoch and its relevance to the Tanakh. The translators of *The Dead Sea Scrolls Bible* note that "[t]he caves at Qumran have produced twenty manuscripts of Enoch—as many as the book of Genesis" (481). They describe the Qumran community as having existed from some point in the middle second century BCE until about 70 CE, so the scrolls are at least that old (xv). The oldest functionally complete version of the Book of Enoch (1 Enoch) is the Ethiopian text, dated by Michael A. Knibb and Edward Ullendorff to somewhere in the fourth- through sixth-century CE (22).[3] No complete text of the Book of Giants exists, but both the Manichean fragments and those from the Dead Sea Scrolls seem to be an expansion of the first part of the Book of Enoch, the Book of the Watchers.

The origin of the Nephilim in 1 Enoch starts nearly identical to that in Genesis but soon diverges by naming "the angels, the sons of heaven ... Semyaza, who was their leader, Urakiba, Ramiel, Kokabiel, Tamiel, Ramiel, Daniel, Ezeqiel, Baraqiel, Asael, Aramos, Batriel, Ananel, Zaqiel, Samsiel, Saratel ..., Turiel, Yomiel, Araziel. These are the leaders of the two hundred angels, and of all the others with them" (1 Enoch 6:2, 7b–8). This listing of angels will later be repeated in a litany of skills taught by these rebel angels and is similar to the listing of angels for magical purposes in the Sepher Ha-Razim.

These angels are called Watchers, or Grigori, after the Greek word for watcher (*Egregori*):

> [T]hey took wives for themselves, and everyone for himself one each. And they began to go in to them and were promiscuous with them. And they taught them charms and spells, and showed to them the cutting of roots and trees. And they

became pregnant and bore large giants, and their height (was) three thousand cubits ... and they devoured one another's flesh and drank the blood from it. (1 Enoch 7:1–4,5b)

This may or, as we will see, may not be the end of the Nephilim but not of the Watchers' sin and punishment:

Azazel taught men to make swords, and daggers, and shields and breastplates. And he showed them the things after these, and the art of making them: bracelets, and ornaments, and the art of making up the eyes and of beautifying the eyelids, and the most precious and choice stones, and all (kinds of) coloured dyes. And the world was changed. (1 Enoch 8:1)

Other angels proceed to give their Promethean gifts, including magic, astrology, and herbology.

Initially it seems that it is the Nephilim's hunger that drives them to destroy one another, but the 1 Enoch goes on to state that part of the judgment against the Watchers is that their sons will destroy each other: "And the Lord said to Gabriel ... send them [the Nephilim] out, and send them against one another, and let them destroy themselves in battle" (1 Enoch 10:9). This, like the two creation stories in Genesis, creates parallel and incommensurable events: in this case, of the destruction of the Nephilim. Either their hunger compelled them to it or they were set up by Gabriel.

The Qumran Book of Giants offers a third explanation: that the giants did not fight each other or the Watchers but struggled against the host of heaven and lost. John Reeves "With the strength of my powerful arm and with the power of my might/... (a)ll flesh, and I did battle with them, but I (am) not able to prevail for us (?), for my adversaries/ sit (in heaven), and they dwelt with the holy ones, and no/... (the)y are stronger than I" (Reeves, 65). This creates an image of the Nephilim that is tragic and human, heroes, giants, or otherwise. These Nephilim were condemned for their ancestry, cut off from heaven and human kin alike, and left to fight a hopeless war against a superior power. The Qumran Book of Giants is fragmentary and it is impossible to say what has been lost, but there is no mention in what we have of it of the Nephilim being cannibalistic: if that wasn't part of the oldest text, when was it added, and to what purpose?

The Watchers are punished more harshly than their children, and their punishment is cruelly ironic: "When all their sons kill each other, and when they see the destruction of their beloved ones, bind them for seventy generations under the hills of the earth until the day of their judgment and their consummation" (1 Enoch 10:12). They were tasked to watch and not interfere, and because they became involved, they are forced to watch one last event, the slaughter of their children before being deprived of even their function: watching.

The importance of being denied the ability to watch is emphasized in the fate of Azazel, who is singled out for especially harsh treatment:

And further the Lord said to Raphael: " Bind Azazel by his hands and his feet, and throw him into the darkness. And split open the desert which is in Dudael, and throw him there. And throw on him jagged and sharp stones, and cover him with darkness; and let him stay there for ever, and cover his face, that he may not see light." (1 Enoch 10:1–5)

Azazel is covered with darkness twice, the second time explicitly to deny him the ability to see, to be a Watcher.

Azazel is mentioned in the Torah, and Azazel's fate in 1 Enoch gives contest to the "scapegoat" rite of Leviticus 16, in which two goats are prepared "one marked for the Lord, and the other marked for Azazel" (Lev. 16:8b). The Lord's goat is sacrificed, along with a bull, and the temple is ritually cleansed, after which "the live goat shall be brought forward. Aaron shall lay both hands upon the head of the live goat and confess over it all the iniquities and transgressions of the Israelites, whatever their sins, putting them on the head of the goat;" after this, Aaron is to "send it off to the wilderness for Azazel" (Lev. 16:21a, 10b). In the notoriously error-ridden Tyndale Bible and the largely Tyndale-based King James version: "Azazel" is mistranslated as "(e)scape."

Azazel the Watcher, teacher of humans and father of Nephilim, is the original scapegoat, a kind of lodestone of covenant breaking upon which lesser failures may be placed, thereby rendering the people "more" *chasid*. This mirrors the religious exemption from military service for Hasidic Jews: they are allowed to be more *chasid* by the moral sacrifice of soldiers who may do un-*chasid* things for them.

The war between Nephilim and angels may sound like the Miltonian Christian narrative of war in heaven but it is different in a number of key aspects, most importantly that it does not have the same moral polarization. The element of good versus evil present in the Ethiopian Book of Enoch may have come out of the more-or-less lost Manichean Book of Giants, specifically the Zoroastrian influence on that text. The ambivalence between the ravenous giants of 1 Enoch and the "heroes of old" of Genesis may be resolved in the lost passages of the Qumran Book of Giants. In the end, the Nephilim may be people of great power, doers of great deeds, who nonetheless had to be destroyed because their appetites would have stripped the world bare and left it lifeless.

Osterman plants another hint at a redemptive narrative in Gath with the inclusion of Merkavah mysticism. The Merkavah, or Chariot of the Lord, appears in Ezekiel, in the H'aggada, and in mystical texts. Genesis 5:24 says that "Enoch walked with God; and then he was no more, for God took him." 1 Enoch and the H'aggada expand on this, adding in the Merkavah from 1 Ezekiel. In Louis Ginsberg's collected H'aggada, it is said that "Enoch was carried into the heavens in a fiery chariot drawn by fiery chargers." The Merkavah is described in Ezekiel:

> I could see that there were four wheels beside the cherubs, one beside each of the cherubs ... and when they moved, each could move in the direction of any of its four quarters ... Their entire bodies—backs, hands and wings—and the wheels, the wheels of the four of them, were covered all over with eyes. It was these wheels that I heard called "the wheelwork." Each one had four faces: One was a cherub's face, the second a human face, the third a lion's face, and the fourth an eagle's face. (Ezek. 10:9a, 11a, 12–13)

The Merkavah has powerful symbolic significance: in 1 Enoch, the Watchers ask Enoch to carry their petition for mercy to God, because they cannot enter his presence. The Merkavah is associated with the intense presence of God, and one has to be worthy to see it and live—in the Ginsberg H'aggada after Enoch was carried up in the chariot, "They found snow and great hailstones upon the spot whence Enoch had risen, and, when they searched beneath, they discovered the bodies of all who had remained behind with Enoch [after being told to leave]."

In Osterman's Gath the player can continue to practice Blood Magic, but she or he can also pursue the difficult goal of summoning the Merkavah. In this way, the giants who were denied a chance to repent in 1 Enoch and the Book of Giants can be brought into the covenant and made right with the heavens. After extensive preparation, including disciplined frugality by the player, as the spell requires 222 astral pearls, more than any other spell in the game, the Merkavah will descend and (literally, in game terms) bless giants and humans alike. In the player-enabled narrative in which the Merkavah descends on Gath and the Abbas have put an end to human sacrifice, the remaining *chasid* (faithful to the covenant) giants then slot into place as the "lost tribe" of Israel.

Joann Sfar posits just such a lost tribe of Jewish Giants in *The Rabbi's Cat 2*. In it, the titular cat accompanies the titular Rabbi, an Algerian Sephardic Jew, his Muslim cousin, a blonde, blue-eyed Russian Ashkenazi Jewish artist, and his black ex-slave African bride on a quest to find a hidden city, home to the lost tribe. After a great many confrontations with prejudice, including the patronizing attitude of a young Belgian reporter (a parody of Herge's Tintin), they meet a lascivious older European artist who tries to convince the Ashkenazi painter that it is anatomically correct to draw black people with monkey-like features. The Ashkenazi painter strikes the European artist, then explains, in the French his wife has been teaching him: "In country of me, they make same drawing on Jews" (122).

Sfar's rejection of racial caricature, carried through his proxy, the nameless Russian painter, does raise additional questions. Sfar, through his art, does reject racial caricature, but he may veer in the "opposite" direction with the painter's African wife-to-be, who conforms to western ideals of beauty. This unnamed character is drawn with large but also high and "firm" breasts, a thin waist, modest derrière, and a tiny nose. The offensive European suggests to the painter that he should ask her to pose naked, but the impact of this satirization of European painters like Gauguin and their nudes of "native women" may be lessened by the fact that while the painter does not draw the African woman naked, Sfar does, in intimate scenes with the painter. The result is a complicit critique which participates in sexual idealization and objectification even as it rejects racial superiority and colonial power.

This complicity prepares us for the ambivalent encounter with the Lost Tribe of African Jewish giants that concludes the book. When the titular Rabbi's cat, the artist, and his wife find the city, and it is populated with giants, dark-skinned Jewish giants dripping with golden jewelry. They are "Blacks whom nobody ever enslaved. Jews who never left the land of their ancestors. Happy, balanced people who radiate self-confidence" (126). The combination of Semitic, African, and "classical" traits is interesting: the Giant in the bottom-right panel has an exaggerated "Jewish" nose (unlike the Ashkenazi painter); the boy or man in the bottom-left is built like Adonis but has "Hasidic" forelocks; and the women in the middle-right and lower-left panels might almost be Greek statues as well but for their African hair and skin color. That color itself is a dark, cool gray, almost bluish, contrasting with the warm terracotta color of the artist's wife's skin and foreshadowing their rejection by these too-complete, too-self-sufficient people.

Because of their perfect confidence and safety, their isolated history in their hidden city, suffering neither the oppressions heaped upon Africans nor Jews, these happy, balanced people are unable to perceive these smaller, less happy people as their kin and take offense when tells them that he is Jewish, like them. The cat, who understands the giants' speech, translates their answer as: "He says there's no such thing as a white Jew. He says they are the real Jews. He says you've offended them and we have to leave" (128). Sfar's Jewish Giants are isolated by their history. He implies that if such a people existed, they couldn't possibly recognize their kinship to either Jew or African, as they cannot understand how subjugation and suffering have (here seemingly literally) diminished them. Without those experiences, the giants are just as proud and insular (thus the cool, unconcerned gray) as those who have oppressed Jew and African alike.

This is an ironic echo of the Rabbi's words of much earlier: "[N]obody's ever seen such a thing as black Jews ... [L]ook: blacks, they have slavery; Jews, they have pogroms. It's a lot to bear. Now imagine a people that has both at the same time. It just can't be" (84). The Lost Tribe of black, giant Jews has neither pogroms nor slavery. It is a fantasy of absolute freedom from those oppressions, which is the real reason the artist and his wife can't stay there: they are living contradictions to the fantasy these giants represent. Sfar sees his walled city of giants as appealing but also as both impossible and undesirable.

Additionally, there is something interesting going on in Sfar's art in the bathhouse scene, as the titular Rabbi and the French Rabbi are drawn in almost entirely different styles, the former cartooned with a hemispheric "Charlie Brown" nose and the latter rendered in a much more detailed, anatomically correct style. Sfar's relative even-handedness with nudity and willingness to switch-up art style without transition gives the art an intersubjective quality: we seem to see characters as they are seen by others. This may explain the relatively "European" look of the painter's wife. We see his bride as he sees her. He knows she is beautiful, so we see her through the lens of what he has been taught it means to be beautiful.

A different but parallel lesson on gianthood can be found in *Exit Wounds*. Rutu Modan's comics reflect on the individual human tragedy of the Israeli-Palestinian conflict and how that tension both brings people together and, seemingly more powerfully, pushes them apart. Numi, an IDF soldier known as "the Giraffe" because of her great height, is the central figure but not the protagonist of Modan's *Exit Wounds*, where she is held up against and contrasted with Koby Franko, the book's jaundiced protagonist.

The Giraffe is tall, fit, and androgynous in appearance, frequently looming over Koby as she does on the books cover. She clearly does not benefit from the "Hot Jew" phenomenon that Libicki describes. The revelation of her sexual appetite winds up being personally tragic for her, like the sex drive of the Watchers and the hunger of the Nephilim is to them. She sets the plot in motion by telling a distrustful and disinterested Koby that his estranged father, Gabriel, may be dead, an unidentified victim of a terrorist bombing. Her only evidence is an adornment: a scarf she hand-knit for Gabriel, which she saw on TV at the site of the bombing. Despite being bigger, stronger, and more privileged than Koby (her family lives in a palatial estate), she needs something from him: his blood. "A simple blood test can prove if it's your father" (17). This blood sacrifice is not for Koby's sake but Numi's: she was having an affair with Gabriel until he disappeared.

The slowly reconstructed backstory of Numi and Gabriel plays out in slips of the tongue and accidental confessions, like the fragmentary Book of Giants. It is Gabriel this time, not Azazel, who breaks a sexual taboo (Numi being a third of his age), and Gabriel who is entombed in the desert (by the time Numi convinces Koby to give his blood, the body has been buried), but in both stories Gabriel betrays the giant(ess). We eventually discover that Gabriel is still alive and has had at least two more affairs, one with a woman much closer to his age whom he marries. Koby, a cabdriver, is no more effective a messenger than Enoch, as Numi, like the Watchers and their Nephilim children, never sees Gabriel again. In this version of the story, Koby plays out a version of *Waiting for Godot* (1953) with Gabriel' new wife until he finally decides to leave. His existential question "How long can you wait, alone in the dark?" inverts the binding of Azazel as he gives up his perpetual absentee father to chase the Giraffe (164).

The taboo nature of the Nephilim hangs heavy on Numi, who seems isolated on the page even when she's in Koby's company or with her aggressively feminine mother and sister. Her giant status is associated with unattractiveness, and sex seems to be the Giraffe's bane, presaging the end of her relationship with Gabriel and souring her developing connection with Koby. Their relationship begins slowly, with Numi distant, still obsessed with Gabriel, and Koby quick to affirm that the Giraffe is not his girlfriend. The breakthrough comes after Numi meets the first of Gabriel's other lovers, a woman who is clearly older than her own mother. Koby comforts her and they begin to make love, awkwardly, as Numi seeks to keep her body covered. Then, in mid-coitus, she says "Like father, like son" (137). Koby is so offended that he withdraws and ends their nascent relationship right then.

Gianthood and isolation is a theme of Gauld's *Goliath*, whose titular character hates fighting and has only the strength of his arm, not the conviction of faith with which to face a religious fanatic (Gauld's version of David). In Sturm's *The Golem's Mighty Swing*, gianthood is also alienating. In this graphic novel, a barnstorming pre-league baseball team whose gimmick is that they're all Jewish accommodates a black player, their power-hitter, with the fiction that he is from the "Lost Tribe." Later in the story, he is instead costumed as the titular golem, transformed from a large man into a giant, and hidden behind a mask in the image of the golem from the 1915 film *Der Golem*. That movie infamously reinscribes the image of the Old Jew as diabolist by conflating Kabbalah with demonology, among other things, substituting a pentagram for the Star of David. Mask, lie, and libel ring that version of the Jewish giant about like a moat, precluding any possibility of closeness.

This seems to be the danger that Sfar's work cautions against, the isolation that precludes empathy. *Exit Wounds* follows up on that isolation, showing the loss of ability to make meaningful human contact experienced by Numi, Koby, and even the absentee Gabriel, who, it is implied, is already cheating on his new wife. Modan offers an "out" at the end of her story, however, when Koby comes to tell Numi that Gabriel is alive after all. He is treed by her family's dogs, and she offers him only one escape from his elevated, precarious position. "Just jump ... I'll catch you" (171). The last panel of the comic is Koby falling. That uncertain element is key. Numi is, after all, a giantess who demanded his blood and wanted him to exhume the dead.

Numi, however, is not defined by the past, and can use her gianthood without losing her humanity. As with Osterman's Abbas, and Libicki's desire to recover the individual IDF soldier from the fetishization of the "New Jew," she can be *chasid*: covenant-abiding (albeit, perhaps not in the Hasidic sense), possessing "loving-kindness," and perhaps most importantly, merciful. The danger of becoming a giant in the land is in thinking that one is defined by gianthood, set apart from humanity. A *chasid* giant, however, is not defined by gianthood but by humane action.

Notes

1   All Tanakh citations in this essay are from the JPS version.
2   Historically, "Gittite" simply referred to Philistines from the city of Gath.
3   All citations from 1 Enoch are from the Knibb and Ullendorff edition.

Bibliography

Introduction

Aldama, Frederick Luis. *Your Brain on Latino Comics: From Gus Arriola to Los Bros Hernandez*. Austin: University of Texas Press, 2009. Print.

Aldama, Frederick Luis, ed. *Multicultural Comics: From Zap to Blue Beetle*. Austin: University of Texas Press, 2010. Print.

Andrae, Thomas, and Mel Gordon, eds. *Siegel and Shuster's Funnyman: The First Jewish Superhero, from the Creators of Superman*. Port Townsend, WA: Feral House, 2010. Print.

Baskind, Samantha, and Ranen Omer-Sherman, eds. *The Jewish Graphic Novel: Critical Approaches*. New Brunswick, NJ: Rutgers University Press, 2008. Print.

Brod, Harry. *Superman Is Jewish?: How Comic Book Superheroes Came to Serve Truth, Justice, and the Jewish-American Way*. New York: Free Press, 2012. Print.

Brooks, Vincent. *Something Ain't Kosher Here: The Rise of the "Jewish" Sitcom*. New Brunswick, NJ: Rutgers University Press, 2003. Print.

Brown, Jeffrey A. *Black Superheroes, Milestone Comics, and Their Fans*. Jackson: University Press of Mississippi, 2001. Print.

Brownstein, Charles, and Diana Schutz, eds. *Eisner/Miller: A One-on-One Interview Conducted by Charles Brownstein*. Milwaukie, OR: Dark Horse, 2005. Print.

Buhle, Paul. *Jews and American Popular Culture*. 3 vols. Westport, CT: Praeger, 2006. Print.

Buhle, Paul, ed. *Jews and American Comics: An Illustrated History of an American Art Form*. New York: New Press, 2008. Print.

Crumb, R. *The Book of Genesis Illustrated*. New York: Norton, 2009. Print.

Duffy, Damian, and John Jennings. *Black Comix: African American Independent Comics, Art and Culture*. New York: Mark Batty, 2010. Print.

Epstein, Lawrence J. *The Haunted Smile: The Story of Jewish Comedians*. Cambridge, MA: PublicAffairs, 2002. Print.

Fingeroth, Danny. *Disguised as Clark Kent: Jews, Comics, and the Creation of the Superhero*. New York: Continuum, 2007. Print.

Hoberman, J., and Jeffrey Sandler. *Entertaining America: Jews, Movies, and Broadcasting*. Princeton, NJ: Princeton University Press, 2003. Print.

Howard, Sheena C., and Ronald L. Jackson II. *Black Comics: Politics of Race and Representation*. London: Bloomsbury Academic, 2013. Print.

Jones, Gerard, and Will Jacobs. *The Comic Book Heroes*. Rev. ed. Rocklin, CA: Prima Publishing, 1997. Print.

Kaplan, Arie. *From Krakow to Krypton: Jews and Comic Books*. Philadelphia, PA: Jewish Publication Society, 2008. Print.

Kaplan, Arie. *Masters of the Comic Book Universe Revealed!: Will Eisner, Stan Lee, Neil Gaiman, and More*. Chicago, IL: Chicago Review Press, 2006. Print.

Katchor, Ben. Message to author. July 6, 2006. E-mail.

Kotek, Joël. *Cartoons and Extremism: Israel and the Jews in Arab and Western Media.* Trans. Alisa Jaffa. Portland, OR: Mitchell Vallentine, 2009. Print.

Lightman, Sarah. *Graphic Details: Jewish Women's Confessional Comics in Essays and Interviews.* Jefferson, NC: McFarland, 2014. Print.

Most, Andrea. *Making Americans: Jews and the Broadway Musical.* Cambridge: Harvard University Press, 2004. Print.

Niles, Steve. Interview by Derek Royal. "Episode 55.1: Talking with Creators at the October Dallas Comic Con: Fan Days." *Comics Alternative* October 7, 2013. Web. May 15, 2015. <http://ComicsAlternative.com>.

Rogen, Michael. *Blackface, White Noise: Jewish Immigrants in the Hollywood Melting Pot.* Berkeley: University of California Press, 1996. Print.

Roth, Laurence. "Drawing Contracts: Will Eisner's Legacy." *The Jewish Quarterly Review* 97.3 (2007): 465. Print.

Roth, Philip. "The Conversion of the Jews." *Goodbye, Columbus and Five Short Stories.* 1959. Boston, MA: Houghton, 1989. 141–142. Print.

Royal, Derek Parker. "Coloring America: Multi-Ethnic Engagements with Graphic Narrative," Spec. issue of *MELUS* 32.3 (2007). Print.

Sheyahshe, Michael A. *Native Americans in Comic Books: A Critical Study.* Jefferson, NC: McFarland, 2008. Print.

Simon, Joe, with Jim Simon. *The Comic Book Makers.* New York: Crestwood/II Productions, 1990; Lebanon, NJ: Vanguard Productions, 2003. Print.

Stömberg, Frederik. *Black Images in the Comics: A Visual History.* Seattle, WA: Fantagraphics, 2003. Print.

Stömberg, Frederik. *Jewish Images in the Comics: A Visual History.* Seattle, WA: Fantagraphics, 2012. Print.

Tabachnick, Stephen E. *The Quest for Jewish Belief and Identity in the Graphic Novel.* Tuscaloosa: University of Alabama Press, 2014. Print.

Weinstein, Simcha. *Up, Up, and Oy Vey!: How Jewish History, Culture, and Values Shaped the Comic Book Superhero.* Baltimore: Leviathan Press, 2006; Fort Lee, NJ: Barricade Books, 2009. Print.

Yang, Jeff, Parry Shen, Keith Chow, and Jerry Ma, eds. *Secret Identities: The Asian American Superhero Anthology.* New York: New Press, 2009. Print.

Zurawick, David. *The Jews of Prime Time.* Lebanon, NH: Brandies University Press, 2003. Print.

Chapter 1

Andelman, Bob. *Will Eisner: A Spirited Life.* Milwaukie, OR: M Press, 2005. Print.

Carrier, David. *The Aesthetics of Comics.* University Park: Pennsylvania State University Press, 2000. Print.

Dauber, Jeremy. "Comic Books, Tragic Stories: Will Eisner's American Jewish History." *Association for Jewish Studies Review* 30.2 (2006): 277–304. Print.

Eisner, Will. *Comics & Sequential Art.* Tamarac, FL: Poorhouse Press, 1985. Print.

Eisner, Will. *The Dreamer.* New York: DC Comics, 1986. Print.

Eisner, Will. *Eisner/Miller: A One-on-One Interview Conducted by Charles Brownstein.* Milwaukie, OR: Dark Horse Books, 2005. Print.

Eisner, Will. *Graphic Storytelling and Visual Narrative.* Tamarac, FL: Poorhouse Press, 1996. Print.

Eisner, Will. "Keynote Address from the 2002 Will Eisner Symposium." *ImageTexT* 1.1 (2004). Web. November 8, 2013.

Eisner, Will. *Life, in Pictures: Autobiographical Stories*. New York and London: Norton, 2007. Print.

Feiffer, Jules. *The Great Comic Book Heroes*. New York: Bonanza Books, 1965. Print.

Flagg, Gordon. "Life, in Pictures: Autobiographical Stories by Will Eisner." Review. *Booklist* 104.2 (2007): 56. Print.

Harvey, Robert C. "An Affectionate Appreciation." *Comic Journal* 267 (2005): 80–91. Print.

Harvey, Robert C. *The Art of the Comic Book: An Aesthetic History*. Jackson: University Press of Mississippi, 1996. Print.

Hatfield, Charles. *Alternative Comics: An Emerging Literature*. Jackson: University Press of Mississippi, 2005. Print.

Hirsch, Marianne. "Collateral Damage." *PMLA* 119.5 (2004): 1209–1215. Print.

Jacob, Dale. "Mulimodal Constructions of Self: Autobiographical Comics and the Case of Joe Matt's *Peepshow*." *Biography: An Interdisciplinary Quarterly* 31.1 (2008): 59–84. Print.

Kitchen, Denise. "Editor's Notes." In Eisner *Life, in Pictures*, 13–17. Print.

Kitchen, Denise. "Life, in Pictures." Review. *The New Yorker* 83.37 (2007): 167. Print.

McCloud, Scott. "Introduction: A Will to Change." In Eisner *Life, in Pictures*, 9–12. Print.

McCloud, Scott. *Understanding Comics: The Invisible Art*. New York: HarperCollins, 1993. Print.

Miller, Nancy. "The Entangled Self: Genre Bondage in the Ag of the Memoir." *PMLA* 122.2 (2007): 537–548. Print.

Morrison, Toni. "The Site of Memory," in *Inventing the Truth: The Art and Craft of Memoir*, ed. William Zinsser. Boston, MA: Mariner, 1998. 185–200. Print.

Roth, Laurence. "Drawing Contracts: Will Eisner's Legacy." *The Jewish Quarterly Review* 97.5 (2007): 463–484. Print.

Royal, Derek Parker. "Introduction: Coloring America: Multi-Ethnic Engagements with Graphic Narrative." *MELUS* 32.3 (2007): 7–22. Print.

Schlam, Helena Frenkil. "Contemporary Scribes: Jewish American Cartoonists." *Shofar* 20.1 (2001): 94–112. Print.

Takaki, Ronald. *A Different Mirror: A History of Multicultural America*. New York and Boston, MA: Little, Brown and Company, 1993. Print.

Varnum, Rrobin, and Christina T. Gibbons, eds. *The Language of Comics: Word and Image*. Jackson: University Press of Mississippi, 2001. Print.

Whitlock, Gillian. "Autographics: The Seeing 'I' of the Comics." *Modern Fiction Studies* 52.4 (2006): 965–979. Print.

Whitlock, Gillian, and Anna Poletti. "Self-Regarding Art." *Biography* 31.1 (2008): v–xxiii. Print.

"Will Eisner Official Web Site." Web. Nov. 8, 2013. <http://willeisner.com/>.

"Will Eisner's *Life, in Pictures*." Review. *Publishers Weekly* 254.40 (2007): 43. Print.

Chapter 2

Antin, Mary. *The Promised Land*. New York: Penguin Books, 1997. Print.

Bergland, Betty. "Rereading Photographs and Narratives in Ethnic Autobiography: Memory and Subjectivity in Mary Antin's *The Promised Land*," in *Memory, Narrative, and Identity: New Essays in Ethnic American Literatures*, eds. Amritjit Singh, Joseph T.

Skerrett Jr., and Robert E. Hogan. Boston, MA: Northeastern University Press, 1994. 45–88. Print.

Chametzky, Jules. "Chapter 1: Rethinking Mary Antin and *The Promised Land*," in *Modern Jewish Women Writers in America*, ed. Evelyn Avery. New York: Palgrave MacMillan, 2007. 17–27. Print.

Corman, Leela. Interview by Eli Rosenblatt. "Introducing a New Graphic Novel: Leela Corman's 'Unterzakhn.'" *The Jewish Daily Forward*. The Jewish Daily Forward, February 28, 2008. Web. August 28, 2014.

Corman, Leela. *Unterzakhn*. New York: Schocken Books, 2012. Print.

Eisner, Will. *The Contract with God Trilogy: Life on Dropsie Avenue (A Contract with God, A Life Force, and Dropsie Avenue)*. New York: W. W. Norton & Company, 2005. Print.

Elahi, Babak. "The Heavy Garments of the Past: Mary and Frieda Antin in *The Promised Land*." *College Literature* 32.4 (Fall 2005): 29–49. Print.

Gabler, Neil. "Yiddishkeit: An Introduction," in *Yiddishkeit: Jewish Vernacular & the New Land*, eds. Harvey Pekar, and Paul Buhle. New York: Abrams Books, 2011. 9–10. Print.

Glenn, Susan A. *Daughters of the Shtetl: Life and Labor in the Immigrant Generation*. Ithaca, NY: Cornell University Press, 1990. Print.

Hoffman, Eva. *Lost in Translation: A Life in a New Language*. New York: Penguin Books, 1990. Print.

Jirousek, Lori. "Mary Antin's Progressive Science: Eugenics, Evolution, and the Environment." *Shofar* 27.1 (2008): 58–79. Print.

Kellman, Steven G. "Lost in the Promised Land: Eva Hoffman Revises Mary Antin." *Prooftexts* 18 (1998): 149–159. Print.

Portnoy, Edward. "Re: Comics …" Message to the author. March 16, 2012. E-mail.

Salz, Evelyn. *Selected Letters of Mary Antin*. Syracuse, NY: Syracuse University Press, 2001. Print.

Sollors, Werner. "Introduction," in *The Promised Land*, ed. Mary Antin. New York: Penguin Books, 1997. xi–xlx. Print.

Weinberg, Sydney Stahl. *The World of Our Mothers: The Lives of Jewish Immigrant Women*. Chapel Hill: The University of North Carolina Press, 1988. Print.

Wirth-Nesher, Hana. "Linguistic Passing: Mary Antin," in *Call it English*. Princeton, NJ: Princeton University Press, 2006. 52–75. Print.

Yezierska, Anzia. *Bread Givers*. New York: Persea Books, 1975. Print.

Yezierska, Anzia. "Hunger," in *How I Found America: The Collected Stories of Anzia Yezierska*. New York: Persea Books, 1991. 17–29. Print.

Chapter 3

Babylonian Talmud Tractate Megillah. Print.

Babylonian Talmud Tractate Sanhedrin. Print.

Barthes, Roland. "Rhetoric of the Image," in *Image, Music, Text*. New York: Noonday Press, 1977. Print.

Beal, Timothy K. *The Book of Hiding: Gender, Ethnicity, Annihilation, and Esther*. New York: Routledge, 1997. Print.

Brenner, Athalya. "Introduction," in *A Feminist Companion to Esther, Judith and Susanna*, ed. Athalya Brenner. Sheffield, England: Sheffield Academic Press Ltd, 1995. 11–25. Print.

Fewell, Danna Nolan. "Feminist Reading of the Hebrew Bible: Affirmation, Resistance and Transformation." *Journal for the Study of the Old Testament* 12.3 (1987): 77–87. Print.

Gal, Nissim. "The Language of the Poor: *Bible Stories* as a Critical Narrative of the Present." *Images* 4.1 (2010): 82–108. Print.

Hotlz, Barry. "Midrash," in *Back to the Sources: Reading the Classic Jewish Texts*, ed. Barry Holtz. New York: Summit Books, 1984. 177–212. Print.

Ibn Ezra. *Mikraot Gedolot: Commentary on Megillat Esther*. Print.

Katz, Jackson. "Not-So-Nice Jewish Boys: Notes on Violence and the Construction of Jewish-American Masculinity in the Late 20th and Eary 21st Centuries," in *Brother Keepers: New Perspectives on Jewish Masculinity*, eds. Harry Brod, and Shawn Israel Zevit. Harriman, TN: Men's Studies Press, 2010. 57–74. Print.

Klein, Lillian R. "Honor and Shame in Esther," in *A Feminist Companion to Esther, Judith and Susanna*, ed. Athalya Brenner. Sheffield, England: Sheffield Academic Press Ltd., 1995. 149–175. Print.

Komlosh, Yehuda. "Targum Sheni." *Encyclopedia Judaica*. 2nd Edition. Print.

"National Jewish Population Survey Report 2000–2001." 2002. United Jewish Communities. Print.

Rashi. *Mikraot Gedolot: Commentary on Megillat Esther*. Print.

Soltes, Ori Z. "Images and the Book of Esther: From Manuscript Illumination to Midrash," in *The Book of Esther in Modern Research*, eds. Leonard Greenspoon, and Sidnie White Crawford. London: T&T Clark International, 2003. 137–175. Print.

Soltes, Ori Z. "The Graphic Novel From Diaspora to Diaspora: James Sturm's *The Golem's Mighty Swing* and J.T. Waldman's *Megillat Esther* in the Tree of Contexts." 2009 Conney Conference on Jewish Arts: Madison, WI, 2009. Presentation.

Targum Sheini. *Mikraot Gedolot: Megillat Esther*. Print.

Wafish, Barry Dov. *Esther in Medieval Garb: Jewish Interpretation of the Book of Esther in the Middle Ages*. Albany: State University of New York Press, 1993. Print.

Wafish, Barry Dov. "Kosher Adultery? The Mordecai-Esther-Ahasuerus Triangle in Talmudic, Medieval, and Sixteenth-Century Exegesis." *The Book of Esther in Modern Research*, eds. Leonard Greenspoon, and Sidnie White Crawford. London: T&T Clark International, 2003. 111–136. Print.

Waldman, J.T. *Megillat Esther*. Philadephia: The Jewish Publication Society, 2005. Print.

Zaeske, Susan. "Unveiling Esther as a Pragmatic Radical Rhetoric." *Philosophy and Rhetoric* 33.3 (2000): 193–220. Print.

Chapter 4

Baade, Christina L. "Jewzak and Heavy Shtetl: Constructing Ethnic Identity and Asserting Authenticity in the New-Klezmer Movement." *Monatshefte* 90.2 (1998): 208–219. *JSTOR*. Web. Aug. 30, 2009.

Boyarin, Jonathan, and Daniel Boyarin. "Diaspora: Generation and the Ground of Jewish Identity," in *Theorizing diaspora*, eds. Jana Evans Braziel and Anita Mannur. Malden, MA: Blackwell, 2003. 85–118. Print.

Boym, Svetlana. *The Future of Nostalgia*. New York: Basic, 2001. Print.

Bérubé, Patrick. "A Guide to European Comic Book Publishers Part 3: l'Association." *Comic Book Bin*, December 23, 2008. Web. March 27, 2010.

Grainge, Paul. *Monochrome Memories: Nostalgia and Style in Retro America*. Westport, CT: Praeger, 2002. Print.

Radhakrishnan, R. "Ethnicity in an Age of Diaspora," in *Theorizing Diaspora.*, eds. Jana Evans Braziel and Anita Mannur. Malden, MA: Blackwell, 2003. 119–131. Print.

Sfar, Joann. *Klezmer: Book One:Tales of the Wild East.* Trans. Alexis Siegel. New York: First Second, 2006. Print.

Sfar, Joann. "Notes," in *Klezmer: Book One: Tales of the Wild East.* Trans. Alexis Siegel. New York: First Second, 2006. Print.

Starobinski, Jean. "Rivers, Bells, Nostalgia." *The Hudson Review* 61.4 (2008): n. pag. Trans. Richard Peaver. *JSTOR.* Web. March 27, 2010.

Chapter 5

Adams, Henry. *Selected Letters*, ed. Ernest Samuels. Cambridge, MA: Harvard University Press, 1992. Print.

Bellow, Saul. *Dangling Man.* 1944; New York: Penguin, 1996. Print.

Epstein, Lawrence J. *The Haunted Smile, The Story of Jewish Comedians in America.* New York: Public Affairs, 2001. Print.

Feiffer, Jules. *Backing into Forward.* New York: Doubleday, 2010. Print.

Feiffer, Jules. *Explainers: The Complete Village Voice Strips (1956–1966).* Seattle, WA: Fantagraphics Books, 2008. Print.

Feiffer, Jules. *Jules Feiffer's America: From Eisenhower to Reagan.* ed. Steven Heller. New York: Knopf, 1982. Print.

Feiffer, Jules. "Op-Art," *New York Times* July 27, 1997: A 17. Print.

Feiffer, Jules. "Opinion," Universal Press Syndicate. June 1997. Web. August 19, 2014. <http://www.uexpress.com>.

Feiffer, Jules. *Tantrum.* New York: Alfred Knopf, 1979. Print.

Groth, Gary. "Introduction," in *Explainers.* Seattle, WA: Fantagraphics, 2008. v–xviii. Print.

Howe, Irving. "Introduction," in *Jewish-American Stories.* New York: New American Library, 1977. Print.

Manso, Peter. *Mailer, His Life and Times.* New York: Simon & Schuster, 1985. Print.

Sendak, Maurice. "An Appreciation," in *The Phantom Tollbooth*, Norman Juster. Illustrations Jules Feiffer. 1961. New York: Random House, 1996. Print.

Wisse, Ruth R. *The Schlemiel as Modern Hero.* Chicago, IL: University of Chicago Press, 1971. Print.

Chapter 6

Andelman, Bob. *Will Eisner: A Spirited Life.* Milwaukie, OR: M Press, 2005. Print.

Brodkin, Karen. *How the Jews Became White Folks and What That Says about Race in America.* New Brunswick, NJ: Rutgers University Press, 1998. Print.

Eisner, Will. *The Contract with God Trilogy: Life on Dropsie Avenue.* New York: Norton, 2005. Print.

Eisner, Will. *Dropsie Avenue: The Neighborhood.* 1995. New York: Norton, 2006. Print.

Fingeroth, Danny. *Disguised as Clark Kent: Jews, Comics, and the Creation of the Superhero.* New York: Continuum, 2007. Print.

Groensteen, Thierry. *Comics and Narration*. Trans. Ann Miller. Jackson, MS: University Press of Mississippi, 2013. Print.

Ignatiev, Noel. *How the Irish Became White*. New York: Routledge, 1995. Print.

Jacobson, Matthew Frye. *Whiteness of a Different Color: European Immigrants and the Alchemy of Race*. Cambridge: Harvard University Press, 1998. Print.

McCloud, Scott. *Understanding Comics: The Invisible Art*. 1993. New York: HarperPerennial, 1994. Print.

Omi, Michael, and Howard Winant. *Racial Formation in the United States: From the 1960s to the 1990s*. 2nd ed. New York: Routledge, 1994. Print.

Roth, Laurence. "Drawing Contracts: Will Eisner's Legacy." *The Jewish Quarterly Review* 97.3 (2007): 463–484. Print.

Royal, Derek Parker. "Sequential Sketches of Ethnic Identity: Will Eisner's *A Contract with God* as Graphic Cycle." *College Literature* 38.3 (2011): 150–167. Print.

Chapter 7

Aguirre-Sacasa, Roberto, Valentine Delandro, Mizuki Sakaibara, et al. *Marvel Knights 4: Impossible Things Happen Every Day*. New York: Marvel, 2006. Reprints issues #19–24. Print.

Bilefsky, Dan. "Hard Times Give New Life to Prague's Golem." *New York Times*, May 10, 2009. Web. September 10, 2009.

Boganove, Jon, and Louise Simonson. *Superman: Man of Steel* #80–82. New York: DC Comics, 1998. Print.

Burden, Bob, and Rick Geary. "Behold the Golem," *Gumby* #2, Wallnut Creek, CA: Wildcard Productions, 2006. Print.

Carycomix, "The Golem." *Marvel Universe Database*. 2006. Web. September 10, 2009.

Chabon, Michael. *The Amazing Adventures of Kavalier & Clay*. New York: Picador, 2001. Print.

Chomiak, Bohdan. "Letters to the Golem," in *Strange Tales* #176, Mike Friedrich, Tony DeZuniga, et al.. New York: Marvel, October 1974. Print.

Christiansen, Jeff, Sean McQuaid, Michael Hoskin, et al. *Marvel Legacy: The 1960s–1990s Handbook*. New York: Marvel, 2007. Print.

Comtois, Pierre. *Marvel Comics in the 1960s: An Issue-By-Issue Field Guide to a Pop Culture Phenomenon*. Raleigh, NC: TwoMorrows, 2009. Print.

Daniels, Les. *Marvel Five Decades of the World's Greatest Comics*. New York: Henry Abrams, 1992. Print.

Defalco, Tom, Peter Sanderson, et al. *Marvel Chronicle*. New York: DK, 2008. Print.

Ellstein, Abraham, and H. Leivick. *The Golem: An Opera in Four Acts*. New York: Program Publications, 1962. Print.

Eshed, Eli, and Uri Fink. *HaGolem: Sipuro Shel Comics Israeli*. Ben Shemen, Israel: Modan, 2003. Print.

Federation of American Scientists. "Heavy Water Production." *Federation of American Scientists: Weapons Primer*. 1998. Web. September 18, 2009.

Friedrich, Mike, Tony DeZuniga, and Steve Austin. *Strange Tales* #177. New York: Marvel, December 1974. Print.

Giffen, Keith, Eduardo Francisco, Bob Campanella, et al. *Nick Fury's Howling Commandos* #2 and #6. New York: Marvel, January 2006 and May 2006. Print.

Harde, Roxanne. "Give 'em Another Circumcision: Jewish Masculinities in the *The Golem's Mighty Swing*," in *The Jewish Graphic Novel*, eds. Samantha Baskind, and Ranen Omer-Sherman, New Brunswick, NJ: Rutgers University Press, 2008. 64–81. Print.

Inglourious Basterds, Dir. Quentin Tarantino. A Band Apart, 2009. Film.

Kaplin, Arie. *From Krakow to Krypton: Jews and Comic Books*. Philadelphia, PA: Jewish Publication Society, 2008. Print.

Lee, Edward. *The Golem*. New York: Leisure, 2009. Print.

Leivick, H. David Fishelson adapt., and Joseph C. Landis trans., *The Golem*. New York: Dramatists Play Service, 2001. Print.

Levin, Neil W. *Jewish Operas, Volume 1*. Hong Kong: Naxos, 2004. 4–5. Print.

Marvel Editors. "Letters to the Golem," in *Strange Tales* #177, Mike Friedrich, Ton DeZuniga, and Steve Austin. New York: Marvel, December 1974. Print.

Marvel Editors. "Okay Axis Here We Come," in *Invaders* #17. New York: Marvel, June 1977. Print.

McQuaid, Sean, Al Sjoerdsma, and Michael Hoskin. *Marvel Legacy 1: 1970s Handbook*. New York: Marvel, 2006. Print.

Meyer, Richard. "The Golem." *Comic Book Profiles*. 2003. Web. September 16, 2009.

Meyrink, Gustav. *The Golem: A Novel*. New York: F Ungar, 1962, originally published in 1915. Print.

Neugroschel, Joachim, ed. *The Golem: A New Translation of the Classic Play and Selected Short Stories*. New York: W. W. Norton and Co., 2006. Print.

Pratchett, Terry. *Feet of Clay*. New York: HarperTorch, 2007. Print.

Raab, Alan. "Ben Gurion's Golems and Jewish Lesbians: Subverting Hegemonic History in Two Israeli Graphic Novels," in *The Jewish Graphic Novel*, eds. Samantha Baskind, and Ranen Omer-Sherman, New Brunswick, NJ: Rutgers University Press, 2008. 214–233. Print.

Roberts, Jaime Morgan. *Golem*. Quincy, MA: Pop Art Productions, 1994. Print.

Sanderson, Peter. *Marvel Universe*. New York: Abradale Press, 1996. Print.

Scholem, Gershom. *Kabbalah*. New York: Quadrangle/New York Times Book Club, 1974. Print.

Singer, Isaac Bashevis, and Uri Shulevitz. *The Golem*. New York: Farrar, Straus and Giroux, 1982. Print.

Steranko, Jim. *Steranko History of Comics*. Reading, PA: Supergraphics, 1970. Print.

Strum, James. *The Golem's Mighty Swing*. Montreal, Canada: Drawn and Quarterly, 2002. Print.

Thieberger, Friedrich. *The Great Rabbi Löew of Prague: His Life and Work and the Legend of the Golem, with Extracts from His Writings and a Collection of the Old Legends*. London: East and West Library, 1955. Print.

Thomas, Roy. e-mail message to author, September 14, 2009.

Thomas, Roy. *Hulk* #134. New York: Marvel, December 1970. Print.

Thomas, Roy, Dave Hoover, and Brian Garvey. *The Invaders* #1–4. New York: Marvel, May–August 1993. Print.

Thomas, Roy, Bill Mantlo, and Bob Brown. *Marvel Two-In-One* #11. New York: Marvel, September, 1975. Print.

Thomas, Roy, Frank Robbins, and Frank Springer. *Invaders* #11. New York: Marvel, December 1976. Print.

Thomas, Roy, Frank Robbins, and Frank Springer. *Invaders* #12. New York: Marvel, January 1977. Print.

Thomas, Roy, Frank Robbins, and Frank Springer. *Invaders* #13. New York: Marvel, February 1977. Print.

Wein, Len, John Buscema, and Jim Mooney. *Strange Tales* #174. New York: Marvel, June 1974. Print.

Weiner, Robert G. *Marvel Graphic Novels and Related Publications: An Annotated Guide.* Jefferson, NC: McFarland, 2008. Print.

Wiesel, Elie. *The Golem: The Story of a Legend.* New York: Summit Books, 1983. Print.

Wisniewski, David. *The Golem.* New York: Clarion Books, 1996. Print.

Chapter 8

Boyarin, Daniel. *Unheroic Conduct: The Rise of Heterosexuality and the Invention of the Jewish Man.* Berkeley, CA: University of California Press, 1997. Print.

Breines, Paul. *Tough Jews: Political Fantasies and the Moral Dilemma of American Jewry.* New York: Basic, 1990. Print.

Brod, Harry. *Superman is Jewish? How Comic Book Superheroes Came to Serve Truth, Justice, and the Jewish-American Way.* New York: Free Press, 2012. Print.

Caplan, Gregory. "Militarism and Masculinity as Keys to the 'Jewish Question' in Germany," in *Military Masculinities: Identity and the State*, ed. Paul R. Higate. Westport, CT: Praeger, 2003. 175–190. Print.

Chaykin, Howard. *American Flagg!* #2. Chicago, IL: First Comics, November 1983. Print.

Chaykin, Howard. *American Flagg!* #7. Chicago, IL: First Comics, April 1984. Print.

Chaykin, Howard. "An Afternoon with Howard Chaykin," by Brannon Costello, in *Howard Chaykin: Conversations*, ed. Brannon Costello. Jackson: University Press of Mississippi, 2011. 250–288.

Chaykin, Howard. *Dominic Fortune* #1–4. New York: Marvel Comics, October 2009– January 2010. Print.

Chaykin, Howard. "Howard Chaykin Puts It All Back Together Again," by Kim Thompson, *Howard Chaykin: Conversations*, ed. Brannon Costello. Jackson: University Press of Mississippi, 2011. 79–108. Print.

Chaykin, Howard. "I Have a Hard Time with Vigilantes: An Interview with Howard Chaykin." By Gary Groth. *The Comics Journal* (July 1986): 70–104. Print.

Chaykin, Howard. "The Messiah in the Saddle Resolution," in *Marvel Super Action* #1. New York: Marvel Comics, January 1976. 60–74. Print.

Chaykin, Howard, and Bill Morrison. "Jewish Influences in Comics: Panel with Bill Morrison and Howard Chaykin part 1/3." YouTube.com. July 28, 2011. Web. March 15, 2012.

Chaykin, Howard, and Bill Morrison. "Jewish Influences in Comics: Panel with Bill Morrison and Howard Chaykin part 3/3." YouTube.com. July 28, 2011. Web. March 15, 2012.

Chaykin, Howard, and Dennis O'Neil. "All in Color for a Crime," in *The Hulk!* #21, New York: Marvel Comics, June 1980. Print.

Coogan, Peter. *Superhero: The Secret Origin of a Genre.* Austin, TX: MonkeyBrain Books, 2006. Print.

Feiffer, Jules. "The Minsk Theory of Krypton," in *The Last Word: The* New York Times *Book of Obituaries and Farewells: A Celebration of Unusual Lives*, ed. Marvin Siegel. New York: HarperCollins, 1999. 156–157. Print.

Fingeroth, Danny. *Disguised as Clark Kent: Jews, Comics, and the Creation of the Superhero.* New York: Continuum, 2007. Print.

Goldberg, Jeffrey. "Hollywood's Jewish Avenger." *Atlantic Monthly* September 2009: 74–77. *Academic Search Complete*. Web. April 4, 2012.

Harvey, R.C. "Chaykin's Crusade." *The Comics Journal* (March 23, 2010). Web.

Itzkovitz, Daniel. "Secret Temples," in *Jews and Other Differences: The New Jewish Cultural Studies*, eds. Jonathan Boyarin, and Daniel Boyarin. Minneapolis: University of Minnesota Press, 1997. 176–202. Print.

Kaplan, Arie. *From Krakow to Krypton: Jews and Comic Books*. Philadelphia, PA: Jewish Publication Society, 2008. Print.

Klein, Uta. "The Military and Masculinities in Israeli Society," in *Military Masculinities: Identity and the State*, ed. Paul R. Higate. Westport, CT: Praeger, 2003. 191–200. Print.

Legman, Gershon. "From *Love and Death: A Study in Censorship*," in *Arguing Comics: Literary Masters on a Popular Medium*, eds. Jeet Heer, and Kent Worcester Jackson: University Press of Mississippi, 2004. 112–121. Print.

Rosenberg, Warren. *Legacy of Rage: Jewish Masculinity, Violence, and Culture*. Amherst: University of Massachusetts Press, 2001. Print.

Royal, Derek Parker. "Jewish Comics; or, Visualizing Current Jewish Narrative." *Shofar: An Interdisciplinary Journal of Jewish Studies* 29.22 (2011): 1–12. Print.

Weinstein, Simcha. *Up, Up, and Oy Vey! How Jewish History, Culture, and Values Shaped the Comic Book Superhero*. Baltimore, MD: Leviathan, 2006. Print.

Chapter 9

Benson, John. "A Conversation with Harvey Kurtzman and William M. Gaines," in *The Complete Mad*. Vol. I–IV, West Plains, MO: Russ Cochran, 1985. Print.

Bronstein, Daniel M. "Comedy and Comedians," in *The Cambridge Dictionary of Judaism and Jewish Culture*. ed. Judith R. Baskin. New York: Cambridge University Press. 2011. Print.

Buhle, Paul. "Are Comics a Jewish Art Form?" *New York Jewish Week*. Web. October 3, 2011. <http://TheJewishWeek.com>.

Chicken Fat: The Will Elder Documentary Project. Web. October 8, 2015. <http://www.WillElder.net>.

Corliss, Richard. "That Old Feeling: Hail, Harvey!" *Time*. Web. May 5, 2004. <http://Time.com>.

Cuddihy, John Murray. *The Ordeal of Civility: Freud, Marx, Levi-Strauss, and the Jewish Struggle with Modernity*. New York: Dell, 1974. Print.

Decker, Dwight R., and Gary Groth. "An Interview with William M. Gaines," *The Comics Journal TCJ* 81 (May 1983): 53–84. Print.

Elder, Will. "The Night Before Christmas," *Panic* 27.1 (1953). Print.

Grimes, William. Will Elder Obituary, *New York Times* May 18, 2008. A 31. Print

Groth, Gary. "The Will Elder Interview," *TCJ* no. 254, 2003. 78–135. Print.

Groth, Gary, Daniel Clowes, Greg Sadowski, eds. *The Mad Playboy of Art*. Seattle, WA: Fantagraphics Books, 2003.

Hajdu, David. "Will Elder: His Mad World," *New York Times Magazine*, December 24, 2008. 28. Print.

Kelman, Ari Y., ed. *Is Diss a System: A Milt Gross Reader*. New York: NYU Press, 2010. Print.

Kitchen, Denis, and Paul Buhle. *The Art of Harvey Kurtzman: The Mad Genius of Comics*. New York: Abrams Comicarts, 2009. Print.

Kurtzman, Harvey, and Will Elder. *Playboy's Little Annie Fanny, Vol. 2: 1970–1988*. Milwaukie, OR: Dark Horse, 2001. Print.

Portnoy, Eddy. "Follow My Nose: Self-Caricature in Cartoons of the Yiddish Press." *International Journal of Comic Art* 6.2 (2004). 285–303. Print.

Reidelbach, Maria. *Completely Mad: A History of the Comic Book and Magazine*. New York: Little, Brown, 1991. Print.

Rourke, Constance. *American Humor: A Study of the National Character*. New York: Doubleday, 1931. Print.

Tubbs, Keith E. "*Mad Mumblings* Presents: Part II - A Conversation with Willy," an interview with Will Elder. *Mad Mumblings*. Web. 2005. <https://web.archive.org/web/20080518132751/www.madmumblings.com/Elder_Interview.html>.

Vandenbergh, Gary. "Will Elder: Mad Magazine's Yiddishe Kup," *New Jersey Jewish Standard*, May 15, 2009. Electronic.

Veri, Rob. "An Interview with Bill Elder," *TCJ*, no 177, 1995. 101–118. Print.

von Bernewitz, Fred, and Geissman, Grant. "Interview with Albert Feldstein," *Tales of Terror: The EC Companion*. Seattle, WA: Fantagraphics, 2000. 87. Print.

Webb, H. Brook. "The Slang of Jazz," *American Speech* 12.3 (1937): 179–184. Print.

"Will Elder." (Notes from the 1972 EC Fan Convention.) Web. October 8, 2015. <http://pics.livejournal.com/scottedelman/pic/00034e6k>.

Wochner, Lee. "Mad Times with Jack Davis," *TCJ* #153. Print.

Chapter 10

Auerbach, Yehudit. "National Narratives in a Conflict of Identity," in *Barriers to Peace in the Israeli-Palestinian Conflict*, ed. Yaacov Bar-Siman–Tov. Jerusalem: The Jerusalem Institute for Israel Studies, 2010. 99–134. Print.

Bartana, Or-Zion. *Generations in the States' Fantasy Literature: A Study of the Works of Yorm Kaniyuk, Yitzchak Averbouch-Orpaz & David Shahar* [הפנטסיה בסיפורת דור המדינה: אורפז ודויד שחר – יצחק אוורבוך, יורם קניוק דיון ביצירתם של]. Tel Aviv: Papyrus, 1989. Print.

Duvdevani, Shmuel. "Magic Realism in Israeli Cinema [ריאליזם מאגי בקולנוע הישראלי]," in *With Both Feet On the Clouds: Fantasy in Hebrew Literature—A Selection of Essays* [עם שתי הרגליים עמוק בעננים: פנטסיה בספרות העברית – מבחר מאמרים], ed. Hagar Yanai, and Daniela Gurevitch. Tel Aviv: Graf Publishing, 2009. 61–81. Print.

Eshed, Eli. *From Tarzan to Zbeng—The Story of the Popular Hebrew Literature* [ועד זבנג הסיפור של הספרות הפופולארית העברית—מטרזן]. Tel Aviv: Bavel Publishing, 2002. Print.

Eshed, Eli. "Yoske Mayor: The Israeli Comics as a Historical Epos [יוסקה מאיור: הישראלי כאפוס היסטורי הקומיקס]." January 19, 2009. *E-Mago: Culture & Content Magazine*. Web. March 17, 2011.

Fink, Uri. "A Word from the Creators—Epilogue [מכתב מהיוצרים—אחרית דבר]," Fink, Uri, Koren Shadmi and Michael Netzer, in *Profile 107*, Ben Shemen, Israel: Modan, 1998. 66. Print.

Fink, Uri, Koren Shadmi, and Michael Netzer. *Profile 107* [107 פרופיל]. *Uri Fink & Michael Netzer (w). Uri Fink & Koren Shadmi (a). Michael Netzer (i), Koren Shadmi (c & l). Ben-Shemen: Modan, 1998*. Ben Shemen, Israel: Modan, 1988. Print.

Gaon, Galit. "How to Write Comics in Hebrew," in *Israeli Comics //Part I—The Early Years (1935-1975)*, eds. Galit Gaon, Zachi Ferber, and Eli Eshed. Holon, Israel: The Israeli Caricature and Comics Museum, 2008. 8–13. Print.

Goldberg, Leah (w), and Arieh Navon (w, a). "Little Soldier Ktina [קטינא החייל]." *Davar Leyeladim* 1941. Print.

Goldberg, Leah (w), and Arieh Navon (w, a). "Topsy-Turvy World [עולם הפוך]." *Davar Leyeladim* 1938. Print.

Gulst, Moshik. "Meet the Creators- Lecture at the Israeli Caricature and Comics Museum." Holon, February 10, 2011. Public Talk.

Gulst, Moshik. *Revolt.* [מרד] Vol. 1. Self-Published, 2010. Print.

Hareven, Gayil. "About Inconceivable Things [על דברים שלא יעלו על הדעת]," *With Both Feet On the Clouds: Fantasy in Hebrew Literature—A Selection of Essays* [מבחר מאמרים – עם שתי הרגליים עמוק בעננים: פנטסיה בספרות העברית], eds. Hagar Yanai, and Daniela Gurevitch. Tel Aviv: Graf Publishing, 2009. 43–58. Print.

Kohn, Matan. *Angels* [מלאכים]. Self-Published, 2002. Print.

Landman, Shiri. "Barriers to Peace: Protected Values in the Israeli-Palestinian Conflict," *Barriers to Peace in the Israeli-Palestinian Conflict*, ed. Yaacov Bar-Siman–Tov. Jerusalem: The Jerusalem Institute for Israel Studies, 2010. 135–177. Print.

Manheim, Noa. "The Grand Old Witch of Dreams [המכשפה הגדולה של החלומות]," in *With Both Feet On the Clouds: Fantasy in Hebrew Literature—A Selection of Essays* [עם שתי הרגליים עמוק בעננים: פנטסיה בספרות העברית – מבחר מאמרים]," eds. Hagar Yanai, and Daniela Gurevitch. Tel Aviv: Graf Publishing, 2009. 130–135. Print.

Merlock-Jackson, Kathy, and Mark D. Arnold. "Baby-Boom Children and Harvey Comics after the Code: A Neighborhood of Little Girls and Boys." *ImageText: Interdisciplinary Comics Studies* 3.3 (2007). Web.

Morag, Amir. "Zbeng, but we're not done yet [זבנג ולא גמרנו]." *Fuse supplementary edition, Yedioth Achronot* July 21, 2005: 5. Print.

Raab, Alon. "Ben Gurion's Golem and Jewish Lesbians: Subverting Hegemonic History in Two Israeli Graphic Novels," in *The Jewish Graphic Novel: Critical Approaches*, eds. Samantha Baskind, and Ranen Omer-Sherman. Rutgers: The State University, 2008. 214–233. Print.

Reshef, Nimrod. *Uzi—Urban Legend* [עוזי – אגדה אורבנית]. 1–4 vols. Tel Aviv: Storyboard-Hai Comics Publishing, 2005–2009. Print.

Rothman, Giora. "The Ghost from Hirbet-el-Jath [הרוח מח'ירבת אל-ג'ת]." *Ha'aretz Shelanu* 1975. Print.

Rothman, Giora. "Meet the Creators—Lecture at the Israeli Caricature and Comics Museum." Holon, June 20, 2008. Public Talk.

Rothman, Giora (w, a), and Dov Zigelman (w). "Yoske Mayor [יוסקה מאיור]." *Ha'aretz Shelanu* 1972–1974. Print.

Sade, Pinchas (Yariv Amatzia), and Elisheva Nadel. "The space kids' mystery, or a journey to 20,000 light years [תעלומת ילדי החלל – או מסע אל 20,000 שנות אור]." *Ha'aretz Shelanu* 1962. Print.

Samooha, Sami. "The Option of the Status Quo: Israel as an Ethnic Democracy: A Jewish-Democratic State," in *Seven Roads: Theoretical Options for the Status of the Arabs in Israel*, eds. Sara Ozacky-Lazar, Ahmed Ghanem, and Ilan Pappe. Givat Haviva: Institute for Peace Research, 1999. 23–77. Print.

Sandi, Amitay. "Comics' Ability to Convey Messages—A talk at Icon Sci-Fi & Fantasy Festival." Tel Aviv, October 05, 2009. Public Talk.

Shamir, Shlomo. *–At any cost—to Jerusalem* [לירושלים -בכל מחיר]. Tel Aviv: Ma'arachot, 1994. Print.

Tzadok, Erez. *Zoo'la Stories* [סיפורי זולה]. 1–2 vols. Self-Published, 2008 and 2010. Print.

Yanai, Hagar. "Is it Allowed to Imagine in Hebrew? [?מותר לדמיין בעברית]," in *With Both Feet On the Clouds: Fantasy in Hebrew Literature—A Selection of Essays* [עם שתי הרגליים עמוק בעננים: פנטסיה בספרות העברית – מבחר מאמרים], eds. Hagar Yanai, and Daniela Gurevitch. Tel Aviv: Graf Publishing, 2009. 7–10. Print.

Zanzuri, Ofer (w) and Ofer & Moshe Zanzuri (a). *Azure Giants—You Can Never Know Which Side You're On* [אדירי התכלת - אתה אף פעם לא יכול לדעת באיזה צד אתה], ed. Ofer Berenstein. 1–6 vols. Ashdod: Zanzuria Comics Publishing, 2004–2009. Print.

Zanzuri, Ofer. "Behind the Scenes of Azure Giants—A talk at the 10th Caricature-Animation-Comics Festival." Tel Aviv, August 17, 2010. Public Talk.

Chapter 11

Bible. *The Five Books of Moses, The Schocken Bible: Volume 1*, Everett Fox (trans). New York: Schocken Books, 1997. Print.

Browning, Christopher. *Ordinary Men: Reserve Police Battalion 101 and the Final Solution in Poland*. New York: HarperCollins, 1992. Print.

Heuvel, Eric (artist), Heuvel, Ruud van der Rol, Lies Schippers (author), and Lorraine T. Miller, (trans.) *The Search*. New York: Farrar, Straus, and Giroux, 2009. Print.

Hoberman, J., et al. "*Schindler's List*: Myth, Movie, and Memory: A Debate." *Village Voice* XXXIX.13 (March 29, 1994): 24–31. Print.

Lagnado, Caroline. "A Novel Approach to Holocaust Education." *Jewish Week* 220.51 (July 25, 2008. Web. March 15, 2010): 50–51.

Lanzmann, Claude. *Shoah: An Oral History of the Holocaust: The Complete Text of the Film*. New York: Pantheon Books, 1985. Print.

Phalnikar, Sonia. "Graphic Novel Tackles Taboo of the Holocaust." Deutsche Welle. January 2, 2008. Web. November 9, 2013. <http://www.dw.de/graphic-novel-tackles-taboo-of-the-holocaust/a-3102723-1>.

Spiegelman, Art. *Maus: A Survivor's Tale: My Father Bleeds History*. New York: Pantheon Books, 1986. Print.

Spiegelman, Art. *Maus II: And Then My Troubles Began*. New York: Pantheon Books, 1991. Print.

Chapter 12

Adler, David, and Karen Ritz. *A Picture Book of Anne Frank*. New York: Holiday House, 1993. Print.

Adler, David, and Karen Ritz. *Hilde and Eli: Children of the Holocaust*. New York: Holiday House, 1994. Print.

Adler, David, and Karen Ritz. *Child of the Warsaw Ghetto*. New York: Holiday House, 1995. Print.

Avnet, Jon, dir. *Uprising*, 2001. CBS Television miniseries.

Baron, Lawrence. *Projecting the Holocaust into the Present: The Changing Focus of Contemporary Holocaust Cinema*. Lanham, MD: Rowman and Littlefield Publishers, Inc., 2005. Print.

Baskind, Samantha, and Ranen Omer-Sherman, eds. *The Jewish Graphic Novel: Critical Approaches*. New Brunswick, NJ: Rutgers University Press, 2008. Print.

Berg, Mary. *The Diary of Mary Berg: Growing Up in the Warsaw Ghetto*, ed. S.L.
     Shneiderman. Oxford: Oneworld, 2007. Print.
Eisenstein, Bernice. *I Was a Child of Holocaust Survivors*. New York: Riverhead Books,
     2006. Print.
Geis, Deborah R., ed. *Considering Maus: Approaches to Art Spiegelman's Survivor's Tale of
     the Holocaust*. Tuscaloosa: University of Alabama Press, 2003. Print.
Gutman, Israel. *Resistance: The Warsaw Ghetto Uprising*. Boston, MA: Houghton Mifflin
     Company, 1994. Print.
Hirsch, Marianne. *Family Frames: Photography, Narrative, and Postmemory*. Cambridge,
     MA: Harvard University Press, 1997. Print.
Holliday, Laurel, ed. *Children in the Holocaust and World War II: Their Secret Diaries*. New
     York: Pocket Books, 1995. Print.
Kaplan, Chaim A. *Scroll of Agony: The Warsaw Diary of Chaim A. Kaplan*. Bloomington:
     Indiana University Press, 1999. Print.
Katin, Miriam. *We Are on Our Own: A Memoir*. Montreal, Canada: Drawn & Quarterly,
     2006. Print.
Kleid, Neil, and Jake Allen. *Brownsville*. New York: ComicsLit, 2006. Print.
Korczak, Janusz. *The Warsaw Ghetto Memoirs of Janusz Korczak*. Translated by
     E.P. Kulawiec. Washington, DC: University Press of America, 1979. Print.
Kubert, Joe. *The Adventures of Yaakov and Isaac*. Vol. 1. Jerusalem: Mahrwood Press, 2004.
     Print.
Kubert, Joe. *Jew Gangster*. New York: ibooks graphic novels, 2005. Print.
Kubert, Joe. *Yossel: April 19, 1943*. New York: ibooks graphic novels, 2003. Print.
Kubert, Joe, et al. *Showcase Presents: Unknown Soldier*. Vol. 1. New York: DC Comics,
     2006. Print.
Lanzmann, Claude, dir. *Shoah*, 1985. Film.
Prager, Brad. "*The Holocaust without Ink: Absent Memory and Atrocity in Joe Kubert's
     Graphic Novel* Yossel: April 19, 1943," in *The Jewish Graphic Novel: Critical Approaches*,
     eds. Samantha Baskind, and Ranen Omer-Sherman. New Brunswick, NJ: Rutgers
     University Press, 2008. 111–128. Print.
Ringelblum, Emanuel. *Notes from the Warsaw Ghetto: The Journal of Emanuel Ringelblum*.
     Translated and ed. Jacob Sloan. 1958; New York: Schocken Books, 1974. Print.
Royal, Derek Parker, ed. "Jewish Comics." *Shofar* 29.2 (winter 2011). Print.
Schelly, Billy. *Man of Rock: A Biography of Joe Kubert*. Seattle, WA: Fantagraphics Books,
     2008. Print.
Spiegelman, Art. *Maus: A Survivor's Tale*. New York: Pantheon, 1986 [vol.1], 1991 [vol. 2].
     Print.
Uris, Leon. *Mila 18*. Garden City, NY: Doubleday and Company, 1961. Print.
Wojcik-Andrews, Ian. *Children's Films: History, Ideology, Pedagogy, Theory*. New York:
     Garland, 2000. Print.

Chapter 13

Bowe, Marisa. "No Laughing Matter." *BOOKFORUM* (June–September 2005): 26–27.
Comics, Actus. *How to Love*. Tel Aviv: Actus Comics, 2007.
Eisner, Will. *Comics and Sequential Art: Principles and Practices of the World's Most
     Popular Art Form*. Tamarac, FL: Poorhouse Press, 1985.

Folman, Ari, and David Polonsky. *Waltz with Bashir*. New York: Metropolitan Books, 2009.

Glidden, Sarah. *How to Understand Israel in 60 Days or Less*. New York: DC Comics, 2010.

"Interview with Joe Sacco." June 2011. *The Believer*. Web. March 14, 2012. <http://www.BelieverMag.com>.

Libicki, Miriam. *Jobnik*. British Columbia, Canada: Real Gone Girl Studios, 2008.

Modan, Rutu. *Exit Wounds*. Montreal, Canada: Drawn and Quarterly, 2010.

Morris, Janice. "Comics Journalism." *Canadian Literature* 201 (2009): 187–188.

New York Times. topics.nytimes.com. Web. Aug. 21, 2014. <topics.nytimes.com/top/news/international/countriesandterritories/israel/index.html>.

Sacco, Joe. *Al Jazeera English Interview with Joe Sacco* Laila El-Haddad. January 2010.

Sacco, Joe. *Footnotes in Gaza*. New York: Metropolitan Books, 2009.

Sacco, Joe. *Palestine*. Seattle, WA: Fantagraphics Books, 2001.

Sacco, Joe. "Ruto Modan Interviewed by Joe Sacco." Drawn & Quarterly, Feb. 15, 2008. Web. January 8, 2016. <http://www.DrawnAndQuarterly.com>.

Scanlon, Molly. "Comics, Journalism and War Discourse." 2011. Web. <http://pkjournal.org/?page id=1443>.

Seliktar, Galit, and Gilad. *Farm 54*. Spain: Fanfare/Ponent Mon Ltd., 2011.

Versaci, R. *This Book Contains Graphic Language: Comics as Literature*. New York: Continuum, 2007.

Weiland, Jonah. "Talking With Amitai Sandy about Israeli Comics and Dimona Comix Group." August 28, 2005. *Comic Book Resources*. Web. December 19, 2011. <http://www.ComicBookResources.com>.

Williams, Kristian. "The Case for Comics Journalism." *Columbia Journalism Review* (March/April 2005): 43–60.

Chapter 14

Baetens, Jan. *The Graphic Novel*. Louvain, Belgium: Leuven University Press, 2001.

Baskind, Samantha. "A Conversation with Myriam Katin," in *The Jewish Graphic Novel: Critical Approaches*, eds. Samantha Baskind, and Ranen Omer-Sherman. 237–243. New Brunswick, NJ: Rutgers University Press, 2010.

Baskind, Samantha, and Ranen Omer-Sherman, eds. *The Jewish Graphic Novel: Critical Approaches*. New Brunswick, NJ: Rutgers University Press, 2010.

Berger, Alan L. *Children of Job: American Second-Generation Witnesses to the Holocaust*. New York: State University New York Press, 1997.

Brown, Robert McAfee, Lucy Dawidowicz, Dorothy Rabinowitz, and Elie Wiesel. *Dimensions of the Holocaust: Lectures at Northwestern University*. Evanston, IL: Northwestern University Press, 1977.

Celan, Paul. *The Selected Poems and Prose of Paul Celan*. New York: W.W. Norton, 2001.

Costello, Lisa. "History and Memory in a Dialogic of 'Performative Memorialization' in Art Spiegelman's *Maus: A Survivor's Tale*." *The Journal of Midwest Modern Language Association* 39.2 (2006): 22–42.

Eaglestone, Robert. *The Holocaust and the Postmodern*. New York: Oxford University Press, 2004.

Eisenstein, Bernice. *I Was a Child of Holocaust Survivors*. Toronto, ON: McClelland & Stewart, 2006.

Elmwood, Victoria A. "'Happy, Happy Ever After': The Transformation of Trauma Between the Generations in Art Spiegelman's *Maus: A Survivor's Tale.*" *Biography* 27.4 (2004): 691–720.

Felman, Shoshana, and Dori Laub. *Testimony: Crises of Witnessing in Literature, Psychoanalysis, and History.* New York: Routledge, 1992.

Frahm, Ole. "'These Papers Had Too Many *Memories*. So I *Burned* Them.' Genealogical Remembrance in Art Spiegelman's *Maus: A Survivor's Tale*," in *The Graphic Novel*, ed. Jan Baetens. Louvain, Belgium: Leuven University Press, 2001. 61–77.

Geis, Deborah R. *Considering Maus: Approaches to Art Spiegelman's "Suvivor's Tale" of the Holocaust.* Tuscaloosa: University of Alabama Press, 2003.

Harris, Miriam. "Releasing the Grip of the Ghostly: Bernice Eisenstein's," in *I Was a Child of Holocaust Survivors. The Jewish Graphic Novel: Critical Approaches*, eds Samantha Baskind, and Ranen Omer-Sherman. New Brunswick, NJ: Rutgers University Press, 2010. 129–143.

Hirsch, Marianne. "The Generation of Postmemory." *Poetics* 29.1 (2008): 103–128.

Hirsch, Marianne. *The Generation of Postmemory: Writing and Visual Culture After the Holocaust.* New York: Columbia University Press, 2012.

Hoffman, Eva. *After Such Knowledge: Memory, History, and the Legacy of the Holocaust.* New York: PublicAffairs, 2004.

Katin, Miriam. *We Are on Our Own.* Montreal, Canada: Drawn & Quaterly, 2006.

LaCapra, Dominick. *Writing History, Writing Trauma.* Baltimore, MD: The John Hopkins University Press, 2001.

Lemelman, Martin. *Mendel's Daughter: A Memoir.* New York: Free Press, 2006.

Levi, Primo. *If This Is a Man and the Truce.* London: Abacus, 2001.

Levine, Michael G. "Necessary Stains: Art Spiegelman's *Maus* and the Bleeding of History," in *Considering Maus: Approaches to Art Spiegelman's "Suvivor's Tale" of the Holocaust*, ed. Deborah R. Geis. Tuscaloosa: University of Alabama Press, 2003. 63–104.

Roth, Laurence. "Contemporary American Jewish Comic Books: Abject Pasts, Heroic Futures," in *The Jewish Graphic Novel: Critical Approaches*, eds. Samantha Baskind, and Ranen Omer-Sherman. New Brunswick, NJ: Rutgers University Press, 2010. 3–21.

Spiegelman, Art. *Maus, A Survivor's Tale I: My Father Bleeds History.* New York: Phantom, 1986.

Spiegelman, Art. *Maus, A Survivor's Tale II: And Here My Troubles Began.* New York: Phantom, 1991.

van Alphen, Ernst. "Second-Generation Testimony, Transmission of Trauma, and Postmemory." *Poetics* 27.2 (2006): 473–488.

Wiesel, Elie. "The Holocaust as Literary Inspiration," in *Dimensions of the Holocaust: Lectures at Northwestern University*, eds. Robert McAfee Brown, Lucy Dawidowicz, Dorothy Rabinowitz, and Elie Wiesel. Evanston, IL: Northwestern University Press, 1977. 5–19.

Young, James E. "The Holocaust as Vicarious Past: Art Spiegelman's *Maus* and the Afterimages of History." *Critical Inquiry* 24 (1998): 666–699.

Chapter 15

al-Ali, Naji. *A Child in Palestine.* London: Verso, 2009. Print.

Allabad, Mahi Ad Dih. "30 Domande," in *L'invenzione Diabolica*, ed. Sesto S. Giovanni. Milan, Italy: Il papiro Editrice, 1990. 33–63. Print.

Baloup. "Témoignage De Natalie Abou Shakra," in *Gaza Décembre 2008—Janvier 2009: Un Pavé Dans La Mer*, ed. Collectif. Paris: Boite à Bulles, 2009. 152–156. Print.

Bartoll, Jean-Claude, and Pierpaolo Rovero. *Mossad—Opérations Spéciales*. Paris: Jungle, 2011. Print.

Bo-huyn, Kim. *Naplouse*. Trans. Amoruso, Kette. Paris: Casterman, 2007. Print.

Boisserie, Pierre, and Frédéric Ploquin. *Les Agents Du Mossad*. Paris: 12 bis, 2011. Print.

Boudjellal, Farid. *Juifsarabes, Intégrale*. Paris: Futuropolis, 2006. Print.

Delisle, Guy. *Jerusalem: Chronicles from the Holy City*. Trans. Helge Dascher. Montreal, Canada: Drawn & Quarterly, 2012. Print.

Demiguel, Jacques. Interview by Scenario.com. "Moussa Et David: Un Espoir De Paix Au Coeur Du Conflit Israélo-Palestinien." *Scenario.com*. 2007. Web. September 4, 2014. <http://www.scenario.com/>.

Duncan, Randy, and Matthew J. Smith. *The Power of Comics: History, Form, and Culture*. New York: Continuum, 2009. Print.

Feldt, Jakob. *The Israeli Memory Struggle. History and Identity in the Age of Globalization*. University of Southern Denmark Studies in History and Social Sciences. Odense: University Press of Southern Denmark, 2007. Print.

Ferra. "4 Jan 2009 (D'après Un Témoignage De Said Abdelwahed)," in *Gaza Décembre 2008—Janvier 2009: Un Pavé Dans La Mer*, ed. Collectif. Paris: Boite à Bulles, 2009. 149–150. Print.

Fink, Uri. *Fink! Tales from the Ragin' Region*. Trans. Gabriel Etinzon. El Sobrante, CA: Hippy Comix, 2002. Print.

Fink, Uri. *Israël-Palestine Entre Guerre Et Paix*. Trans. Marie Lefort. Paris: Berg International éditeurs & Uri Fink, 2008. Print.

Gertz, Nurith, and George Khleifi. *Palestinian Cinema—Landscape, Trauma, and Memory*. Edinburgh: Edinburgh University Press, 2008. Print.

Ghanayim, Mahmud. *The Quest for a Lost Identity. Palestinian Fiction in Israel*. Studies in Arabic Language and Literature. Vol. 7. Wiesbaden, Germany: Harrassowitz, 2008. Print.

Glidden, Sarah. *How to Understand Israel in 60 Days or Less*. New York: Vertigo-DC Comics, 2010. Print.

Harb, Samir. *Oba'den?!* [What Next?!] #2. 2008.

Harb, Samir. "Digging for Gold." *CoPYLefT*. 2008. Web. September 4, 2014. <http://c-left.blogspot.de>.

Harb, Samir. "From the Diaspora to the Diaspora." *Decolonizing Architecture Art Residency*. Web. September 4, 2014. <http://www.decolonizing.ps/site/battir-2/>.

Harb, Samir. "Silent Night." *CoPYLefT*. 2009. Web. September 4, 2014. <http://c-left.blogspot.de>.

Hermans, Analèle, and Delphine Hermans. *Les Amandes Vertes—Lettres De Palestine*. Berlin: Warum, 2011. Print.

Histoire d'en Lire. "Moussa Et David: Deux Enfants D'un Même Pays." 2007. Web. September 2, 2014. <http://www.histoiredenlire.com/>.

Hohenberger, Eva. *Die Wirklichkeit Des Films*. Studien Zur Filmgeschichte; 5. Hildesheim [u.a.]: Olms, 1988. Print.

Israel Ministry of Foreign Affairs. "Suicide Bombing of Egged Bus No 37 in Haifa-5-Mar-2003." 2004. Web. September 2, 2014. <http://www.mfa.gov.il/>.

Issartel, Sandrine. "Maurice Rajsfus: Le Conflit Israélo-Palestinien En Bd." *Regards* Dec. 7, 2007. Web. September 4, 2014. <http://www.regards.fr/>.

Jadallah, Ahmed. "1st Prize, Spot News." *World Press Photo* 2003. Web. September 4, 2014. <http://www.archive.worldpressphoto.org/>.

Jover, José. Telephone interview by Chantal Catherine Michel. April 20, 2012.

Juneau, Thomas, and Mira Sucharov. "Narratives in Pencil: Using Graphic Novels to Teach Israeli-Palestinian Relations." *International Studies Perspectives* 11.2 (2010): 172–183. Print.

Kirschen, Ya'akov. *What a Country! Dry Bones Looks at Israel*. Philadelphia, PA: Jewish Publication Society, 1996. Print.

Kirschen, Yaakov. *Trees ... The Green Testament*. 1993. Private Edition ed. Israel: Yaakov Kirschen, 2011. Print.

Kolton, Batia. "Mon Jour D'indépendance," in *Substance Profonde*. 1998–2003 Actus Tragicus (Hebr.). Trans. Rosie Pinhas-Delpuech. Arles, Paris: Actes Sud, 2005. 39–45 (n. p.). Print.

Layoun, Mary. "Telling Stories in Palestine: Comix Understanding and Narratives of Palestine-Israel," in *Palestine, Israel, and the Politics of Popular Culture*, eds. Rebecca L. Stein, and Ted Swedenburg. Durham, NC: Duke University Press, 2005. 313–337. Print.

Le Roy, Maximilien. "Dimanche, 28 Décembre (D'après Un Témoignage De Baaloucha)," in *Gaza Décembre 2008—Janvier 2009: Un Pavé Dans La Mer*, ed. Collectif. Paris: Boite à Bulles, 2009. 11–18. Print.

Le Roy, Maximilien. *Faire Le Mur*. Brusells: Casterman, 2010. Print.

Libicki, Miriam. *Jobnik! An American Girl's Adventures in the Israeli Army*. Vols. 1–6, 7, 8, 9. Coquitlam, BC: Real Gone Girl Studios, 2008–2011. Print.

Maher, Birgid. "Drawing Blood: Translation, Mediation and Conflict in Joe Sacco's Comics Journalism," in *Words, Images and Performances in Translation*, eds. Rita Wilson, and Brigid Maher. New York: Continuum, 2012. 119–138. Print.

Mahfud, Haider. "L'invenzione Diabolica," in *L'invenzione Diabolica*, ed. Sesto S. Giovanni. Milan, Italy: Il papiro Editrice, 1990. 3–30. Print.

Maluah, Said Ali. "L'inseguimento," in *L'invenzione Diabolica*, ed. Sesto S. Giovanni. Milan, Italy: Il papiro Editrice, 1990. 65–92. Print.

Marie. "Moussa Et David." *Sceneario.com* March 13, 2007. Web. September 4, 2014. <http://www.sceneario.com>.

Massad, Joseph. "The Weapon of Culture: Cinema in the Palestinian Liberation Struggle," in *Dreams of a Nation*, ed. Hamid Dabashi. London: Verso, 2006. 32–44. Print.

Mathieu, Marc-Antoine. *Julius Corentin Acquefacques, Prisonnier Des Rêves*. Vol. 1–5. Paris: Delcourt, 2004. Print.

Matton, Annette. "From Realism to Superheroes in Marvel's *the 'Nam*," in *Comics and Ideology*, eds. Matthew P. McAllister Jr., Edward H. Sewell, and Ian Gordon. New York: Peter Lang, 2009. 151–176. Print.

Mazari, Mohamed. "La Proiezone Continua," in *La Palestina D'oro*, ed. Sesto S. Giovanni. Milan, Italy: Il Papiro Editrice, 1990. 33–63. Print.

McCloud, Scott. *Understanding Comics*. New York: Morrow, 1994. Print.

McGreal, Chris. "The Only Question Was When Revenge Would Come. At Dawn, It Came to Jabaliya." *The Guardian* March 7, 2003. Print.

Michel, Chantal Catherine. "Bericht Oder Propaganda? Dokumentarische Comics Über Den Nahostkonflikt," in *Der Dokumentarische Comic—Reportage Und Biographie*, ed. Dietrich Grünewald. Essen: Verlag, 2013a. 189–206. Print.

Michel, Chantal Catherine. "Panels for Peace: Contributions of Israeli and Palestinian Comics to Peace Building." *Quest. Issues in Contemporary Jewish History* n. 5 (2013b). Web. September 4, 2014. <http://www.quest-cdecjournal.it/>.

Modan, Rutu. *Exit Wounds*. Montréal, Canada: Drawn and Quarterly, 2007. Print.

Modan, Rutu, and Igal Sarna. "Haut Les Mains—Peau De Lapin," in *Le Tour Du Monde En Bande Dessinée*, ed. Vincent Bernière. Vol. 2. Paris: Delcourt, 2010. 6–19. Print.

Nichols, Bill. *Representing Reality: Issues and Concepts in Documentary*. Bloomington: Indiana University Press, 1991. Print.

Rajsfus, Maurice. *Israel-Palestine: L'ennemi Intérieur*. Paris: La Brèche, 1987. Print.

Rajsfus, Maurice. *Palestine: Chronique Des Événements Courants, 1988–1989.* Paris: L'Harmattan, 1990. Print.

Rajsfus, Maurice, and Jacques Demiguel. *Moussa Et David—Deux Enfants D'un Même Pays.* Cachan, France: Tartamudo Editions, 2007. Print.

Rédaction Carrefour Européen du 9e Art et de l'Image. "Le Prix « Melouah Moliterni » 2011." *Aubenas* May 28, 2011. Web. September 4, 2014. <http://www.aubenasbdimage.com/>.

Reiser, Jean-Marc. "Dessin De Presse Redécouverte: Reiser—L'amérique, Israël Et Les Arabes." *Bang! Bande Dessinée-Images-Actualité* 1.1 (2003): 62–71. Print.

Roannie, and Oko. *L'intruse—Une Internationale En Palestine.* Vol. 1–4. Paris: Vertige Graphic, 2010–2012. Print.

Sacco, Joe. *Footnotes in Gaza: A Graphic Novel.* London: Random, 2009. Print.

Sacco, Joe. *Journalism.* New York: Random, 2012. Print.

Sacco, Joe. *Palestine.* 1993. London: Random, 2003 Print.

Saliman, Ammar. "La Palestina D'oro," in *La Palestina D'oro,* ed. Sesto S. Giovanni. Milan, Italy: Il papiro Editrice, 1990. 3–30. Print.

Salomon, Gavriel. "A Narrative-Based View of Coexistence Education." *Journal of Social Issues* 60.2 (2004): 273–287. Print.

Saquer-Sabin, Françoise. *Le Personnage De L'arabe Palestinien Dans La Littérature Hébraïque Du Xxe Siècle.* Paris: CNRS éditions, 2002. Print.

Schwender, Clemens. *Medien Und Emotionen. Evolutionspsychologische Bausteine Einer Medientheorie.* Sozialwissenschaft. 2., aktualisierte Aufl. ed. Wiesbaden: Dt. Univ.-Verl., 2006. Print.

Seliktar, Galit, and Gilad Seliktar. *Farm 54.* Trans. Altman Kaydar, Ronen. Rasquera, Spain: Fanfare, Ponent Mon Ltd., 2011. Print.

Shohat, Ella. *Israeli Cinema: East/West and the Politics of Representation.* London: Tauris I B, 2010. Print.

Soulman, and Maximilien Le Roy. *Les Chemins De Traverse.* Antony: Boite à Bulles, 2010. Print.

Squarzoni, Philippe. *Torture Blanche,* ed. Squarzoni, Philippe. Albi: Les Requins Marteaux, 2004. Print.

Vanderbeke, Dirk. "In the Art of the Beholder: Comics as Political Journalism," in *Comics as a Nexus of Cultures. Essays on the Interplay of Media, Disciplines and International Perspectives,* eds. Mark Berninger, Jochen Ecke, and Gideon Haberkorn. Jefferson, NC: McFarland, 2010. 70–81. Print.

Wiesner, Al. *Shaloman, the Man of Stone/New Adentures of Shaloman/the Legend of Shaloman/Saga of Shaloman/Shaloman the Sequel.* Philadelphia, PA: Mark 1, 1988–2011. Print.

Wolfman, Marv, Mario Ruiz, and William J. Rubin. *Homeland—The Illustrated History of the State of Israel.* 2007. Skokie, IL: Nachshon, 2008. Print.

Woo, Benjamin. "Reconsidering Comics Journalism: Information and Experience in Joe Sacco's Palestine," in *The Rise and Reason of Comics and Graphic Literature. Critical Essays on the Form,* eds. Joyce Goggin, and Dan A Hassler-Forest. Jefferson, NC: McFarland, 2010. 166–177. Print.

Yslaire, Bernar. *Le Ciel Au-Dessus De Bruxelles.* Vol. 1 & 2: Avant/Après. Paris: Futuropolis, 2006–2007. Print.

Zigelman, Dov, and Giora Rotman. "The Adventures of Yoske Mayor." *Ha'aretz Shelanu,* 20-51(1972) and 1-50 (1973), back covers. Print.

Chapter 16

Kahn, Ariel. "From Darkness into Light: Reframing Notions of Self and Other in Contemporary Israeli Graphic Narratives," in *The Jewish Graphic Novel: Critical Approaches*, eds. Samantha Baskind, and Ranen Omer-Sherman. New Brunswick, NJ: Rutgers, 2008. 198–213. Print.

Korver, Steve. "Ben Katchor and Rutu Modan: Comics Artists" (Originally appeared in *The Amsterdam Weekly*.) May 6, 2008. Web. August 17, 2014. <www.stevekorver.com>.

Modan, Rutu. *Exit Wounds*. Montreal, Canada: Drawn and Quarterly, 2007. Print.

Modan, Rutu. *Jamilti and Other Stories*. Montreal, Canada: Drawn and Quarterly, 2008. Print.

Chapter 17

Abrams, Meyer Howard. *A Glossary of Literary Terms*. 1958. Boston, MA: Heinle & Heinle, 1999. Print.

Bender, Hy. *The Sandman Companion*. 1999. New York: DC Comics Vertigo Books, 2000. Print.

Bergson, Henri. *Œuvres*. 1959. Paris: Presses Universitaires de France, 1970. Print.

Brod, Max. *Franz Kafka: A Biography*. 1937. Trans. G. Humphreys Roberts and Richard Winston. Cambridge: Massachusetts: Da Capo Press, 1995. Print.

"Cainite." Encyclopædia Britannica online. Encyclopædia Britannica, Inc. Web. October 12, 2009. <http://global.britannica.com/EBchecked/topic/88487/Cainite>.

Carroll, Robert, and Stephen Prickett, eds. *The Bible, Authorized King James Version*. Oxford: Oxford University Press, 1997. Print.

Cohen, Sarah Blachen, ed. *Jewish Wry: Essays on Jewish Humor*. Bloomington/Indianapolis: Indiana University Press, 1987. Print.

Desproges, Pierre. *Dictionnaire superflu à l'usage de l'élite et des bien nantis*. Paris: Editions du Seuil, 1985. Print.

Fingeroth, Danny. *Disguised as Clark Kent: Jews, Comics, and the Creation of the Superhero*. New York: The Continuum International Publishing Group Inc., 2007. Print.

Gaiman, Neil, et al. *Outrageous Tales from the Old Testament*. London: Knockabout Comics, 1987. Print.

Gaiman, Neil. *Smoke and Mirrors*. London: Headline Publishing Group, 1999. Print.

Gaiman, Neil. *American Gods*. London: Headline Publishing Group, 2001. Print.

Gaiman, Neil. *Adventures in the Dream Trade*. 2002. Framingham, MA: The NESFA Press, 2007. Print.

Gaiman, Neil, et al. *Absolute Sandman, Vol. 2*. 1990–1993. New York: DC Comics, 2007. Print.

Gaiman, Neil, et al. *Absolute Sandman, Vol. 3*. 1991–1993. New York: DC Comics, 2008. Print.

Girard, René. *Violence and the Sacred*. 1972. Trans. Patrick Gregory. Baltimore, MD: The Johns Hopkins University Press, 1977. Print.

Girard, René. *Des Choses cachées depuis la fondation du monde*. Paris: Editions Grasset & Fasquelle, 1978. Print.

Jackson, Kevin. *The Language of Cinema*. Manchester: Carcanet Press Ltd., 1998. Print.

Mairowitz, David Zane, and Robert Crumb. *Kafka*. Seattle, WA: Fantagraphics Books, 2007. Print.

McCabe, Joseph. *Hanging Out with the Dream King: Interviews with Neil Gaiman and His Collaborators*. Seattle, WA: Fantagraphics Books, 2004. Print.

McCloud, Scott. *Understanding Comics: The Invisible Art*. New York: HarperCollins Publishers, 1993. Print.

Mills, Watson E., ed. *The Lutterworth Dictionary of the Bible*. 1990. Cambridge: Mercer University Press, 1994. Print.

Moore, Alan, et al. *Swamp Thing, Vol. 2: Love and Death*. 1984–1985. New York: DC Comics, 1990. Print.

Moore, Alan, et al. *Swamp Thing, Vol. 4: A Murder of Crows*. 1985–1986. New York: DC Comics, 2001. Print.

Otto, Rudolf. *The Idea of the Holy*. 1917. Trans. John W. Harvey, 1923. Oxford: Oxford University Press, 1958. Print.

Schaefer, Eric. *Bold! Daring! Shocking! True! A History of Exploitation Films, 1919–1959*. Durham, NC/London: Duke University Press, 1999. Print.

Schweitzer, Darrell, ed. *The Neil Gaiman Reader*. Holicong, PA: Wildside Press, 2007. Print.

Wagner, Hank, Christopher Golden, and Stephen Bissette. *Prince of Stories: The Many Worlds of Neil Gaiman*. New York: St Martin's Press, 2008. Print.

Witek, Joseph. *Comic Books as History: The Narrative Art of Jack Jackson, Art Spiegelman and Harvey Pekar*. Jackson: University Press of Mississippi, 1989. Print.

Chapter 18

The Dead Sea Scrolls Bible: The Oldest Known Bible Translated for the First Time into English. Trans. Martin Abegg Jr., Peter Flint, and Eugene Ulrich. San Francisco, CA: Harper, 2002. Print

Dominions 3: The Awakening. Illwinter Game Design. Wilmington, NC: Shrapnel Games, 2006. Video game.

The Ethiopic Book of Enoch: A New Edition in the Light of the Aramaic Dead Sea Fragments, Vol. 2. Trans. Michael A. Knibb and Edward Ullendorff. Oxford University Press, 1979. Print.

Ginsberg, Louis, ed. *Legends of the Jews* (H'aggada). *The Internet Sacred Texts Archive*. Modified September 29, 2005. Web. May 5, 2012.

Libicki, Miriam. "Towards a Hot Jew." Unknown: self-published, N.D. Print.

Modan, Rutu. *Exit Wounds*. Montreal, Canada: Drawn and Quarterly, 2007. Print.

Osterman, Kristoffer. "Gath, dev diary or something.".*com.unity Forums > Illwinter Game > Design Dominions 3: The Awakening*. Posted March 19, 2008 (10:35am). Shrapnel Games. Web. May 5, 2012.

Reeves, John. *Jewish Lore in Manichean Cosmogony: Studies in the Book of Giants Traditions*. Cincinnati, OH: Hebrew Union College Press 1997. Print.

Sand, George. *A Woman's Version of the Faust Legend: The Seven Strings of the Lyre*. Trans. George A. Kennedy. Chapel Hill: University of North Carolina Press, 1989. Print.

Sfar, Joann. *The Rabbi's Cat 2*. New York: Pantheon, 2008. Print.

Tanakh: The Holy Scriptures: The New JPS Translation According to the Traditional Hebrew Text. Jerusalem: Jewish Publication Society, 1988. Print.

Index

Actus Tragicus Comics Collective 8,
192–193, 221
Al-Ali, Naji 222
Allabad, Mahi Ad Dih 222
Allen, Woody 1, 67, 68, 71, 75, 116
alternate reality 146–149. *See also* science
fiction
Antin, Mary 8, 29, 30, 31, 35–37, 37nn1–4,
38n8
anti-Semitism xvi, 2, 16, 17, 21, 22, 23,
121, 122, 123, 124, 255n11, 260
Archie 131–132, 140n1
Atom Smasher 6
Auschwitz 7, 158, 159, 161–168, 179,
181, 192, 200, 202–203. *See also*
Holocaust
Avengers 117

B., David 17, 26, 56
Batman 2, 184n15, 248, 249
Baxter, Jack 7
Bechdel, Alison 26, 92n7
Bellow, Saul xvi, 10, 11n10, 21, 67, 73
Bendis, Brian Michael 7
Berman, Shelley 67
Bertozzi, Nick 7
Book of Enoch 260, 262, 264
Book of Esther 8, 41–44
Book of Giants 260, 262–265, 267
Bosch, Hieronymus 132, 133, 134
Boy Commandos 2
Brice, Fanny 139
Brooks, Mel 131, 252
Bruce, Lenny 71, 134, 139
Bruegel, Pieter, the Elder 131, 132, 133,
143
Burns, George, and Gracie Allen 139
Buscema, John 5, 104

Cadmus, Paul 133
Caesar, Sid 130, 131, 138, 139
Cantor, Eddie 139

Captain America 2, 4, 5, 106, 110, 111, 117
Carol Burnett Show 139
Celan, Paul 200–201
censorship 118
Chabon, Michael 3–4, 6, 101, 116; *The
Amazing Adventures of Kavalier &
Clay* 3–4, 6, 101, 116; *Michael
Chabon Presents the Amazing
Adventures of the Escapist* 6. *See also*
Escapist, The
Chaykin, Howard 6, 7, 9, 115–128;
American Flagg! 6; *Black Kiss* 7;
Dominic Fortune 6, 9, 115–128;
Power and Glory 117
Classics Illustrated 242
Cleese, John 139
Clowes, Daniel 4, 7, 132, 138, 194
Cohen, Sacha Baron 260
Colossal Boy 6
Conan 244–245
Corman, Leela 7, 8, 29–37; *Queen's Day*
7; *Subway Series* 7; *Unterzakhn* 8,
29–37
Crane, Roy 134
Croci, Pascal 7
Crumb, Robert 4, 5, 11n10, 17, 138, 139,
247, 253n2, 254n4; *The Book of
Genesis Illustrated* 5

David, Larry 1
Davis, Jack 132
Davis, Vanessa 7
DC Comics xv, 2, 6, 9, 101, 172, 241, 248,
249, 252
Dead Sea Scrolls 260, 262
Deitch, Kim 4, 7, 242
Delisle, Guy 56, 222
Demiguel, Jacques 223, 227–229
Deutsch, Barry 6
Diablo (game), 257, 258
Disney, Walt 131
Dominions 3 257, 258–262

Donald Duck 131
Doom, Dr. 102
Dorkin, Evan 6
Dragnet 135
Dres, Jeremie 7

EC Comics 2, 131–140, 242–243, 245–246,
      249
Eisenstein, Bernice 7, 9, 177, 181, 199,
      200, 208–210
Eisner, Will xvi, 2–3, 6, 8, 10, 15–28,
      38n10, 74, 81–94, 186; and
      autobiography 8, 15–28; *Comics
      and Sequential Art* 19, 27n2; *A
      Contract with God* xvi, 6, 16, 21,
      27n3, 38n10, 81, 83, 91, 92n2,
      92n6, 93n14; "The Day I Became
      a Professional," 16; *The Dreamer*
      6, 16, 17–20, 27n6, 28n8, 28n11,
      90; *Dropsie Avenue* 6, 8, 21, 38n10,
      81–94; *Fagin the Jew* 6, 90; *Graphic
      Storytelling and Visual Narrative*
      27n2; *A Life Force* 6, 21, 38n10,
      81, 91; *Life, in Pictures* 16; *Minor
      Miracles* 90; *The Name of the Game*
      6, 16, 27n4, 28n9; *The Plot: The
      Secret Story of the Protocols of the
      Elders of Zion* xvi, 92n7; *The Spirit*
      xv, xvi, 2, 15, 18, 74; "A Sunset in
      Sunshine City," 16; *To the Heart
      of the Storm* xvi, 6, 16, 17, 20–26,
      28n11, 92n2
Elder, Will 2, 9, 129–140; *Help!*
      (magazine) 139; *Humbug* 139; *Little
      Annie Fannie* 139; "Night before
      Christmas," 136–138; *Trump* 139.
      *See also Kurtzman, Harvey; Mad;
      Panic; and* Playboy
Emerson, Hunt 242
Escapist, The 6. *See also Chabon, Michael*
Eshed, Eli 101, 152
Estrin, Leivbel, and Dovid Sears 6, 114n6

Fantastic Four 2, 5, 102, 107, 112. *See also
      Thing, The*
Faudem, Joshua 7
Feiffer, Jules xvi, 2, 6, 8, 15, 67–79, 116, 139
Feldstein, Al 2, 136. *See also* Mad
Felman, Shoshana 200, 209
femininity/feminism 49, 51, 53

Fiddler on the Roof 55
Finck, Liana 7
Finger, Bill 2
Fingerman, Bill 7
Fink, Uri 101, 143–145, 152, 221, 222
Folman, Ari 9, 186, 191–192, 197
Frank, Anne 158, 163; Anne Frank Center
      158, 160
Friedman, Bruce Jay 75
Friedman, Drew 7, 11n12
Fury, Nick 104, 108

Gaiman, Neil 9, 241–255; *American
      Gods* 241, 242; *Black Orchid* 247;
      *Outrageous Tales from the Old
      Testament* 242–248, 255n10,
      255n12; *Sandman* 9, 241–242,
      248–252; *Violent Cases* 247. *See also
      McKean, Dave*
Gaines, Maxwell "Charlie" 1
Gaines, William 2, 131, 132, 138. *See also*
      Mad
Gantz, David 6
Gauld, Tom 257, 267
Giardino, Vittorio 7
Gibbons, Dave 242
Gilliam, Terry 132, 139
Girard, René 243–244, 252, 254n7
Gleason, Jackie 139
Glidden, Sarah 7, 9, 187–188, 191, 197,
      221
Goldberg, Leah 149–150
golem, in comics 5, 6, 8–9, 101–114;
      legend of 4, 101–102, 114n8
Golem, Der (film) 101, 267
Golem, the (character) 5, 9, 104–109, 112,
      113
Golem, The (book title) 5, 101, 152
Goya, Francisco 133, 134
graphic novel, problems of definitions of
      10n1, 92n3
Green Lantern 2
Gross, Milt 6, 132, 136, 138, 140nn3–4
Guardian 2
Gulst, Moshik 146, 148–149, 152n2

Haggadah 157, 168, 255n18
Haney, Bob 174
Hanuka, Asaf, and Tomer Hanuka 8
Harvey, Robert C. 15, 124

Hebrew Bible 9, 41, 234–235. *See also Old Testament and Tanakh*
Hergé (Georges Remi) 160, 193, 231, 265
Heuvel, Eric 7, 9, 157–168; *A Family Secret* 7, 162–163; *The Search* 7, 9, 157–168
Hoffman, Eva 37n3, 202, 204, 209
Holman, Bill 134
Holmes, Sherlock 135
Holocaust xv, 4, 6–7, 8, 9, 11n11, 20, 55, 57, 58, 108–110, 157–168, 171–172, 177–182, 183n7, 183n13, 185, 186, 199–210, 210n2, 210n5, 211n10, 212n24, 229, 253n1. *See also Auschwitz*
Homer 254n5
Hulk, The 2, 9, 102–104, 107, 113, 118

Intifada 9, 231–240. *See also Israeli-Palestinian conflict*
Invaders, the 108–112
Iron Man 2, 102
Israeli comics 8, 141–152, 191–194
Israeli Defense Forces (IDF) 144, 146, 185, 188, 191, 257–259, 266, 268
Israeli-Palestinian conflict 9, 185–197, 221–230, 258, 266. *See also Intifada*

Jaffee, Al 2
Jewish comics, defining xv–xvi, 1–8,
Jewish Hero Corps 6
Jewish humor 4, 8, 9, 129–140
Jewish identity 7, 8, 23, 45–46, 64, 110, 113, 201, 241, 257; and Ashkenazi culture 4, 56–60, 64, 265; and Israel 59, 61. *See also masculinity*
Justice League 6, 249

Kabbalah 4, 45–46, 102, 106, 111, 260–261, 267
Kafka, Franz 67, 71, 242, 253n2
Kane, Bob 2, 138
Kane, Gil 2
Karlsson, Johan 258
Katchor, Ben 2–4, 6
Katin, Miriam 7, 183n11, 199, 200, 204–206, 208, 211nn13–17
Kaye, Danny 138
Kefauver, Estes 138
Kingston, Maxine Hong 21

Kirby, Jack 2, 103, 118
Kirschen, Yaakov 221
Kitchen, Denis 17, 18, 131
Kleid, Neil 6, 7, 184n15
Kleist, Reinhard 7
Kohn, Matan 150
Kolton, Batia 221
Kominsky-Crumb, Aline 4, 7
Kubert, Joe 2, 7, 171–184; *The Adventures of Yaakov and Isaac* 175–178, 183nn6–7; and Hawkman 172; *Jew Gangster* 7, 184n15; Joe Kubert School of Cartoon and Graphic Art 172, 184n15; and Unknown Soldier 172–174, 179, 182n1, 184n15; *Yossel: April 19, 1943* 7, 175, 178–182, 183n8, 183n11, 184n15. *See also Sgt. Rock*
Kuper, Peter 6
Kurtzman, Harvey 2, 4, 130–136, 138–139, 140n1; *Help!* (magazine) 139, 140n1; *Humbug* 139; *Trump* 139. *See also Mad*
Kushner, Seth 5

Lasko-Gross, Miss 7
Laugh-In 139
Lee, Stan 2, 103
Legion of Super-Heroes 6
Leiber, Larry 2
Lemelman, Martin 7, 9, 199, 200, 206–208, 212n22
Levi, Primo 199, 206, 209
Le Roy, Maximilien 9, 222
Libicki, Miriam 7, 9, 188–191, 197, 221, 257–259, 266, 268

Mack, Stan 6
Mad xv, 2, 4, 9, 129–137, 139–140, 183n6. *See also Elder, Will; Gaines, William; Kurtzman, Harvey*
Magneto 5
Mahfud, Haider 222
Mailer, Norman 11n10, 75, 122
Malamud, Bernard xvi, 11n10, 21, 79n3, 122
Maluah, Said Ali 222
Mandrake the Magician 128n3, 136
Marvel Comics xv, 2, 5, 9, 101–113, 115, 117, 118, 122, 128n3, 244, 253n3; and MAX imprint 123

Marx Brothers 132, 133, 139
Marx, Groucho 1
masculinity 9, 42, 46, 49–53, 76, 115–128
Mathieu, Marc-Antoine 223
Matt, Joe 17, 26
Mazari, Mohamed 222
McCloud, Scott 19, 92n7, 223, 224, 254n6,
    255n12
McCourt, Frank 21
McKean, Dave 247
Melville, Herman 254n5
memory 21–22, 26, 55–64, 162, 191–192,
    199–210, 235; and postmemory
    191, 199–210
Moaveni, Azadeh 21
Modan, Rutu 7, 8, 9, 186, 193–194, 197,
    221, 231–240, 257, 261, 266, 268;
    Exit Wounds 7–8, 193–194, 231–237,
    238, 240, 257, 266–268; "Jamilti"
    231, 237–240; *Jamilti and Other
    Stories* 8, 237; *The Property* 7, 8
Monolith, The 101
Monty Python 132, 139, 252
Moore, Alan 6, 242, 249–250, 252, 254n4
Morrison, Toni 22, 204

Nadel, Elisheva 145
Navon, Arieh 149–150
Nephilim 9, 257–258, 261–264, 266–267.
    See also Rephaim
Netzer, Michael 143–144
Nichols, Mike, and Elaine May 75, 79n2
Niles, Steve 5, 11n10
nostalgia 3, 8, 55–65; definitions of 57–59

Old Testament 241–253. *See also Hebrew
    Bible and Tanakh*
O'Neil, Dennis 118, 128n3
Osterman, Kristoffer 9, 258–261, 264–265,
    268
Ozick, Cynthia 10

Paley, Grace 21
Panic 129, 136–139
parallel universes 142–145. *See also science
    fiction*
Pekar, Harvey 6, 7, 10n2, 17; and Paul
    Buhles 6, 38n9
Phantom, The 128n3
Playboy 139

Poe, Edgar Allan 136
Popeye 131, 136
propaganda 9, 118–119, 187, 221–229
Protocols of the Elders of Zion, The 260
Pryde, Kitty 5

Ragman 5, 6, 101
Rajsfus, Maurice 223, 227–229
Rephaim 9, 257–258, 261. *See also
    Nephilim*
Reshef, Nimrod 152
Riesman, David 70
Robbins, Trina 4, 181
Robinson, Jerry 2
Rol, Ruud van der 9, 158–168
Roth, Philip xv–xvi, 10, 11nn9–10, 21, 67,
    79n1, 122
Rothman, Giora 146–147, 221

Sabra 6, 150
Sacco, Joe 9, 186, 194–197, 222, 258;
    Footnotes in Gaza 194, 196–197,
    222, 223–227; *Journalism* 222;
    Palestine 194–196, 222, 223, 258
Sade, Yizhak 145
Sahl, Mort 67, 73, 139
Saliman, Ammar 222
Sand, George 260
Sarna, Igal 221
Satrapi, Marjane 18, 26, 27n7, 56, 92n7
Saturday Night Live 131, 139
Schippers, Lies 9, 158–168
Schrag, Ariel 7
Schwartz, Julius 2
science fiction 142, 152. *See also alternate
    reality, parallel universes, and "what
    if" narratives*
Seliktar, Galit, and Gilad Seliktar 192, 221,
    222
Severin, John 132, 136. *See also Mad*
Sfar, Joann 7, 8, 9, 55–65, 257, 261,
    265–266, 267; *Klezmer: Tales of the
    Wild East* 7, 8, 55–66; *The Rabbi's
    Cat* 7, 56; *The Rabbi's Cat 2* 257,
    265–266
Sgt. Rock 2, 172, 184n15. *See also Kubert,
    Joe*
Shadmi, Koren 7, 143–144
Shakespeare, William 249, 254n5
Shelton, Gilbert 139

Shuster, Joe 2, 3, 138
Siegel, Jerome 2, 3
Sim, David 7
Simon, Joe 2, 10n2
Spider-Man 102, 117
Spiegelman, Art 4, 5, 6, 9, 17, 18, 26,
    27n7, 158–161, 168, 169n3,
    181, 199–200, 202–204; *In the
    Shadow of No Towers* 27n7; *Maus*
    6, 17, 26, 158–161, 168, 181,
    183n14, 199–204, 210n1, 210n5,
    211nn10–14
Spielberg, Steven 127, 161, 168; *Schindler's
    List* 161, 168, 169n3
Squarzoni, Philippe 9, 222
Sturm, James 6, 101, 257, 267; *The Golem's
    Mighty Swing* 6, 101, 257, 267;
    Market Day 6
Superman xv, 2, 3, 4, 5, 113, 116–117, 122,
    128, 128n3, 130, 131, 136, 179, 181,
    248, 249. *See also Shuster, Joe; and
    Siegel, Jerome*

Tanakh 102, 113n1, 257, 262. *See also
    Hebrew Bible and Old Testament*
Tarantino, Quentin 101, 127
Targum Sheni 45–46
Thing, The 4, 5, 6, 9, 107–108, 112–113.
    See also Fantastic Four
Thomas, Roy 102–104, 107–113
Thor 4
Tractate Megillah 44, 54n2
Tractate Sanhedrin 44
Two-Gun Kid 6
Tzadok, Erez 145

Updike, John 11n10
Uris, Leon 181–182

Valley, Eli 10, 95–98
videogames 9, 257–265
Village Voice 67–72, 75, 161, 168, 169n3

Waldman, J.T. 6, 7, 8, 41–54; *Megillat
    Esther* 8, 41–54; *Not the Israel My
    Parents Promised Me* 7
Warsaw Ghetto 9, 110, 112, 159, 171–182
Wein, Len 5, 104, 106, 118
Weisinger, Mort 2
Wertham, Fredric 118, 246
"what if" narratives 149–150. *See also
    science fiction*
Wiesel, Elie 101, 199, 209
Wiesner, Al 6, 10, 213–218, 221; *Shaloman*
    6, 10, 213–218
Winick, Judd 7
Wolfman, Marv 221
Wonder Woman 133, 248
Wood, Wally 132, 136, 140n1. *See also
    Mad*
World War II 16, 19–23, 55–56, 58,
    87, 108–112, 221, 130, 131, 162,
    171–173, 178–182
Wrightson, Berni 5

X-Men 2, 4, 5, 102

Yakin, Boaz 7
Yiddish xvi, 3, 4, 5, 6, 33–34, 38n7, 38n9,
    39n12, 66n1, 68, 71, 72, 75, 123,
    132, 134, 135, 136, 139, 178

Zanzuri, Ofer 143–144, 152
Zigelman, Dov 146–147, 221
Zionism 9, 59–60, 121–122, 141–152, 221,
    227–229
Zwick, Edward 127

CPSIA information can be obtained
at www.ICGtesting.com
Printed in the USA
LVHW011618090819
627135LV00006B/111/P